BROOKS MEMORIAL

CHARLES A. BROOKS

ANNA CLOYDE BROOKS

THE AMERICAN SYSTEM

THE AMERICAN SYSTEM

A New View of Government in the United States

MORTON GRODZINS

Edited by
DANIEL J. ELAZAR

Transaction Books
New Brunswick (U.S.A.) and London (U.K.)

Transaction edition 1984. Original edition copyright © 1966 by Rand Mc-
Nally & Company.

Library of Congress Catalog Number: 82-8449
ISBN: 0-87855-916-7
Printed in the United States of America

Library of Congress Cataloging in Publication Data

Grodzins, Morton.
  The American system.

  (Political theory series)
  Reprint. Originally published: Chicago: Rand McNally, 1966. (Rand
McNally political science series)
  Includes bibliographical references and index.
  1. Federal government—United States. I. Elazar, Daniel Judah. II.
Title. III. Series. IV. Series: Rand McNally political science series.
[JK325.G78   1984]   321.02′3′0973   82-8449
ISBN 0-87855-916-7

EDITOR'S INTRODUCTION

I

Morton Grodzins devoted the last decade of his life to shaping a new view of the American federal system as pioneering in its efforts to understand the mechanics of democratic government as it was broad in scope. His deep knowledge of the workings of American government had left him dissatisfied with conventional discussions of the nature and impact of federalism as a system of political organization. He clearly recognized that federalism—at least in an age of complexity and interdependence such as ours—was not a matter of isolating governments for separate (and minimal) action but of sharing powers for interdependent accomplishment. Flowing from this was his recognition that in a functioning federal system, the principles of federalism are not confined to a single dimension of "intergovernmental relations" but pervade every aspect of the system's political life.

Grodzins' interest in federal-state-local relations can be traced back to the early days of an academic career that spanned two productive decades. The sources of his interest were varied, ranging from a concern with civil liberties and loyalty to an interest in the problems of sharing power in a nuclear age. No doubt his great insight that federalism is something more than intergovernmental relations was a product of those wide-ranging interests. Through his explorations, he discovered that, in the United States, the "politics" of all such concerns are shaped by the special institutions and processes of the federal system.

Stated broadly, his hypothesis views the American system of government as functionally analogous to a *marble cake* of shared activities and services even though it is formally structured (like a layer cake) in three *planes*. Despite the great increase in the *velocity of government* in the twentieth century, the American system remains decentralized, democratic, and responsive to the public because there is a *little chaos* built into it. At one level, this chaos promotes *sharing* because it prevents any single government or governmental plane from gaining exclusive jurisdiction and power in any area of governmental concern. At a second level, the chaos allows citizens to utilize *multiple cracks* (in the double sense of wallops from outside the system, and fissures in the system itself) to gain their ends. This has the consequence of involving (at least potentially) governments at every plane in the same problems. On the national plane in particular, the existence of a *public-private continuum,* which is used to mobilize local influence, helps translate citizen benefits from the multiple crack into benefits for the states and localities. The *sharing system* is maintained in large measure by the nation's *undisciplined political parties* which are almost caricatures of the system they serve. The constitutionality of the sharing system has been ratified by the decisions of the United States Supreme Court which tend to divert questions about the precise measures and forms of sharing to the political arena. The *sharing system* is effective because there exist *channels of sharing* that bring some order to the process. These include the constitutionally defined mechanisms of federalism and the *mixture of laws* which lies at the root of the sharing process. In a system of this kind, there are perpetual tensions and problems including a perennial search for *balance* between the centers of power, a constant problem of dealing with *squeak points* in the system, and a continuing search for the harmonization of *special interests* with the *general* (or *national*) *interest.* These problems can lead to *antagonistic cooperation* between government (and other elements) in the American system, but it is inevitably cooperation, or sharing, nonetheless. The existence of these problems is not a sign of the system's deficiencies but, rather, a reflection of its vigor and health.

Grodzins was acutely conscious of contemporary work being done in American federalism, and saw his own project as taking it a step further. His aim was to correct the misunderstanding that he saw around him and to provide an alternate set of standards by which to measure the status of American federalism as well as to prescribe for its maintenance in the future. Grodzins' work was done primarily in the 1940's and 1950's. Thus it does not take into account the changes wrought by the election of John F. Kennedy and the later elevation of Lyndon B. Johnson to the presidency. His feeling—supported by the evidence—that the domestic role of the federal government was actually declining *vis-à-vis* that of the states and localities is less appropriate today than it was in the fifties. Much of what he offered as new ideas then is widely accepted now— in no small measure because of his own pioneering work. If some of his conclusions appear less than striking now it should be understood that today in all likelihood, Morton Grodzins would be talking more about the "squeaks and strains" of a very active partnership. More to the point, however, is the way in which his work stands up despite the changes of the past decade.

Grodzins' view of American politics was optimistic, but never "Pollyannaish." He, of all people, was aware of the problems of American political life because he, more than most of his colleagues, devoted much of his time to grappling with these problems on the front lines, as it were. His greatness was that he was never misled into confusing the immediate problems confronting his generation with the long-range virtues of the American system. He was sufficiently insightful to recognize, as he says in Chapter One, that most of the system's ills are defects of its larger virtues and must be handled so as to preserve those larger virtues. This view, clearly reminiscent of the ideas of the founders of the Republic, is curiously at variance with many of the views that have repeatedly attracted public support in the twentieth century, views of those who are willing to "throw out the baby with the bath" because they cannot distinguish between them.

In his manner of teaching and in his life Morton Grodzins was a democrat. Never given to exploiting the work of others, he sought to reach the kind of accommodation with his students and colleagues that allowed all parties to profit in a common partnership. He was no man for disciples— instead wherever he went he served as a catalyst for the creation of a true *res publica* of scholars. At least one student of his believes that it was this almost instinctive sense of working in partnership that drew Grodzins to the study of federalism and gave him the insight to see into the heart of the system he was studying.

The same penchant for partnership may also have given him his sense of optimism, enabling him to believe that a system of government requiring such rare human qualities as self-restraint and concern for the general interest, while interposing fewer barriers to the exercise of less desirable human characteristics than ever before, had a happy and prosperous future before it. Yet his optimism was not facile, nor was he unaware of the difficulties—including the nuclear difficulty—that could at any moment alter his optimistic prognosis.

In his files, Morton Grodzins kept a paper written by his friend Irene Coltman on "Problems of Political Conscience." After agreeing that in an imperfect world, the best of intentions can often lead to the worst of consequences and that counsels of perfection as well as counsels of despair are self-destructive, the paper concludes with a passage which Grodzins underlined:

> [T] here is nothing to do but to go on trying to give, without being so naive as to hope for everything and tolerate nothing, or so disillusioned as to hope for nothing and tolerate everything.

Morton Grodzins valued the American system not because it was perfect but because it seemed to be the best vehicle for carrying out that prescription, a prescription which he made his own as long as he lived.

II

Grodzins launched his formal study of the federal system in the fall of 1955 with the organization of the University of Chicago Federalism Workshop and the launching of a bundle of major projects. The Workshop functioned at peak strength between 1956 and 1961, and it was during those years that the greater part of the field research and theoretical analysis for this book was done. As early as 1958, Grodzins had determined to present his view of federalism in full panorama through a large and comprehensive volume which he aptly titled: *The American System: A New View of Government in the United States.* During his year at the Center for Advanced Studies in the Behavioral Sciences (1958–59), Grodzins was able to write substantially complete drafts of five chapters, one stating the essence of his over-all hypothesis and the others documenting that hypothesis from the local perspective; what was, to him, the hardest case. After 1959, he wrote versions of additional chapters (and rewrote some of his earlier chapters) for publication as articles in response to various requests. Thus, in 1960 he wrote the chapter on federalism which appeared in *Goals for Americans,* the volume resulting from the work of the President's Commission on National Goals, and published a modified version of his first completed chapter in the *Western Political Quarterly.* In subsequent years he presented other segments of the book as lectures, some of which were subsequently published in various volumes. Called to serve on committees dealing with urgent governmental problems, he applied the sharing hypothesis to the study of those problems to suggest important (and occasionally radical) means to meet them. At the same time he broadened his interest in federalism to begin an exploration of central-local relations in other countries. Moreover, his continued interest in the problems of the nuclear age led him to devote an increasing amount of his time to the consideration of the scientist's role in government.

Morton Grodzins' concern for perfection, which he conveyed to his students as he analyzed the "architecture" of their own work and which is abundantly evident in the relatively small stock of his own published writings, reached full flower when it came to completing this volume. For a time, he considered publishing the five substantially completed chapters as a small volume on federal-local relations but apparently hesitated to depart from his larger effort even to that extent. Always he felt that the work needed "just a bit more polishing." Thus, in his search for a projection of style and content characteristic of his life and work, he delayed publication of his cherished work until the matter was no longer in his hands.

After his death, those closest to him decided that, despite the limitations of an incomplete presentation of his ideas, it was important to make Grodzins' final contribution to the study of American politics available to a broader public in the most coherent possible form. The task of assembling and editing the materials he left was given to this writer. As a student of Morton's who was with him from the very beginning of his formal researches into American federalism, I have considered it a privilege and a high obligation to undertake that task and a partial payment of the interest on my debt to him. As his friend, I hope that the editorial effort in some way does him justice.

The material in the following pages is Grodzins' own, with a minimum of editorial imposition. Along with the partially completed manuscript mentioned above, Grodzins left a detailed outline of his proposed work, a small collection of published materials on federalism of highest quality, and substantial pieces of other chapters in the form of lecture notes or segments of manuscript. It is from these sources that this volume has been shaped and given final form. From them it has been possible to reconstruct most of his ideas, though not entirely in his own unique style. The book is substantially in his own words from chapter and section headings to footnotes. No attempt has been made to alter those words or add to them except where absolutely necessary for editorial coherence, to insert more recent data drawn from the author's own files, or to bring the manuscript into conformance with the author's own subsequent intentions. Wherever possible, complete chapters have been used unaltered. In some instances, it was necessary to construct chapters from several manuscripts; this has been indicated. Though I do not accept every interpretation or subscribe to every conclusion drawn in the book, I have tried to the best of my ability to retain the author's views as he clearly expressed them and accept full responsibility for any errors in that attempt.

Grodzins had hoped to complete his book with a section devoted to evaluating the entire system of sharing in light of its larger consequences. As this book demonstrates, he believed in the existence of a group process as one of the key dimensions of American politics, and often compared the role of groups and interests to Madison's description of the role of "factions" in *Federalist 10* and elsewhere. He knew and wrote of multiple loyalties. But he also firmly believed that there was such a thing as the public (or general or national) interest—he used the terms interchangeably —even as he was hard put to define it.

In his lectures, Grodzins spoke of a hierarchy of interests to be served through the political process which together comprise the national interest. First and foremost among the various interests deserving political attention he placed the maintenance of the system, including the systematic pulling and hauling of interest groups and the general concern with securing the greatest good for the greatest number. He believed that the pull and haul of the various groups is the definitional activity of the national interest. Moreover, sometimes the special interest turns out to be the national interest. The example he gave was the Negroes' struggle for their civil rights. Second in his hierarchy came the largest social interests such as survival, food, work, and the like. In them the national interest is clear and is usually formulated through consensus even as the consensus may be slowly changed through interest group conflict. The special interests work within the framework of these largest interests. Third in order is the special interest which is also the national interest, such as the Negro interest in gaining full civil rights. More difficult to define and identify, such special-cum-national interests always exist, and serving them may actually provide the basis for the reforms that lead to continued maintenance of the system. Finally, even where the special interests served are not in the national interest (apparently, directly, or at all), and the latter does not always triumph, there is always someone to raise the question of what the national interest is.

In fact, Grodzins argued, the national interest has always been broad enough to allow virtually everyone to get something of what he wants. But this is in large measure due to the fact that the demands of virtually everyone are rooted in an American consensus. This general consensus on the basic issues of American society can be traced to the founding fathers. As his constant references to the founders indicate, Grodzins' notions were set within an almost creedal framework which caught, for him, the American spirit and provided means for its embodiment in the conduct of American government.

Although much of what Morton Grodzins had hoped to write remained unwritten, substantial traces of his ideas on all his basic themes can be found throughout this book. At the same time, many of his evaluations of the American system can be found in the policy-oriented reports he prepared for various agencies of government, primarily in the last years of his life. Indeed, his concern with the application of the sharing hypothesis in the political realm makes such "practical" products of his intellect a prime source for the discovery of his evaluation of American federalism. In addition, a review of those products reveals the broad perspective from which Morton Grodzins viewed even the most specific problems confronting the nation. The reports are also useful as showpieces demonstrating the way in which he used his methodology for investigative and prescriptive purposes. Consequently, the final part of this volume consists of selections from three of his reports (and some other materials) plus a concluding chapter which summarizes his over-all assessment of the trends and present status of the American federal system and his view of the system's values and goals.

The final four chapters reveal Grodzins' unconventional thinking in several different fields. In Chapter Thirteen, based on his recommendations to the Outdoor Recreation Resources Review Commission, he subtly turned on those who would bring compulsive neatness to the affairs of state to advocate the continued involvement of all levels of American government in the affairs of conservation and recreation. Following his thesis that federal programmatic activities, like federal laws, should be interstitial rather than primary, he suggested places for increased federal activity on the basis of existing deficiencies in the entire bundle of conservation and recreation services, increases whose end result would be to strengthen the states and localities, not to preempt the recreation field from out of their hands.

In Chapter Fourteen, which is taken from his dissenting statement submitted to Secretary of Agriculture Orville Freeman in 1962 as an addendum to the report of the USDA study committee reviewing the Department's farmer committee system, he made a radical suggestion that the federally dominated local governments in agriculture be eliminated and their functions transferred to regularly constituted county (or township) governments under a system whereby federal inducements would be used to upgrade the character and capabilities of rural local government, thus strengthening the weakest element in the American system. Chapter Fifteen, based on an article published in the *National Tax Journal* in 1950, offers a brief discussion of some of the fiscal fallacies of the "home rule" movement and its more recent corollary, the drive for metropolitan consolidation as a means to gain local autonomy. There again, Grodzins utilized the sharing hypothesis as a yardstick against which to measure the chances for successful separation of local and non-local functions and resources.

In the last chapter, based on sections from the *Goals* chapter and drafts of his last publications, the author summarized his thesis and its applications. He related the twentieth-century trends of society and government in the United States to the present status of American federalism. Then he assessed the value of the system according to his own standards of measurement. Finally, he set forth some of the goals appropriate to the American political system in light of basic American values.

There is markedly less emphasis in the last chapter on the undistinguish-able intermixture of institutions, levels, and functions characteristic of the marble cake hypothesis. Among the author's last comments was a certain measure of dissatisfaction with the marble cake analogy. Some of his disenchantment was undoubtedly due to sheer boredom with the term's overuse, but, more importantly, his new sense of the role of the constitutional division of American government into levels caused him to modify starkness of analogy that served best when people had to be alerted to the very existence of pervasive sharing. The very fact that Grodzins began to give constitutional factors more weight lessened his interest in the "marble cake" as a descriptive term. His restored emphasis on the role of the states also played a part in this. Moreover, he had become convinced that "layer cake" thinking is useful in certain situations because it helps bring some measure of rationality and order to what, from the other perspective, often appears to be sheer chaos. Significantly enough, a lecture first prepared at the outset of his work (in 1950, to be precise) seems to best capture his final mood—that the single "sharing system" is simultaneously a system of systems.

III

Unfortunately, in any attempt to thank those who helped Grodzins in his work, the limits of my knowledge will no doubt leave some valuable con-tributors unrecognized. To them, my sincere apologies. I will, however, try to thank those whom I know the author wished to recognize.

The members and associates of the Federalism Workshop, who were closest to him in his work, deserve first mention. Six graduate students formed the core of the Workshop. R. Bruce Carroll was directly responsible for the administrative study conducted in Chicago and Springfield, Illinois. Kenneth E. Gray studied the Congress as a participant observer, emphasiz-ing congressional-executive relations, congressional "case work," and voting patterns. E. Lester Levine was responsible for the state perspective and did his field work in Minnesota. Douglas G. St. Angelo studied the local perspective in depth in an Indiana community, with particular em-phasis on the political (as distinct from administrative) aspects of sharing. Roy Turner studied party cohesiveness in Congress during the Wilson and F. D. Roosevelt administrations. The editor was responsible for the his-torical studies, particularly the evolution of cooperative federalism, con-ducted in Minnesota, Colorado, New Hampshire, and Virginia, and also shared in the local community field studies and the exploration of the problem of special versus general interest. In addition, three scholars participated actively in the Workshop's research. Lewis A. Dexter, an acknowledged expert in congressional politics, was of constant service to the project, providing the author with reams of valuable material on Congress, the national political scene, state and local lobbying in Washington, and data on sharing in Massachusetts and Maryland. Charles Quick, a lawyer with great familiarity in law enforcement matters, worked with the author on the police study. Jacob Cohen, an economist, prepared a thorough study of the fiscal impacts of the sharing system.

After 1959, several other graduate students joined the Workshop, which was broadened in its scope to include comparative studies of central-local relations in other countries. Dennis Palumbo undertook a major study of sharing in the realm of foreign affairs. Ernest Benjamin served as Grodzins' research assistant and filled in many gaps in the research previously undertaken. David Haight began explorations into federalism theory and intergovernmental sharing in Canada. Mark Kesselman's major responsibility was a study of central-local relations in France. William Lighter studied federal stimulation of state legislation during the New Deal. Other active members of the Workshop included Herschel R. Bergman, Edgar A. Hubin, Thomas Landye, Christopher McCarthy, Sylvia Snowiss, and Paul Tennant.

Special acknowledgment is due those of Morton's colleagues who took time to read and comment on the author's various research proposals and drafts of chapters and articles, among them Frank Allen, William Anderson, Edward C. Banfield, Lee Benson, Martin Diamond, Harry H. Eckstein, Joseph Harns, Louis Kriesberg, I. M. Labovitz, Kaspar Naegele, David Riesman, Herbert Storing, and Paul Ylvisaker. Thanks are due Deil S. Wright, who utilized four of the draft chapters in his federalism class to test their efficacy, and made a major contribution to their improvement.

Many people aided the author in his research but special assistance of exceptional character was rendered by Frank Bane, formerly of the Council of State Governments and presently chairman of the Advisory Commission on Intergovernmental Relations; Charles Conlon of the Federation of Tax Administrators; Senator Paul H. Douglas of Illinois; Orville Freeman, former Governor of Minnesota and presently Secretary of Agriculture; Delphis C. Goldberg of the House Subcommittee on Intergovernmental Relations; Paul Lewinson of the National Archives and his staff; John P. Mallan of Massachusetts; Robert E. Merriam, formerly of the President's

Office; Mrs. Selma J. Muskin of the Bureau of the Budget; Arthur Naftalin, former Minnesota Commissioner of Administration and presently mayor of Minneapolis; and Raymond F. Simon, assistant to the Mayor of Chicago.

Over 200 people were interviewed by the author and other members of the Federalism Workshop aside from those who participated in the administrative time study. All of them deserve the warmest acknowledgement. Thanks are also due the many students who contributed to the development of the hypothesis presented in this volume through their research and their questions.

Financial support for the federalism project was generously supplied by the Ford Foundation, the Social Science Research Council, the Social Science Research Committee of the University of Chicago, and the Center for Advanced Study in the Behavioral Sciences. The members of the Department of Political Science of the University of Chicago provided support in numerous other ways.

As editor, I would like to acknowledge the valuable assistance of the Rand McNally staff given both Morton and myself, particularly that of John Applegath, Social Sciences Editor of the College Department and F. Edward Peacock, Vice President of the Education Division.

It would be indeed untoward of me to attempt to acknowledge Ruth Grodzins' role in the creation of this book. But as its editor I can thank her for myself, for asking me to undertake a task that means so much to her, and for making that task as light as possible by her unstinting generosity and cooperation.

                                                    D.J.E.

TABLE OF CONTENTS

Part I

INTRODUCTION

Chapter 1

THE AMERICAN SYSTEM
AS A SINGLE MECHANISM

I. THE CHAOS OF AMERICAN GOVERNMENTS

Democratic government, in the abstract at least, should be simple government, if not simple in process at least structured simply enough to be easily comprehended by the citizenry. For simplicity maximizes fulfillment of an important democratic ideal: that citizens understand public institutions. Without this understanding the public cannot make intelligent judgments, especially cannot know how to reward at the polls those who have done well and penalize those who have done poorly. But government in the United States is not simple, either in structure or process.

The structure of the United States government is chaotic. In addition to the federal government and the 50 states, there are something like 18,000 general-purpose municipalities, slightly fewer general-purpose townships, more than 3,000 counties, and so many special-purpose governments that no one can claim even to have counted them accurately. At an educated guess, there are at present some 92,000 tax-levying governments in the country. A given citizen may be buried under a whole pyramid of governments. A resident of Park Forest, Illinois, for example, though he may know very little else about them, knows that he pays taxes to the following governments:

> The United States of America
> The State of Illinois
> Cook (or Will) County
> Cook County Forest Preserve District
> Suburban Tuberculosis Sanitary District
> Rich (or Bloom) Township
> Bloom Township Sanitary District
> Non-High School District 216 (or 213)

3

Rich Township High School District
Elementary School District, 163
South Cook County Mosquito Abatement District

The Park Forest citizen enjoys more governments than most people in the United States. But he is by no means unique, and although no one has made the exact calculation, it is not unlikely that a majority of citizens are within the jurisdiction of four or more governments, not counting the state and national ones.

The multitude of governments does not mask any simplicity of activity. There is no neat division of functions among them. If one looks closely, it appears that virtually all governments are involved in virtually all functions. More precisely, there is hardly an activity that does not involve the federal, state, and some local government in important responsibilities. Functions of the American governments are shared functions. Consider a case that seems least likely to demonstrate this point: the function of providing education. It is widely believed that education is uniquely, even exclusively, a local responsibility. Almost half of all governments in the United States are school districts. Is this a great simplifying fact? Does it indicate a focussing of educational responsibilities in the hands of single-purpose local governments?

The answer to both questions is a clear "no." That there exist something like 37,000 school districts in the United States does not indicate that the educational function, even in the grade and high schools, is in any sense an exclusive function of those districts. In several states local districts are largely administrative arms of state departments of education, and the educational function is principally a state responsibility. In all states, to a greater or lesser degree—and the degree tends to be greater not lesser—local districts are dependent upon state financial aid, state teacher certification, state prescription of textbooks, and state inspection of performance in areas as diverse as building maintenance and the caliber of Latin instruction. School districts also have intricate and diverse relationships with county and city governments: the latter, for example, often act as tax-levying and tax-collecting agencies for the districts; they are responsible for certifying that standards of health and safety are maintained on school property; they must provide special police protection to students.

Nor is the federal government's finger out of the pie. The United States Office of Education provides technical aids of all sorts. Throughout the 1950's a federal milk and school lunch program contributed more than $250 million annually in cash and produce to supply food and milk at low cost to 11 million children in all 50 states. Federal surplus property supplies many essentials of school equipment. Federal aid to vocational education programs makes possible the employment of special teachers. In many areas "affected by" national government installations, federal funds build and maintain school buildings and contribute to general school support. Federal aid trains high school teachers of science, mathematics, and foreign languages; contributes equipment and books for instruction in these fields; makes possible testing and guidance programs for the identification of superior students; and may be used generally to strengthen state departments of education. All of these were initiated before the passage of recent legislation to enlarge further the national government's participation in education.

All this barely hints at the diverse ways in which all planes of governments in the United States participate in the function of education. It does not consider the political relationships among leaders of city, county, state, nation, and school district that basically establish the level of support that schools receive. Nor does it take into account the informal professional ties among teachers, administrators, and other specialists, ties that criss-cross governmental boundaries and from which a good fraction of new ideas and new programs emerge. A complete description of intergovernmental sharing in education would also have to consider how the school district's job is affected by the *mélange* of private, quasi-private, municipal, state, and federally financed programs and institutions that provide education beyond the high school in the United States. Nevertheless, the larger point is clear: grade and high school education is not simply a function of local school districts. It is not neatly a responsibility of one sort or one "level" of government. Rather, education is provided through the joint efforts of many governments. What is true of the "hard case" of education is also true of virtually all functions performed by the governments of the United States.

Many overlapping governments involved in many overlapping functions produce other attributes of the chaotic American system. Areas of government do not often correspond with problems of government. In order to provide adequate facilities for, and control of, automobile transportation, a given large city will have to deal with literally hundreds of other governments. This lack of congruence between area and function complicates the official's problem; it complicates the citizen's even more so. Where does he go and whom does he blame if super-highways become clogged with cars and the air polluted with their exhaust? What does he do if his water tastes foul? It is purchased from one city, runs in open lines through six others, is filtered and chlorinated by his own municipality, and is affected by the drainage systems of several dozen governments as well as by the septic tanks of several thousand homes in unincorporated areas. How does the citizen begin if he wishes to do something about his deteriorating neighborhood? Slum clearance involves three sets of law—local, state, and federal —and perhaps half a dozen separate administrative agencies, each with its own body of regulations. Points of influence and centers of decision are diffuse and obscure. More often than not the citizen cannot name most of the officers he elects, or describe the responsibilities of the governments that serve him. How can he hope to make them responsive to his wishes?

The chaos of structure and function is matched by a chaos of political process. The political parties play a key role, as later discussion will show, but it is a role different in almost every respect from what political parties are classically supposed to perform. Nominating procedures more often than not deprive the voter of genuine choices. Party platforms are election slogans, not statements of program. Legislative procedures are complex and unpublicized. If it is difficult on the administrative plane to discover what government does what, it is frequently impossible in the legislative halls—of locality, state, and nation—to discover who initiates, who obstructs, who is for or against what. Leadership functions, even in the national government, are typically splintered. Legislation and administration proceed through a system of pushing, hauling, bargaining, and cajoling. Legislative committee and economic interest group compete for influence with the administration, which often speaks through several opposing voices, with party leaders in and out of office, with local and state political chiefs, and with professional associations of all varieties. The two houses of the Congress, unlike any other major legislature in the world, vie with each other for power, the leaders of those houses, even when of the same party, often taking opposite sides on a given issue.

To penetrate this jungle and to bring his influence to bear, the citizen votes, writes to his congressman, joins forces with others in order to promote what he wishes to promote and, more typically, oppose what he wishes to oppose. As a businessman he pays dues to the National Association of Manufacturers; as a father of school-age children he contributes to the National Citizen's Council for Better Schools; as a churchgoer he supports the National Association of Churches of Christ. Frequently when these organizations speak they express the citizen's own views. But not always. He is enraged, because he is a humanitarian, when "his" manufacturer's group opposes a bill before Congress to extend social security. He feels betrayed, because he believes in the local control of education, when "his" committee on education favors federal aid for school construction. He is frightened, because he is opposed to all totalitarian government, when a high officer of "his" church group is accused by a senator of being tinged with Communism. The citizen's interest groups may not represent his interests just as his congressman may seem to represent no interest at all except that of his own re-election.

This view of chaos in government is not one of despair. The system of American government flaunts virtually all tenets of legislative responsibility and administrative effectiveness. It appears always to be wasteful of manpower and money. At times it threatens the very democracy it is established to maintain. But it works, it works—and sometimes with beauty.

II. GOVERNMENT BY CHAOS AND COOPERATION

Lord Bryce commented on the "working relations" of the national and state governments in the following words:

> The characteristic feature and special interest of the American Union is that it shows us two governments covering the same ground, yet distinct and separate in their action. It is like a great factory wherein two sets of machinery are at work, their revolving wheels apparently intermixed, their bands crossing one another, yet each set doing its own work without touching or hampering the other.[1]

Classic works are sometimes responsible for classic errors. We will see in Chapter Two that Lord Bryce was wrong, even for the period of his own observations, in describing the federal government and the states as "each . . . doing its own work without touching or hampering the other." Subsequent chapters will demonstrate how fallacious this description is for the contemporary American scene. Yet it cannot be said that the error has been, or is, widely recognized. During the very years that Bryce was in the United States the Supreme Court announced:

> There are within the territorial limits of each state two governments, restricted in their sphere of action, but independent of each other, and supreme within their respective spheres. Each has its separate departments, each has its distinct laws, and each has its own tribunals for their enforcement. Neither government can intrude within the jurisdiction of the other or authorize any interference therein by its judicial officers with the action of the other.[2]

The misunderstanding persists today. Lip service is frequently paid to the high degree of collaboration between the units of government in the American system. And there are a few scholars who have explicated some

---

[1] James Bryce, *The American Commonwealth* (New York: The Macmillan Company, 1916), Vol. I, p. 318.
[2] *Tarble's Case*, 13 Wall. 397 (1871).

aspects of the collaborative pattern.[3] But the general view is the view of the three-layer cake of government, the institutions and functions of each "level" being considered separately.

In fact, the American system of government as it operates is not a layer cake at all. It is not three layers of government, separated by a sticky substance or anything else. Operationally, it is a marble cake, or what the British call a rainbow cake. No important activity of government in the United States is the exclusive province of one of the levels, not even what may be regarded as the most national of national functions, such as foreign relations; not even the most local of local functions, such as police protection and park maintenance.

If you ask the question "Who does what?" the answer is in two parts. One is that officials of all "levels" do everything together. The second is that where one level is preponderant in a given activity, the other makes its influence felt *politically* (here the voice of the peripheral power units are heard most strongly) or through *money* (here the central view is most influential) or through *professional associations*.

The actual joint sharing of functions is easily illustrated in the field of public welfare. Here the national, state, and local governments together administer public assistance programs; the national government alone administers the old age insurance program commonly known as "social security"; the national government and the states (without the local governments but with the assistance of local business groups) administer employment security; the states and the local governments (without the national government) handle general assistance; and, to complete the circle of possible combinations, all three branches of government together administer child welfare services.

This is only the formal view. The informal aspects of welfare administration illustrate the second part of the answer. Even in general assistance programs, where the states and localities formally have exclusive jurisdiction, the national government's standards of professional conduct are greatly influential and becoming more so all the time. Even in a welfare field of so-called exclusive federal concern—hospital care for military veterans, for

[3] For example, William Anderson, *The Nation and the States, Rivals or Partners?* (Minneapolis: University of Minnesota Press, 1955); the series of monographs, *Intergovernmental Relations in the United States as Observed in Minnesota,* edited by William Anderson and Edward W. Weidner and published by the University of Minnesota Press; Henry M. Hart, Jr., and Herbert Wechsler, *The Federal Courts and the Federal System* (Brooklyn: Foundation Press, 1953). An important early work, limited to describing "some of the ways in which the federal and state governments have cooperated and how effective their joint activity has been," is Jane Perry Clark, *The Rise of a New Federalism* (New York: Columbia University Press, 1938).

example—the states and localities exercise controlling power over many fundamental decisions. They can, for example, make it difficult, in some cases impossible, for the national government to close a hospital or to move it from one site to another.

That one set of officials is paid out of the national treasury, one out of state funds, and a third from local budgets is the least important aspect of the matter. If one looks closely at the route of payments, the fact of common concern becomes clear again. All levels collect taxes from the same people. And the government that collects the tax frequently does not pay the officer; intergovernmental transfers, for example, account for a very large fraction of both state and local welfare expenditures. Consider the health officer, styled "sanitarian," of a rural county in a border state. He embodies the whole idea of the marble cake of government. The sanitarian is appointed by the state under merit standards established by the federal government. His base salary comes jointly from state and federal funds, the county provides him with an office and office amenities and pays a portion of his expenses, and the largest city in the county also contributes to his salary and office by virtue of his appointment as a city plumbing inspector. It is impossible from moment to moment to tell under which governmental hat the sanitarian operates. His work of inspecting the purity of food is carried out under federal standards; but he is enforcing state laws when inspecting commodities that have not been in interstate commerce; and somewhat perversely, he also acts under state authority when inspecting milk coming into the county from producing areas across the state border. He is a federal officer when impounding impure drugs shipped from a neighboring state; a federal-state officer when distributing typhoid immunization serum; a state officer when enforcing standards of industrial hygiene; a state-local officer when inspecting the city's water supply; and (to complete the circle) a local officer when insisting that the city butchers adopt more hygienic methods of handling their garbage. But he cannot and does not think of himself as acting in these separate capacities. All business in the county that concerns public health and sanitation he considers his business. Paid largely from federal funds, he does not find it strange to attend meetings of the city council to give expert advice on matters ranging from rotten apples to rabies control. He is even deputized as a member of both the city and county police forces.

The sanitarian is an extreme case, but he accurately represents an important aspect of the whole range of governmental activities in the United States. Functions are not neatly parceled out among the many governments. They are shared functions. It is difficult to find any governmental activity which does not involve all three of the so-called "levels" of the federal system. In the most local of local functions—law enforcement or education, for example—the federal and state governments play important roles. In what, *a priori,* may be considered the purest central government activities— the conduct of foreign affairs, for example—the state and local governments have considerable responsibilities, directly and indirectly.

The federal grant programs are only the most obvious example of shared functions. They also most clearly exhibit how sharing serves to disperse governmental powers. The grants utilize the greater wealth-gathering abilities of the central government and establish nationwide standards, yet they are "in aid" of functions carried out under state law, with considerable state and local discretion. The national supervision of such programs is largely a process of mutual accommodation. Leading state and local officials, acting through their professional organizations, are in considerable part responsible for the very standards that national officers try to persuade all state and local officers to accept.

Even in the absence of joint financing, federal-state-local collaboration is the characteristic mode of action. Federal expertise is available to aid in the building of a local jail (which may later be used to house federal prisoners), to improve a local water purification system, to step up building inspections, to provide standards for state and local personnel in protecting housewives against dishonest butchers' scales, to prevent gas explosions, or to produce a land use plan. States and localities, on the other hand, take important formal responsibilities in the development of national programs for atomic energy, civil defense, the regulation of commerce, and the protection of purity in food and drugs; local political weight is always a factor in the operation of even a post office or a military establishment. From abattoirs and accounting through zoning and zoo administration, any governmental activity is almost certain to involve the influence, if not the formal administration, of all three planes of the federal system.

So the functions of government are not in neat layers. Rather, they are all mixed up: marbled, to use the baker's term. And in no neat order: chaotic, to use the reformer's term. Unless one sees the American federal system from this perspective, he misses the most important fact of all: the system is, in effect, one government serving a common people for a common end.

III. THE MEANING OF "SHARING"

The term "shared functions" needs definition. It is one thing for a man to share his wife's bed and an altogether different thing to share the car in his commuter train with 150 fellow suburbanites. The significance of "sharing" depends upon the meaning given the word. In using the word, we will restrict its meaning. "Sharing" or "shared functions" will designate one or more of the following conditions:

(a) In the formulation of any given program, significant decision-making power is exercised both by those in the federal government and those in state and local governments.

(b) Similarly, where officials of all governments exercise significant responsibilities in the administration of a given activity, this will be called a "shared" function.

(c) Finally, where representatives of all governments exert significant influence over the operations of a given program, it will be considered a form of sharing.

All three statements are deceptive in their simplicity and none is easy to test against actual events. They are further complicated because sharing can take different forms. In the American system there is sharing by design (the grant-in-aid programs), sharing by politics (river and harbor improvement), and sharing by professionalization (staff functions). Stated so formally, these are "ideal types." They are not mutually exclusive in practice and, indeed, are frequently combined in the same programs.

The greatest complications arise when attempting to determine the locus of decision-making power. For example, it cannot be assumed that members of the national legislature or of the national executive speak only in the "nation's view" while state and local offices represent only parochial non-national views. In fact the non-national view is frequently supported by national officials, acting under a variety of influences. An analogous problem is the way in which special interest groups—date growers or electric train manufacturers, for example—will identify themselves as representing the local or state interest when the burden of their position is one of avoiding national regulation. Under such circumstances, can it be said that the state, and localities, are actually represented in the decisional process by the date growers? Even when states and localities are speaking for themselves, it is often not easy to determine whether their views are distinct from the national view. This problem is exacerbated by the universal tendency of all Americans to legitimate all their actions in terms of the national interest. "What is good for electric train makers is good for the nation." Finally, it must be said that froth, rather than substance, may separate the national and the state-local views, even when distinct views are readily identified. "The Republic will collapse," said an Indiana governor, "if the local security administration refuses to let us publicize the names of our relief clients." It is easy to dismiss the substance of the claim and yet, here as elsewhere, what men believe to be true, rather than truth itself, determines their action.

The following pages supply an overview of the basic patterns through which governmental sharing is achieved. But it should not be thought that the modes of sharing are exhausted by this schematic outline. In later chapters it will be seen that the sharing process operates in the interstices as well as on the principal grids of the system; it exists even when those who profit or suffer from it are not aware of the source of their achievement or frustration. Where a given property of any institution is diffused throughout its entire structure, attempts to specify the property may conceal as well as reveal its importance. The process is akin to attempting to describe how love is manifest in a tightly knit family. Cataloguing observed specific affectionate acts may have the results of hiding the basic point that the entire household relationship is based upon affection. An observer who is not a member of the network of affection may easily miss the subtleties and indirections of the affectionate act. Even reprimands, argument, and an occasional harsh word have special affectionate meanings in such a situation. The point is not that the federal-state-local relationship is one of love. It is, rather, that the acting-together of governments is not often the subject of discussion; it is not fully understood, it is marred by occasional jurisdictional squabbles or interlevel expressions of hostility, but it is always a principal mode of action, always assumed, taken for granted as love is in a household characterized by love.

These are difficulties of analysis that cannot be completely solved. The tactic of the following chapters is to make minimum claims: the real contribution of both federal and state-local views to a given decision must be apparent before it is labeled a shared decision; and the real participation of both sets of officials must be apparent before a given activity is labelled a shared function. This does not preclude attempting to take account of the subtleties of the system. Yet it is clear that what is revealed in the nature of sharing from this sort of evidence is not the whole picture. The distortion, however, is a conservative one. What is unrevealed, in order not to stretch the evidence, cannot be taken as contrary to the view of sharing.

IV. AN OVERVIEW OF PRINCIPAL THEMES

The task of describing and analyzing the chaotic American government has been done many times by many hands in many ways for many purposes.

Yet it is a job that must always be done again. Circumstances are ever changing. New methods of observation supply new data. And most of all, the phenomena themselves are complex and baffling. What is nearest at hand may be furthest from understanding. Familiarity robs one of perspective. Froude's observation about human nature is equally true of human institutions:

> Every one is a perplexity to himself and a perplexity to his neighbors; and men who are born in the same generation, who are exposed to the same influences, trained by the same teachers, and live from childhood to age in constant and familiar intercourse, are often little more than shadows to each other, intelligible in superficial form and outline, but divided inwardly by impalpable and mysterious barriers.[4]

Stress must be placed upon the difficulty of unlocking the "impalpable and mysterious barriers" that separate the observer from even the most familiar institutions. It is the only justification for presenting a view of American government that differs markedly from previous views. A new scheme of analysis of American government is no virtue in itself. Whatever advantage it may have can be gauged only in terms of how successfully it fulfills its objectives. And the objectives are the standard ones of democratic political inquiry; to add something to the scholar's aggregate of knowledge and stock of theory; to provide the student with insight, understanding, and some basis for further observation; to contribute to the comprehension and competence of the citizen; and to make clearer to the reformer what are the appropriate (and inappropriate) levers for change.

This volume is organized on three planes.

First and central is a plane of general description. The principal question here is *how*. How do the many governments get the job done? Which units of government do what, and how is this determined? How is it decided that certain tasks will be undertaken by government, others not?

Description is impossible without guide lines for the collection and organization of materials, guide lines that the researcher calls hypotheses. The central hypothesis of the descriptive chapters of this book, stated in its extreme form, is this: all levels of government in the United States significantly participate in all activities of government.

Every chapter attempts in its own way to supply the documentation, and necessary qualifications, for this hypothesis. The very way the question is stated makes it inappropriate to follow the usual procedure of books in American government, the procedure of examining "level by level" the

[4] James Anthony Froude, *History of England* (New York: Charles Scribner's Sons, 1872), Vol. IV, p. 1.

institutions and politics of the federal, state, and local governments. Instead, we look first (Part Two) at programs of government devoting primary attention to "hard cases," functions such as police protection, on the one hand, and recreation on the other, that seem least likely to demonstrate sharing. This section is concluded by showing how the mixture of functions is ultimately reflected in a mixture of laws as well. The focus is then shifted from functions to people and institutions at the most immediate level of action, in the local community (Part Three). Here we examine the sharing hypothesis from the perspective of the actors in the system: people, interest groups, various governmental units.

These descriptive chapters, if they are successful, will demonstrate the various and subtle means by which the many governments in this country intermesh with each other to produce what we call the "marble cake" of American government. The argument will be extended to the proposition that the American federal system, far from being three separate "levels" of institutions, can profitably be viewed as a single mechanism of government.

Part Four shifts emphasis from *what* the system is to *why*. Specifically: Why does the system operate the way it does? Here the leading hypothesis is that the peculiar and unique nature of American political parties provides the dynamics of the system: that the chaos of party explains the chaos of governments and the characteristics of government that flow from this chaos. The parties are reflexes of the larger social system, and they are viewed as institutions mediating between governments, on the one hand, and population groups, on the other. At the same time the parties are seen as independent forces, directly shaping and being shaped by political institutions. Constitutional factors are usually given primary importance in explanation of the forces shaping American political institutions. They are here seen in a less immediately important, *which is not to say an unimportant,* role.

A summary concept shorthands the importance of the party dynamics. We call this the concept of the multiple crack. The term "crack" has two meanings. First, it means fissure, an opening for individuals and groups to make their views known; in this meaning "crack" is almost synonymous with what the literature discusses as "access."[5] But access alone is too static a concept. Crack also means a wallop, a smack at government in an attempt to influence policy. Both the availability of the fissures and the multiplicity of the wallops result primarily from the operations of the party system. The normal process of policy-making is one in which individuals and groups take their crack at influencing governmental policy at literally

[5] Pendleton Herring, *The Politics of Democracy* (New York: W. W. Norton and Company, 1940), p. 431; David B. Truman, *The Governmental Process* (New York: Alfred A. Knopf, 1951), pp. 507–8.

uncountable points in the legislative-administrative process. The process produces, among other things, the characteristic collaborative chaos of the American system.

On the final plane of analysis (Part Five), the sharing hypothesis is applied to specific problems. The focus is no longer *how* or *why*, but *with what result?* Here an attempt is made to cast the image of *what is* against standards of *what should be,* derived from the over-all hypothesis. Only selected issues are considered, and the point is to demonstrate the utility of the analysis for evaluative (and reform) purposes. The disadvantages of the American system—particularly the difficulty of achieving national consensus in a period of crisis—are not trivial. But they are often magnified without giving sufficient weight to correcting mechanisms or compensating factors. Special interest is found often to be congruent with, not opposed to, national interest. The American system has within it a number of built-in balances. If even right solutions are necessarily compromised in the course of navigating the chaos of decision-making, neither of two prevalent, if mutually cancelling, fears are justified: The strength of special and local interests is not effacing the national welfare. Nor is the steep trend towards centralization and bureaucratization effacing the strength of the peripheral units. Lack of simplicity in government is a vice of the system's virtues. Dangers exist because the world of the hydrogen atom is a world of danger. But advantages for both the individual and the nation are found in chaos.

One more point—current theories deny any possibility of defining the national or general interest except in terms of the temporary, successful agglomeration of special "selfish" interests. And this seems to be inadequate. One of the central purposes of this book is to show how, in all the welter of atomistic individuals, groups, and institutions, something that can be called a general interest does and can make itself felt.*

The data presented in the following chapters show (recent theories to the contrary) that decisions are widely shared. They also show that in almost every decision, someone, some place, somehow expresses and makes felt the larger view—for the future of the system, for the processes of free choice, for the greater number, for the whole nation rather than a part. Built-in balances and the influence of particular sorts of leaders and of "do-good" organizations (which are themselves evidence of the openness of the system) aid this process. The fact that the system does not always

---

*Editor's note: The following paragraphs are based on a letter to David Reisman, dated August 5, 1959, amplifying the author's views on the problem of the "general interest." For further discussion of these views see his *The Loyal and the Disloyal* (Chicago: University of Chicago Press, 1954).

work and that it runs the risk of not working on the biggest issue of all—
peace in a nuclear age—are temptations to think of junking it. But, in fact,
most of its ills are defects of larger virtues.

A root difficulty of handling the whole matter of the general interest in
a study like this is that it does not easily fit into the mechanistic views of
history and social change that social scientists use as naturally as breath-
ing. Louis Brownlow, himself a man who devoted his life to seeking and
serving the public interest, tells a story in his autobiography:

> I was greatly impressed and influenced by the attitude of the corporation
> counsel . . . of the District (of Columbia). . . . He was Conrad H.
> Syme, a lawyer of course, a West Virginian, a quick-motioned person with
> tousled hair, a perpetually belligerent personality, a sharp tongue, and a
> biting wit.
> I remember Connie Syme telling me . . . after he had assumed his duties
> that he had . . . an odd and curious experience. "Heretofore," he said,
> "in all the years I have been at the bar, I have held it to be my chief duty
> and principal concern to be faithful in my relationship with my clients and
> vigilant in the protection of their interests . . . but during the last week
> I have experienced a new and startling feeling. Every time I go out on the
> street, I am struck with the fact that every person I see on the sidewalk,
> every person I see in the streetcar, every person I see in the stores, all
> these people, every one of them, is my client. It is a realization that has
> sunk in upon my consciousness and my conscience that it is my duty to be
> vigilant in the protection of the interest of all the people in Washington.[6]

Mechanistic social scientists have no way of handling the Symes of the
world. They can only assert that such people do not exist.

[6] Louis Brownlow, *A Passion for Anonymity* (Chicago: University of Chicago
Press, 1958), p. 32. Copyright © 1958 by the University of Chicago.

Chapter 2

THE PERSPECTIVE OF HISTORY[1]

America was a common enterprise long before it was a nation; and the colonies, long before they became states, were parts of a whole. The founders attempted to attain unity with diversity through the Articles of Confederation and the Constitution. Their solution makes it clear that from the beginning the national government and state governments lived together in two basic dimensions. That is no less true today. One dimension is the social fact of the American nationality; here, the national and the state governments have always been committed to a common existence in the face of common cares. The second dimension is the practical division of powers between the units concerned in the federal system; here, the American experiment in self-government has passed through several distinct stages.

The American federal system has never been a system of separated governmental activities. There has never been a time when it was possible to put neat labels on discrete "federal," "state," and "local" functions. Even before the Constitution, a statute of 1785, reinforced by the Northwest Ordinance of 1787, gave grants-in-land to the states for public schools. Thus the national government was a prime force in making possible what is now taken to be the most local function of all, primary and secondary education. More important, the nation, before it was fully organized, established by this action a first principle of American federalism: the national government would use its superior resources to initiate and support national programs, principally administered by the states and localities.[2]

[1] I profited greatly in writing this chapter from Daniel J. Elazar's dissertation, "Intergovernmental Relations in Nineteenth Century American Federalism," Department of Political Science, University of Chicago, 1959.

[2] While the emphasis in this chapter is on federal-state relations, it is not a new fact that federal and state governments perform what by any definition must be considered local functions. Paul N. Ylvisaker considers it a "popular myth" that

17

We can discern four major periods in American experience with the division of powers between the national government and the states. The first period, before the Constitution, raised almost all the primary problems, without providing many of the answers. The second, or Federalist period—from the adoption of the Constitution to about 1800—was employed in exploring the meaning of the constitutional premises. Among the meanings developed was a large measure of cooperation between the national government and the states. The third period, from 1800 to 1913, was one of cross currents dominated first by the great national-regional conflict that climaxed in the Civil War, and later by the unification of the country. Throughout the period there existed conflicting trends: one pushing toward the separation of the national government and the states, the other encouraging their close collaboration. The fourth period, from 1913 to 1948, was one in which forces long conducive to solidarity of national and state policy came to the surface and became visible to all.

I. QUESTIONS WITHOUT ANSWERS BEFORE 1787

In the period before the Constitution, the fact of major significance was the relative powerlessness of central authority. Yet, even when the sovereignty of a central government was hardly a problem at all, except in the sense of its absence, an American national government did control certain areas of power. The Confederation government possessed a large public domain in the West. In 1785 Congress dipped into this inheritance by providing that section 16 of each township in the public domain should be set aside for the maintenance of public schools. Reaffirmed by the Northwest Ordinance of 1787, this was the first act by which the national government used its resources to encourage the states to follow a national policy.

The significance of this move for national-state relations was tremendous, but largely for the future. At the time, executive confusion characterized

there "was once a golden age in [Blue Earth County's] history when government at the grass roots was completely local and unfettered."
Even during the years of settlement, the community's government was much as it is today—a complex of local, state (territorial), and national action. Except in degree the situation has never been otherwise; at no time has either the state or the federal government retired from the field and left local units to enjoy complete or unremitted control over the community's affairs.
See Paul N. Ylvisaker, *Intergovernmental Relations at The Grass Roots* (Minneapolis: University of Minnesota Press, 1956). The validity of Ylvisaker's assessment for the rest of the country is documented in Daniel J. Elazar, *The American Partnership* (Chicago: University of Chicago Press, 1962).

the relations between the national government and the states. This confusion resulted from ambiguous financial interdependence, intermingled sovereignties, and constitutional uncertainty. Under the articles, a congressman was both a state ambassador to the national government and a federal administrator. It was he who conveyed the decisions of the Continental Congress to the state legislatures, and it was he who brought back the remonstrances, the refusals, and the acquiescences. Until 1781 the congressmen themselves administered most of the national government through a clumsy system of committees.

II. FEDERALISM AND ADJUSTMENT: 1787–1800

THE CONSTITUTION

As a result of their experience in the Confederation, the founders wrote the Constitution with an eye to the fact that a congressman who was also an executive, and a state ambassador who was also a federal administrator, faced constant peril of self-paralysis. By analogy, this problem of powers represented a large part of the constitutional problem as a whole.

The founders solved these problems by deciding to derive the power of the Constitution not from the states, but from the people of all the states; and to exercise its powers not only in direct relation to the states, but to the individual citizens as well. To Madison, in retrospect, this solution appeared as a major accomplishment of the Convention. He argued that a national government working on a purely national-to-state basis would have to possess compulsive powers which might well result in "equal calamities to the innocent and the guilty, the necessity of a military force, both obnoxious and dangerous, and in general, a scene much more resembling a civil war than the administration of a regular government. Hence was embraced the alternative of a Government which, instead of operating on the states, should operate without their intervention on the individuals composing them."

Madison's formula, "without their intervention," is an oversimplified interpretation of the part that the states were to play in the federal system. Since the very beginning, at least some aspects of the national administration have always required the mediation of the states before they took effect on individuals.

The events of the period dating from the ratification of the Constitution to 1800 demonstrate the narrowness of Madison's view. This was a time of adaptive adjustment between the national and state powers, and the adjustments were many. They involoved not only the general divisions of power laid down by the Constitution but more specific matters as well. The Constitution designed new distinction between national and state financing and between national and state administration. These adjustments had to be made without delay.

QUESTIONS OF PURSE

In terms of the fiscal framework to which we are accustomed today, the national and state budgets of the Federalist period involved only petty funds. Therefore, it is not easy to describe realistically the immediate effects of the Constitution on national and state financial powers and on the relation between them. Yet the principals involved are basic, and it is essential to see the matter as it appeared to the citizen of that day.

The informed citizen of this period was used to the idea that the debts created by the states during the Revolution were the chief fiscal problem of the nation. He was used to the idea that import duties and excises were the chief revenues of governments. He was used to the idea that government, with the exception of defense and war, should limit itself to providing only such basic services as courts and coinage. Finally, he was used to the idea that a fairly simple bureaucracy sufficed to maintain approved services and to collect required revenues. Within this framework of usage, the period brought about changes that can be summarized as follows:

1. The national government assumed the Revolutionary War debts of the states. This lifted some budgets into a surplus position. More important, the national government's assumption of a standing debt and debt service was one of the factors that committed it to a long-range revenue policy.

2. The Constitution deprived the states of their import duties. While this established free trade among all the states, it took from them a great tax resource.

3. The national government, with the power to levy excise taxes, was now in a position of potential conflict with states that also depended on excises.

4. The national government took over and accepted full responsibility for financing, administering, and manning such services as national defense, foreign affairs, the mails, customs, the national judiciary, etc.

5. Finally, the national government strengthened the states by its establishment of patterns in the disposal of public funds. In a final settlement of Revolutionary War accounts, it paid clearing balances to creditor states without bothering to collect clearing balances from debtor states. And in the land grants of the Northwest Ordinance, it opened to the states a vast source of revenue not based on taxes.

ADMINISTRATIVE PROBLEMS

With these principles of purse and power settled by the Constitution and early legislation, the new government was ready to administer them. At the very outset, it was necessary to determine whether the national government should use its own administrative machinery to put into effect the exclusive powers granted to it by the Constitution. When it was suggested that the states might be employed to collect federal taxes, James Madison and others succeeded in legislating a purely national machinery for that purpose. Congress decided along the same lines for the postal service, the Navy, and the conduct of foreign affairs.

But this early treatment of the exclusive powers should not blind us to the fact that the Constitution actually assumed a broad and deep cooperation between the national government and the states. In the very election process itself, the Constitution set forth a method that depended heavily on the active efforts, as well as the good will, of state officers. It also provided explicitly for a joint administration of the militia, and allowed the states to call on the national government to repel invasion or suppress insurrection. Correspondingly, it required all state officials to take an oath in support of the national government. Finally, it tied the states into the national scheme not only by the amendment idea itself, but also by each state's control of its own participation in the amendment process.

ADMINISTRATIVE SOLUTIONS

Points of Power

The adjustment period was required to deal with at least two broad points of power within the new system: the matter of militia, and the matter of courts.

The organization and governing of the state militias raised some difficulties for national-state relations between 1789 and 1800. The constitutional clause (art. I, sec. 8, clause 16) was clear enough, but cooperation was not generally forthcoming. Congress passed an act to establish a uniform militia in 1792. The states did not uniformly carry out the provisions of the act and, since the states were charged with officering, paying, and governing the militia except in a national emergency, little could be done. Nevertheless, in the Whiskey Insurrection crisis (1794), the four state militias that were called out—although not all organized and trained as Congress had prescribed—responded without delay.

The organization of the courts proved somewhat less difficult to deal with. The Judiciary Act of 1789 (sec. 25) allowed the state courts to try cases in which there existed a federal question, while the right of review by a national court remained. Practice, pleadings, and forms of proceeding in federal civil cases were to conform so far as possible to those in the states where the proceedings in question were to take place. Any local or state judicial officer might take the depositions of witnesses in a federal case where the use of national machinery for this purpose was inconvenient. Federal offenders might be haled before any justice of the peace for arrest, commitment, and bail. Probably the most thorough intermeshing of national and state machinery occurred in the court structure.

Points of Law

The adjustment period assumed an experimental approach toward the coordination of national and state statutes. From the very beginning, Congress left the administration of national elections to the states. In 1790 it authorized federal collectors to assist in the enforcement of state quarantine laws—despite some objections that this form of personnel assistance was an unconstitutional interference with states' rights. The licenses of state auctioneers were accepted as a qualification for federal auctioneers. Lacking jails, the national government entered into contracts with the states to use state jails for federal prisoners at the rate of 50 cents a month per prisoner plus cost of maintenance. National officers were authorized to use state courts in suits to collect fines or forfeitures. National jurors were to be selected in the manner employed in each state to select its own jurors. State laws were adopted as the basis of rules of decision in common law trials. In 1792 the powers of United States marshals were prescribed to include the same powers in executing national laws as the state sheriffs possessed in executing state laws.

From 1789 to 1800 the state government went through a series of adjustments to bring their laws into conformity with the Constitution and the national laws enacted in pursuance of it. Laws regarding coinage, legal tender, admiralty, naturalization, and Indian affairs were amended or repealed. But few men in either national or state governments had clear ideas of how the working relationship should be arranged, and the national government was not yet in a position to carry out its new powers thoroughly. As a result, in the first few years of the new government, the states performed tasks which violated the theory of the new Constitution. Nor did the busy national government insist on the letter of the law. True, a federal circuit court declared a Rhode Island state law invalid; and Virginia and Connecticut laws conflicting with provisions of the Treaty of 1783 were voided. These were exceptions, however, and the states, for a while, ran up an impressive list of violations.

In the decade of 1790, tne states let their banks issue bills of credit—

a practice which was later upheld by the Supreme Court, although Story and others doubted its constitutionality. Massachusetts and Georgia enacted laws taxing imports. A number of the states maintained and manned forts. Others managed Indian affairs as in the past. Rhode Island, Pennsylvania, and Virginia operated some diplomatic services. And most states had naturalization laws that differed from the uniform law passed by Congress. Uncertainty, legislative inertia, and adherence to states' rights doctrine were some of the chief factors contributing to this confusion.

In administrative matters falling within the area of concurrent jurisdiction, inevitable conflicts were eased by cooperation. State and national officers often worked together voluntarily, sometimes with the added support of permissive legislation by states and the national government. Congress passed laws prescribing cooperation in several spheres. A congressional resolution ordered that copies of federal laws be transmitted to each state within ten days of passage. The states helped publicize national laws, even in some cases appropriating money for printing and distributing them. State proclamations ordering state officers to carry out national laws were common. A New York law, for example, required pilots to report all vessels sighted to the harbor master, who was obliged to forward the reports to national customs officers. The national government, in return, ordered that all state pilot laws be obeyed.

Points of Personnel

The problems of power and problems of law on their way toward harmony, the new system still was faced with one of the most sensitive subjects of all. It had to answer the question: Who is to do the job? The transition from Confederation to Constitution brought most of the Confederation personnel into corresponding positions under the Constitution. Officers to man the new administrative positions of the national government were found among holders of equivalent preexisting state positions. The new court system drew mainly from men of experience on the state benches. In short, the states provided the training ground for many of the national personnel; and an influential, though unplanned, community of interest between state and national administrations resulted.

The problem of dual officeholding raised not only administrative difficulties, but a states' rights issue as well. The Constitution prohibits only two kinds of dual officeholding. It forbids congressmen and persons holding offices of trust or profit under the United States from being appointed as electors of the President. It also prevents any officer of the United States from being at the same time a member of Congress. On the other hand, the state legislatures, and especially their anti-Federalist members, wanted to protect state officers from national temptation and to preserve the separation of powers. They took steps before 1800, except in Rhode Island and Massachusetts, to prevent individuals from holding both national and state offices at the same time.

A Point of Contact: Interstate Compacts

Finally, the new system had to make up its mind about a tradition that had a long history before the Constitution and that was destined to revive in powerful forms during the twentieth century. This was the tradition of interstate compacts. They dealt with fishing rights, commercial rights on waterways, port regulations, and boundary arrangements. The Constitution required congressional consent to any new pacts. Such consent was given to the Virginia-Kentucky territorial agreement of 1789 when Kentucky was admitted to the Union. In 1793, after the failure of the states to settle extradition disputes amicably under the express provision of the Constitution (art. IV, sec. 2, clause 2), Congress set forth the procedure to be followed in extraditing a fugitive from one state to another. The development of interstate compacts in general was encouraged by the willingness of Congress to tolerate some compacts it did not explicitly approve. Absence of dissent was taken to mean assent.

SUMMARY: THE FEDERAL PERIOD OF ADJUSTMENT (1787–1800)

Cooperation Assumed

In this formative time, the Constitution did not set up rigidly independent administrative establishments in both national and state governments. On the contrary, cooperation between the national government and the states was assumed from the very first. Although the scale of administration at both state and national levels was small, and the areas of government were few, general practice already included the major forms of national-state administrative relationships known to us today. These may be summarized as follows.

With respect to powers:

1. State and national laws were brought into alignment with each other, in some cases by the adoption of state laws as national laws and vice versa.

2. The states engaged in interstate compacts.

With respect to purse:

1. The national government and the states evolved a substantial division of revenue resources.

2. The national government made its first grants-in-aid in the form of land grants.

3. The national government gave relief to the states through the assumption of state debts.

With respect to administration:

1. State and national officials cooperated—informally or under statutory authority—in the performance of joint or related activities.

2. Administrative arrangements were completed for both states and the national government to undertake functions in fields within the other's authorized jurisdiction; in some cases state officers were paid by the national government and vice versa.

3. States performed national governmental activities through contractual arrangements.

III. THE PERIOD OF CROSS-CURRENTS:
1800–1913

CHARTING THE CURRENTS

The Federalist age, ending in the early 1800's, showed inclinations toward cooperative federalism. During the next century, the centralism of the Federalist Party was challenged many times in the executive, legislative, and judicial forums of the nation, and once on the battleground.

Formation of the anticentralist Republican Party of Jefferson at the turn of the nineteenth century signalized the political challenge to the supremacy of a centralist view. All arms of the national government shared in the burden of the dispute, but the judiciary bore the brunt—partly because of the Supreme Court's role as an arbitrator and partly as a result of Chief Justice Marshall's enlargement of its review powers.

The results of this tendency to carry the issues to the courts by no means formed a consistently clear pattern. Even today, experts in the judicial developments of the nineteenth century do not thoroughly agree in their interpretations of the period. Yet, while they differ in opinion, the authorities seem to agree that the nineteenth century reveals two opposing juridical trends. In the earlier years of the century, the Supreme Court was heavily weighted with Federalists who successfully sought to extend the national power at the expense of the states. Their object was the unification of the nation, but their efforts stimulated the states to become increasingly aware of their side of a dual power system. In the later years of the century, this duality was emphasized by the Court in quite a different way. The Court, in the postbellum years, was more inclined to pare down the national powers and reserve more rights to the states. It tried to set the national and state governments at arm's length. Thus, in the long run, the Supreme

Court's decisions during the nineteenth century show a strong tendency toward dual federalism—toward carving out separate fields of authority for the national government, on one hand, and for the states, on the other hand. This tendency persisted until the 1930's.

An obvious struggle for power between the national and state governments followed. But the dual system did not supplant the old cooperative system; it was added to it. In other words, there existed throughout this period two sets of relationships: (a) between the national government and the states within the new system of separated governments (dual federalism); (b) between the national government and the states within the continuing older system of interlocking governments (cooperative federalism).

We cannot intelligibly chart these cross-currents of nineteenth-century federalism unless we study the two-level approach in some detail; recount the shifts in power from national to state government and back again; and recognize, when it appears, the power vacuum that finally presents itself between the two parts of a dual system. Conversely, even while the dual federal scheme was dominating public attention by its frequent appearance in the courts, the older cooperative federalism was slowly redeveloping its own forms, such as the grant-in-aid, in response to new conceptions of the general need.

The major channels of these currents lay in the constitutional law itself—particularly the amendments that followed the Bill of Rights—and the application of constitutional powers, such as the commerce clause, to both foreign and domestic affairs.

The fiscal policies that paralleled the rise of new governmental relations in this period were linked, in the first place, with a general growth in size, income, and expense of all types of government. Secondly, the financial responsibilities of the national government increased enormously. This was not reflected, except during the Civil War period, by large increases in national expenditures. The new responsibility was not so much that of a tax collector and tax spender, but rather that of distributing the riches of the national domain.

Finally, significant administrative beacons guiding the flow of national and state powers were erected in this period. We see a willingness on the part of the national government to share with the states some of the regulatory powers which it acquired in the post-Civil War period. We see, moreover, the growth of new programs, some involving national grants, that resulted in increasing administrative cooperation between the nation and the states. It was these programs that largely served as the cooperative counterweight to the judicially defined theory of dual federalism.

THE CURRENTS OF LAW

The Amendments: Toward Cooperation

The amendment process influenced the relation between the national government and the states in several significant ways. In terms of the way they divided power, the amendments increased national power at the expense of the states. Of the 11 amendments since the Bill of Rights, two may be considered to have strengthened the role of the states in the federal structure, seven to have diminished it, and two not to have materially changed it.

Two which ostensibly accrued to the benefit of the states were the Eleventh, prohibiting the national judiciary from taking cognizance of suits against a state by citizens of another state or of a foreign state, and the Twenty-first, granting state option on interstate commerce in intoxicating liquors.

The seven arbitrating against the states were the Civil War amendments (Thirteenth, Fourteenth, and Fifteenth); the income tax amendment (Sixteenth), which increased enormously the taxing capacity of the national government; the Seventeenth, which recognized a growing tendency on the part of the states themselves to make senators elective by popular vote; the Eighteenth (prohibition amendment); and the woman's suffrage amendment (Nineteenth).

The Twelfth Amendment (regulating the election of the President and Vice President in the absence of a majority of electoral votes) and the Twentieth ("lame duck" amendment) had no important consequences for national-state relations. It should be noted that the Eighteenth, the prohibition amendment, while it allowed congressional legislation to ban the manufacture and sale of intoxicating liquors anywhere in the United States, gave the states concurrent power to enforce the amendment by appropriate legislation.

For the purpose of this survey, the major consideration is that the amendment power and the amendment process have always been in the hands of the states. Thus, while the concurring states recognized a decrease of their power in many amendments, they accepted them in view of considerations that outweighed considerations of power. A good example is the Nineteenth Amendment. By forbidding the abridgment of the right of suffrage on account of sex, the amendment took away from the states the right to determine their own policy in the matter. The states appear to have valued the proposed benefits of the amendment more than the power they surrendered to obtain them.

The Nineteenth Amendment is a fairly simple case; some of the other amendments were not so simple in their ultimate effects on the relation between national and state powers. They illustrate the possibility that an amendment, when it comes to be applied beyond the scope of the situation which produced it, may prove to operate in ways unforeseen. The Fourteenth Amendment demonstrates this. It denies to the states the right to deprive any person of "life, liberty, or property without due process of law." Large additional areas of state power, unexamined when this amendment was written, were taken away from the states in the late nineteenth century when the Court decided that "persons" included corporations. This decision nullified any of the business-control statutes passed by the various states in the decades following the Civil War.

On the other hand, the Court, in interpreting the Fourteenth Amendment, handed back tremendous powers to the states. In the Slaughterhouse cases (1873) and the Civil Rights cases (1883), the question was whether the state government, without interference by the national government's influence under the Fourteenth Amendment, were free to exercise and enforce large powers over the rights, privileges, and immunities of citizens. These cases decidedly limited interference on the part of the national government.

Whether these be reversals or reconsiderations of Supreme Court judgment, they suggest that the amendment process during the nineteenth century is pertinent to this study not for its power implications—since it cut both ways—but for another reason. The amendment process demonstrates the interdependence of nation and state.

Commerce: Toward Duality

The policy makers of the nineteenth century found themselves returning to constitutional considerations not only through the amendment process, but through the interstate commerce clause. They did so for the same reason that makes the commerce clause an important issue to consider here. The clause involved a basic application of national versus state powers and its economic and legislative implications crosscut the major social issues of the century. The clause offers an important perspective from which to view the whole course of national-state relations. For the judges turned their neatest and hardest distinctions between national and state power on the pivot of the commerce clause.

The national powers, in their earliest influential application, were directed toward foreign commerce and affairs rather than toward the domestic arena. Although there has never been any doubt that the Constitution awards to the national government complete power over foreign affairs, the national government could afford to be magnanimous toward the states in many of these matters. In settling the northeastern boundary dispute with England in the early nineteenth century, the negotiations were strongly influenced by the states involved. Maine, for example, intervened, memorialized, and protested with persistence over the slow progress of the settlement. States also intervened not as formal parties, but as affected jurisdictions, in the Oregon and southeastern settlements. The voice of the states has been heard recently in connection with Great Lakes-St. Lawrence deep water-way plans. Yet in the later nineteenth century, as in more recent years, the national government has amply demonstrated its right to use foreign commerce powers even over matters ultimately domestic. It has extended its control in the field of health, drugs, white slavery, obscene literature, migratory birds, and the livestock industry.

It is in the field of domestic commerce that two landmark decisions of the Supreme Court provide us with our clearest examples of the construction of nineteenth-century dual federalism.

The tones of John Marshall are heard clearly in the first case. Before 1824, the states often regulated commerce that only by some stretch of the imagination might be called intrastate. In *Gibbons* v. *Ogden* (1824), the first case before the Supreme Court regarding the commerce clause, Marshall defined the national power as sovereign, complete, and as broad as if it were vested in a single government rather than in a federal one. The states might regulate only completely internal commerce, which would include such matters as inspection laws, quarantine laws, health laws, turn-pike roads, or ferries. This decision recognized no rights of the states in respect to interstate commerce at all. The supremacy clause of the Constitution, in fact, was cited by Marshall as eliminating all possible doubts in areas where the congressional power conflicted with state power. The idea of a basic residue of reserved power of the states, which is untouchable by any principle of national supremacy in interstate commerce, arose as a part of the political struggle over slavery. It did not win a single case before the Court until after the Civil War.

After the war the principle won many cases, but the climax of its victory came in the twentieth century. In *Hammer* v. *Dagenhart* (1918), we hear the late nineteenth-century voice that opposed itself to Marshall speak out in firmest tones. In this case the Court declared unconstitutional an act of Congress prohibiting the interstate transportation of goods in the manufacture of which children had taken part. The Court held that "the grant of authority over a purely federal matter was not intended to destroy the local power always existing and carefully reserved to the states in the tenth amendment to the Constitution." The decision insisted upon the doctrine that interstate commerce must be regulated by Congress as commerce, and not for "ulterior" purposes. And it insisted upon the complementary doctrine that production of goods that would enter into interstate commerce could not be regulated in the process of regulating the traffic itself.

In terms of power, the two decisions—*Gibbons* v. *Ogden* and *Hammer* v. *Dagenhart*—were contradictory. The first extended the powers of national government; the second limited them. In terms of dual federalism, however, the second was completely consistent with the first. It confirmed the duality of powers in the very act of redressing a balance between them. Such an outcome might have been predicted as early as 1871, when the decision in Tarble's case drew the verbal hairline on which the earlier and the later cases were finally balanced:

There are within the territorial limits of each state two governments, restricted in their sphere of action, but independent of each other, and supreme within their respective spheres. Each has its separate departments, each has its distinct laws, and each has its own tribunals for their enforcement. Neither government can intrude within the jurisdiction of the other or authorize any interference therein by its judicial officers.

The Tarble decision did not, and could not, foresee one result of its own doctrine that became plain only when the 1918 case had completed the work of the decision of 1824. When state powers had been awarded to one area and the national powers to another, it was already beginning to be noticed that the two areas together did not cover the field. Between them existed a vacuum. The issue of child labor affords an excellent example of the effects. At a period when the individual state could not exercise its power to control child labor without pricing itself out of the market, dual federalism prevented the national government from exercising its power in this field to act in behalf of the general welfare.

Judicial rhetoric is not always consistent with judicial action, and the Court did not always adhere to a separatist doctrine. Indeed, its rhetoric sometimes indicated a positive view of cooperation. In any case, the Court was rarely, if ever, directly confronted with the issue of cooperation versus separation as such. Rather it was concerned with defining permissible areas of action for the central government and the states; or with deciding with respect to a point at issue whether any government could take action. The Marshall Court contributed to intergovernmental cooperation by the very act of permitting federal operations where they had not existed before. Furthermore, even Marshall was willing to allow interstate commerce to be affected by the states in their use of police power. Later courts also upheld state laws that had an impact on interstate commerce, just as they approved the expansion of the national commerce power, as in statutes providing for the control of telegraphic communication, or prohibiting the interstate transportation of lotteries, impure foods and drugs, and prostitutes. Similar room for cooperation was found outside the commerce field, notably in the Court's refusal to interfere with federal grants of land or cash to the states. Although research to substantiate the point has not been completed, it is probably true that the Supreme Court from 1800 to 1936 allowed far more federal-state collaboration than it blocked.

POLITICAL BEHAVIOR AND ADMINISTRATIVE ACTION

Political behavior and administrative action of the nineteenth century provide positive evidence that, throughout the entire era of so-called dual federalism, the many governments in the American federal system continued the close administrative and fiscal collaboration of the earlier period. Governmental activities were not extensive. But regarding what governments did, intergovernmental cooperation during the last century was comparable with that existing today.

Occasional presidential vetoes (from Madison to Buchanan) of cash and land grants provide some evidence of constitutional and ideological apprehensions about the extensive expansion of federal activities which produced widespread intergovernmental collaboration. In perspective, however, the vetoes are a more important evidence of the continuous search, not least by state officials, for ways and means to involve the central government in a wide variety of joint programs. The search was successful.

Grants-in-land and grants-in-services from the national government were of first importance in virtually all the principal functions undertaken by the states and their local subsidiaries. Land grants were made to the states for, among other purposes, elementary schools, colleges, and special educational institutions; roads, canals, rivers, harbors, and railroads; reclamation of desert and swamp lands; and veterans' welfare. In fact whatever was at the focus of state attention became the recipient of national grants. (Then, as today, national grants established state emphasis as well as followed it.) If Connecticut wished to establish a program for the care and education of the deaf and dumb, federal money in the form of a land grant was found to aid that program. If higher education relating to agriculture became a pressing need, Congress could dip into the public domain and make appropriate grants to states. If the need for swamp drainage and flood control arose, the federal government could supply both grants-in-land and, from the Army Corps of Engineers, the services of the only trained engineers then available.

Aid also went in the other direction. The federal government, theoretically in exclusive control of the Indian population, relied continuously (and not always wisely) on the experience and resources of state and local governments. State militias were an all-important ingredient in the nation's armed forces. State governments became unofficial but real partners in federal programs for homesteading, reclamation, tree culture, law enforcement, inland waterways, the nation's internal communications system (including highway and railroad routes), and veterans' aid of various sorts. Administrative contacts were voluminous, and the whole process of interaction was lubricated, then as today, by constitutent-conscious members of Congress.

The essential continuity of the collaborative system is best demonstrated by the history of the grants. The land grant tended to become a cash grant based on the calculated disposable value of the land, and the cash grant tended to become an annual grant based upon the national government's superior tax powers. In 1887, only three years before the frontier was officially closed, thus signalizing the end of the disposable public domain, Congress enacted the first continuing cash grants.

The National Wealth and the Grant System

General View. A principal point of interest is the growth of grants-in-aid. Their place in the fiscal development of the federal system cannot be understood without a general budgetary view of the period.

In the early nineteenth century, it became apparent that the national government had financial resources in excess of its spending programs. The states had been spending freely on extensive internal improvements and were heavily in debt. From $13 million in 1820, state indebtedness had increased to over $174 million in 1837. Meanwhile, the national government had paid off its own debts, and current revenues exceeded total expenditures each year.

Sectional opposition, bolstered by constitutional doubts, prevented the use of national income for internal improvements. Jackson vetoed Clay's bill of 1832 to distribute revenues from the sale of the public domain to the states for education or internal improvements. In 1836 Congress agreed on an unconditional distribution of the federal Treasury surplus among the states according to their national representation. Since Jackson opposed an outright gift of the money, the sums were declared to be deposits which the United States Treasury might recall if needed. In 1837 three quarterly distributions were made, totaling $28.1 million. A depression intervened, and further payments were not made. Both national and state revenues dropped sharply, but by 1850 the national government was running surpluses again. After the interruption of the Civil War, the Treasury had surpluses from 1866 to 1893, with the exception of 1874. Very few national expenditures followed; pensions, public buildings, and river and harbor improvements were principal items.

Grants and the Public Domain. The national government's grant-in-aid system appeared first in the land grants of 1785 and the Northwest Ordinance of 1787. Following 1789, the earliest grants were justified either by specific clauses in the Constitution or by the power of Congress to dispose of the national domain for the common benefit. Thus, the public domain demanded immediate attention in any consideration of the role played by national grants in the destinies of the states. Many aspects of national-state relations have been influenced by the national domain.

If we look at the domain as a possible source of governmental income, we see that the prevailing policy of the national government has been to make the states the principal direct beneficiaries of the sale or exploitation of public lands.

If we look at the national domain as a source of purse-power for the national government, one drift is clear. From the beginning, the national government conditioned its land grants to the states on state fulfillment of certain requirements. Over the years, these conditions have become increasingly specific in tone and based on an increasing alertness to provide the national donor with administrative checks on the state recipient.

The proceeds of the national domain were used, as time went on, for a variety of purposes. The earliest land grant, under the Northwest Ordinance, was earmarked for a broad purpose of welfare—free public education. Later, grants to subsidize the construction of roads, canals, and railroads shot ahead of all other types in their influence on national development. Still later, the withdrawal of millions of acres from the disposable public domain, on conservation principles, put a brake on the whole land-grant procedure.

When we examine the grants to the states in terms of the fiscal pattern which they established, one development is especially important: the land grant tended to become a cash grant based on the land's disposable value, and the cash grant tended to become an annual grant based on national tax powers.

The Grants: Education. The 1785 land grant for schools, reaffirmed in the Northwest Ordinance of 1787, was the first use of national funds to encourage the states to follow a national policy. In the years that followed, the pattern was applied again and again. Although grants to Ohio (1802) and four other states put the lands directly into the hands of the townships, later grants were made to the governments of the states. In 1848, the grant was increased to two sections per township, and 14 states entered the Union with this more generous endowment. The total count of lands distributed by the national government for common school purposes exceeds 130 million acres.

The same pattern was applied to public education at progressively higher levels. Beginning in 1787, Congress provided two townships in each state as an endowment for institutions of higher learning. Such grants ranged from 160,000 to 800,000 acres. More than 2.6 million acres went for universities, and 1.36 million acres for state normal schools. Then, in 1818 Congress added to its endowment of state schools by providing that 5 per cent of the proceeds of the sale of remaining national lands within the state should flow into the state treasury. Much, though not all, of this revenue was expended for educational purposes.

The precedent of coupling the public domain with educational policy was substantially extended in 1862. Representative Morrill, of Vermont, in 1857 introduced in Congress a bill donating land to each state for the "endowment, support, and maintenance of at least one college where the leading subject shall be, without excluding other scientific and classical studies, and including military tactics, to teach such branches of learning as are related to the agriculture and the mechanic arts." Both Houses passed the bill by a slim margin, but President Buchanan, after declaring it an unconstitutional disposition of public lands, vetoed it. Morrill finally pushed this bill through in 1862. It granted each existing and future state a basic endowment of 60,000 acres and 30,000 additional acres for each of its congressional representatives. If states were short of national land within their own borders, they were given federal land scrip with which to claim public domain in other parts of the country. These funds could not be used for construction, which had to be provided by each state itself; the principal had to be invested in approved securities and left untouched, and the expenditures had to be reported annually to Congress.

The Grants: Agriculture. Congress extended and deepened the Morrill design in following years. The second Morrill Act, passed in 1890, provided an annual cash grant rising to $25,000 per state wherever national requirements were met, and the Nelson amendment of 1907 not only doubled the grant but extended the purposes for which it might be used. Congress kept in mind its experience with the first Morrill bill when it made the national government a patron of agricultural research. The Hatch Act of 1887 authorized $15,000 a year in land sale proceeds for the establishment of state agricultural experiment stations at agricultural colleges. The central government specified annual fiscal reports and, beginning in 1895, imposed a national audit on expenditures. The Adams Act of 1906 doubled these allotments. Congress followed more or less the same lines in 1911 when the Marine School Act offered to states that would match it a grant of $25,000 for schools of seamanship.

The Grants: Internal Improvements. The history of the national subsidy of state, local, and private enterprise in internal improvements is complex. In the first place, "internal improvements" has not always been a clear classification. Widely different enterprises were included in this category at different times in the nineteenth century. In the second place, a good many of the land grants used for canals and other expenditures were originally given to the states for the quite different purpose of flood control and drainage. The effects of internal improvement subsidies on state governments were debated vociferously and from a variety of viewpoints throughout the entire nineteenth century.

The debates did not prevent action. The national government, in the days of wagons, gave away 3.25 million acres for the support of wagon roads. When canal building boomed, it gave 4.5 million acres for this purpose to Illinois, Indiana, Michigan, Ohio, and Wisconsin; and 2.25 million acres to Alabama, Iowa, and Wisconsin to improve river navigation. It gave about 64 million acres to the states for flood control and to drain marshy lands. When steam rode the rails, it gave grants for railroad construction. For many reasons, the national government finally decided to subsidize the railroads directly.

The roster of statesmen of 1800 to 1850 who viewed these grants with Old Roman alarm is studded with eminent names. Madison, in the early 1800's, vowed that the national government was debarred from the field of internal improvements by nothing less than "a defect of constitutional authority." He promptly vetoed the bonus bill of 1817, which made provisions for internal improvements. Both Monroe and Jackson vetoed bills providing national funds for local roads. Jackson, in 1832, vetoed Henry Clay's bill to distribute land sale proceeds to the states as endowments for both internal improvements and education. Other opponents of specific-purpose grants were Polk, Pierce, and Buchanan. This tradition of alarms and vetoes was renewed in the debate over the creation of the Department of the Interior in 1849. Until that year, the Secretary of State administered those few domestic affairs the national government had in hand. Argument for the Department of the Interior bill, based on the claim that i would promote efficiency in administration, was countered by the prediction that it would increase national patronage and power at the expense of the states. President Polk remarked as he signed the bill: "I fear its consolidating tendency."

The Grants: Forestry. National forestry legislation, aimed at enforcement of forest protection, gave the national government considerable powers over state administration. The President in 1891 acted under his power to create forest preserves and set aside millions of acres of the public domain. Western discontent with the act led to the practice of rebating a portion of the revenues from the forests to the states in which they stood. The rebates, which climbed from 10 per cent in 1906 to 25 per cent of total receipts in 1908, were earmarked for education and roads.

In 1911 Congress passed the Weeks Act. It authorized the Secretary of Agriculture ". . . to cooperate with any state or group of states, when requested to do so, in the protection from fire of the forested watersheds of navigable streams. . . ." This enactment was legislative news. It not only made federal aid conditional upon advance approval of state plans for forest guardianship, but also provided federal inspection of state procedure. Whereas previous grants-in-aid were embodied in directives of a general nature, the states were now subjected to national scrutiny intended to be both continuing and particularized.

The Weeks Act, besides requiring state matching, also described in some detail how the state as well as the national contribution should be overseen by national officers. The full machinery of the Weeks Act was not promptly and fully applied, and its operations were not costly. Total national payments did not exceed $100,000 a year until after 1920, and the national grants were often paid in salaries to national patrolmen who held state commissions.

The Grants: Welfare. Throughout the nineteenth century, there was little fear of a "consolidating tendency" in the field of welfare, since there was little national tendency to deal with welfare problems at all. Indiana in 1830 called upon Congress to open its purse to "minister consolation to all whom casualty or misadventure may render dependent upon benevolent protection." Four years later Indiana asked for the construction of national hospitals within the state, with the Ohio River boatmen as likely clients. Other states brought similar projects to the attention of Congress and, by 1861, 24 marine hospitals were built, many of them on navigable lakes and rivers.

But almost to the end of the nineteenth century, America appears to have held the opinion that a citizen's ill health or incapacity was not the concern of Congress. When Congress in 1854 proposed to grant public lands to the states for the benefit of the insane, President Pierce vetoed the proposal. He feared that "the dignity of the states shall bow to the dictation of Congress by conforming their legislation thereto" and that this, in terms of state powers, would be "the beginning of the end." Not until 1879 was the next cautious step taken by Congress. The Education of the Blind Act provided funds to the American Printing House for the Blind.

This was apparently the first act to set up the principle of allotment according to need: the $10,000 worth of books and equipment produced under the grant each year was distributed to the states according to the number of blind pupils enrolled in the public institutions of each state.

In 1888 Congress voted an annual appropriation of $25,000 for the care of disabled soldiers and sailors in the state soldiers' homes, at the rate of $100 per inmate per annum. An amendment the following year took the memorable step of requiring the states to match federal funds as a condition for receiving them.

Only after the start of the new century did the national interest in local health take a new turn. A statute of 1902 is indicative: it authorized the Surgeon General of the United States to call meetings of national and state officials and to furnish assistance to state officials.

The Grants: Militia. National assistance to the National Guard began in 1808, when Congress granted an annual sum of $200,000 to the states to arm and equip their militia. Congress imposed no conditions of supervision. Many citizens criticized the manner in which the states spent the money, but it was not until 1886 that Congress attached to its increased grant of funds ($400,000) the condition that each state must provide 100 militiamen for each Senator and Representative. Congress increased the funds in 1901, 1906, and 1908, until the appropriation reached $4 million. The Dick Act of 1903 provided for the standardization of arms and equipment from federal stocks and paid the National Guard from national funds during national military exercises. It also authorized inspection of state performance. However, while the national government could advise, make regulations, and threaten to withhold pay, the state governments retained administration and command.

The Grant as an Interactive Device. The historical development of the grant system displays changes in attitude toward the administration of the grant as well as changes in the source, size, and function of the grant funds. In the early years, grants were largesse—primarily in the form of land, cash based on land sales, and Treasury surpluses—from the national government to the states. The national government attached general, simple, and generous conditions to those early grants, sometimes designating the broad purposes for which they were to be used, but left the states almost complete freedom in disposing of their proceeds. Beginning with the first Morrill Act, however, Congress, took care to write into the grant enactments an increasing number of administrative prescriptions. These prescriptions assumed and encouraged cooperation between the national government and state governments. The total effect of the growth pattern of grants was to provide a new and important field of collaboration.

ADMINISTRATIVE AND FISCAL STREAMS: 1800–1913

Administrative Interaction in Nongrant Fields

Legislative Cooperation. In this period the national system of grants was not the only device that encouraged national-state collaboration. In nongrant fields cooperation between the national and state governments was set in motion by legislative acts ranging from election procedures and controls over dual officeholding to regulatory statutes.

Elections and Dual Officeholding. The administration of elections is a case both of dual officeholding and national-state administrative cooperation. The Constitution, providing that "the Congress may at any time make or alter such regulations" as the states prescribe for holding elections, gave the national government an area of wide potential influence that it has never fully exercised. In 1842 an act was passed declaring that members of the House of Representatives should be elected on the district plan. Again in 1866 Congress provided for regulating the election of senators by the state legislatures, all this while state officers were administering national elections. And the national laws controlling congressional elections, enacted in the reconstruction period, were virtually all repealed by 1894.

Nevertheless, in 1880, in the case of *Ex parte Siebold,* the Supreme Court upheld the prosecution of state officers for violation of the federal code despite the protests of certain states that their officers were not forced to administer federal law. The Court replied that national functions were constitutionally designated to be performed by state officers. *Ex parte Clarke* (1880) and *Ex parte Yarbrough* (1884) approved this position. This congressional power has recently been extended to cover primaries for national officers (*U.S.* v. *Classic,* 1941). But little positive regulatory legislation exists, and the administrative machinery available to enforce national law on state officers is practically nonexistent.

The use of state officers to carry out national law continued through the nineteenth century even after it became explicitly acknowledged that no compulsion lay with state executives to carry out national laws. During the slavery controversy such cooperation inevitably declined, but it picked up after the Civil War and increased greatly in later years.

In *Wayman* v. *Southard* (1825) the Court assumed that the national government might properly designate state officers as its agents. In *Prigg* v. *Pennsylvania* (1842) such action was approved in connection with giving local magistrates power to arrest fugitive slaves, and, in the absence of express prohibition by the states, the state was assumed to have consented to such delegation of tasks. However, grave doubt was cast on the power of the national government to compel state officers to perform national tasks, and in *Kentucky* v. *Dennison* (1818) the Court held that the national government could not compel a state executive to surrender a fugitive demanded by another state. Thus the limits of national encroachment on the affairs and discretion of state officers were reached and defined. In *Levin* v. *U.S.* (1904) a United States circuit court declared the practice as defined in the preceding decisions so old and established that it might be considered the law.

Just as the question of discretion was answered in *Kentucky* v. *Dennison,* the question of disqualification was handled by *U.S.* v. *Hartwell* (1868); the Court held that, in applying state laws forbidding dual officeholding, the term "federal office" embraced "the ideas of tenure, duration, emolument, and duties." Since, in most cases of cooperative activity, the duration of the cooperation is indeterminate and the salary of the secondary office of no fixed nature, such state provisions have not interfered with formal cooperation on the administrative level.

On the national level, problems in connection with dual officeholding were from time to time encountered when national officers also held state places of prominence. President Grant issued a still-surviving executive order against this practice in 1872, but it exempted the minor offices. Orders of Presidents Theodore Roosevelt, Taft, and Wilson allowed dual officeholding for specific offices, and an important order of President Coolidge in 1926 commissioned local officers with powers to enforce national prohibition. The Selective Service Act of 1918, the civilian conservation program, and the National Industrial Recovery Act of 1933 utilized the technique of dual officeholding, and the practice is to be found in a number of more recent programs which the nation and state jointly administer.

Regulatory Cooperation. When Congress began to attempt a regulation of business for reasons of the general welfare, the courts were inclined to pick up the loose threads of the theory of states' rights. The theory appeared to be opposed to national intervention in economic affairs. The courts did this despite the many ways in which the states and the nation depended on one another for sustenance and vitality. Thus, judicial events both before and after the Civil War blocked many natural channels of mutual and beneficial cooperation between nation and states. Furthermore, as illustrated by the matter of child labor legislation, it also created a power vacuum in which neither could operate.

Yet, despite the judicial tendency of the 1800–1913 period to insist on dual federalism in many areas of government, public action of quite a different tenor was not lacking. The Supreme Court, in the act of sustaining certain forms of cooperative legislation, or at least in tacitly approving them, permitted considerable flexibility in national-state relations. This flexibility was the opposite of dual federalism, since it implied and actively nurtured national-state cooperation. For example, the Constitution and the Court gave the national government authority to restrict state police powers with respect to the importation of certain goods. Yet Court and Congress, by action or inaction, permitted a considerable freedom to the states in commerce regulation.

This, however, did not mean that the national government surrendered the field. In 1889 it entered the area aggressively with the Interstate Commerce Act. But here again, it provided methods for cooperation with states. The Interstate Commerce Commission, two years after its establishment in 1889, arranged a conference with state agencies working in the field of railroad regulation. The conference resolved to meet annually "with a view of perfecting uniform legislation and regulation concerning the supervision of railroads." It adopted bylaws and a constitution and named itself the National Association of Railroad Commissioners.

In 1897 the National Association recommended adoption of an amendment to the ICC law authorizing the Commission to appoint accounting examiners and to establish a bureau of statistics and accounts to regulate carriers' books. The Hepburn amendment of 1906 gave the required power; and the best results of national-state cooperation came precisely in the matters of accounting and statistics. The National Association also assisted the ICC in valuation of railroad property for rate-making purposes under the Valuation Act of 1913. The ICC, without specific statutory sanction, also held joint meetings, with state commissions. But informal cooperation, based solely on good will without legal status, hardly could guarantee the public interest in transportation or bring national order to conflicting rate structures.

CROSS CURRENTS: CONCLUSION

Pattern of Conflict

The crowded years from 1800 to 1913 present a bewildering variety of growth impulses at work on both the national and state governments. To Americans of the nineteenth century the great problem was to balance the power of the national government with the powers of the states and the sections. They did not solve that problem without resort to arms. Appomattox decided in favor of the North's belief that, whatever the powers of the states might be, secession was not one of them. By removing this issue from the forum, the Civil War made it possible for later comers to see that Americans of the nineteenth century were struggling to solve another question as well. They were trying to find answers to the problem of dual versus cooperative federalism, an issue that emerged as a by-product of the states' rights battle itself.

Which Federalisms?

The Supreme Court, faced with the problem of arbitrating, tended to move in the direction of dual federalism—separating the activities of nation and state. But the judicial decisions of the early nineteenth century, while they extended the national government's power, were not intended to make the states the mere servants of a national master; and the decisions of the late nineteenth century, while carving out additional prerogatives for the states, were not intended to veto national-state collaboration.

The most convincing evidences of cooperative federalism, however, are found outside the conflict-laden dockets of the courts. The national grant-in-aid programs are an example. They served the common purpose of nation and states and heavily relied on state cooperation in the task of dividing and allotting an empire twice as large as France. When the national government and the states collaborated to carry out these programs, they renewed old administrative bonds and formed new ones.

At the turn of the century, the problem of national versus state power had long been decided by the Civil War. The problem of dual versus cooperative federalism was preparing to take a new turn.

IV. THE TRIUMPH OF COOPERATIVE FEDERALISM:
1913–48

Long-term trends account for the increased activity of government at all levels and the increased collaboration of the national government and the states. But recurring national crises lent impetus to those trends. World War I, World War II, and the depression were great historical forces that changed the public bookkeeping and the role of government itself.

Industrial interdependence and urbanism, with their consequent changes in population and family life, largely explain the variety of popular needs that challenged government from 1913 to 1948. The disappearance of the geographic frontier, the increase of the aged in a society less able to give them family care, and, above all, the wage dependency of the masses of the people added up to a social structure that could afford little less than continued prosperity. Prosperity proved discontinuous. When the depression of 1929 struck the nation, it upset an already precarious social balance. The national government, in pump priming operations of various kinds, rapidly stepped up its grant expenditures in such typical fields as public works, welfare, social security, and agriculture. These operations were adapted to the exigencies of fiscal and administrative policies of World War II, a period which further emphasized the economic unity of the United States. Thus, depression and war speeded the response of both the national and state governments to many challenges once considered to be outside the governmental sphere of concern. Crisis, in short, at once dramatized and accelerated the role of government.

A TWILIGHT PERIOD

These new forces were well in motion by 1913, before any significant increase in the extent of national-state cooperation. Because of the sudden penetrating changes in the economy and society, many political leaders and theorists were perplexed as to the future role of the states in the federal system. There was little use in appealing to the simplicities of the Jeffersonian theory, based on the assumption that Americans were to live and work in a small-scale freeholding, agricultural economy. There was little use in appealing to the simplicities of the Hamiltonian scheme, based on the assumption that the self-interest of a substantial financial and manufacturing class alone was sufficient to insure a successful operation of the great modern industrial plant. In unmodulated form neither of these postulates could be applied realistically to twentieth-century problems of national-state relations.

GOVERNMENT GROWS

Government finance responded to the changing conditions of the years 1913–48 with basic changes in approach and method. The year 1913 was a turning point in the history of America's intergovernmental relationships. Total national expenditures then amounted to only $700 million (grants were $3 million), contrasted with state and local expenditures of about $2 billion.

While jurists and theorists were exploring the twentieth-century setting of Hamiltonian and Jeffersonian theses, political leaders brusquely ushered in the modern period with two far-reaching enactments. In 1913 the national government entered the field of income taxation on a permanent basis. At the same time, the Smith-Lever bill, the first major twentieth-century grant program, was being debated in Congress and was soon to be enacted into law. These two events signalized victory for the theory of active government in the United States.

The income tax soon proved to be a readily expandable source of revenue which, as World War I demonstrated, could funnel billions into the national Treasury. The war's end brought a reduction in national expenditures, although not to the 1913 level. The Congress and the Executive were thus in possession of a financial tool of the first magnitude.

The Smith-Lever Act of 1914, establishing the Agricultural Extension Service, represented an initial cash grant of unprecedented size from the national government to establish a continuing state-aid program. The act itself climaxed a widely supported movement to strengthen farming. The county agent program, previously dependent on private and local funds and on small sums from the Department of Agriculture, now received an initial amount of $480,000. These funds, to be matched by the states dollar for dollar, ballooned to $4.2 million in seven years.

By 1916, the total program of cooperative agricultural extension work was using $1.1 million of Smith-Lever money matched by an additional $597,924 from the states. To these funds were added $1.1 million from the Department of Agriculture, $873,000 from state and college funds, $973,000 from county funds, and $277,000 from philanthropic and other funds.

These large expenditures, the importance of the program, and the many groups involved in it all focused national attention on the system of conditional grants. Once accepted as a useful combination of national money with local needs, in a program of national, social, and economic interest, the grant device was now ready for further evolution. Public opinion and official thinking seized upon it as a basis for new social and economic programs. Consequently, in the years immediately following the Smith-Lever Act, a number of influential programs developed, including the Federal Aid Road Act of 1916, the Smith-Hughes Act of 1917, the Chamberlain-Kahn Act of 1918, and the Sheppard-Tower Act of 1921.

FEDERALISM IN THE DEPRESSION

The results of underlying economic and social changes showed themselves markedly during the economic recessions of 1921 and 1929. Particularly after 1929, the number of persons who depended on day-to-day earnings, and who lost this means of self-support in the economic crisis, reached proportions beyond the management of state and local governments. Fiscal resources of both local and state governments proved inadequate to support the strain of urgent new responsibilities, and the national government stepped in. Thus in December, 1930, Congress appropriated $80 million as an "advance" to the states for highway programs in lieu of state matching funds. This was the beginning of extensive emergency aid from the national government to states and localities during the depression crisis. Regular and emergency highway grants made up almost 90 per cent of the $183.5 million expended as federal grants in 1931.

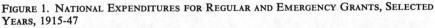

FIGURE 1. NATIONAL EXPENDITURES FOR REGULAR AND EMERGENCY GRANTS, SELECTED
YEARS, 1915-47

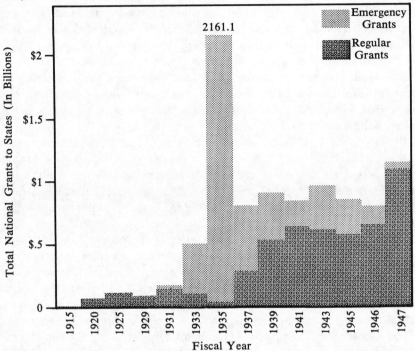

Source: U. S. Treasury, *Combined Statements of Receipts, Expenditures and Balances* and *Annual Report* for various years.

Figure 1 illustrates the course of the emergency grants. Between 1931
and 1933 national grants more than doubled, reaching the half-billion dollar
mark, and rising from 5 per cent of federal expenditures to about 13 per
cent. By 1933 emergency grants amounted to approximately three times the
regular grants, and in 1935 a high point in national grants was reached.
Over $2 billion was involved—some 30 per cent of all national expendi-
tures. As for the dependency of the states, it was estimated that receipts
from national aid constituted 23 per cent of all state revenues in 1933 and
48.5 per cent in 1935. By 1937, the WPA had taken over the emergency
spending function, largely on a nongrant basis, and emergency grants
dropped to the $.5 million level.

When World War II began, a new series of smaller emergency grants
was voted, but the depression emergency grant system was on its way out.
At the same time new permanent federal grant programs were being in-

augurated beginning with the Wagner-Peyser Act of 1933 and capped by a series of programs contained in the Social Security Act of 1935: old age assistance, aid to dependent children, aid to the blind, unemployment compensation, and several of lesser importance. After World War II, the school lunch program was established on a continuing grant-in-aid basis, the Hospital Survey and Reconstruction Act authorized grants for hospital facilities, and the 1946 Federal Airport Act provided grants for airport construction. Concern for national security caused Congress to tighten specific controls over grants to the National Guard. Thus, a few grant programs, once begun, were abandoned, and there was a continuous demand for new ones.

At the same time, the national government experimented with regional, multi-purpose programs, which in some ways stood as alternative methods of administration. The Tennessee Valley Authority is the most important case in point. Organized as a corporation for widely ranging activities over a number of states, TVA has developed a whole new system of state-national and local-national relations. Furthermore, during the depression years especially, the national government increased its direct contact with local governments.

The activities of the national government had a profound effect on the situation of the states in the federal system. Both state and national governments greatly increased their functions and expenditures and, as these functions grew, they forced constant reconsideration of the place of nation and state in American federalism. The sum of the development was that cooperative federalism acquired a wider and deeper meaning than it had ever had before World War I.

COLLABORATION TO THE FORE

While the grant programs, because of their size, received most of the attention given to national-state administrative relations between 1913 and 1948, other national and state activities moved toward closer collaboration. National, state, and local police developed a number of continuing contacts without benefit of financial arrangements or statutory requirements. The national government's regulatory laws increasingly provided for forms of cooperation between national and state agencies. The Interstate Commerce Commission, the Food and Drug Administration, the Federal Power Commission, the National Recovery Administration, the Federal Deposit Insurance Corporation, the Federal Communications Commission, the Federal Trade Commission, and, to a slight extent, the Securities and Exchange Commission adopted collaborative techniques to promote better administration of mutual tasks.

The states themselves, far more frequently than before, employed inter-state compacts, uniform state laws, reciprocal or contingent legislation, and administrative cooperation.

THE COURT DISPOSES

The Broad Bases

In the twentieth century, decisive policies have depended on the attitude of the Supreme Court toward the national government's increasing tendency to legislate and spend for such general social ends as social security, stabilized farm prices, education, and highways. In the midst of rapid administrative and fiscal developments, the Supreme Court moved toward a new point of view. It approached cases involving national-state relations with increasing liberality and enlarged its approval of efforts at cooperation in national-state activities. It allowed both the national government and the states to move more freely into each other's area of power, and the two levels of government were encouraged to develop both their individual programs and cooperative relations on their own initiative. In short, the Court's decisions in the twentieth century have evolved in the direction of cooperative federalism.

Evidences of the New Judicial View

Twentieth century interpretations of the commerce clause demonstrate this shift. It is also noticeable in the construction of the general welfare clause, the taxation clauses, and in decisions relating to still other parts of the Constitution.

After almost a century of building a separate federal "common law," the Supreme Court in 1935 *(Erie Railroad* v. *Tompkins)* dissolved the whole of that law. Since 1935 the only common law recognized by the federal courts has been the common law of the several states. The Supreme Court has also looked favorably upon a number of state laws that indirectly laid burdens upon interstate commerce while protecting the citizens of the states against threats to their health or interests from the outside. When the Court has acknowledged problems arising from interstate barriers, it has placed the responsibility for solving them on the national and state legislatures.

The Supreme Court has not destroyed state powers acquired as a result of nineteenth-century decisions. In several important ways it has fostered states' rights. Certain nondiscriminatory and nonburdensome state taxes affecting national instrumentalities have been upheld. Absolute tax immunity has disappeared, and the fiscal disadvantages of immunity have been partially mitigated. In commerce, while allowing to the national government a wider measure of tolerance and erasing the distinction between "production for commerce" and "engaged in commerce," the Court has allowed a noticeable extension of the state police and tax powers over interstate commerce. In sum, the Court has given more scope to legislative discretion, with the result that the state and federal jurisdictions interpenetrate each other with a flexibility and freedom unknown since the first days of the Republic.

The Welfare Clause

The conditional grant device moved from the protection of specific empowering clauses into the wider shelter of the general welfare clause. The Court has accepted the Hamilton-Story theory: "to provide for the general welfare" is a separate, broad federal power. In *Massachusetts* v. *Mellon* (1923), the Court refused to hear an attack on the constitutionality of the Sheppard-Towner maternity care grant of 1921. Declaring its lack of jurisdiction in the absence of a justiciable controversy, the Court also remarked that it failed to see that the states were being coerced because they were being offered national financial aid upon the satisfaction of certain conditions. Decisions of the Court in *Steward Machine Co.* v. *Davis* (1937), *Carmichael* v. *Southern Coal & Coke Co.* (1937), *Alabama Power Company* v. *Ickes* (1937), and *Duke Power Co.* v. *Greenwood* (1937) strengthened the constitutional position of the grant system. In the first of these cases, the Court recognized the welfare premises of the unemployment-compensation grants, and declared that the tax on employers imposed by Title IX of the Social Security Act of 1935 was permissible under the power of Congress to levy taxes to provide for the general welfare. A parallel decision in *Helvering* v. *Davis* (1937) upheld the old age insurance feature of the Social Security Act, a program exclusively administered from Washington.

A Sweeping Power

In view of these and other decisions, the general welfare clause appears to give Congress ample authority to legislate widely on national social welfare and, if Congress wishes, to provide for an administration that is completely national. Programs that Congress can tax and spend for, it can probably administer through its own agencies directly without the intercession of the states. The larger part of all regulatory activity, in which there has developed an appreciable amount of national-state cooperation in recent years, falls in the same category. Thus the most important test of how a public function should be undertaken seems to be not the legality of the method, but the prospective administrative efficiency and social productivity.

FISCAL DEVELOPMENTS IN FEDERAL-STATE RELATIONS, 1913–48

The legislative and judicial activities of government from 1913 to 1948 were accompanied by fiscal developments, the major outlines of which are revealed in sharp, simple form by Table 1. This table makes three major points:

TABLE 1

GOVERNMENTAL EXPENDITURES IN THE UNITED STATES

(in billions of dollars)

	1913	1932	1942	1946
Expenditures from own sources:				
National	0.7	4.4	35.1	61.9
State and Local	1.8	8.2	9.2	10.7
Total	2.5	12.6	44.3	72.6
Expenditures for own functions:				
National	.7	4.2	34.2	61.1
State and Local	1.8	8.4	10.1	11.6
Total	2.5	12.6	44.3	72.6

Source: Adapted from reports of Bureau of the Census and Secretary of the Treasury. Figures include transfer of social-insurance taxes to trust accounts.

First is the speedy growth of all governmental expenditures: from less than $3 billion to more than $70 billion within 25 years.

The second point relates to the composition of this 29-fold increase. At the beginning of the period, the national budget was less than half as large as the combined state and local budgets; at the end it was six times larger.

The third point is more localized, historically, but it is unmistakable in the table. The national government, in 1946, spent almost $1 billion more from its own sources than for its own functions. Table 2 shows the character of those expenditures between 1915 and 1947. The state and local governments, on the other hand, spent almost $1 billion more than they collected from their own sources. In each case, of course, the sum was the same money, transferred by national grants from the national to state-local column. National grants in 1913 were so small that they have not been included in the table.

All three of these points are better understood if the second—the national government's rise to the top rank as a public spender—is more clearly

TABLE 2

National Expenditures for Regular Grants-in-Aid, by Program, 1915–46

(in thousands of dollars)

Program	1915	1920	1925	1929	1931	1933	1935
Highways	—	62,535	95,750	82,097	135,593	101,266	12,657
Agricultural experiment stations	1,438	1,440	1,440	3,840	4,340	4,359	4,384
Agricultural extension work	480	4,472	5,879	7,151	8,650	8,607	8,580
Agricultural and mechanical colleges	2,500	2,500	2,550	2,550	2,550	2,550	2,550
Forestry aids	70	95	399	1,393	1,779	1,817	1,547
Vocational education	—	2,477	5,615	6,879	7,879	7,726	9,997
Vocational rehabilitation	—	—	520	665	933	993	1,029
Public health	—	2,324	611	650	887	421	264
Maternal and child health	—	—	933	777	—	—	—
Crippled children	—	—	—	—	—	—	—
Child welfare	—	—	—	—	—	—	—
Old-age assistance	—	—	—	—	—	—	—
Aid to dependent children	—	—	—	—	—	—	—
Aid to the blind	—	—	—	—	—	—	—
Employment security	—	—	—	—	—	—	1,927
Annual contributions, public housing	—	—	—	—	—	—	—
School milk and lunch program[a]	—	—	—	—	—	—	—
Minor grants[b]	1,000[c]	1,272	781	640	577	947	669
Total, regular	5,488	77,115	114,478	106,642	163,188	128,686	43,604

(continued on next page)

TABLE 2

NATIONAL EXPENDITURES FOR REGULAR GRANTS-IN-AID, BY PROGRAM, 1915–46 (CONTINUED)

(in thousands of dollars)

Program	1937	1939	1941	1943	1945	1946	1947
Highways	86,602	161,084	165,900	86,112	33,375	44,480	183,245
Agricultural experiment stations	5,611	6,538	6,861	6,922	6,972	7,195	7,190
Agricultural extension work	16,343	17,822	18,477	18,784	18,715	23,148	26,455
Agricultural and mechanical colleges	4,030	5,030	5,030	5,030	5,030	5,030	5,030
Forestry aids	1,737	1,883	2,081	3,787	6,058	7,078	8,454
Vocational education	9,695	19,533	20,068	20,911	19,811	20,153	20,493
Vocational rehabilitation	1,585	1,799	2,217	2,803	7,155	10,764	12,363
Public health	7,765	10,346	16,236	20,374	21,765	28,411	34,078
Maternal and child health	3,002	3,739	5,471	5,708	5,486	6,056	10,672
Crippled children	1,991	3,029	3,928	3,848	3,839	4,151	7,430
Child welfare	969	1,521	1,532	1,583	1,363	1,278	2,010
Old-age assistance	124,585	210,160	259,781	319,176	345,738	368,524	491,091
Aid to dependent children	14,789	31,467	62,991	67,927	53,891	60,127	108,429
Aid to the blind	4,560	5,272	7,073	8,520	10,355	10,482	14,312
Employment security	12,243	62,338	66,199	36,480	34,419	55,726	102,218
Annual contributions, public housing[a]	—	—	4,764	9,883	8,722	7,136	5,667
School milk and lunch program[b]	—	—	—	—	—	—	3,548
Minor grants[b]	751	1,089	2,786	3,309	2,834	2,782	3,548
Total, regular	296,258	542,650	651,395	621,157	585,528	662,521	1,119,733

Source: U.S. Treasury, annual reports, and combined statements of receipts, expenditures, and balances for various years; Bittermann, *State and Federal Grants-in-Aid*, pp. 132–135; *Tax Systems*, 8th ed. (1940), p. 311; and unpublished data from U.S. Bureau of the Budget.

[a] Emergency program prior to 1947.
[b] Homes for disabled veterans, marine schools, wildlife restoration projects.
[c] Estimated.

visualized. Table 3 breaks down spending into three columns—national, state, and local. It carries the figures back to 1800. The statistical result puts the spotlight on the national and local governments as the principals in a reversal of fiscal roles between 1890 and 1946. In 1890, the national government spent 36.2 cents out of every public dollar, the localities 55.6 cents. In 1946, the national government spent 85.2 cents out of every public dollar, the localities 7.2 cents.

TABLE 3

PERCENTAGE DISTRIBUTION OF GOVERNMENTAL EXPENDITURES FROM
OWN SOURCES,[a] SELECTED YEARS, 1890–1946

Year	National	State	Local	Total
1890	36.2	8.2	55.6	100.0
1902	32.5	12.0	55.5	100.0
1913	29.2	15.1	55.7	100.0
1932	35.4	20.0	44.6	100.0
1942	79.2	10.7	10.1	100.0
1946	85.2	7.6	7.2[b]	100.0

Source: Bureau of the Census and Annual Reports of the Secretary of the Treasury.
[a] National and state figures include transfer of social-insurance taxes to trust accounts.
[b] Estimated.

Tables 1 and 3 somewhat obscure the rapid growth in the revenues and expenditures of the state governments. Although still collecting and disbursing less than either the national government or the localities, the states' rate of expansion has been far more marked than the local increase. From 1913 to 1946, for example, the states experienced a spectacular increase in revenues from their own sources as compared to local revenues from local sources. (The figures thus exclude both national and state grants.) Whereas the total revenues of localities were almost four times greater than total revenues of states in 1913, local revenues exceeded those of states in 1946 by less than 15 per cent (excluding unemployment compensation taxes from the state total). If unemployment compensation taxes are included as a part of state revenues, the state total exceeds local collections.

Figure 2 shows that for the shorter 1926–42 period, state tax collections rose almost 170 per cent, compared to an increase of less than 20 per cent for localities.

Just as national grants to states have become increasingly important in recent years, so has state aid to localities. Throughout the twenties, state aid was relatively small; but the picture changed drastically in the thirties, and by 1942 state aid constituted approximately 25 per cent of the total revenue of all local units of government (including counties, school districts, and other localities, as well as cities).

The result of all the fiscal trends, from the viewpoint of the taxpayer, is summed up in a single index: the total cost of government in the United States increased from about $26 per capita in 1913 to $518 in 1946.

How was the money spent? Table 4 illustrates increases in the cost of

TABLE 4

PER CAPITA GENERAL GOVERNMENTAL EXPENDITURES 1913, 1932, AND 1941

	At Current Prices			At 1941 Prices[a]	
	1913	1932	1941	1913	1932
Total expenditures	$26.07	$99.49	$174.15	$50.48	$115.50
General control	3.18	8.33	9.07	4.97	9.00
War and protection	6.59	17.60	55.97	10.65	19.10
Military forces	2.79	6.03	46.27	2.87	6.19
Veterans' pensions	1.86	6.21	4.21	4.42	7.35
Police	.94	3.07	3.09	1.63	3.18
Fire	.66	1.50	1.49	1.15	1.46
Inspection and regulation	.34	.79	.91	.58	.82
Transportation	4.06	15.48	14.77	8.75	19.84
Highways	3.57	14.80	12.18	7.53	18.92
Waterways and other	.49	.68	2.59	1.22	.92
Natural resources	.35	4.81	10.85	.87	6.50
Agriculture	.22	3.16	8.84	.54	4.22
Forestry, reclamation, floods, other	.13	1.65	2.01	.33	2.28
Health and sanitation	1.24	3.35	3.12	2.43	4.23
Health	[b]	.93	1.24	[b]	1.02
Sanitation	[b]	2.42	1.88	[b]	3.21
Welfare, hospitals, and correction	1.93	8.34	27.37	3.79	8.58
Welfare	[b]	4.29	22.70	[b]	4.33
Hospitals	[b]	2.87	3.45	[b]	2.91
Correction	[b]	1.18	1.22	[b]	1.34
Social insurance	—	1.61	14.42	—	1.60
Schools	5.94	18.22	18.21	14.21	19.50
Libraries	.13	.37	.41	.15	.41
Recreation	.60	1.53	1.53	.70	1.67
Contributions to credit corporations and public service enterprises	.44	7.31	1.93	1.09	11.11
Public employee pensions	.11	.88	1.99	.16	.88
Interest	1.50	10.44	12.59	2.08	9.43
Miscellaneous	.38	3.31	1.93	.63	3.63

Source: J. F. Dewhurst & Associates, *America's Needs and Resources* (New York: Twentieth Century Fund, 1947), pp. 468–469.
[a] For explanation of indexes used to convert 1914 and 1932 expenditures at current prices to the 1941 price level, see (Dewhurst) table 156 and accompanying text, and appendix 27.
[b] Separate figures not available.

FIGURE 2. PERCENTAGE INCREASES IN STATE AND LOCAL TAX COLLECTIONS: 1926-42

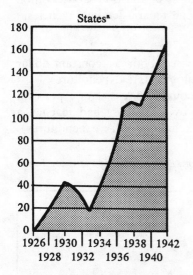

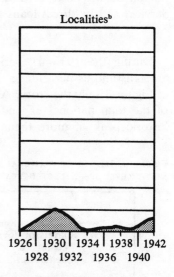

ᵃ Exclusive of unemployment compensation taxes; inclusive of local shares.
ᵇ Includes cities, counties, townships, school districts, and other local units.
Source: Computed from Report to the Secretary of the Treasury, *Federal, State, and Local Government Fiscal Relations* (Washington, D. C., 1943), Tables 35, 37.

specific governmental services in per capita terms. A per capita measurement is not the most perfect one for this purpose, since it may suggest that governmental expenditures can be expected to grow in 1-to-1 ratio with population. Such a ratio neglects many other factors that affect governmental budgets, including the results of urbanization and the changing age pyramid. Nevertheless, Table 4 provides a useful historical and functional view. The chosen periods, 1913 to 1932, and 1932 to 1941, reveal the economists' conviction that there were actually two distinct periods of budget growth. The first period shows all governmental functions engaged in consistent growth, with emphasis on agriculture, schools, highways, forestry, reclamation, and pensions.

The second period shows explosive growth. War, welfare, social insurance, and agriculture, in that order, account for the biggest percentage increase in funtional expenditures. Two peacetime items, welfare and agriculture, are precisely those that are most directly dependent on national grants. The increase in the agriculture item, however, is due only in minor degree to grants to the states (about 4 per cent of the total). It has been caused primarily by public subsidies to farmers amounting to about $586 million by the costs of direct federal operation of the Soil Conservation Service, and by direct loans to farmers through federal lending agencies.

THE GRANTS

During the 1913–41 period grants increased both as constant-dollar amounts and as percentage shares of national and state expenditures.

Figure 3 tells the story. Although grants composed less than 1 per cent of the total national expenditures in 1915, by 1935 they had reached a historic peak of more than 30 per cent (excluding WPA expenditures).

FIGURE 3. IMPACT OF NATIONAL GRANTS ON NATIONAL EXPENDITURES AND ON TOTAL STATE REVENUES, SELECTED YEARS, 1915-47

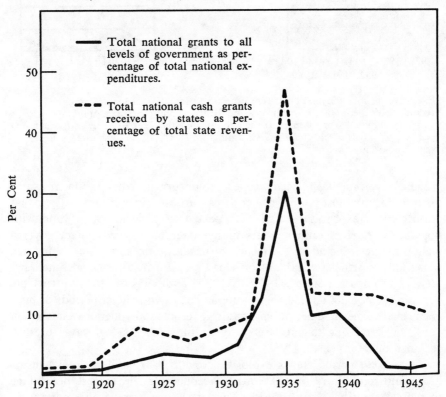

Source: *Annual Report of the Secretary of the Treasury* for various years; Bittermann, *State and Federal Grants-in-Aid;* Bureau of the Census, *State Finances* for various years, and *Historical Review of State and Local Government Finances.* All data are for fiscal years ending June 30. National expenditures exclude debt retirement, trust accounts since 1930, and postal expenditures. State revenues include unemployment compensation taxes.

Later, while their dollar amounts increased in absolute terms, their percentage of the swollen national war budget of the years 1940–48 fell off sharply. The story is remarkably similar for the state side of the transaction. Figure 3 adds grants to state revenues and measures the grants as a percentage of total state revenues. It shows that, whereas grants composed only 1.2 per cent of state revenues in 1915, by 1935 they made up almost half of such revenues. After 1935 both the dollar total and the percentage share of the grants fell off sharply, for emergency measures declined and states were able to meet modestly expanded expense schedules with substantially increased wartime tax revenues.

CONFLICT AREAS

A broad survey of national-state fiscal relations between 1913 and 1948 indentifies several points of friction. Before World War I there was an almost complete separation of revenue sources between the national government and the states. The states leaned heavily on property taxes; the national government depended largely on customs and on liquor and tobacco levies. After 1910 there was a noticeable increase in the number of state taxes modeled after national taxes, and the central government entered some tax fields, such as the tax on gasoline. Experience during the depression demonstrated an extreme lack of coordination between national and state fiscal policies, and the grant programs of the national government created areas of difficulty for both the national government and the states.

From 1930 to 1949, organized efforts at fiscal coordination multiplied. In all, almost 50 major federal, state, local, and private agencies went into the jungle of fiscal affairs and came forth with findings and conclusions Yet, except for some state use of national tax administration facilities, some interstate exchange of reports and information, and a certain amount of working cooperation between national and state tax officers, no important measure of fiscal coordination was achieved before World War II. Important advances were made during and after the war. Nevertheless, a great need for further national-state collaboration persisted.

FEDERALISM IN TWO WARS

The two world wars in which the nation engaged increased the centralizing trend in the federal union. The transportation and supply needs of war industry, the teeming interstate migration of war workers, the subsequent problems of displaced populations and overcrowding, and the great financial burdens of war itself—all these factors concentrated many demands for action on the national government. Some 10 million persons moved their homes between VJ-day and October, 1946; almost as many moved between states as within states. With national functions increasing in many areas, a heavy national budget, weighted by military expenditures, cut deeply into tax resources.

Although functions, power, and prestige tended to slip into the hands of the central government, state machinery was relied on more heavily in administering emergency programs during World War II than in World War I. In part this was the result of a record successful administration of joint activites between the wars.

The states were used to set up the Selective Service System after polling places had been adjudged more fitting than post offices as centers from which to conduct the national recruiting program. The local and district draft boards were composed of state appointees, and the responsibility for selecting men for service fell upon state officers acting as federal agents. Thus the state and local governments were responsible for the establishment and effective administration of much of the selective service machinery. The national government, again working through the state governments, was able to set up quickly a nationwide system of rationing boards. Civilian defense was organized and manned in large part by state and local officers in state councils of defense. The victory home food supply program received support from the many state organizations established to conserve food and encourage garden production. Transport regulations, such as enforcement of the 35-mile-per-hour speed limit throughout the country and the expedition of truck transport, ordinarily encumbered by some state barriers, were accomplishments of state and local executives, acting voluntarily and rapidly. A Joint Federal-State-Local Committee of Fiscal Policies and Practices was put into operation in an advisory capacity. A state drafting committee, in liaison with the Special War Policies Unit of the Department of Justice, drew up a wide variety of proposals for war legislation—suggestions which in almost all cases the states enacted into law.

World War II rapidly increased the scope and number of grants. Grants were a prominent means of national-state wartime cooperation for education of defense workers, access roads, maternity and infant care, a strategic highway network, highway surveys and plans, and flight strips. Total national defense-grant programs amounted to $208 million in 1944. An additional $135 million was spent for community facilities through grants-in-kind.

V. CONCLUSION: THE PAST AS A POINT OF VANTAGE

A long, extensive, and continuous cooperative experience is the foundation of the present system of shared functions characteristic of the American federal system. It is a misjudgment of our history and our present situation to believe that a neat separation of governmental functions could exist without drastic alterations in our society and system of government.

The whole period reviewed in this part of the study is a point of vantage from which modern developments can be surveyed. In the modern period the competition between theories of dual and cooperative federalism is no longer the issue. A cooperative pattern began to emerge before the Constitution itself, grew during the Federalist era, and continued side by side with the dual pattern in the long period between 1800 and 1913. After 1913, and especially after 1935, it became supreme. The cooperative idea cultivated new programs and added new dimensions to old ones.

The Supreme Court, whose pronouncements both established and defined the old dual balance, changed roles and spoke strongly in favor of the new cooperation. In 1937 (*Carmichael* v. *Southern Coal & Coke Co.*) the Court commented on the issue of whether a state statute had been unconstitutionally forced into existence by the federal Social Security Act:

> Together the two statutes now before us embody a cooperative legislative effort by state and national governments, for carrying out a public purpose common to both, which neither could fully achieve without the cooperation of the other. The Constitution does not prohibit such cooperation.

This is the touchstone of the period discussed in the remaining parts of this study.

Part II

THE MARBLE CAKE OF GOVERNMENT

Chapter 3

BASIC PATTERNS OF
THE "SHARING" SYSTEM

I. SHARING DESIGN: THE GRANTS-IN-AID

The grant-in-aid programs, by any standard one chooses, have been the foremost forces to bring about planned national-state collaboration. They have transferred more funds between national and state governments, involved more civil servants, framed more far-reaching policies, and led to greater administrative interaction than any other single factor in the national-state operation. Their scope is ever increasing. Table 5 lists the 21 grant programs inaugurated before 1961 in chonological order, showing the amount of federal funds allocated for each in fiscal years 1960, 1961, and 1962.

The range of specific expenditures in the regular grant programs from 1915 to 1947 was presented and tabulated in Table 2 of the preceding chapter. It showed in some detail how grant expenditures of under $5.5 million in 1915 soared to $1.1 billion by 1947, a 220-fold increase in 32 years. Table 5 shows the comparable growth of federal grant expenditures from $1.6 billion in 1948 to $7.4 billion in 1962, an increase of nearly seven times in the last 15 years. Because of the proliferation of grant programs, the figures are presented by functional categories.

The growth of interlevel grant programs has had profound effects both on the day-to-day activities and the long-run power position of the national and state governments. The national government now has a large financial stake in the effective operation of state programs. The acts of the national Congress have an immediate and profound effect upon state budgets and state administration. The states are dependent upon the national government for a large portion of their revenue, and the administration of many state activities is carried out under the supervision of national authorities. Extensive programs covering a variety of fields are being operated at a

TABLE 5

FEDERAL GRANTS-IN-AID TO STATE AND LOCAL GOVERNMENTS, 1948–1962, BY MAJOR FUNCTIONAL CATEGORIES

(thousands of dollars)

Year	Veterans Service & Benefits	Health, Welfare & Labor	Education & General Research	Agriculture & Agricultural Resources	Other Natural Resources	Commerce, Housing, Transportation, Communication	Total[a]
1948	84,977	1,024,488	37,154	70,940	11,473	387,461	1,616,493
1949	31,587	1,231,538	36,921	86,631	13,997	442,225	1,842,899
1950	15,277	1,562,252	38,614	106,276	16,957	475,006	2,214,382
1951	8,998	1,637,185	48,814	98,344	17,740	433,970	2,245,051
1952	6,656	1,661,957	122,234	83,865	19,755	481,699	2,376,166
1953	6,326	1,811,136	230,958	97,337	22,771	594,384	2,762,912
1954	6,863	1,890,389	203,210	213,173	24,938	630,299	2,968,872
1955	7,686	1,854,170	239,303	247,730	25,932	723,634	3,098,455
1956	8,091	2,109,270	208,672	389,277	26,606	873,715	3,615,631
1957	8,217	2,178,892	204,570	381,786	26,577	1,016,359	3,816,401
1958	8,326	2,523,430	165,881[b]	278,195	31,330	1,723,940	4,731,102
1959	8,316	2,777,160	296,747[b]	322,470	34,481	2,877,781	6,316,955
1960	7,880	2,923,591	363,558[b]	275,268	35,335	3,241,641	6,847,273
1961 (est.)	9,096	3,105,400	384,525[b]	297,937	33 108	3,273,917	7,103,983
1962 (est.)	9,024	3,243,596	306,417[b]	322,632	33,742	3,481,610	7,397,021

Source: Advisory Commission on Intergovernmental Relations.

[a] Data in this table are drawn from tabulations made in prior years by the Labor and Welfare Division, Bureau of the Budget, and for more recent years from special analyses dealing with grants-in-aid and accompanying the President's Budget. Figures shown do not tally precisely with other figures used in the text of the report for the reason that Budget Bureau classifications encompass a few additional items not falling within the definition of grant-in-aid used in this report. These differences in no way affect the orders of magnitude or trends of federal grants-in-aid as defined herein.

[b] Federal aid highway program financed for these years out of emergency relief funds.

high level of performance as a result of the participation of the national and state governments.

The importance of the grants in national-state administrative relations is partially indicated by the amount of money involved. Yet the impact of these enactments on the state governments increased by more than the increase in the amount of the money grants themselves. The grants, taken together, left the practice of national-state relations not only to a new quantitative level in fiscal terms, but also to a new administrative level. No small measure of their importance is based on the fact that their organizational influence is deeper, wider, more organic than even the large sums involved can suggest. The grant programs, in effect, decrease the area of free policy-making by state legislatures; but they have enabled the states to expand their activities greatly. The grant programs have subjected state administrators to national supervision; but that supervision, with some notable exceptions, has been cordial, cooperative and constructive.

THE NATIONAL PURPOSE

The grant programs have supplied a cooperative method for achieving results that might never have been achieved if the grant technique had not been developed. In the early decades of the century, a wide gap appeared between the need for nationwide economic and social legislation and the ability of the lower-than-national levels of government to meet that need. The availability of the grant method provided legislators with a tested and traditional formula for policy. It made possible the allocation of responsibilities between the levels of government according to criteria of administrative and fiscal efficiency. These criteria can be simply stated: the national government assumed partial responsibility for supplying funds and primary responsibility for establishing minimum standards of service, because the national government possessed superior fiscal resources and was concerned with the general welfare of the residents of all states. The states (and their political subdivisions) assumed primary responsibility for administration, because they were in the better position to interpret and meet local needs. The very interaction of the national government and the states, as well as the device of matching, prevented any absolute separation between financing and the establishment of standards on the one hand and administration on the other. Instead, the entire process of policy determination, financing, and administration became a circular, cooperative process.

The grants have been successful in (1) providing a basis for the achievement of broad national purposes and (2) providing a fiscal and administrative mechanism characterized by national-state cooperation and the division or responsibilities in the shared functions. The grants, therefore, have avoided both overweening centralization and the inadequacy of complete decentralization in large-scale programs.

The sharing relationships developed through grant programs and related forms of national-state activity can be viewed in two main and overlapping categories. The first category includes all those relationships that principally emerge as the result of the substantive policy lines laid down by the national government. The second category includes the procedures that govern the day-to-day activities of national and state administrators.

THE PROBLEM OF NATIONAL POLICIES

Most grant programs and almost every cooperative activity within the federal system involve both the national and state legislatures. The responsibility of the national legislature is primary in that it sets the larger program framework, and its purse power is inevitably a strong influence on state legislatures. Congress has at least three large obligations in legislating for intergovernmental programs:

First, Congress is always required to use a precise pen in defining the broad policies within which state and national administrators exercise their power. The difficulty of this task is multiplied by the difficulty of providing the necessary areas of discretion when two sets of officials are involved.

Second, in facing this problem of discretion with the directness that it deserves, Congress must make room not only for national and state officers, but for their cooperative initiative. This latter area can be a large and fruitful one. For the fact is that the discretion of either the national or the state official does not necessarily mean a lack of discretion for the other.

Third, Congress has the major responsibility for achieving balance within the federal system in at least two ways:

1. *With respect to the means chosen to achieve national purposes.* The grant enactments should balance a truly national purpose with the appropriate means for attaining it. By and large, the grants have been the greatest single lever within the area of national-state relations capable of working toward a minimum standard of public services throughout the country. Other federal commonwealths have employed the grant system for purposes of equalization—the balance between one citizen and another—but none has attempted it on the geographical, social, and fiscal scale of the United States.

2. *With respect to fiscal and administrative responsibilities.* There must be balance between the fiscal and administrative aspects of a program. In

other words, there must be balance in power terms between the national government, which largely controls the purse strings, and the states, which largely control the administrative implementation of the enactment.

OVER-ALL VIEW: NO OVER-ALL PROGRAM

The grant programs have been enacted in response to public demands for the purpose of meeting public needs. The end result is the lack of any over-all system of national grants. Each program is legislated separately; its relation to other programs is unplanned and unclear, and is certainly not based on any total picture of national purpose. Comparisons of various programs present illustrations of this state of affairs. Welfare grants are large, but no national funds go for general relief. In 1962, more money was granted to the states by the national government for hospital construction ($167 million) than for school construction ($57 million) and highways received nearly 25 times as much as both combined ($3 billion). Eighteen separate allocations were made in 1962 for various public health purposes.

Similar conditions are found in some nongrant programs such as river-basin development. In most programs, however, coordination between state and national administrators has been achieved informally without the need for specific congressional action.

ADMINISTRATIVE PROCEDURES

All national grant programs are contingent upon states meeting certain standards of administration and service. The mechanisms and devices employed in effecting national guidance include reports, inspection, advice, personnel standards, advance approval of plans, review, orders, and—in extreme cases—withdrawal of national funds. In all national grant programs, the national government exerts a certain degree of control. But the national agencies, in most cases, do not customarily make the day-to-day decisions; nor do they exercise uninterrupted direction and supervision. There has been a tendency for some national agencies to relax national supervision in proportion to the degree of excellence achieved by each state administration. A formalistic overview of the operating functions in grant programs will make this clearer.

PLANNING AND BUDGETING

There can be a wide gap between the determination of national policies affecting the states and the administration of those policies. This is as true of the grant programs as of others. Their purposes, of course, are various. Grants have been used to stimulate particular state activity, to establish minimum national standards, to equalize competitive differences between the states, and to finance specific state services. The stake of the states in such programs is immense, for the programs commit a large proportion of the states' personnel and finances to directed ends, and the grants represent a considerable share of the governmental services received by the citizens of the states.

Stage 1: Prestatutory

The first and crucial relationship between the national government and the states occurs when the grant enactment is being considered by Congress. In some cases there is informal consultation between national and state officials before the statutes are presented in draft. States may send representatives to legislative committee hearings, and state governors may hold conversations with their congressmen and senators. However, it is characteristic of the grant programs that they have offered no full-dress discussion between state and national officers representing their respective levels of government with respect to matters of administration and budget before the final enactment of the bills. The consultations that do take place are between professionals at the various levels, often through their professional associations.

Stage 2: Implementation

Once an activity has been legislated into existence, state planning is encouraged and, in some cases, enforced.

In many jointly financed and administered programs, advance approval of contemplated state action is required. Such approval applies to current operations and is in addition to the initial conditions that must be met by states in qualifying for grants. The need for advance approval leads to the formulation of state plans and budgets, especially in those cases in which considerable discretion is allowed the states.

Advance approval of state action has proved an effective method for dealing with a wide variety of state situations, adjusting state programs to conform with broad national purposes, and stimulating a planning attitude and a periodic examination of state programs. Generally, when there is need for variation in accordance with conditions in particular states, a considerable latitude is allowed each state in preparing its plans.

Public assistance and highway programs provide examples of the independent state planning initiative achieved within a general framework laid down by the national government. Approval of public assistance plans is actually not an advance approval of specific actions to be taken, but rather an advance acceptance of the methods and general rules to be employed by the states in providing these services. This procedure allows for a relatively wide discretion in state administrative planning.

In some other programs state initiative is more limited. In the National Guard, for example, a high degree of uniformity is required, and national policies are implemented by rules, regulations, and general orders rather than by the formulation of advance plans and budgets.

The correct execution of congressional policy is the basic justification for the device of advance approval. But the technique serves other functions of equal significance. For example, grants to the states may be spent in accordance with the letter of statutory requirements, and yet the services rendered may be of indifferent quality. Periodic reconsideration and review allows state administrators to profit from unusually successful methods employed in other states or from ideas and findings developed through the experience and research of the national administrative agency.

In most federal aid functions, the amounts available are fixed by statutory or administrative formulas; thus the question which dominates the ordinary budget review is already settled when the state request for funds is submitted. The purpose of the national review, then, is not to determine whether the money shall be appropriated, but whether it will be spent in accordance with statutory policies and in keeping with accepted administrative and technical practices.

Periodic submission of plans and budgets tends to create an attitude of planning on the part of state administrators. In the process of planning and reviewing plans, responsible administrators, both national and state, are compelled to ask themselves periodically how much of the task they have been doing, what they have been neglecting, and whether they could perform the work more effectively. The submission of plans for national review is, at times, a mechanical formality; but in most functions there has been significant success in stimulating the development of alert administration. The scope of the plan and the attitude of national administrators toward the problem greatly affect the attitude with which state administrators engage in planning activities.

Planning cannot do everything. It may lead, for example, to the kind of paper perfection which is carried so far that the plan itself has relatively little relation to work in the field. The requirements regarding preliminary conditions, the procedures of preparation, and submission of the plan may become so complex that the whole process could become meaningless, or an exercise in deceit whereby the state administrators prepare paper plans for approval and then find ways to go about their own business ignoring the approved design.

Planning: A Case Study of Success

The Federal Aid Road Act of 1916 laid the foundation for a national system of highways by clearly defining the mutual and separate responsibilities of the national and state governments in the construction of rural roads during the succeeding five years and authorized national participation up to 50 per cent of the total cost. The outline of the present national highway system emerged several years later. The present program dates from the Federal Aid Highway Act of 1944 which, for the first time, provided for national-state cooperation in a completely integrated program of highway improvement involving city as well as primary and secondary rural highways.

The principal means employed by the Bureau of Public Roads in carrying out the policies of the Federal Aid Highway Act is advance approval of action to be undertaken by state highway departments. This procedure accomplished its goal with a minimum of friction. National representatives and state engineers confer during the preparation of plans; and the value of such close contact can hardly be overestimated.

However, issues have arisen between state highway departments and the Bureau of Public Roads about the location of the roads themselves. The national agency considers projects from the standpoint of the national interest, while state highway departments are generally responsive to local interests. The determination of whether a particular project should be undertaken rests exclusively with state authorities. Occasionally a state highway department is unwilling to accept or is compelled by local conditions to reject the views of the Bureau of Public Roads on a question of location or type of construction. The national government may participate in financing most of a route across a state and then find that the sections of the road involving disputed locations are built entirely with state funds and according to the state's views. This seriously impairs the utility of the entire road for national purposes.

More comprehensive planning has been used since 1932 in an effort to prevent national-state conflicts of this type. Regulations under the current national aid appropriation require an annual program from each state. The plan must indicate the county, the length of road proposed, character of construction, total estimated cost, and the amount of national funds desired for each project. On examination and review of this program, the Bureau of Public Roads can suggest the exclusion, inclusion, or postponement of projects. Although the potentialities of this device have not been fully realized, the national agency now possesses a formalized procedure for dealing with conflict situations. On the whole, success of the national-state highway program is generally acknowledged by most administrators.

REPORTS, INSPECTIONS, AND AUDITS

National agencies commonly require periodic financial and operating reports from state agencies administering grant programs. Such records furnish gross measurements of administrative competence as well as of compliance with conditions of national grants.

Inspection

Periodic inspection by national field representatives is one of the most important means of reviewing state actions. The intensity, frequency, and thoroughness of inspections vary considerably from function to function.

National inspection may be continuous. For example, the system of inspection of the Bureau of Public Roads is the most thorough of any operated by a national grant agency. Field representatives constantly inspect every mile of road constructed with the aid of national funds and all other activities of state highway departments under their supervision.

There is less thorough inspection when the aided function is regarded as a matter of particular state interest. This is especially noticeable in educational and agricultural functions. The Office of Experiment Stations, for example, sends its agents to the state stations once a year. These officials extend their inquiries to those research projects supported solely from state funds as well as those carried on with national assistance. They can do little more than determine whether a workmanlike job is being done and approximately evaluate the caliber of the personnel employed in research. The national agency for vocational education sends out regional agents at intervals. A considerable part of the time of each visit is devoted to consultative and advisory work with the state staff and with teacher-training institutions.

Inspection of an aided function such as agricultural extension, which is administered largely on the local level, must be conducted so that intensive inspection of local work does not atrophy the action of state supervision. Thus the Agricultural Extension Service obtains a much more complete knowledge of state-level activities than it does of county work. Its policy is to stimulate the development of a state staff that can bring about competent work in the counties.

The potentialities of the promotional and advisory role of the field services of national agencies have been demonstrated amply in the administration of most of the older grant programs. The function of the national government in this respect is in many ways a form of friendly, expert advice.

Periodic inspections and suggestions from competent outsiders constitute an intangible but effective method of raising standards. The inspectors become interstate carriers of administrative ideas. The major strategy of a national agency in its advisory and promotional role is to bring about creative collaboration between itself and the state agency, and among the states themselves.

Audits

Not all payments to the states are followed by national audits; but whenever specific purposes are stated in the national statutes, audits are made. In each case it is a post-audit; that is, it is made after the funds have been spent by the state. The rules defining the purpose of an enactment form the general basis of the audit.

While post-audit is the conventional form of fiscal control, there are really two types of post-auditing activity by the national government. Under the first type, the plan of work and the budget are approved in advance in considerable detail. The task of the auditor is merely to ascertain that there is evidence to support the disbursement in accordance with the approved program, that the required matching funds have been spent or offered by the state, and that all other financial requirements have been met. This type of control is exercised by a number of national agencies, including the Bureau of Public Roads, the Extension Service, and the Forest Service.

A second type of audit is considerably more searching. In vocational rehabilitation, and in various types of public assistance, advance approval is given by the national agency only in terms of general rules. The state is to decide the administrative conclusion of particular cases and the corresponding disbursements. The national audit thus serves to determine whether these individual cases have been decided in accordance with the rules laid down by the national government.

WITHDRAWAL OF NATIONAL FUNDS

The right to suspend or withhold national grants is the most formidable power possessed by the national government to insure that operations are conducted in accordance with the requirements laid down by Congress. Yet, while the statutory conditions and procedures under which it may be exercised are numerous, the practical limitations of the device are equally numerous. It has been invoked with relative infrequency.

Temporary suspensions of payments have been used to help raise state action to national standards. If an engineer of the Bureau of Public Roads finds that a road built by a state with the aid of national funds is not properly maintained, the state agency is notified that within a certain time it must correct this condition. If this is not done, no national funds are forthcoming for highway construction in that state until the highway is maintained in accordance with national standards.

The power of revocation of national cooperation for any state not fulfilling its obligations was first sketched in general terms in the second Morrill Act, which extended aid to land-grant colleges. Soon the agencies administering agricultural extension, experiment stations, and vocational education and rehabilitation were armed with the revocation device. When revocation action is taken under this group of laws, the state agency may appeal to Congress directly. When grants to Georgia for agricultural research were discontinued in 1918 by the Office of Experiment Stations, the withdrawal was revoked by Congress.

Some acts contain provisions that place considerable emphasis on such procedures as notice and hearing prior to withdrawal of cooperation, and set up specific conditions under which action may be taken. Under the Social Security Act, grants may be withheld only if the national agency makes certain findings after reasonable notice and provides an opportunity for hearings. The importance of hearings cannot be overestimated.

Still another group of enactments sets up no specific procedure to be followed in taking action. The broad authorization of the Secretary of Agriculture under the Clarke-McNary Act to cooperate under such conditions as "he may determine to be fair and equitable" furnishes legal authority for agreements with the states. A uniform provision of the agreement is that it may be terminated by either party upon 30 days' notice, thereby enabling withdrawal of national cooperation.

States have withdrawn from a cooperative program, either by failure to appropriate matching funds or by refusing positive legislative action. Such withdrawal may be temporary or may suspend particular grant services in a state for a longer time. In 1925 Montana failed to match its share of national highway funds in time to receive the national grant and thus had to wait until the following year to resume cooperation. More serious situations arise where grant services conflict with important economic or other interests in a cooperating state.

It is primarily the large issues, such as the failure of the legislature to grant proper powers or adequate appropriations to the state agency, or extravagant and improper administration, that bring about the exercise of the power to withdraw funds. This power is of little use in the correction of a weak state agency which commits no serious offenses and exhibits a modicum of activity. The fact is that national agencies usually hesitate to withdraw aid because of a genuine desire to promote the affected activity in the state. A state forest protection system, for example, may be relatively ineffective, but it may be better than none; and the Forest Service is primarily interested in seeing that the forests are protected.

II. SHARING THROUGH PROFESSIONALIZATION:
THE FUNCTIONAL ASSOCIATIONS

As the various grant programs have been developed into routine and continuing cooperative operations, a new means of sharing—through the common professional interests and aspirations of the officials of all levels of government—has developed. This sharing by professionalization now fosters a high degree of cooperation among equals regardless of the governments they serve. The tendency of professional workers at each level of government to identify themselves with the function to be performed, rather than with the particular government served has become more pronounced as the number of workers at the several levels who are products of the same professional training increases. Here one may find cohesive groups among professional workers in public health, welfare, education, and other fields. Their own standards of professional conduct, their interest in the job to be performed, and the pressures exerted by their clients produce a guild-like loyalty that transcends their identification with that government which happens to pay their salary.[1]

This type of identification is strong in some fields and in some areas. But it never completely effaces the worker's identification with his own unit of government. In some cases, ambivalent and conflicting loyalties may be entertained.[2]

Sharing through professionalization is, in part, a result of attempts by the government to professionalize the state employees handling grants-in-aid. All problems of national-state administrative relationships, no matter how completely they seem dependent on nonpersonnel aspects of the orga-

[1] See R. Bruce Carroll, "Intergovernmental Administrative Relations," unpublished Ph.D. dissertation, Department of Political Science, University of Chicago, 1963; also statement of Professor William Anderson, *Joint Hearings before the Subcommittees on Intergovernmental Relations of the Committees on Expenditures in the Executive Department* (Washington, D.C.: Government Printing Office, 1949), p. 124.

[2] Even when the functional loyalties of professional workers are strong, the chief political officers of both municipalities and states maintain their separatist attitudes and a certain degree of competitiveness and combativeness in their relationships with each other. Social cohesiveness along lines laid down by the unit of government is still dominant among those who determine basic policies, including tax policies.

nization, ultimately must rely upon the quality of the men in the job. Congress has consequently recognized the importance of qualified personnel to the successful administration of national grants. Unsatisfactory experience with unrestricted national and state patronage in the period of large work relief appropriations during the depression demonstrated in dramatic fashion the need for placing personnel as far as possible on a merit basis.

The national government now exercises some control over the personnel of almost every grant program. Even in the nongrant functions it is common for national agencies to certify certain state officials as being qualified to act for the national government. Examples of this practice are common in the grading and inspection of grain, butter, eggs, and other agricultural commodities. Certified state officials also engage in national law enforcement activities such as the pure food and drug laws, game and bird laws, and forest protection laws.

Method 1: Merit Systems

In recent years, the national government has tended to require that the states maintain a formalized merit system of personnel administration as a condition for the receipt of grant funds. The chief characteristics of these merit systems are (1) open competitive examinations for all except top policy-determining positions; (2) establishment of formal position classification and compensation plans; (3) protection against discharge for reasons other than unsatisfactory performance of the job; and (4) promotion within the ranks based on efficiency and merit. National legislation now requires state merit systems of this kind in public assistance, child welfare service, unemployment compensation, public employment service, and public health programs, to name only the major ones.

Method 2: Certification

The older grant programs, if they required any personnel standards at all, did not prescribe so formal a pattern. They usually asked that the appointing state authorities select personnel who had been certified as having minimum training and experience. No recourse to an examination list was necessary. This method is currently in force in grant programs that affect the fields of education, agricultural extension, forestry, highway construction, and a number of other areas.

Methods Compared and Evaluated

Certification is a means of establishing minimum standards; a competitive merit system aims at selecting the best person for a given job. The latter, therefore, has many theoretical advantages over the former. But neither is foolproof. Merit systems, when operated by appointees without merit, accomplish little.

National insistence upon state-wide merit systems for particular programs has undoubtedly improved the administration of those programs. Experience with merit systems in grant programs has also influenced a considerable number of states to extend these systems to other departments. In addition, many state civil service agencies have been strengthened and revitalized by the services rendered them by the Division of Technical Advisory Service to States of the Social Security Administration.

Certification has proved effective in a variety of programs which are well established and possess generally accepted professional standards. Highway construction supervisors, for example, are universally expected to have graduated from courses in civil engineering. Teachers are expected to have graduated from approved teachers' colleges or universities, and foresters from colleges of forestry. Programs which have operated on the basis of professional certification over a long period appear to function at very satisfactory levels of efficiency.

Personnel Supervision: A Case Summary

The rapid expansion of the social security program in the late 1930's posed a new and difficult problem for both national and state administrators. Unemployment compensation, employment service, and public assistance called for large numbers of administrative personnel with a range of training and experience that did not exist at the time. Personnel standards for such positions as employment counselors, claim adjustment clerks, public assistance investigators, and numerous others simply did not exist. While people were being recruited for these positions, the positions themselves had to be evaluated, analyzed, and classified. From 1935 to 1939, the social security programs worked under no consistent system of personnel supervision, and program difficulties consequently existed in a number of states. Following a congressional amendment to the statute, a formalized merit-rating system was made mandatory upon all states participating in the national social security grant programs. Since then the national agency has emphasized personnel supervision, and the caliber of the entire administration has been generally high.

The technical leadership of the national agencies is another integral factor in promoting professionalization in administration. And, by itself, it stands as an important means of achieving national-state cooperation.

The national government, with its more central outlook and its concentration of resources, has been able in most instances to exert a constructive influence on the technical quality of state administration. The results of research studies conducted by the national agencies have been published and widely circulated; demonstration projects in agriculture are often operated in connection with state agencies and the results made available to all concerned. In most of the jointly administered programs the national administrative agency maintains staffs of expert consultants, who are available upon the call of the states.

There are a number of outstanding examples of national leadership in technical matters. In public health, for example, the promotion of rapid treatment centers for venereal disease control and the use of mass X-ray surveys in discovering active tuberculosis are recent and outstanding contributions.

Technical assistance constitutes a fruitful way of providing administrative leadership to state agencies. In the words of a national official: "If we can't convince the states that our requirements have real merit, then coercion and the use of authority will in the long run also fail to secure desired results."

PROFESSIONAL ASSOCIATIONS AND CONFERENCES

The productive use of technical assistance depends, in the long run, on an established and skilled personnel. An important means for developing the needed skills—and discovering them when they are developed—is provided by professional associations and conferences. The semiformal relationships built up in these organizations serve many purposes. Not the least of their services is that they satisfy a basic need for personal give-and-take on official problems outside the official frame of the everyday job.

Examples are numerous enough. The Interstate Commerce Commission, finding that national-state interests often diverge sharply in the field of its concern, set the stage for informal meetings with the railroad commissioners of the states. Although these conferences had no sanction in state or national law, they continued over a long period of years and accomplished valuable work. The social security program has made extensive and profitable use of conferences and committees. The meetings of the American Association of State Highway Officials and the State and Territorial Health Officers' Association provide forums of great usefulness for the discussion of points of difference between national and state officials. Out of these meetings have developed many procedures later adopted as standard by national and state governments.

On the whole, discussion of administrative aspects of national-state relations leads up to a simple point: the states now possess a rich variety of administrative tools for building their own plans and programs in a cooperative federal scheme; and the national government's most effective means for aiding the states are the persuasive devices.

This merely indicates that national supervision should not be confused with national control. National supervision has been most effective when it has allowed the states to profit from its superior technical facilities and greater experience. The emphasis in national supervision now rests to a large extent on building up the quality or personnel within state agencies. Merit systems are only the first important step in this process. Additional devices of importance include budgeting and planning aid; information, advice, and technical assistance; conferences and inspections. These instruments of cooperation, not coercion, lead to increasingly effective administrative cooperation.

III. SHARING THROUGH PROXIMITY: THE REGULATORY AGENCIES

The Interstate Commerce Act of 1889 and succeeding regulatory acts carved out an important area of national-state cooperation that differs markedly from that outlined by the grant system. The grants involve transfers of large amounts of money; the regulatory acts do not. The grants introduced national supervision of intrastate activities as the by-product of programs based on the national revenues; the regulatory acts introduced a minor exchange of funds, chiefly for administrative expenses, as the by-product of bringing certain state policies into collaboration with national policy. Intergovernmental sharing in the regulatory field occurs primarily because the several levels of government have the power to regulate, and, in exercising that power, are brought into proximity with one another. The record of the nation's lending regulatory agencies indicates that cooperation develops simply through proximity even without material incentives.

THE INTERSTATE COMMERCE COMMISSION

The beginnings of cooperation between the Interstate Commerce Commission and state commissions, noticeable before World War I, continued thereafter. The New England Conference of 1917 was a strikingly successful example. The ICC and all of the New England railroad commissions joined together in discussion and hearings on a proposed rate increase, and the final agreement was approved by all participants.

The Transportation Act of 1920 intensified national-state collaboration. It required the ICC to notify state regulatory commissions when any proceedings before the Commission brought into issue orders or regulations of state commissions, and it permitted the ICC to avail itself of state records and facilities. The act stipulated that, if both national and state agencies desired cooperation, they should hold conferences to decide on the desirability of a joint hearing. The ICC was encouraged to consult with the state commissions prior to final disposition of its cases. The act of 1920, though not coercive in nature, was well drawn to encourage interofficial courtesy and permit flexibility in handling national-state problems. Hundreds of joint hearings on rate, construction, and abandonment cases have been held since the act was passed. Despite the apparent success of this continuous cooperative mechanism, the number of joint hearings has declined in recent years. This trend has been the subject of some controversy between the state and national agencies, and attempts have been made in recent years to make cooperative hearings more frequent and meaningful.

When the Motor Carrier Act of 1935 was passed, the state agencies were again incorporated into the national administration. Previously, all states except one had agencies concerned with regulating busses or trucks; but they were limited by the Constitution's prohibition of state interference in interstate commerce. While the new law increased national control over intrastate commerce, it also gave the states an active role in the national government's administration. For example, it directed the ICC to refer certain cases for initial hearing and provisional determination to joint boards of representatives of the state governments involved in the issue. These were cases that affected no more than three states and dealt with licenses, mergers, or complaints on violation, rates, and charges. The proportion of joint hearings to all hearings under the Motor Carrier Act of 1935 has exceeded considerably the proportion of joint hearings under the Interstate Commerce Act.

THE FOOD AND DRUG ADMINISTRATION

Soon after enactment of the Federal Food and Drugs Act of 1906, the Food and Drug Administration, under pressure from state officials engaged in similar enforcement, set up a Division of State Cooperation. A policy was established of heading the Division with a man experienced in state food and drug administration. Former state officers have filled the position since the Division was established.

All states except one enacted laws similar to the national law within a few years before and after its enactment. When the national law was substantially modified in the Food, Drug and Cosmetic Act af 1938, state legislative response was not as prompt. Only 13 states passed laws substantially similar to the national one. The act of 1938 provided explicitly for the commissioning of state officers as national examination and inspection agents. An appreciable amount of collaboration developed. National and state agencies freely exchange information, reports, and records; they often coordinate work plans; and they have formed a Joint Committee on Definitions and Standards. The joint committee's chairman is the head of the FDA, and the states are represented by four members.

THE FEDERAL TRADE COMMISSION

The Federal Trade Commission Act of 1914 and the Clayton Act of the same year, which together block out the main outlines of the Federal Trade Commission's powers and duties today, do not contain provisions requiring active cooperation with the state governments. However, state agencies frequently have called the Commission's attention to abuses prohibited by the acts; and state marketing departments, purchasing bureaus, testing laboratories, and inspection services have often furnished information and witnesses to support Commission complaints. The Commission has found that the nature of its cooperative relations with the states is such that a formal definition of it, in rule and regulation, would only be redundant or would render the working channels more rigid than necessary. National-state contacts have been on an informal basis rather than systematic and continuous. The Federal-State Relations Section of the Department of Justice, a unit originally established through the efforts of the Council of State Governments, has assisted the FTC in recent years in its attempt to bring national and state laws into uniformity.

Two other recent acts of Congress that confer authority on the Commission, the Wool Products Labelling Act of 1939 and Public Law 15 (1945) covering insurance, do make provision for administrative cooperation. The Wool Act authorized the Commission to cooperate with any state or political subdivision, and the Commission, in letters to the governors, invited such cooperation. The Insurance Act was designed to give the states full opportunity to adjust their statutes to the new interstate character assumed by insurance as a result of the Supreme Court decision in *U.S.* v. *South-Eastern Underwriters Association* (1944).

The reaction of the states to the changed status of insurance was immediate. Within three years they had explored the implications which the South-Eastern Underwriters case and Public Law 15 held for their regulatory laws. They decided on policies and enacted legislation to govern their state systems in the light of the new legal position of the insurance business. They began to examine the possibilities of interstate cooperation in insurance regulation.

None of the laws administered by the Securities and Exchange Commission provides explicitly for collaboration with state agencies. However, cooperative relations have developed through interchange of information, through joint action in securities issuance, and in the investigation of frauds. The SEC joined the National Association of Securities Commissioners, and the association's annual reports testify to many instances of informal collaboration.

THE FEDERAL POWER COMMISSION

Established originally as a weak interagency commission by the Federal Water Power Act of 1920, the Federal Power Commission was reorganized in 1930 as an independent regulatory body. Under the act of 1920, it was given authority to regulate the rates, services, and securities of power licensees, to prescribe their manner of keeping accounts, and to investigate national water power resources. The Federal Power Act of 1935 brought FPC into the interstate electricity movement. The act of 1938 carried it into the interstate transportation and wholesale sale of natural gas. Still other acts and resolutions committed it to long-term studies in the power field.

In both 1935 and 1938 Congress provided for a pattern of national-state relations. While the intergovernmental policy of the 1920 act had been one of national deference to state regulation, and two levels of government were conceived as operating in the same field without any essential relations, the more recent legislation emphasized collaboration as the essence of power law administration.

In addition to limiting by statute the intrusion of national over state regulation, Congress has permitted and required a variety of working relationships between FPC and the states. In some cases, where the state itself is a licensee, FPC is the regulating body. Generally, FPC requires that license applicants present satisfactory evidence of having complied with state laws and, where state control existed prior to national entrance on the scene, it frequently limits the licensee's control of rates, services, and securities. Private licensees are subject to both national and state accounting procedures, which have been uniform since 1936.

THE FEDERAL DEPOSIT INSURANCE CORPORATION

Under the Federal Deposit Insurance Corporation Act of 1933, state banks, operating solely under state authority, were permitted to apply to the Federal Deposit Insurance Corporation for deposit insurance. Several types of national-state administrative relations developed. In view of the speed with which the program was put into effect, certificates of solvency by the supervising state agency were instrumental in determining the immediate inclusion of state banks under the Corporation's benefits. Subsequently the FDIC encouraged state legislatures to pass acts facilitating the Corporation's work. The FDIC found state authorities helpful in conducting inquiries into the conduct of particular institutions and in making surveys of state banks. The FDIC significantly hastened the improvement and standardization of state procedures in chartering and regulating banks.

THE FEDERAL COMMUNICATIONS COMMISSION

The Communications Act of 1934, establishing the FCC, included several provisions which acknowledged the interests of the states. State commissions were authorized to file complaints against any common carrier in the communications field. The FCC was directed to give advance notification to the governor of each state in which it was proposed that a new line be operated. States affected by individual corporate applications to consolidate, merge, or purchase telephone companies were granted hearings. FCC was permitted to exempt certain carriers from its accounting rules when the carriers were subject to regulation by state commissions; and it had to hold hearings before it prescribed standards of accounts or records for local carriers. Although empowered to define whether or not a carrier was "interstate," the FCC was obliged to give prior notice of such action and to grant hearings to the states concerned.

Unlike the Motor Carrier Act, the Communications Act did not compel joint hearings. It merely authorized them. In practice, joint hearings have been few, partly because there existed previously no extensive state regulation of telephone and telegraph. In its relations with the states the Commission has concerned itself principally with providing them with information otherwise unavailable to them. The National Association of Railroad and Utility Commissioners, an organization of state officials, has from time to time cooperated with the FCC in gathering information and presenting briefs in telephone cases. In 1938, the Association assisted an FCC hearing on a request for a rate increase affecting all the states. In the large-scale study of telephone companies undertaken by the FCC in 1935, the state commissions lent the national agency a number of their staff members.

REGULATORY ACTIVITIES: SUMMARY

Although there is variety among the particular materials that constitute the object of regulation in acts that follow the example of the FCC, a pattern of comparable collaboration has nonetheless emerged. This pattern usually takes form first in the empowering statutes. They provide for national-state cooperation or they make it implicit in declarations of policy; in grants of powers on a contingent basis subject to the absence of state regulation in the area; in definitions of terms which take cognizance of states as parties or as affected interests; in acceptance of existing state regulation as national practice or law; or in specific limitations upon grants of authority in order to prevent invasion of state jurisdictions.

As a result, the national administration regularly employs certain useful techniques of collaboration with the states. Notice of issues pending are sent to state agencies with invitations to cooperate in the proceedings; private parties are required to conform to state regulations as a condition for receiving national licenses; joint hearings are conducted, joint conferences are held, joint investigations are made, and joint boards are formed; there is an increasing amount of information exchanged; and the lending of personnel from one agency to another has become a familiar practice.

This whole process has not developed without friction. Difficulties are inherent in cooperation of any kind, and unusual strains and stresses exist in the fields of economic regulatory activity. Conflicts have stemmed from transitory conditions; from the presence of established state agencies; from the adjustments of new—and sometimes not very precise—laws to complex situations; from constitutional and legal difficulties in settling the framework of regulation. There have been continuing difficulties owing to the faulty organization of some national and state commissions. Conflicts arising from personal differences and clashes between the national and local interest have been experienced. Finally, because of the volatile nature of the matters regulated, the problem of pressure groups often has been acute. In some cases private economic interests have been able to set state and national agencies at loggerheads.

Despite all these difficulties, the development of formal and informal national-state cooperation in the nongrant fields has been consistent and productive.

IV. THE BACKGROUND OF SHARING:
THE MIXTURE OF LAWS

A root fact of sharing is the nature of American law. In virtually no field does the complete body of law with respect to a given governmental activity have its source in one of the so-called levels of government. In the typical case a mixture of federal, state, and local regulation covers an area of regulation or activity.

The point does not even need documentation with respect to the intermingling of state and local law. Without pausing to consider whether municipalities in fact make law, the important fact is that they are legal creatures of the states. Their rule-making powers rest completely upon a body of state constitutional and statutory provisions. This is often true to an apparently ludicrous extent; for example, some years ago it was discovered that Chicago needed a state enabling act if the city wished to license peanut vendors on its pier. In other situations, state laws permit far greater local discretion. But even in these cases it is not possible to separate state and local jurisdictions, state and local areas of administrative action, or state and local bodies of law. They can be considered only as a single entity. No local act can be divorced from its source in state law.

The relationship between state and federal law does not differ greatly. The states of course have a constitutional sanctity that municipalities lack. Certain bodies of private and commercial law are set forth as entities in states, although almost never without their coming into contact with federal law. As for the latter:

> Federal law is generally interstitial in its nature. It rarely occupies a legal field completely, totally excluding all participation by the legal systems of the states. This was plainly true in the beginning when the federal legislative product (including the Constitution) was extremely small. It is significantly true today, despite the volume of Congressional enactments, and even within areas where Congress has been very active. Federal legislation, on the whole, has been conceived and drafted on an *ad hoc* basis to accomplish limited objectives. It builds upon legal relationships established by the states, altering or supplanting them only so far as necessary for the special purpose. Congress acts, in short, against the background of the total *corpus juris* of the states in much the way that a state legislature acts against the background of the common law, assumed to govern unless changed by legislation.[3]

Hart and Wechsler speak of the interstitial character of federal law as being of "surprising generality and force." They affirm that "the strength of the conception of the central government as one of delegated, limited authority is most significantly manifested on this mundane plane of working, legislative practice."[4]

Examples of the interstitial character of federal law are at every hand:

Criminal Law. Federal criminal statutes often utilize state standards in defining federal crimes.[5] As early as 1789 Congress provided that violators of federal law were to be arrested, imprisoned, and bailed by United States officers "agreeably to the usual mode of process against offenders in such state."[6] The present federal law regulating the control of intoxicating liquors has as its object the use of federal penalties to prevent the shipment

[3] Hart and Wechsler, *op. cit.,* p. 435.

[4] *Ibid.,* p. 436.

[5] 1 *U.S. Stat.* 91 (1789) cited in Richard F. Schier, "State Adoption of National Law: A Study in Federalism" unpublished Ph.D. dissertation, Department of Political Science, University of California, Los Angeles, August, 1951, p. 14.

[6] See, for example, 18 *U.S.C.,* paras. 13, 43, 1073, 1153, 1201, 1262, 1342, 1821, 1911; also Hart and Wechsler, *op. cit.,* p. 457.

of alcoholic beverages into a state in violation of the state's law. The federal statute provides that in determining violators of the federal law "the definition of intoxicating liquors contained in the laws of such state shall be applied."[7]

In addition to the incorporation of standards of state law in federal criminal statutes, incorporations are found in other fields. This is true in statutes establishing judicial procedures. Recovery of tort claims against the United States is possible, according to the legislation, only "under circumstances where the United States, if a private person, would be liable to the claimant in accordance with the law of the place where the act or omission occurred."[8]

Licensing. Federal licensing requirements also incorporate state standards. The national government, for example, issues licenses for the construction and operation of dams, powerhouses, and electric transmission lines. The legislation provides, however, that federal requirements cannot be fulfilled unless the applicant has previously met all licensing requirements established by the appropriate state laws.[9] Similar provisions exist in the federal statutes covering licensing in other fields. The federal government has even incorporated state licensing acts into its own laws when defining criminal acts as an adjunct to the regulation of interstate commerce. For example, the Federal Denture Act of 1942 makes it unlawful for a person making dental plates to send through the mails (or any instrumentality of interstate commerce) any denture "the cast of which was made by a person not licensed to practice dentistry in the state into which the denture is sent."[10] Even more numerous are the cases in which the Supreme Court has given meaning to ambiguous congressional enactments by making state law the appropriate national rule even in matters that on their face are areas of the national government's primary concern.[11]

State Adoptions of Federal Law. Direct state adoption of federal law occurs more frequently than federal adoption of state laws. Virtually all states have adopted policies, definitions, and standards of the federal law with respect to the regulation of foods and drugs; and more than a third of the states have provided in their laws for the automatic state adoption of new federal standards. As the Congress alters the federal law, the state regulations automatically change accordingly. Federal standards for grad-

---

[7] 18 *U.S.C.* 1262. The Twenty-first Amendment itself says, "The transportation or importation into any State. . . for delivery or use therein of intoxicating liquors, in violation of the laws thereof, is hereby prohibited."

[8] 28 *U.S.C.* 1346 (b).

[9] 41 *U.S. Stat.* 1663 (1920), December 9, 1920.

[10] 18 *U.S.C.* 420 (f), (g), (h).

[11] *Board of County Commissioners* v. *U.S.,* 308 U.S. 343 (1939); *Cope* v. *Anderson,* 331 U.S. 461 (1947).

ing grain, vegetables, fruit, and other commodities are also more or less automatically followed in many states. The same system prevails, though by no means uniformly, over such diverse fields as the hunting season for waterfowl and the important area of taxation. With respect to the former, a Montana law is typical:

> Laws relating to migratory birds are prescribed by the United States Department of Agriculture. Open season, bag limit and other rules and regulations are announced each year by proclamation by the President of the United States. After each proclamation, the state fish and game commission by proper action will adopt, advertise and enforce such proclaimed regulations as may be applicable to the State of Montana.[12]

With respect to taxation, many states base their income taxes upon net income as defined by national statutes and administrative regulation. The taxpayer thus need only compute his income once; he then pays state taxes according to the rate levied by the states.[13]

The process of literal adoption of the laws of one government by the other is the least important aspect of the sharing process, as illustrated by the legal system. Of far greater importance is the manner in which federal legislation stimulates corresponding, or supplementary, state laws, and vice versa.

In the Soil Conservation Law an administrative action by the Secretary of Agriculture was required before state laws became necessary for states participating in the program. Other federal legislation makes state laws mandatory. For example, the 1935 federal law for the protection of land against soil erosion provided that "as a condition to the extending of any benefits under this Act . . . the Secretary of Agriculture may . . . require (1) the enactment . . . of state and local laws imposing suitable permanent restrictions in the use of such lands and otherwise providing for the pre-

---

[12] *Mont. Laws* 1921, c. 238, sec. 20, *Mont. Rev. Codes* (1947), sec. 26–320. Quoted in Schier, *op. cit.,* p. 33.

[13] On the problems of state adoption of federal law see Schier, *op. cit.;* also Arthur N. Holcombe, "The States as Agents of the Nation," *Southwestern Political Science Quarterly,* Vol. I (1921), reprinted in Association of American Law Schools, *Selected Essays on Constitutional Law,* Vol. III (1938), pp. 1187–1202, at 1201–2; Milton Conover, "National, State and Local Cooperation in Food and Drug Control," *American Political Science Review,* Vol. XXII (1928), p. 913; W. Brooke Graves, "Federal Leadership in State Legislation," *Temple Law Annual,* Vol. X (1936), pp. 308–405; Jane P. Clark, "Interdependent Federal and State Law as a Form of Federal-State Cooperation," *Iowa Law Review,* Vol. XXIII (1938), p. 542; Samuel Mermin, "Cooperative Federalism Again," *Yale Law Journal,* Vol. LVII (1947), pp. 1–26, 201–18; Note, "State Legislation Adopting Federal Standards," *Columbia Law Review,* Vol. XXIII (1923), p. 674; Note, "Supreme Court Review of State Interpretations of Federal Law Incorporated by Reference," *Harvard Law Review,* Vol. LXVI (1953), pp. 1948.

vention of soil erosion."[14] The Secretary of Agriculture determined that erosion control should be undertaken by the Federal Soil Conservation Service only through legally constituted local agencies. State legislation, making possible the establishment of local soil conservation districts, thus became necessary. Officials of the Department of Agriculture, with the consultation of state officials and farm leaders, drafted a suggested state law. It was subsequently adopted by all 48 states, in some cases with minor amendments. At least one state was apparently so anxious to qualify its farmers for federal aid that the state legislature even enacted the footnotes in the model act, footnotes intended simply to give advice to state officials with respect to alterations in the model that would be necessary to "fit" it to the situation of particular states.

Similar situations are the rule for virtually all grant-in-aid programs, which cover many of the principal governmental services: road building, social security, public health, and others. Hence the intermeshing of laws is continuous and complex. In the Illinois welfare statutes, for example, there is hardly a page or a paragraph that, explicitly or implicitly, does not refer to federal statutes in administrative regulations. There is, of course, continuous consultation between federal and state officers concerning the adequacy of existing federal and state laws and the need for their amendment.

TAXATION AND THE LAW

Federal tax laws are largely concerned with property relations created and defined by state law. Some federal taxes are, in effect, returned directly to states (if these states levy similar taxes), as in levies on estates and on employers for unemployment benefits. A complex of congressional and judicial legislation covers state taxation of goods in or affecting interstate commerce, which is permissible under some conditions and forbidden under others. Though, as Justice Frankfurter has written, perhaps ruefully, "The history of this problem has been spread over hundreds of volumes of our Reports,"[15] and clear answers are still difficult to find, the states continue to tax such goods in multifarious ways and are sustained in doing so by court decisions that further confuse the laws.

DIVERSITY OF CITIZENSHIP AND STATE LAW

The same intermeshing may be seen in rules evolved by the Supreme Court that have arisen out of cases that come to the Court because of the litigants' diverse citizenship. In 1842 the Supreme Court decided, in effect, that cases in common law coming before it—i.e., cases where there were no state constitutional or statutory provisions applicable—would be decided

[14] Public Law No. 46, 74th Congress (Approved April 27, 1935), sec. 3.
[15] *Freeman* v. *Hewit*, 329 U.S. 249, 251 (1946).

according to "the general nature and doctrines of jurisprudence."[16] The decision held that in such subjects the decisions of state courts were entitled to attention and respect but they could not be binding in the federal courts. This led in time to an attempt by the Supreme Court to construct a separate common law not only in the field of commercial law but in other important fields of unwritten law. The consequences were to establish two systems of law, especially over a wide area of private commercial transactions, with the outcome of a suit depending in large part upon whether it was brought before a federal or a state court. This duality was ended only in 1938 (*Erie RR* v. *Tompkins*). Decisional rules of state courts were held no longer to be inferior to state statutes. Mr. Justice Brandeis declared for the Court: "Except for matters governed by the Federal Constitution or by Acts of Congress, the law to be applied in any case is the law of the state. And whether the law of the state shall be declared by its Legislature in a statute or by its highest court in a decision is not a matter of federal concern. There is no federal common law." This left unsolved a number of problems, including the basic one of whether federal or state law was applicable in a given case. But there was no longer any doubt about the necessity of federal courts to give effect to state common law. If anything they may have been overzealous. The larger point here is again the intermeshing of state and federal bodies of law. While the Court has retreated somewhat from its 1945 position that: "A federal court adjudicating a state-created right solely because of the diversity of citizenship of the parties is for that purpose, in effect, only another court of the state,"[17] the federal courts have assiduously adhered to the 1938 rule.

These are easy cases of intermeshed laws. The important point is to recognize the hard cases: where there are no federal funds directly involved and where a given service may seem on its face to be purely that of a "single level" of the federal system. In fact, it is hard to find bodies of either federal or state law that preempt a complete field.

THE MESHING OF JUDICIAL ENFORCEMENT

Substantive rights defined in federal statutes may have their enforcement left wholly or partially to the states. Even more often the national law supplies "protection against infringement by the states of rights which the states themselves have created."[18] Thus state actions allegedly impairing contracts made under state law are adjudicated by the Supreme Court

[16] *Swift* v. *Tyson* (16 Pet. 1.).

[17] *Guaranty Trust Co.* v. *York,* 326 U.S. 99, 108–9 (1945).

[18] Henry M. Hart, Jr., "The Relations Between State and Federal Law," in Arthur W. Macmahon (ed.), *Federalism, Mature and Emergent* (New York: Doubleday & Company, 1955), p. 197.

under the contract clause of the Constitution. Similarly, the constitutional "due process" may be held infringed by state action in cases involving property rights established by previous state action.

Even where the Constitution allows the central government to exclude state participation, Congress has not—we will see later that it cannot—fully used the power legally available to it.

> The Constitution . . . empowers Congress "to dispose of and make all needful Rules and Regulations respecting . . . property belonging to the United States." Grants pursuant to the exercise of this power are the foundation of a large proportion of the land titles in the country. Conceivably, Congress might have attempted to impose conditions on these grants governing the rights and powers of grantees and subsequent holders. But as a Supreme Court has read the legislation, it provided instead that the interests of the grantees should be assimilated into the general mass of property interests in the state, and subject thereafter to the governance of the general land laws of the states. . . . And in another early instance the Court upheld the power of Congress to create the Bank of the United States and to authorize it to sue and be sued in a Federal Circuit Court. But it is assumed that the state law would determine the rights and duties of the bank incident to ordinary banking transactions. To add a similar recent example, from among a host of others, the Court has decided that the statutes providing for federal licensing of a radio broadcasting station and federal approval of transfers of licenses, are not to be construed as removing contracts concerning the operation of the stations and transfers of their property from the basic control of the state law.[19]

PATENTS: A "HARD CASE"

The Constitution (art. 1, sec. 8) provides that Congress shall have power "to provide the Progress of Science and useful Arts, by securing for limited Times to Authors and Inventors the exclusive Right to their respective Writings and Discoveries." On this base, Congress has built the edifice of patent law. On its face the combination of constitutional and statutory provisions seems to involve a "pure" federal function. States cannot and do not issue letters of patent. Nevertheless, the mixture of laws exists in even this field. Patent laws do not displace either the police or taxing functions of the states. Patent rights are subordinate to a given state's authority over property within its limits. Royalties received from patents are taxable under state law.[20] A state may condemn the use of devices it finds injurious to health and safety even though the device has been

---

[19] *Ibid.*, p. 201. For discussion of Congress giving to the states power that the Supreme Court has declared to be national, see below, Chapter Ten.

[20] *Fox Film Corp.* v. *Doyal*, 286 U.S. 123 (1932) overruling *Long* v. *Rockwood*, 277 U.S. 142 (1928).

granted a patent.[21] A state may regulate the transfer of patent rights so as to protect purchasers against fraud.[22] In suits involving damages or other property rights, a plaintiff enjoys ample leeway in determining whether he will take his case to a state or a federal court. If he pivots his case on the allegation that he is due damages for slander or libel against his patented product, including the claim that the patented product is merely an infringement of another patent, then his case must go to the state courts.

> A suit for damages to business caused by a threat to sue under the patent law is not itself a suit under the patent law. . . .[whether the defendent's act] is wrong or not depends upon the law of the state where the act is done, not upon the patent law, and, therefore, the suit arises under the law of the state.[23]

Bodies of state laws in some cases occupy a complete field, more so than do bodies of federal law. In matters of divorce, custody of children, the administration of estates, no federal law exists and federal courts do not take direct jurisdiction even in cases of diverse citizenship. Similarly, one can say that state law is a more or less complete entity in matters governing the ownership and control of automobiles and other personal property. This is so despite the fact that federal law touches this matter at many points: in statutes supplying penalties for the interstate movements of stolen automobiles, for example; or in the manner in which federal courts exercise jurisdiction over substantial damage cases involving diverse citizenship, for another. Even in the extreme "hard case" of divorce, where the Supreme Court has said flatly "the whole subject of the domestic relations of husband and wife . . . belong[s] to the laws of the states and not to the laws of the United States,"[24] it is possible to find cases closely related to divorce proceedings where federal courts have taken action. Thus a federal district court has enforced against a wandering husband in Wisconsin an award of alimony granted by a New York state court;[25] and the Supreme Court has had occasion to declare that the constitutional "full faith and credit" must be accorded a divorce decree in the state court by the courts of another state.[26]

By stretching the concept of intermeshed laws, one can clearly hold that all law of the United States is intermeshed. The nature of the American constitutional system as it was initially outlined, establishing the national government as one of limited powers, has clearly produced a body of law

[21] *Patterson* v. *Kentucky,* 97 U.S. 501 (1879).

[22] *Ozan Lumber Co.* v. *Union County Bank,* 207 U.S. 251 (1907).

[23] *American Well Water Co.* v. *Lane and Bouler Co.,* 241 U.S. 257 (1916).

[24] *In re Burrus,* 136 U.S. 586, 593 (1890).

[25] *Barker* v. *Barker,* 21 Harv. 582 (U.S. 1859).

[26] *Williams* v. *North Carolina,* 317 U.S. 287 (1942) and 325 U.S. 226 (1945).

in which the federal-state mixture is extreme and pervasive. Just as clearly, some bodies of state law stand largely independent, touching federal law and the federal courts relatively infrequently and on relatively peripheral points. For any individual litigant, facing a specific legal problem, these points may of course be the crucial ones.

In summary, then, the statute and case books do not contain neat packages of law covering a given area that can be labelled "all federal" or "all state." The typical situation is that bodies of state and federal law cover the same field of regulation or substantive service. More exceptions are to be found in state than in federal law. The courts have looked with increasing favor on this mutual penetration of the legal systems. Judicial leniency has extended to the direct incorporation of state laws in federal legislation and of federal laws in state legislation.[27] It has also extended to a new view of the cooperative nature of federal-state functions. In 1937 the court commented on the issue of whether a state statute had been unconstitutionally forced into existence by the federal Social Security Act:

> Together the two statutes now before us embody a cooperative legislative effort by state and national governments, for carrying out a public purpose common to both, which neither could fully achieve without the cooperation of the other. The Constitution does not prohibit such cooperation.

Where programs mesh so must law. The programs do not always mesh easily and without conflict: this produces a large part of the political problems the country faces. The laws do not mesh without undefined gaps and contradictory interpretation; and this is responsible for a large share of the business of the federal and state courts.

The mixture of laws is largely a product of history. The American common law background has discouraged attempts at summary and codification of law which might have led to the development of areas of exclusiveness in order to promote "rationality." The fact is that the constitutional fathers established a national government of limited functions; the further fact that this national government has added continuously to its responsibilities, and at an increased velocity during the past half-century, contributes to the development of the necessity to mix laws and the number of points of contact. These are historical considerations contributing to the mixture of federal-state legal systems. To view the process of American legislation and administration in operation is simply to catch this history in the present tense. The rest of this book, excluding only the last evaluative section, is an attempt to do exactly that.

[27] *Carmichael v. Southern Coal & Coke Co.*, 301 U.S. 495 (1937).

Chapter 4

SHARING OF FUNCTIONS:
THE "NATIONAL" POLICE SYSTEM

Police work is often considered an example *par excellence* of a "purely local" function. The evidence is quite the contrary. Here as elsewhere there exists the most intimate federal-state-local collaboration. Primary responsibilities over a wide range of police functions remain in state-local hands. But the federal government has carved out an extensive area of police activities. More fundamentally, there is hardly a local police force, however small and parochial it may be, that does not depend upon federal assistance in its day-to-day activities; and hardly a federal police activity that is not dependent upon local aid.

The Director of the Federal Bureau of Investigation has placed himself on record as being "vigorously opposed to anything savoring of a national police force."[1] A fully national police force—one in which all criminal activities are defined by a single body of law and enforced by a centrally directed corps of officers—does not exist in the United States. But if the nation has not produced a national police force, it has developed what can accurately be called a national police system. J. Edgar Hoover has himself set the tone for this system. "I like to think of the Federal Bureau of Investigation of the United States Department of Justice," he has said, "not only as an arm of the United States government, but as an agency maintained by and for each and every State, every county, every crossroad." Federal-state-local cooperation has produced in fact what Mr. Hoover stated in 1935 as belief: ". . . no unit of apprehension and detection can be self-

[1] Testimony of J. Edgar Hoover, *Hearings,* Subcommittee on Appropriations, U.S. Senate (1950), as reprinted in Federal Bureau of Investigation mimeographed document (1950), p. 127.

sufficient . . . crime is no longer local, but nationalized, and . . . nationalized methods are necessary to combat it."[2]

Here are three examples of how the national police system operates:

1. In a small midwestern town, two citizens almost simultaneously called the local police. A housewife complained of a prowler in her yard; a janitor of a church reported that someone had tried to break open the church safe. In response to the first call, a policeman trailed the prowler by footprints in the snow, almost immediately picked him up, and lodged him in the city jail. In response to the second call, another policeman found the church office in a shambles. A window had been broken. The safe had been beaten and bent, and quantities of fireproof packing from the space between the safe's inner and outer walls had been scattered about. The policeman at the church had been taught to preserve criminal evidence in a training course given by one of his colleagues (the latter having learned the techniques at the National Police Academy of the Federal Bureau of Investigation). In separate envelopes he put samples of the broken glass, of the paint chipped from the face of the safe, and of the fireproofing materials. He found under the safe a small bit of metal that he preserved in still a fourth envelope. Returning to the jail to make his report, the officer became curious about the prowler who had been detained. He consequently searched the prowler's automobile, in which he found a screwdriver with its tip broken off. The piece of metal he had discovered under the church safe seemed to correspond to the missing end of the screwdriver. When the prowler was confronted with this evidence, he denied that the metal pieces were at all identical and denied any knowledge whatsoever of the attempted church burglary.

As a routine matter, all the evidence that had been collected at the church was sent to the FBI laboratories in Washington. So was the broken screwdriver. The suspect was relieved of his clothes so that they could be dispatched to Washington. The FBI laboratories promptly reported to the local police chief that (1) the piece of metal found under the church safe had, without doubt, been broken off the screwdriver; (2) the suspect's clothes contained many microscopic bits of the paint chipped from the safe; (3) a quantity of the safe's fireproof packing was in the cuffs of the suspect's trousers; (4) slivers of glass impregnated in the suspect's jacket

[2] *Address of J. Edgar Hoover, before Convention of the International Association of Chiefs of Police,* Atlantic City, New Jersey, July 9, 1935 (Washington, D.C.: Government Printing Office, 1935), pp. 3–4. Mr. Hoover has consistently maintained this stand through the years. Thus, from the *FBI Law Enforcement Bulletin* of February, 1960: "The answer to nationwide crime is nationwide law enforcement, with each agency—local, state, and federal—forming a united, cooperative front against professional criminals."

were probably from the broken church window. Confronted with this evidence, the suspect confessed to the attempted robbery. After having sat in jail in his underclothes for some days, he was given his clothes so that he might stand trial.

Confessions are the usual result of this sort of evidence. If, however, the suspect had not admitted his guilt, the FBI's services to the small, local police department would have continued. The technicians who had established the correspondence between the church office evidence and the suspect's clothes would have been dispatched from Washington to testify at the local trial. They would have brought with them enlarged microphotographs and detailed technical analyses, and would have remained in the locality until their services were no longer needed. Their appearance, like their technical work in Washington, would be at no cost to the local government. That no federal statute was involved made no difference; FBI technical services are given freely to local governments without regard to issues of formal jurisdiction.

2. Another small town robbery, this one in Texas, was more successful. The safe in a bus station was emptied by a person who apparently hid himself in the men's room before the station was closed for the night. After opening the safe, the robber left without triggering automatic door and window alarms by chopping a hole through the roof. Local investigation demonstrated that there were no fingerprints of any sort on the safe. The local police chief, a graduate of the FBI's National Academy, thought that envelopes in the safe, which the thief had rifled, might contain latent fingerprints. The local police force did not have the technical facilities to search for fingerprints on paper. Consequently the chief wrapped the envelopes carefully and sent them to the FBI Washington laboratory, along with fingerprints of all employees of the bus station whose prints might normally be on the envelopes. Bureau technicians discovered no fewer than seven single prints on the envelopes that did not belong to station employees. Almost simultaneously, the local police chief was told by an informer that a safe cracker named Malone used the through-the-roof escape technique and that Malone had once served a term in the New Mexico penitentiary. The chief wired the New Mexico state police to ask if a fingerprint record of Malone were available. It was supplied to him, and he sent it to the FBI. The FBI conclusively demonstrated that the latent fingerprints on the bus station envelopes were identical to those of Malone. From this initial identification, both Washington and New Mexico were then able to supply from their records a complete description of Malone, his family, and his habits of work and play. The local chief had this information broadcast throughout the state, utilizing the facilities of the Texas Rangers, the state's principal

criminal investigation agency. And under the provisions of the federal
Fugitive Felon Act, Malone's description was supplied by the FBI to all
police officers in the United States. The local police chief had no doubt
that Malone would be caught. "The fix on him is so certain that we will find
him if he's not dead," the chief said.

3. In a large eastern city, officers on the narcotics detail of the local
police force became concerned when they noticed that a number of known
addicts were not appearing in their usual haunts. One of the police department's paid informers said that there appeared to be a new and cheap
source of heroin available in the city. Local officers discussed this development with agents of the Federal Bureau of Narcotics (Treasury Department) in the course of their routine, daily meetings. It was decided that a
major effort should be made to discover and cut off the new heroin supply.
Local police officers would attempt to make a "buy." The federal agency
would supply funds for this effort. Federal agents would make inquiries
throughout the country to see if similar developments were discernable
elsewhere and, especially, to discover the origin of the new heroin supply.
These inquiries proved fruitless, and the local scene became the focus of
action. A disguised member of the local police force made his purchase.
The "pusher" was an inexperienced young addict. It was obvious that he
was being utilized as a seller of heroin because he had no previous record
of narcotics convictions. Local and federal officers together questioned him.
He knew very little. He had agreed to sell in return for his own supply of
the drug. He readily supplied a description of two men who, he alleged,
were the owners of the heroin he had in his possession when arrested. One
of these two people—call him Brown—was known to the local police, and
police records included several addresses indicating where he might be
found. A "stake" on these places soon revealed Brown's presence; and he
was observed in the company of the other person—Bell—who had been
described by the arrested pusher. Since no record on Bell was available
locally, the FBI searched its photograph file of habitual criminals and Bell
was identified as a known addict from an eastern city. A federal narcotics
agent, in the company of a local policeman, observed Messrs. Bell and
Brown talking with still a third person—Jones—in a barroom. Jones was
immediately identified by the local police as a suspected recipient of stolen
goods, not previously connected with the narcotics trade. Though not certain that any of these three persons was the kingpin of the new heroin
trade, local and federal officers feared that one or more of the group might
disappear (or sell whatever supply of heroin they had on hand), and it was
therefore decided that they should be arrested immediately. State search
warrants were obtained. Federal agents served as leaders of the actual raid-

ing parties, with manpower supplied by the local police force. Three raids were made simultaneously, concerted by the local short-wave radio. Heroin was found in two of the three places raided. Some evidence was also found indicating the possibility of connecting these finds with a known narcotics peddler in another city. It was decided to try all three men in the federal court, since clear evidence of interstate traffic was involved and since one of the men had a previous record of narcotics convictions. (Federal penalties for second offenders were greater than state penalties.) All the evidence collected by the local police was turned over to the federal narcotics units for transmittal to the United States District Attorney. The young man originally arrested was also given over to federal custody, though it was agreed that he would be penalized lightly because of the information he had supplied.

*　　*　　*

These cases illustrate many facets of federal-state-local cooperation in police administration, including the importance to local police forces of federal training programs, federal laboratory facilities for the identification of criminal evidence, the federal fugitive felon law, and federal fingerprint and photographic files. Just as important, the last case makes clear the dependence of federal law enforcement agencies on the information and manpower resources of local police forces. The cases do not reveal the tension and disharmony occasionally exhibited among the nation's many law enforcement agencies, but properly emphasize their characteristic day-to-day collaboration. In short, the cases illustrate the national police system at work.[3]

I. BACKGROUND FOR POLICE COOPERATION

Root causes for collaborative police activities are found in the nature of the American federal system. The individual criminal has become mobile. He may flee or fly across state boundaries, and he can plan a robbery in one state, execute it in another, dispose of his loot in a third, and look for sanctuary in a fourth. Criminal activities, moreover, tend like other forms of endeavor to evolve through handicraft to industralized stages. Crime becomes organized into larger units, "mobs" or "syndicates" dividing territories into quasi-monopolistic units for the provision of prostitution, boot-

---

[3] Of the three cases, the first two are of a type that occurs so frequently that anonymity of sources has been assured only by using pseudonyms and altering trivial details, including the section of the country in which they occurred. Greater alterations in the third case have been made.

leg whiskey, gambling, narcotics, and stolen goods. Customers for such services exist everywhere, and the larger the population concentration, the greater the supply of consumption units. Where a natural market does not exist, the underworld, especially when organized and disciplined, can supply an artificial market. Here are found the more or less pure rackets: "protection" for restaurants, laundries, and garages; "leadership" for bogus unions; "services" to truckers, manufacturers, and others—all forms of blackmail to prevent threatened violence. Industrialized vice and industrialized racketeering readily and ordinarily cross state lines. The telephone, telegraph, and other modern modes of communication and transportation make control from central points feasible and easy. Operating members of the mobs, including specialists in violence, are moved from place to place as a measure of efficiency. Stolen goods, prostitutes, or narcotics can be produced on order from widely scattered places.[4]

MANY LAW ENFORCEMENT AGENCIES

The response of the American governments to these and other crime control problems has been characteristically piecemeal. Local law enforcement units, as the Kestnbaum Commission's Advisory Committee on Law Enforcement remarked, are so numerous and so difficult to classify or describe that they cannot even be counted exactly. The total number of state and local police units is "approximately 39,000." They differ enormously in size and professionalization. More than 3,000 counties have elected sheriffs. Their offices may not even contain a typewriter; on the other hand, a sheriff's establishment may include a large staff and a considerable laboratory, and it may display a high degree of professional sophistication. The more or less independent police agencies include one-man constabularies (most of whom are part-time employees) in many of the nation's 20,000 townships. At the other extreme, the police department of New York City had (as of 1958) a budget exceeding $160 million and more than 23,000 employees, a force roughly equal to the entire field staffs of all federal law enforcement agencies. Each of the 50 states except Hawaii maintains a police unit, and they too vary widely in size, technical training, and the

---

[4] Robert Tieken, U.S. District Attorney for the Northern District of Illinois, supplied an example in 1957: ". . . a Chicago 'fence' early one day received an order for the sale of a truckload of pens from a Boston outlet. By that evening, pens meeting specifications . . . were stolen in Dayton, Ohio, brought to Chicago, trans-shipped and delivered in Boston by the third day after the original order was placed. This is not an isolated example . . . furs from Las Vegas and Hollywood, whiskey from Peoria, jewelry from New York. I could go on and on giving illustrations. . . ." Address before the Chicago Crime Commission, Chicago, Illinois, October 23, 1957 (mimeographed press copy), pp. 5–6.

limits of their jurisdiction. In the majority of states, the state police are principally concerned with highway patrol even when formal jurisdiction extends over the full police power. Some states—New York, and Texas, for example—assign state officers to a wide range of crime problems, maintain effective criminal identification laboratories, and carry on extensive training activities for local police forces.[5]

There is a corresponding lack of neatness in the organization of police work within the national government. Enforcement responsibilities for criminal statutes are widely dispersed: there are at least 34 investigative and enforcement agencies in the federal government organized under 16 separate departments, commissions, and agencies. Since the Revenue Cutter Service was established in 1790 to control smuggling and to aid in the collection of taxes, federal law enforcement agencies have been characterized by limited jurisdiction. The separate agencies possess strong traditions of independence, and there is no federal mechanism to focus the activities of federal agencies (to say nothing of state and local ones) on general problems of law enforcement.

The Federal Bureau of Investigation is the largest national agency concerned with the enforcement of criminal laws and the one with the widest jurisdiction. In addition to responsibilities for enforcing the espionage, sabotage, and treason statutes, it is charged with maintaining more than 150 other federal criminal laws, including those covering kidnaping, bank robberies, extortion, and automobile thefts. Its "investigative jurisdiction" indeed extends to all matters in which the United States is, or may be, a party, but in practice it has simplified its work by not giving attention to matters specifically assigned by Congress to other agencies. A group of five Treasury Department agencies covers a wide and overlapping field of criminal law enforcement. (1) The Intelligence Unit of the Bureau of Internal Revenue has numerous responsibilities but specializes in the investigation of income tax frauds. (2) The Enforcement Division of the Alcohol Tax Unit is concerned with violations of several national firearms acts as well as liquor tax laws. (3) The Division of Investigation and Patrol of the Bureau of Customs has primary responsibility over illegal imports and exports (the Treasury's Coast Guard shares some of these responsibilities). (4) The Secret Service Division enforces counterfeiting and forgery laws, as well as a number of banking and related statutes, and also has the task of protecting the President and his family. (5) Finally, and

[5] See *Compilation of Comparative Data for State and Provincial Law Enforcement Agencies* (Washington, D.C.: International Association of Chiefs of Police, 1950); Robert L. Mawhinney, "State Police and Patrol Compensation," *State Government,* Vol. XXVI, No. 2 (February, 1953), pp. 52–54.

of first importance, the Bureau of Narcotics is charged with enforcing all federal statutes aimed at controlling the use of narcotics and other harmful drugs.

Still other federal agencies have important law enforcement responsibilities. The inspection service of the Post Office is concerned with mail theft, fraudulent use of the mails, forgery of money and postal savings certificates, mailing of obscene matter, and other criminal acts related to the mails. The Border Patrol of the Immigration and Naturalization Service (Department of Justice) has as its duty the prevention of unlawful entry of aliens and the apprehension of persons who are illegally resident in the country. Other agencies concerned with criminal law enforcement include the various branches of the Military Police, whose concern extends to military personnel off duty as well as to deserters and those "absent without leave"; the Food and Drug Administration of the Department of Health, Education, and Welfare, whose work centers on preventing the sale of misrepresented or poisonous materials; and branches of the Department of Agriculture concerned with plant and animal diseases, meat inspection, and pest control. Many other federal agencies have police authority that shades off from other regulatory or service functions.[6]

[6] The Advisory Committee on Law Enforcement of the Kestnbaum Commission in its unpublished memorandum (pp. 6–9) listed the following federal departments as having developed "law enforcement units easily recognized as such": 1. *Department of Justice:* Federal Bureau of Investigation; Immigration and Naturalization Service. 2. *Commerce Department:* Civil Aeronautics Administration; Maritime Administration; Bureau of Foreign and Domestic Commerce, Office of International Trade. 3. *Defense Department: Department of the Air Force:* Office of Special Investigations. *Department of the Army:* Criminal Investigation Division; Counter Intelligence Corps; Office of Inspector General; Corps of Engineers; *Department of the Navy:* Office of Naval Intelligence; Office of Inspector General; Office of Provost Marshal; 4. *Health, Education and Welfare Department:* Food and Drug Administration; Social Security Administration; Children's Bureau. 5. *Department of the Interior:* Federal Petroleum Board; Fish and Wildlife Service; Bureau of Mines. 6. *Department of Labor:* Wage, Hour and Public Contracts Division. 7. *Post Office Department:* Office of Chief Inspector. 8. *Treasury Department:* Alcohol Tax Unit and Intelligence Unit (both in Bureau of Internal Revenue); Bureau of Customs; Bureau of Narcotics; Coast Guard; Secret Service.

The Advisory Committee also listed the following federal governmental units as having law enforcement responsibilities "by reason of being charged with the administration of laws possessing criminal sanctions or requiring the performance of investigative duties. . . ." 1. Agriculture Department, 2. Civil Service Commission, 3. Federal Communications Commission, 4. Federal Trade Commission, 5. Housing and Home Finance Agency, 6. Interstate Commerce Commission, 7. Security and Exchange Commission, and 8. Veterans Administration.

For discussion of federal law enforcement agencies, see Bruce Smith, *Police Systems in the United States* (New York: Harper and Brothers, 1949); also James H. Grisham, *"Crime Control: A Study in American Federalism,"* unpublished Ph.D. dissertation, Department of Political Science, University of Texas, 1953.

MANY LAWS

The many law enforcement agencies must cope with a "spectacular increase in the number and types of functions delegated to American systems of criminal justice."[7]

When Congress determined that kidnaping was a federal crime, a federal agency (the FBI) was assigned the task of enforcing the statute, and a new link of federal-state-local police collaboration was forged. If Congress had not made the determination, there would be one fewer item of interaction. If there were no state or local prohibition or alcoholic tax laws, there would be no moonshiners or bootleggers. The total increase in the work load of police forces is even more the consequence of state laws and local ordinances than it is of federal legislation. Roscoe Pound referred to this total development when he said that "of one hundred thousand persons arrested in Chicago in 1912, more than one-half were held for violation of legal precepts which did not exist twenty-five years before." A more recent estimate holds that ". . . the number of crimes for which one may be prosecuted has at least doubled since the turn of the century."[8] The development of the national police system has in part been the consequence of the sheer increase in criminal law legislation.

FEDERAL CRIMINAL LEGISLATION

The main body of criminal law is state law, and the administration of justice is largely in the hands of the state courts. The Constitution on its face provides limited crime control powers for the central government. They relate to treason and counterfeiting; piracy and felony on the high seas; and the law of nations.[9] In addition, the Thirteenth Amendment gave Congress authority to enforce the prohibition of slavery; the Eighteenth Amendment provided concurrent authority to Congress for prohibiting "the manufacture, sale, or transportation of intoxicating liquors," and the Twenty-first Amendment left the national government with responsibility for aiding in the enforcement of prohibition in states with prohibition laws.

[7] Francis A. Allen, "The Supreme Court, Federalism, and State Systems of Criminal Justice," *The University of Chicago Law School Record*, Vol. VIII, No. 1 (Autumn, 1958), special supplement, p. 3.

[8] Both quotations are cited in Allen, *loc. cit.*, p. 19. The first is from Roscoe Pound, *Criminal Justice in America* (New York: Henry Holt & Company, 1930), p. 23; the second from Bolitha J. Laws, "Criminal Courts and Adult Probation," *National Parole and Probation Association Journal*, Vol. III, p. 354.

[9] The Constitution also vests in Congress exclusive jurisdiction in criminal matters over the District of Columbia and other places completely under national authority, e.g., forts, magazines and arsenals, and national territories (art. 1, sec. 8, clause 17 and art. IV, sec. 3). In practice jurisdiction over many such places (national parks, for example) is shared with states and localities.

In addition to these specific provisions, the national government is also authorized "to make all laws which shall be necessary and proper for carrying into execution" the powers granted to it,[10] and this general authorization is the source of the largest fraction by far of federal criminal law. Thus Congress has made it a criminal offense to rob, destroy, or obstruct the mail (from the power "to establish post offices and post roads"); to evade taxes (from the power "to lay and collect taxes"); to obstruct interstate commerce by robbery or violence (from the power "to regulate commerce"). Federal criminal statutes are in some cases built upon a pyramiding of implied powers: thus the Federal Bank Robbery Act of 1934 rests upon the national power to charter banks which in turn is implied from the power to regulate the currency.

Many federal criminal statutes, based upon the necessary and proper clause, are in fact aimed at aiding states in their police functions or substituting federal penalties in cases where state action has been ineffective. As early as 1890 a statute was aimed at assisting states to enforce their own prohibition laws. In 1900 Congress provided criminal penalties for anyone transporting in interstate commerce game killed in violation of a state law. In 1910 federal penalties were provided for those transporting a woman for immoral purposes in interstate or foreign commerce, and in 1919 for those transporting a stolen automobile across state lines.

Legislation of this nature reached a high point in the 1930's as a reaction to prohibition and its aftermath, the sensational kidnaping and murder of Charles A. Lindbergh, Jr., a series of spectacular bank robberies, and a gang massacre. (There was considerable debate over the possibility of a national police force to combat crime which, it was said, could not be dealt with by the states alone.) Federal criminal laws provided penalties for those using interstate commerce for kidnaping, bank robbery, stolen property, and extortion. Subsequent years saw this list further extended to such items as gambling devices and racketeering. Federal taxes, and penalties for their nonpayment, were utilized to control narcotics, firearms, and certain gambling operations.

Perhaps the most significant federal laws in direct aid of state and local police work are those covering fugitive felons and witnesses, and persons attempting to avoid custody or confinement after conviction.[11] These statutes, among other things, make it a federal offense if a person crosses a state line ("to move or travel in interstate commerce") to avoid prosecution under state laws for murder, kidnaping, burglary, robbery, mayhem, rape,

---

[10] Art. 1, sec. 8.

[11] 48 *U.S. Stat.*, 782 (1934); *F.C.A.* 18, sec. 1073; 60 *U.S. Stat.*, 789 (1946); *F.C.A.* 18, sec. 1073.

assault with a dangerous weapon, or extortion. Penalties range up to five years in prison and a $5,000 fine. No initial federal offense need be involved. The federal offense is simply the act of attempting to avoid state prosecution. This legislation was passed at the request of state and local law enforcement officers who have subsequently (1950) unsuccessfully attempted to have the statute broadened to cover all felonies.[12]

The participation of the federal government in criminal law enforcement thus rests upon statutes (1) to punish antisocial conduct of distinctive federal concern, as in the case of treason; (2) to secure compliance with federal regulatory and tax programs; and (3) to supply penalties for specified criminal activities.[13] In the last field, federal laws compensate for the ineffectiveness of, and bring aid to, state-local law enforcement efforts. To steal an automobile is to break a state law; to transport the stolen automobile across state lines is to break a federal law. This illustrates the complementary quality of federal and state criminal legislation. Their complete overlapping is illustrated in the case of robbery of a bank with federally insured deposits: here the single act is subject to both state and federal penalties. Whether complementary or overlapping, the mixture of laws inevitably leads to close collaboration among law enforcement officers. Collaboration, however, is by no means limited to those cases involving clear complementary or overlapping statutes. The mutual help relationship among federal, state, and local enforcement officers extends over the total area of their activity. There are in practice no "pure" federal or state or local fields of police work.

The states themselves have tried to overcome the disadvantages of limited geographical jurisdictions through interstate compacts and uniform laws. For example, the interstate compact for the supervision of parolees and probationers, enacted by all states except Alaska, facilitates capture of criminals who have violated the terms of their freedom and crossed state

[12] See the resolution of the Law Officers' Conference of 1950, cited in *The Attorney General's Conference on Organized Crime* (Washington, D.C.; Department of Justice, 1951), p. 65. Exposures of organized crime by a Senate Investigating Committee (the Kefauver Committee) in 1950 and in 1951 set off new demands for federal criminal legislation. See, for example, Morris Ploscowe, "The Significance of Recent Investigations for the Criminal Law and Administration of Criminal Justice," *University of Pennsylvania Law Review*, Vol. C, No. 6 (April, 1952), pp. 805–31. A number of bills, principally aimed at racketeers and professional gamblers, were introduced by Senator Kefauver and his colleagues. Congressional investigation also stimulates state legislation and police reform at the local level. With respect to state laws see the Council of State Governments' mimeographed report, "Major Developments in the Field of Crime Control and Law Enforcement" (undated, late 1953 or 1954).

[13] See Bernard Schwartz, "Federal Criminal Jurisdiction and Prosecutors' Discretion," *Law and Contemporary Problems*, Vol. XIII, No. 4 (1948), pp. 64–66; Hart and Wechsler, *op. cit.*, pp. 1095–1100.

lines; the compact also encourages rehabilitation by permitting the supervised interstate movement of parolees and probationers.[14] As the historians of the compact movement have remarked, "One of the most prominent uses to which the interstate compact has been put is crime control."[15] Both the number of compacts, and the number of signatories, increase yearly. Uniform state statutes in the crime control field are even more numerous than compacts. Two organizations—The National Conference of Commissioners on Uniform State Law and the Drafting Committee of The Council of State Governments—are the chief avenues by which uniform crime control statutes are brought to state attention. The National Conference has recommended legislation since 1892; among crime control measures, its statute on securing attendance of out-of-state witnesses has been adopted by 48 jurisdictions; on narcotic control by 50; on criminal extradiction by 45.[16] The Drafting Committee of the Council of State Governments works closely with the National Conference, frequently recommending the latter's statutes, and itself develops texts of model acts and suggested interstate compacts.[17] The efforts to achieve interstate cooperation or uniformity seem, on their surface, not to involve the federal government. In fact, federal crime control agencies often are the source of suggested uniform laws,[18] and federal officials work in many drafting sessions of both the National Conference and the Drafting Committee. The federal government's involvement in interstate compacts is even more direct. Compacts require federal approval before becoming effective. In 1934 Congress gave a blanket advance approval to interstate compacts directed at the control of crime.[19]

Uniform laws and interstate compacts work toward a national uniformity of criminal law procedures. Decisions of the Supreme Court have tended in the same direction. Since its 1932 decision in *Powell* v. *Alabama* the Court has scrutinized under the due process clause of the Fourteenth Amend-

---

[14] See *Book of the States 1956–57* (Chicago: Council of State Governments, 1956), pp. 35–36.

[15] Frederick L. Zimmerman and Mitchell Wendell in *Book of the States 1958–59*, p. 216. See the same authors' *The Interstate Compact since 1925* (Chicago: Council of State Governments, 1951).

[16] The data cover 52 jurisdictions—the 50 states plus Puerto Rico and the District of Columbia—and are given as of November, 1963, in the *Book of the States, 1964–65*, p. 104.

[17] Other organizations working to achieve uniformity in crime control measures include a private group, the American Bar Association (through its Commission on Organized Crime), and an organized group of public officials, the National Association of Attorneys General. The Council of State Governments Drafting Committee attempts to coordinate all such efforts.

[18] See below, Chapter Six. Congressional investigating committees also make recommendations for state laws and local ordinances. For Kefauver Committee recommendations, see *Senate Reports 307* and *725*.

[19] 48 *U.S. Stat.* 909.

ment a continuously enlarging area of state criminal procedures. The Powell case held that due process was abrogated when illiterate defendants in a murder trial were denied the right to secure their own counsel. Due process has been abrogated in state criminal proceedings, according to subsequent Court decisions, in cases where police have physically coerced confessions,[20] or where defendants have been unduly detained, confined incommunicado, moved from place to place during interrogation, or questioned for prolonged periods.[21] Court decisions have also put limits on police search and seizures[22] and, utilizing the equal protection clause, have invalidated criminal convictions when racial discrimination was evident in the selection of juries.[23] Other manifestations of unfair trial have also been condemned.[24]

The net effect of the Supreme Court's decisions on day-to-day police practices is difficult to gauge. A court decision invalidating a coerced confession does not end police brutality. Yet some direct impact of Supreme Court rulings can certainly be found at the local scene; and indirect effects follow state statutes which are at least partially the consequence of court decisions. The impact of the Court is by no means uniform with respect to states or to areas of police activity. And the major portion of criminal law administration remains relatively unaffected, either because of the slowness of states and localities to respond to court decisions, or because of the deference of the court to state authority,[25] or because criminal procedures

[20] *Brown* v. *Mississippi,* 297 U.S. 278 (1939); *Chambers* v. *Florida,* 309 U.S. 227 (1940); *White* v. *Texas,* 310 U.S. 530 (1940).

[21] *Ashcraft* v. *Tennessee,* 322 U.S. 143 (1944); *Watts* v. *Indiana,* 338 U.S. 49 (1949); *Turner* v. *Pennsylvania,* 338 U.S. 62 (1949); *Harris* v. *South Carolina,* 338 U.S. 68 (1949). These cases and others are cited in Allen, *loc. cit.* I have drawn upon this article for the substance of the paragraph above, and have also profited from conversation with Mr. Allen.

[22] *Wolf* v. *Colorado,* 338 U.S. 25 (1949). The decision here held that freedom from unreasonable search and seizure was "basic to a free society" and therefore repugnant to due process; but since Colorado did not follow the federal government's rule of excluding from the trial evidence illegally seized, the Supreme Court did not invalidate the state court's decision based upon such evidence.

[23] *Strauder* v. *West Virginia,* 100 U.S. 303 (1880); *ex parte Virginia,* 100 U.S. 339 (1880).

[24] *Moore* v. *Dempsey,* 261 U.S. 86 (1923); *Tumey* v. *Ohio,* 273 U.S. 510 (1927); *Griffin* v. *Illinois* 351 U.S. 12 (1956).

[25] The Wolf case, cited above, was followed in the subsequent ten years by six other search and seizure cases. In only one was the state action overruled by a Supreme Court decision: *Rochin* v. *California,* 342 U.S. 165 (1952). In this case evidence was secured when a suspect's stomach was pumped for the purpose of obtaining narcotics he had swallowed. Five years later, however, the Court refused to invalidate (*Breithaupt* v. *Abram,* 352 U.S. 432) a conviction based upon the withdrawal of a blood sample from an unconscious person suspected of drunkenness (who had just previously been involved in a fatal automobile accident). The entire series of cases is reviewed by Glendon A. Schubert, *Constitutional Politics* (New York: Holt, Rinehart and Winston, 1960), pp. 609–21, 670–80.

have been untested—and are perhaps untestable—under prevailing court doctrine and practice. Nevertheless, the Supreme Court's decisions are clearly another nationalizing force in police work and criminal law administration.*

The principal fabric of the national police system is not to be found in Supreme Court decisions or interstate compacts or uniform state legislation. It is not to be found in occasional sensational local clean-up campaigns or congressional investigations. The national police system is principally found in the support given each other by federal, state, and local officers who in common do the nation's job of law enforcement.

II. LOCAL DEPENDENCE ON NATIONAL SERVICES

SERVICES-IN-AID

Local police units maintain their most continuous and important federal relationships with the FBI. The FBI national fingerprint file—containing in 1960 the classified prints of more than 150 million people—is the prime point of contact. Virtually every police force, as a matter of course, fingerprints all persons suspected of more than trivial offenses. The fingerprinting is done according to FBI instructions on FBI forms, and sets are routinely mailed to the FBI laboratory, using franked FBI envelopes. The FBI gives rapid service to localities in making identifications from the fingerprint records. Fingerprint identification in turn supplies to local police dossiers of a suspect's criminal career. Nothing is more satisfying to a local police officer than this service. It provides a quick means for establishing the existence of criminal history, confounding or confirming a given suspect's statements of prior lawfulness. Where only fingerprints are available at the local scene, the FBI service can supply descriptions of the persons concerned, their characteristic modes of work, places of residence and, in many cases, their photographs.

The FBI also maintains extensive records of the handwriting specimens of known forgers and "cold check" passers, and a skilled staff for identify-

*Editor's note: Recent Supreme Court decisions have carried the trend toward national uniformity in criminal law even further, reinforcing Grodzins' basic thesis. *Mapp* v. *Ohio*, 367 U.S. 643 (1961) overturned *Wolf* v. *Colorado* to apply the federal rule in search and seizure questions. In *Gideon* v. *Wainwright*, 372 U.S. 335 (1963), the court extended federal right-to-counsel rules to the states. The "assistance of counsel" doctrines derived from the Sixth Amendment were extended to the states in 1964 through *Escobedo* v. *State of Illinois*, 378 U.S. 478. In *Fay* v. *Noia*, 372 U.S. 391 (1963), the Supreme Court eliminated some of the barriers to federal court review of state criminal convictions through the use of the writ of habeas corpus.

ing new samples of forged and bad checks. Local police forces use this service continuously and as a matter of course; next to the fingerprint service it is perhaps the federal service-in-aid most frequently used by local units. The national FBI laboratory has special resources for the analysis and identification of many other sorts of evidence: these include ash from wood and other materials; restored printed matter from burned paper; blood and other stains; casts of shoe prints, heelprints, and tire treads; typewriting, printed matter, paper, watermarks on paper, and erasures and obliterations on paper; gunpowder stains; soil, toolmarks; wood, hair, and fibers; metal fragments; poisons; and bullets and cartridge cases. Through FBI publications and public relations programs, most local police officers know about the existence and utility of these services for the identification of criminal evidence. And through police training programs, largely directed or influenced by the FBI, there is widespread knowledge about the detection and preservation of evidence for transmittal to the FBI. Not only are the services widely known; the skills to make use of them are also widely dispersed.

Most large cities maintain their own criminal evidence laboratories and are less dependent upon national facilities than are smaller communities. Even the largest city nevertheless often finds records or data in Washington —for example, the extensive FBI file of tire treads—that are not available on the local scene. Private and university laboratories are also used by local police forces. Proximity gives them an advantage. But usually they demand a fee which local police are reluctant to pay in the light of the free services supplied by the FBI. A number of state police forces, whose leading personnel is likely to be composed of ex-FBI agents or those trained at the National Police Academy, also maintain fingerprint files and laboratory identification facilities. California, Massachusetts, Georgia, Texas, and Michigan have such establishments. Local officers, as a matter of state pride or speed, or out of friendship, often use these rather than national facilities. FBI services will still be used when the states' prove inadequate.[26] Despite overlapping and partially competing services, the FBI facilities are of utmost importance to local police forces. They make possible a level of police work that, in the words of one local chief, would be "absolutely impossible with our own resources."

Local use of Washington laboratory facilities is only one aspect of the

[26] The FBI, rather than state, criminal identification services may also be preferred merely for purposes of sheer window-dressing. Issues of greater efficiency need not be involved. A state prosecutor, for example, told an interviewer: "In a difficult case, it is nice to have an FBI rather than a state-police witness, and FBI rather than state exhibits." They would show exactly the same thing, he explained, "but the FBI label is impressive to a jury, and we need every bit of advantage that we can get." Field notes, May, 1959.

local dependence on federal services. On the local scene, whatever the size of the community or the particular criminal problems facing it, important local-federal relationships are almost certain to exist. For example, the police department of a rural area of Oklahoma or Arkansas may find that bootlegging and moonshining are among its most difficult police problems. If local police believe that whiskey is being illegally distilled, they will ask a Treasury Department investigator to look into the matter. (In a small town local officers may be so well known that they cannot do this sort of investigation.) The national officers will in many cases turn over their evidence to the local police chief. Where substantial amounts of illegal liquor are concerned, local and federal officers will collaborate in their investigation. Joint "raids" are commonplace.

The extent and kind of local-federal collaboration is largely dependent upon the sorts of problems facing local enforcement officers. Stolen cars in transit or for sale may plague an Ohio or California highway town, and this will lead to close, daily contacts with the FBI. Communities close to military installations find it necessary to work out detailed arrangements with military police units. It may be agreed, for example, that all drunks picked up by the Military Police will be turned over to the local police for detention and punishment; local police in return aid in tracking down deserters and those AWOL and will hold them in the local jail (even though no state laws are involved) until they can be transferred to the appropriate military installation. In other areas, special aid will be received from and given to the Border Patrol, or the Customs Service, or the Post Office inspector's office.

Crimes, like other aspects of life, follow fads and fashions, and a given community may find itself facing a "wave" of bank robberies or filling station holdups. The first sort of case almost certainly involves federal laws; the second does not. The significant point is that local and federal officers will work in common on both sorts of problems. Evidence against a bank robber may be developed by the local police and the suspect incarcerated by local officers. But the prisoner will be interrogated by a joint team of FBI agents and local officers, and an amiable agreement will be reached between state and federal prosecuting attorneys concerning the best jurisdiction in which to try the suspect. Despite the absence of federal legislation with respect to filling station robberies, the FBI will supply all sorts of technical aids to the local police, including descriptions of characteristic work habits of known filling station thieves. FBI personnel will be alerted to apprehend suspected persons.

In the event that the local police believe that a suspect has left the state (thus becoming a fugitive felon), the nationwide resources of the FBI are brought directly into play. The fleeing person is subject to arrest by federal agents throughout the country.[27] The fugitive felon warrant also results in the suspect's picture and description being distributed throughout the country to FBI agents, post offices, and local and state police forces. From the point of view of local police officers, the fugitive felon law makes their effective jurisdiction nationwide, "transforming all FBI agents in fact into a part of our local force," as one chief told an interviewer.

One way to summarize the interaction of local-federal police forces, and particularly the extent of local dependence on federal services, is by looking more closely at a single local police department. The chief of police in a midwestern city of approximately 50,000 population recently outlined the federal contacts of his force in the following terms: (1) The local force used the FBI fingerprint file daily. Prints of all persons arrested on criminal charges (and of all who applied for local police jobs) were sent routinely to Washington for reports. (2) On from ten to 15 occasions a month, cases involving bad checks and forgery made it advisable to send handwriting specimens for analysis to the FBI laboratories in Washington. (3) In the preceding 12 months, evidence on "from eight to a dozen cases" was sent for analysis and identification to the FBI laboratory. Evidence transmitted included casts of tires and shoes, and a blood-stained automobile seat. (4) FBI men visited the local police department two or three times a week "collecting information for their own uses." (5) Exchange of information on matters of mutual concern—with respect to narcotics, bootlegging, stolen mail, and stolen cars, for example—was "continuous." (6) Investigative work collaboratively carried on within the city was not uncommon, "but there is not much occasion for it here" ("We haven't had a bank robbery in many years."). (7) When crimes occurred in neighboring towns, outside the area of the local police radio system, the FBI notified the local police "as a matter of routine courtesy." (8) The relationship with local FBI activities was particularly close because one of the resident agents had formerly been a member of the local force, and "we're good friends." (Two members of the state police force were ex-officers of the local force, and this made for excellent state-local collaboration.) (9) The chief and his assistant were graduates of the (FBI) National Police Academy. (10) One local officer had recently been graduated from a special school operated by the Department's Bureau of Narcotics. (11) A number of local officers had attended a state-sponsored police training school, directed by an ex-FBI

[27] Though the suspect may be tried in a federal court for attempting to avoid arrest, he is usually returned to the state from which he fled, to be tried in a state court. If he is acquitted in this court for the felony originally suspected, federal prosecutors can get a "second crack" at him on the fugitive charge.

agent. (12) Professional and social contacts with national police were also maintained through the state and international associations of chiefs of police. ("We don't only get speeches. At a recent state meeting, two Bureau men gave a demonstration of how to take a couple of bank robbers who had barricaded themselves in a home with a hostage.") (13) When the chief and several of his associates in neighboring towns established a special joint squad for vice and narcotics work, they were advised on matters of organization and technique by both FBI and Narcotics Bureau personnel.[28]

This picture of continuous local-federal collaboration in police matters is duplicated in all parts of the country. In rural areas and in cities of fewer than 50,000 population dependence upon federal services from Washington is greater than it is for larger places. On the other hand, the larger the local unit, the more frequent the federal-local collaboration in actual investigative work on the local scene, and the more often do the local police use the federal fugitive warrant. In big cases—a bank robbery or kidnapping—police of all governments strive to organize their work as if they were a single unit, though interagency and interlevel conflicts over evidence and publicity may also occur. Where state police agencies are active and organized, exactly the same sort of close federal collaboration occurs.[29]

TRAINING PROGRAMS

Police training programs sponsored by national agencies are of the first importance in the development of the national police system. The FBI's National Police Academy, established in 1935, enrolls an increasing number of state and local officers each year for intensive 12-week courses in the latest methods of police investigation and administration. Places in the academy are limited, and local officers consider it a high honor to be chosen for admission. The federal government assumes all costs, except living expenses, of those in training. The complete resources of the FBI are utilized in the courses, which range from firearm training, to technical methods for the identification of criminal evidence, to the best ways of organizing local departments. Each graduate is expected to organize police schools in his home town, this being "the basic purpose behind the formation of the Academy."[30] The Academy has graduated over 4,000 law enforcement officers. More than one-quarter of them are executive heads of their own agencies, as local chiefs, county sheriffs, state chiefs, or in analogous capacities. Other graduates hold leading positions in state or private police schools.

[28] Field notes, August, 1947.
[29] I am indebted to Robert H. Marden for a detailed report, based upon interviews with the officers involved, concerning the close relationships of the Division of State Police, Massachusetts Department of Public Safety, and federal police officials.
[30] Don Whitehead, *The FBI Story* (New York: Random House, 1956), p. 151.

Graduates of the National Academy, as well as personnel of the FBI itself, carry on intensive training programs in the field. Universities, state police departments, and state and regional associations of local police officers are all involved in the training effort. FBI personnel are usually the leading faculty members, whether at a state-sponsored school or at the headquarters of a single, small police department. At the request of a police chief, FBI specialists in such fields as pistol firing or bank robbery investigations will give courses to local personnel on their home grounds. This service, like all FBI aid to local governments, is supplied without cost to the locality.[31] In addition to courses sponsored by state and local agencies, the FBI itself initiates regional conferences. In 1955, for example, these conferences were devoted to the protection problems of banking institutions. In all, 178 conferences in all parts of the country drew a total attendance of 17,000 people representing more than 8,500 banking institutions and local and state police forces.[32]

The FBI is by no means the only federal agency involved in supplying training aids to local police. The Narcotics Bureau of the Treasury Department established a school for local policemen in 1956. Various district offices of the Narcotics Bureau have for a number of years given classes for local policemen in the field. Narcotics agents of the Chicago office, for example, hold classes collaboratively with the FBI, traveling from place to place for lectures and demonstrations. Indianapolis' narcotics squad members in 1955 spent a 30-day training period in the Chicago offices of the Bureau of Narcotics.[33] Training for local officers is also provided by national meetings such as the periodic White House Conferences on Traffic Safety, the Attorney General's Conference on Organized Crime (1939 and

---

[31] The following description from the *New York Times* of October 12, 1958, describes one phase of instruction at the Bergen County (New Jersey) police academy and is typical:

"The present two-week course, called the Investigative Case School, is now at the halfway point. Fourteen members of local departments, attending on their own time, were instructed this week by Gay Shahan, a member of the Federal Bureau of Investigation.

"Under Mr. Shahan's guidance, the students simulated a bank robbery in their classroom at the Civic Center in Hackensack. Two men taking the part of the criminals escaped after the robbery by jumping out a window and fleeing in a car.

"The others dusted for fingerprints, gathered physical evidence and looked for witnesses. The information amassed was used to pick up the criminals. Questioning produced enough facts to warrant taking the suspects before a magistrate in Hackensack, who held them for the Grand Jury."

[32] *Report of the Attorney General*, 1956, pp. 225–26.

[33] *Traffic in, and Control of, Narcotics, Barbiturates, and Amphetamines, Hearings*, Subcommittee of the Committee on Ways and Means, House, 85th Congress (October, 1955–January, 1956) (Washington, D.C.: Government Printing Office, 1956), pp. 1070–71 (cited hereafter as *Narcotics Hearings*).

1950), and the National Conference on Parole (1939 and 1956), sponsored jointly by federal and state agencies. Other national training aids include programs of the Bureau of Standards, Department of Commerce, for instruction in police radio work and the analysis of criminal evidence; of the Federal Communications Commission, for the development of local police radio systems; of the Coast Guard, Treasury Department, for special courses in harbor policing; and of the Army Provost Marshal School, Department of Defense, for technical training in a number of fields, including the use of lie detector equipment. The federal vocational education (George-Deen) act provides funds, through state departments of vocational education, for expenses of police training programs.[34]

Training programs under direct federal supervision—or established by states and localities under federal definitions of what is needed and desirable—simultaneously introduce new police techniques and raise standards of police personnel. The trend is not uniform from place to place, but it moves clearly in the single direction of developing more highly professional police workers everywhere. The standards that become accepted and the friendships that are formed in the process of these training activities produce easy intergovernmental cooperation as a matter of course and without special effort. Each new evidence of the payoff of professional cooperation gives additional impetus to new training programs which, in turn and in time, produce further collaboration among the police workers of the many governments involved.

III. LOCAL AID TO NATIONAL POLICE AGENCIES

Police collaboration, as we have indicated, does not go only in one direction. Dependence of national police agencies on local forces is as great as local dependence on national forces. The sheer preponderance of manpower resources at the local level largely accounts for this. There are an

---

[34] The professional associations of local officers, in police as in other fields, often provide the impetus for federal programs. For example, the International Association of Chiefs of Police in the 1930's requested the United States Civil Service Commission to prepare standard tests for the selection of police personnel; this was done and subsequently the test was utilized by more than 100 police departments (see Donald C. Stone, "Reorganization for Police Protection," *Law and Contemporary Problems*, Vol. I, No. 4 [October, 1934], p. 458). Even when a federal program is initiated by federal officers, it is often discussed and approved by local officials before being made the subject of federal legislation. Mr. Hoover's recommendation to establish the National Police Academy, for example, was discussed and approved by the Attorney General's Crime Conference, a meeting attended by state and local police executives, before it was implemented.

estimated 250,000 officers in local police forces; all the national enforcement personnel in the field do not total one-tenth this number. In a large city like Chicago, to take one example, federal enforcement agents must look to local officers for information and manpower assistance of all kinds. The Federal Bureau of Narcotics in 1955 had a total of 22 agents to cover the three states of Illinois, Wisconsin, and Indiana;[35] at this time the Chicago police force alone had 60 persons detailed to narcotics work. Federal agents daily examined files in the Chicago bureau, looked to Chicago police officers for detailed reports on narcotics sales and consumption (the sort of information available only to those with intimate knowledge of the local situation), and heavily depended upon local personnel in raids and arrests.

With respect to such matters as stolen automobiles in interstate commerce, federal officers (in this case from the FBI) must rely even more heavily on local police. Full-time federal officers assigned to the recovery of stolen cars are few in number. In contrast, big city police forces maintain specialized, stolen car details and, in fact, the total personnel of local forces is involved in the recovery of stolen cars. The stolen auto division of a local department routinely receives from the FBI descriptions of automobiles stolen in other states. This information is logged as a part of the local record system while, simultaneously, advice is also received on every automobile involved in every recorded local crime. In the nature of the situation, the preponderant number of stolen automobiles that are recovered, including those that have moved in interstate commerce, are turned up by local police. If the individuals apprehended with stolen interstate automobiles cannot be charged with more serious crimes, they are turned over to federal authorities for prosecution under United States law for transporting the cars across state lines. In any case, a stolen car in interstate traffic can be labelled "recovered." As one former FBI agent remarked, "The statistics of FBI recoveries of stolen automobiles in interstate traffic are largely statistics testifying to local assistance given to the federal agency in this matter."

In a very similar manner, federal law enforcement officers must look for local aid in the control of prostitution, bootlegging, counterfeiting, mail thefts, illegal immigration, and other matters. A concomitant of the local force's larger personnel is an intimate knowledge of local conditions. In a big city, for example, a local officer in a prostitution detail "can tell pretty rapidly when new girls are being imported into the city—because he knows all the local prostitutes pretty well."[36] Frequently rotated federal officers rarely have this sort of insider's view of local conditions. As for smaller

[35] *Narcotics Hearings,* p. 1071.
[36] Field notes, Chicago, February, 1958.

places, a single FBI agent may be the only federal law enforcement officer on the scene and he may have to "cover" a half-dozen communities. He will drop by the local police station once or twice a week. His dependence upon local police for information concerning federal crimes is well nigh complete.

Other federal police agencies are in a similar situation. Success of the Treasury Department's Alcohol Tax Unit "is largely dependent upon the assistance that it receives from state and local police authorities."[37] The Treasury's Secret Service Division "depends materially on the continuous cooperation of police departments and other local law enforcement agencies" in its work of apprehending forgers and counterfeiters as well as in protecting the President. In a number of cities local police officers are detailed to give full time to aiding the secret service operators in charge. The Division "could not function effectively" without this sort of help. The Division estimates that it would "probably require a field personnel ten times as great as the present Secret Service force to operate without the assistance rendered by local agencies."[38]

The flow of information from local to federal agencies covers matters over which local police have no concurrent jurisdiction. The FBI, for example, has extensive responsibilities for enforcing statutes with respect to espionage and sabotage and for the collection of loyalty-security dossiers on government workers as well as workers in defense-related industries. Precise information concerning investigations of this type is not readily available. Yet local police forces are obviously a prime source of information for individuals under investigation by the FBI. Some local officers complain about the fraction of their time taken by FBI agents asking questions and searching for records about individuals who, as far as the local police are concerned, are "clean" and in some cases outstanding citizens. One chief in a small town estimated that the FBI agent who visited him regularly about such matters "must spend at least half of his time in this town—and must collect more than half of the information he gets here—right in my office." Considerations of jurisdictional niceties have little place in the national police system.

IV. THE SYSTEM IN OPERATION

The national police system is not adequately described in terms of mutual aid rendered by local and federal officers in discharge of others' duties. In

[37] The International City Managers' Association, *Municipal Police Administration* (Chicago: the Association, 1950), p. 915.
[38] *Ibid.*, p. 914.

actual practice, when the law enforcement agents work together, they do so virtually as if there were no distinctions among them. Unified by a common task, they work in unity. The area of narcotics control provides a convenient example.

NARCOTICS CONTROL

All states, as well as the federal government, provide criminal penalties for the unauthorized possession or sale of narcotics. In addition, a number of state laws and local ordinances make it illegal to be "under the influence" of narcotics.[39] Great publicity has been given the detrimental effects of narcotic addiction and the criminal acts performed by addicts seeking money to buy narcotics. Peddlers have become a prime target of congressional investigation and public distaste, especially for their alleged distribution of the drugs to persons of high school age. There exists throughout the country a high public and police interest in the control of narcotics.

Many branches of government act in concert, though not always without friction, to control the sale of narcotics and narcotics addiction. Collaboration exists at the minor points of the control system, as well as at the most important ones. To take an example involving governmental units not usually considered in the network of control, federal customs officers, patrolling a section of the Mexican border, wished to concentrate their efforts on persons attempting to smuggle narcotics into the United States. The federal agents could not deal adequately with addicts "under the influence of" narcotics, people who in effect were internally transporting narcotics across the border. On the advice of the federal officers, the California county in which the principal United States-Mexican border station was located passed an ordinance imposing severe penalties for those under the influence of narcotics. Subsequently, federal customs officials simply turned over to the county sheriff all persons returning from Mexico under the influence of narcotics. "Many persons have been so prosecuted and sentenced to jail for their violations."[40] The arrangement allowed the customs officers to concentrate their full attention on searching for narcotics peddlers.

---

[39]City ordinances, like state legislation, are heavily influenced by advice and persuasion from federal officials. The Federal Bureau of Narcotics has advised cities to adopt an ordinance, and "many have been provided with a model draft, which would class drug addiction as a communicable disease and require compulsory treatment." Statement of H. J. Anslinger, Commissioner, Bureau of Narcotics, Treasury Department, in *Narcotics Hearings,* p. 1403. By 1955, 43 states had passed a uniform narcotics law which, though handled as a purely state matter, had been approved and recommended by federal officials, and only three states were considered to have inadequate narcotics legislation. Statement of Congressman Sidney R. Yates, *ibid.,* p. 949.

[40]Statement of Rae V. Vader, customs agent in charge, San Diego, California, *Narcotics Hearings,* p. 837.

Those centrally concerned with narcotics control, the Federal Bureau of Narcotics and the local police departments, also collaborate closely and in the process bring other agencies into the scheme of control. In Seattle, Washington, the chief of police said that "members of the . . . Police Department Narcotics Squad and the Federal Bureau of Narcotics work very closely together . . . the main objective being to make cases against these people (addicts and peddlers) regardless of who initiates them, and in most cases both (federal and state officers) work on them."[41] The Seattle district office of the Food and Drug Administration, the state Board of Pharmacy, and the local Board of Health were also involved in enforcing narcotics statutes. An effective liaison and division of labor were achieved. At the request of the district supervisor of the Federal Bureau of Narcotics, for example, the state Pharmacy Board had "taken over almost all investigations which involve drugstores, hospitals, nursing homes, forged prescriptions. . . . This leaves more of . . . [the federal] men free to investigate illegal imports and actual peddlers." The cooperation and especially the exchange of information proved "invaluable to both departments." The same sort of relationship was worked out with the federal Food and Drug Administration in the control of barbiturates. "Cases which involve only Washington state laws have been turned over to us by the Food and Drug Administration, and those cases which involve interstate shipments have been referred by us to them."[42]

The United States Commissioner of Narcotics has for some years encouraged and aided local police departments of larger cities in establishing special units for the control of narcotics. More than two dozen cities have adopted this suggestion, including Chicago, which established a Narcotics Bureau in 1950. By 1955 the Bureau had grown to a force of 60 men (New York's force numbered 200). Specialized squads of this sort maximize points of collaboration between local and equally specialized federal officers. The officer in charge of the Chicago Narcotics Bureau has testified that "The United States Bureau of Narcotics and the Narcotics Bureau of the Chicago Police Department have worked in close cooperation on many investigations, arrests, and prosecutions and, in particular, on cases involving major violators."[43] The District Supervisor of the Bureau of Narcotics has echoed this statement: "The cooperation between [the Chicago Narcotics

[41] *Ibid.*, p. 915. The district supervisor of the Federal Bureau of Narcotics fully corroborated the chief's statement. ("We work very closely with the police department narcotics squads.") *Ibid.*, p. 888.

[42] Testimony of Earl V. Acker, secretary of the Washington Board of Pharmacy, *ibid.*, pp. 929, 931.

[43] Memorandum of Lt. Joseph J. Healy, quoted in testimony of Timothy J. O'Connor, Commissioner of Police, Chicago, *ibid.*, p. 966.

Bureau] and the Federal Bureau of Narcotics has been 100 per cent. We work on most cases together and if he (Lt. Healy, in charge of the Chicago squad) runs into an interstate trafficker, before he even investigates he will call our office and we will figure out ways and means in which to build up a better and stronger case against the alleged violator."[44] The Chicago police provide the federal bureau with records of every local narcotics arrest.[45] Contacts between the two groups are continuous and intimate. Local and federal officers frequently act together in making raids. Federal funds are often used by the local police to make "buys" of narcotics in the process of building up evidence for an arrest. If the local police inadvertently arrest an addict who turns out to be a paid informer for the federal agency, the local police turn him over to their federal colleagues (whether or not a federal offense is immediately involved), mark the case "closed," and do not concern themselves with what dispositions the federal agency makes of the prisoner.[46]

PRISONER EXCHANGE

The national police system is illustrated with particular clarity in the common practice of police and prosecutors in their exchange of prisoners and evidence so that punishment will be maximized. A person who has allegedly abrogated both state and federal statutes may be apprehended by local police, but turned over to a federal prosecuting attorney, along with the evidence collected against him, to be tried in a federal court; and similarly federal officers may transmit prisoner and evidence to state prosecuting officers. The transfer usually takes place when penalties seem to be more assured or more severe in the other court.

This practice is well illustrated in narcotics work. From 1927 to about 1930, Chicago police turned over a large fraction of those arrested on narcotics charges to federal officers for federal prosecution. The state law provided penalties that were small, and even hardened dealers received small fines, "the equivalent of a license to deal in narcotics." New Illinois laws and a specialized Narcotics Court in Chicago (whose judges are noted for giving heavy penalties), have made this type of transfer far less frequent.[47] Indeed, the "turnover" of cases is now more likely to go in the other direction. Federal district judges, when relatively small amounts of narcotics are involved, were, in the late 1950's, less likely to convict (under

---

[44] Testimony of Albert F. Aman, *ibid.*, p. 1065. For corroborating statement by United States District Attorney Robert Tieken, see *ibid.*, pp. 1057–61.

[45] *Ibid.*, p. 1066.

[46] Field notes, Chicago, February, 1958.

[47] Field notes, Chicago, March 5, 1958.

a federal statute with minimum penality of two years) then local judges were (under a state statute providing two years to life).[48]

The actual choice of court is handled from case to case. A former Cook County state's attorney has said:

> Cooperation with Federal authorities in this area . . . is excellent. . . . Federal laws are essentially based on revenue laws. Our state laws are criminal laws. The result is that in some fields it is easier to get convictions under the federal law than under the state law. In some fields, we (the state) can give a little more punishment, particularly with our specialized court. So it has been very necessary that we have had that complete interaction and I can speak nothing but highly of the cooperation we are getting from the federal department.[49]

The state's attorney said that each narcotics case involving both state and federal agencies "becomes a matter of individual consideration as to who should act first. . . . There has been much interchange and interaction in the cause of justice, and the courts to be used have been determined after consultation."[50]

This is a widespread practice. Indiana in 1955, for example, provided a minimum penalty of 20 years in prison for second offenders in narcotics sales cases. The federal minimum penalty for the same offense was five years. ". . . We will try prosecuting second offenders in the state courts of Indiana," the district supervisor of the Bureau of Narcotics said.[51] By this he meant that federal police officers would provide prisoners and evidence to state prosecuting officers so that trials could be held in the state courts.

It should not be supposed that the transfer of prisoners and evidence occurs only in the narcotics field. It is, in fact, common in every area of law enforcement where overlapping statutes make it possible. An extreme case in point is that of one Alfonse Bartkus. Bartkus was tried and acquitted in a federal district court on a charge that he had participated in a robbery of a federally insured savings and loan association. The FBI agents and federal prosecutor who had assembled the evidence against Bartkus were "highly displeased" with the verdict.[52] They decided immediately after the

[48] Field notes, Chicago, February 26, 1958.
[49] Testimony of John Gutknecht, state's attorney of Cook County, Illinois, *Narcotics Hearings*, p. 939.
[50] *Ibid.*, p. 948.
[51] *Ibid.*, p. 1068.
[52] All quotations in this paragraph are from the dissenting opinion of Mr. Justice Brennan in *Bartkus* v. *Illinois*, 359 U.S. 121 (1959). The Supreme Court heard this case because of Bartkus' claim that the two trials subjected him to double jeopardy. The Court denied his claim.

trial "to make a second try" at convicting Bartkus. Since the defendant could not be tried again in the federal court because of Fifth Amendment protection against double jeopardy, federal officers contacted the state prosecutor, who agreed to try Bartkus under the state bank robbery law. "It is clear that federal officers solicited the state prosecution." (The attorney for Illinois said: "The Federal officers did instigate and guide this state prosecution" and "actually prepared this case.") Federal officers postponed the sentencing of two witnesses who had confessed their part in the crime in the federal court until after the state trial. An FBI agent who had participated in the federal prosecution against Bartkus strengthened the state's case materially by uncovering a new witness, Grant Pursel, who testified damagingly as to Bartkus' guilt. ". . . the FBI arranged no interview between Pursel and any state authority. The first time that Pursel had any contact whatsoever with a state official connected with the case was the morning that he testified [in the state case]."[53]

V. STRAINS IN THE SYSTEM

As in all other aspects of American government, police activities exhibit a lack of neatness and order. The development of nationwide interdependence in police activities is no evidence of nationwide uniformity in skills or diligence, nor of any evenness in the extent of federal-state-local collaboration. And the development of the national police system has not occurred without interforce antagonisms.

It is a common complaint that FBI field agents seek information from local police officers but do not divulge information in return. (Requests by local police for information from FBI field agents, unless honored because of personal acquaintanceship and trust, are referred as a matter of policy to Washington.) An officer in a big city police department expressed this view in an extreme fashion when he told an interviewer that he regarded "the FBI field men as Mr. Hoover's personal spy ring. They snoop around our files, ask questions of our men, and clam up when we ask them for anything." This complaint—that the flow of information between local and federal officers is a "one-way street"—is frequently voiced at professional meetings of police officials. State attorneys general and governors have also

---

[53] Since *de facto* double jeopardy appears to be a violation of the spirit of the Bill of Rights through the mechanisms of federalism, it should be pointed out that Illinois has since changed its laws to prevent state "retrials" of this character. Even at the time of the Bartkus case, 15 states prohibited such actions by statute.

urged less secrecy on the part of federal agencies as an aid to greater efficiency in police work.[54]

Suspicion and mistrust may go hand in hand with the recognition of common purposes, the need to pool manpower and information, and even comradeship. One striking example of this antagonistic cooperation—and of the resulting bitterness—was described by a veteran police officer of a large city. He spoke with pride of the close relationship he and other members of a local narcotics detail had with federal Treasury officers. But when the Treasury called upon local forces for aid in staging a raid, no detailed information was given in advance to the local squad. Rather, a meeting was arranged immediately prior to the raid itself at some place outside police quarters, and federal officers would then inform the local group where the raid was to be held and who was being sought. The local officer was proud of the dependence of the federal personnel on local information and local manpower; but he was wrathful that federal distrust of the local police was such that even those who worked closest with federal officers were kept uninformed.[55]

The same officer, however, admitted that when planning a raid exclusively with local officers he tried to avoid "leaks" by confining information to the fewest men possible. This, he said, was a "normal" police precaution. The federal authorities, in his view, were going beyond the range of normalcy in keeping secrets from even the leaders of the local squad. From the federal point of view, on the other hand, no matter what confidence was placed in a local police force as a whole, a single unreliable person in that force might prejudice an entire action. To avoid this consequence, they justified complete secrecy until the time of the raid.

In some cases federal agencies will act without informing local police at all. For example, federal Treasury agents in Boston staged a large series of raids in October, 1959, in an effort to clean up what was described as a "$500,000-a-week bookie ring." The entire complex operation was apparently carried out by federal officers without consultation with the Boston police force. More than nine months of preparation preceded the raids. One of them took place place "within 100 yards of the East Boston Police Station. . . . Yet not one of the complement of officers at the station knew what was going on until after it took place. Several detectives from the station stood gaping in awe along with hundreds of spectators as the raids were being conducted. . . ."[56] An event of this sort clearly indicates a dom-

[54] See, for example, the report of the round table on law enforcement at the 1951 Governors' Conference in *State Government,* Vol. XXVI, No. 11 (November, 1951), p. 285.
[55] Field notes, January, 1958.
[56] See the *Boston Daily Globe,* October 31, 1959.

inant distrust, expressed publicly, of local forces by the federal officers concerned.[57]

Even when police work follows the more normal line of mutual help, interlevel hostilities occur. There is prevalent especially in larger cities' resentment over the manner in which federal agents, in the words of one local officer, "build their case on information we supply, and then grab off all the headlines." This officer continued: "Of course we get sore at the FBI, they harass us for information, accept everything and give out nothing. Our department gave the FBI agents just about everything they needed to get *Williams* and *Gilbert* in the *Ross* kidnaping case.[58] Then the FBI sealed them off from the local police, made the arrest, got all the publicity, and made our force look bad. In the FBI reports, the local help wasn't even acknowledged." Headline hunting (or attempts to prevent local leaks) may also contribute to secrecy, with unhappy results. An extreme variant of this situation occurred when the San Antonio police force arrested a "hot narcotics suspect," only to discover that "he was an undercover man for the federal Customs agency." The local chief of police was wrathful. He said it was "unfair" for the federal agencies "to play such low, deceptive tricks" and threatened that he would "immediately sever relationships" with federal agencies if such a thing happened again.[59]

J. Edgar Hoover's own statements have not always been reassuring to local police departments. On the one hand, he has paid tribute to the need for strong forces at the local level. "There is never any doubt within the FBI that the home-town law enforcement agency must be in the forefront of crime control."[60] On the other hand, he has, in the eyes of some local police officers, been arrogant in assuming that the FBI National Police Academy is the "West Point of Law Enforcement" and its graduates "a national faculty," as if no other effective training facilities existed or were possible. More than this, Mr. Hoover has suggested in many statements that local police departments are often dominated by "corrupt politics," and that their forces represent "a dumping ground . . . for some ward politician to use in repaying his obligations to his political party." Mr. Hoover has said that the FBI is "willing and ready" to cooperate with all law enforcement agencies. "The only exceptions are when officers of the

[57] But even an example of such a complete breakdown in collaboration does not indicate an over-all local-federal hostility. There were many evidences in Boston itself during 1958–59 of close working relationships between the local and state police, on the one hand, and the FBI, the Bureau of Narcotics, the Customs Office, and the several military police forces, on the other.

[58] Italicized names are pseudonyms.

[59] *The Austin Statesman*, June 17, 1952, p. 10, cited in Grisham, *op. cit.*, p. 151.

[60] J. Edgar Hoover, in preface to Whitehead, *op. cit.*, n.p.

law are corrupt and controlled by venal politicians; when they can't keep a confidence and be trusted; or when they are so incompetent that to cooperate with them would defeat our purposes."[61] Such statements may inspire local police to throw off corruption, political control, and incompetence. But to many police officers they represent an unwarranted aspersion with respect to local abilities, and an unwise suggestion that local police are morally and professionally inferior to the FBI and other national forces.

Some critics believe that federal police activities, especially those that overlap state-local responsibilites, actually weaken local police forces because they "devitalize" incentives for effective local action. Henry L. Stimson, who at one time served as a United States attorney, expressed this view as early as 1934: "The great bulk of crime is local, and responsibility for its apprehension and punishment should remain imposed upon the localities where it occurs. To throw this burden upon the federal government will . . . atrophy and weaken the sense of responsibility of local officials. . . ."[62] The practical manifestation of this view may be seen in the resentment of some local police officers with respect to duplicating surveillance. "Why should I break my back on the case," one of them said, "when I know the federal boys are in it up to their neck."

Causes for the strains in federal-state-local police relationships are not difficult to discover. They are in the first place the simple consequence of many more or less independently organized and directed forces working in the field. The national police system has developed without any design or mandate (as in a statement of legislative intent) and without widespread public awareness. It rests upon no compulsion, and depends essentially upon the free exchange of services among workers engaged in a common task. The splintering of jurisdictions has basically encouraged the nationalizing trend: poverty of local resources in many places and the easy mobility of criminals across jurisdictional boundaries has increased local dependence upon national facilities. At the same time, the very number of police jurisdictions and their relative independence has resulted in the uneven development of collaboration and expertise. It has also led inevitably to jealousies, rivalries, resentments, and tensions.

Second, the many police forces are by no means socially or professionally homogeneous. Though no data exist to demonstate the point precisely, there is no doubt that federal police officers are recruited from a higher

[61] *Ibid.*, p. 152.
[62] From a speech before the Attorney General's Crime Conference, quoted in Max Lowenthal, *The Federal Bureau of Investigation* (New York: William Sloane Associates, 1950) p. 417. Lowenthal presents further evidence to this point, pp. 414 ff.

social stratum than local ones. They have more professional training, receive higher salaries, and enjoy greater public esteem. They also have a more secure career line inside and outside their service. Differences of this sort are sometimes expressed in mutual disesteem, in expressions of local resentment and in demonstrations of federal "high handedness."

Third, political factors operate differentially and produce conflict among the cooperating police forces. Mr. Hoover might not acknowledge the fact, but his success in bringing the FBI to its present strength and prestige rests in good measure upon the political support that he has built in years of skillful liaison with Congress. Local police forces similarly must find support from political leaders. But national and local political demands may not coincide. In the extreme case local political control of police activities results in condoned and protected lawlessness, widespread racketeering, payoffs by the underworld, and the consequent deterioration of professional standards of law enforcement.[63] Under such circumstances collaboration exists, if at all, only on the basis of relationships of trust built among federal-local workers, as individuals.

Complete breakdown of local law enforcement rarely takes place. A more frequent occurrence is the local protection of a single unlawful area. Local police, for example, may protect prostitution because of political pressures. They may even share in the payoff. And they may justify their action by holding that protected prositution is the best means of control, or by arguing that "going along" at this point allows them to work unhampered by politics in other areas of law enforcement. No justifications for protected prostitution, however, are persuasive to significant national constituencies or political leaders. Congressional committees and national police agencies may demand energetic enforcement of statutes aimed at ending commercialized prostitution. The political bases for local-federal police conflict are thus established.

Political pressures operate in diverse ways, however, and not always to limit local enforcement of the laws. In 1958, for example, the Treasury Department in a Republican administration apparently accepted the invitation of state Republican leaders (and Republican newspapers) to investigate the tax returns of Democratic political workers to determine that whatever income received from "honest graft" (in this case the rental of lawn

---

[63] It is a short step between protecting a thief and performing a theft. During the winter of 1960 a number of police officers in Chicago were revealed to have acted cooperatively with a burglar, patrolling the block while he stole for them and using police cars to haul away the loot. See the *Chicago Daily News* for January and February, 1960, for a daily account of the revelations. Subsequently, similar situations were uncovered in several other cities around the nation.

mowers and other equipment) had been accurately reported in their income tax statements. Here political pressures led to a higher level of enforcement of the laws against the interests of the local politicians.

Finally, local-federal conflict becomes most acute when it mirrors not merely the narrow political differences of constituencies but, in addition, reflects basic social cleavages. A Poplarville, Mississippi, lynching in 1959 illustrates the point. The Negro victim, accused of raping a 23-year-old pregnant white woman, had been dragged from the local jail and brutally murdered. The Governor asked for FBI aid "to show the world that the people of Mississippi do not believe in mob rule." An intensive investigation was carried out by the FBI, which had, at one time, as many as 60 agents in the town of 1,852. The press and public opinion of the nation condemned the lynching, "but the Poplarville area whites were staunchly on the side of the lynchers."[65] At least many of them were opposed to investigation by the FBI team of "Yankees." Local citizens accused FBI men of browbeating witnesses and harassing the community. One suspect, after repeated questioning, threatened to shoot the next FBI agent who came to his door. A federal spokesman deprecated the local criticism and said that it came from persons "who obviously do not desire the case to be solved." Thus fundamental cultural differences between the local and the national communities produce strains in the national police system.[66]

The factors that produce strains within the national police system as a whole are also responsible for the same sort of difficulties within a given police system and within one of the so-called "levels" of government. In all parts of the country, for example, city police and sheriffs may be found at loggerheads, the latter often being accused of staging raids within city boundaries only for political purposes, including the purpose of embarrassing the city administration when it is of the opposite party. The more highly trained big city police official may look with disdain on elected "red neck" rural officers. Splintered jurisdictions within a metropolitan area produce hostilities and competition and not infrequently ineffective police

[64] *Boston Globe*, August 27, 1958. Conversely, political pressures may also be used to attempt to quash income tax investigations.

[65] *Life*, Vol. XLVI, No. 22 (June 1, 1959), p. 19.

[66] See the series of *New York Times* articles on the Poplarville lynching case, especially those of May 23, 26, and 29, 1959. It is peripheral to the immediate point in the text, but relevant to the larger discussion of the national police system, that the FBI withdrew from the case on May 25, 1959, because in the opinion of the Attorney General, no federal law had been violated. The lynching victim had not been carried across state lines and "no successful federal prosecution could be maintained." All the evidence collected by the FBI team was turned over to the Governor of Mississippi, who announced that he would have the case presented to the grand jury. FBI spokesmen in Washington let it be known that their report included the names of the men in the lynching mob. Subsequently, neither a regular nor a special grand jury returned any indictments in the case.

work, as when, in a Chicago murder case, the city police, the county sheriff, the county coroner, a park police force and several suburban forces all collected evidence and, in the process, clearly impeded the total investigation.[67]

Within the federal government itself, the complex of agencies with overlapping and duplicating jursidictions provides the basis for the "entire gamut of bureaucratic rivalry, distrust, and intrigue,"[68] no less intense than that found among competing local agencies. Or, in the words of an earlier observer:

> . . . conflict among federal agencies is evidenced by an unwillingness on the part of one agency to give credit to another; by feverish bursts of self-advertising; by a lack of cordial personal contacts among officials; by indirect attacks of one agency upon another; in at least one case . . . by an attempted "investigation" by Secret Service agents of certain activities of the Bureau of Investigation; and by the frequent use of other petty "sniping" tactics. The situation is generally recognized to be unwholesome and to militate against maximum efficiency.[69]

A curious by-product of intragovernmental difficulties is that they may in some cases lead to greater intergovernmental collaboration. Thus a federal officer may prefer to share information with local police rather than with federal workers of another agency because he dislikes the "headline hunting" tactics of the latter group. Conversely, a police captain of a medium-size midwestern town told an interviewer that he preferred in every case possible to act in concert with federal officers so that arrests could be made by federal men and trials held in the federal courts. He explained that "our locally-elected judges too often play games with our most prominent local crooks."

VI. CONCLUSION

Strains in the federal-state-local police system—whether within or among governments—are strains of propinquity. They are products of closeness, not of distance. They arise out of many groups working together. They are publicized because they are departures from expected, usual standards. They are evidences of rivalry, ill-will, and cross-purposes within vastly

---

[67] See the *Chicago Daily News* accounts of the investigations following the murder of the Schuessler brothers and the Peterson boy in the Chicago area late in 1955.

[68] Smith, *op. cit.*, p. 119.

[69] Arthur C. Millspaugh, *Crime Control by the National Government* (Washington, D.C.: The Brookings Institution, 1937), p. 105. This work is dated, but the quotation is still relevant.

more important and more pervasive evidences of amity and collaboration.

Modern technologies produce criminal activities that in no way correspond to the jurisdictional boundaries of the many local, state, and federal law enforcement units. Moreover, criminal activities do not correspond to the specialized tasks assigned to a particular unit: a narcotics addict may rob a bank, a bank robber may murder, and a murderer may also be a confidence artist. The task of the many enforcement agencies is to produce a total system of law enforcement surmounting jurisdictional boundaries as well as the nongeographical boundaries of specialized missions. The task is one of enforcing laws that grow more and more numerous and that continuously add to the kinds of acts labeled "criminal." Finally, it is the task of surmounting the parochialism, jealousies, and suspicions of workers at all "levels" and in different units of government.

We have seen the police of the many American governments attempt to accomplish these tasks through a well institutionalized system of mutual help. The total network of police relationships produces nationwide standards of professionalization—of conduct and effectiveness. It produces friendships that easily bridge the accidental fact that officers draw salaries from different "levels" of government. Widely accepted professional standards, the easy working together of colleagues, and the sharing of information and problems among friends are both evidence and cause of the national police system. They are often symbolized in the bare offices of local police chiefs: the most notable objects are frequently an autographed photograph of J. Edgar Hoover and a diploma certifying graduation from the National Police Academy.

National agencies are undoubtedly responsible for establishing standards of organization and conduct. They are dominant in training programs and in scientific crime detection. National standards exist for everything from state laws to the desirable public relations activities of a local chief. The Bureau of Narcotics defines heroin addiction and the FBI's *Law Enforcement Bulletin* (circulated "confidentially" to some 8,000 state and local forces) offers authoritative advice on the proper organization of police files. National standards are recognized for all phases of criminal investigation, and FBI forms and categories produce whatever uniformity there exists for reporting and publishing criminal statistics. It may even be said that national agencies provide many effective definitions of crime itself. Within the wide ambit of what the statutes define as criminal behavior (and the statutes themselves are crucially affected by professional opinion), police emphasis winnows out the effective definition: that behavior which is in fact punished. Mr. Hoover, for example, has great resources—through speeches, magazine and newspaper articles, radio and television appearances, congressional testimony, and training programs—to influence police forces throughout the country so that they will give greater attention to, say, the sale of narcotics than to highway homicides, to juvenile delinquency than to homosexuality.[70]

If the cues for police action come from national bureaus and national leaders, action on most criminal law fronts remains in the hands of locally selected police. They possess the widest jurisdiction in law, and they possess the preponderant manpower. Local officers are not unaware of their dependence on national agencies. Neither are they unaware of their own independent status. One police chief said: "I use the FBI every day. But only at my own initiation. J. Edgar Hoover is a great cop. But he has no control over me. If he came into this office tomorrow and asked me to do something I did not want to do, there would be nothing to prevent me from booting the great Edgar out the door."[71] This independence exists in law. In fact, however, over most of the country, police standards of the national bureau have become nationally accepted standards. A local officer follows the edicts of Mr. Hoover not because he has been told to—certainly not because in law he has to—but because Mr. Hoover's standards are almost always his own.

Universal adoption of common professional standards is handicapped by a number of factors, principally that some communities wil not tolerate complete law enforcement and many local police forces are small, unspecialized, and financially underprivileged. Officers in some small towns still utilize the published roster of National Academy graduates (and of the Association of Former Special Agents of the FBI) before asking aid of other local forces whose members are unknown. "If I can find someone on the roster," one chief explained, "I know that I can get competent help and that the crook I am chasing won't be tipped off by some dishonest cop."[72] This procedure, however, is rarely necessary in most parts of the country.

The "single bad egg in the case" can be more prejudicial to police work than to most other administrative operations; yet an officer in one community can with increasing confidence expect a professional response to his request from other localities. The training programs in Washington and in the field, with their secondary and tertiary consequences of students becoming teachers, are one strong factor in the direction of molding a single group of professionals. The routine of frequently working together on

[70] The process of effective definition is complicated. Mr. Hoover's statements are not produced in a vacuum. Rather they are based upon professional assessments of the factual situation, a refined sensitivity to public and political opinions, and consultation with local and state police officials. These affect his statements just as his statements affect them. It remains true that national police leaders, in effect, define many acts punished as criminal.

[71] Field notes, February, 1958.

[72] Field notes, January, 1958.

cases, and of exchanging information, has the same effect, and the easy transferability of personnel also cements unity: an FBI agent will have previously worked on a local police force; or the local chief will have had experience in one of the federal agencies. All this not only establishes the standards of law enforcement as such. It also produces definitions of what a "proper" policeman should be, personally and technically, and it ties the police forces of the country together into a single group, some sharing a common alma mater but a far larger number sharing definitions of the desirable and the proper.[73]

Professional ties are cemented through an elaborate and extensive network of police organizations. The group of top local leaders—the International Association of Chiefs of Police—usually has J. Edgar Hoover as the principal speaker at its annual meetings. State organizations of chiefs and groups such as the Fraternal Order of Police are meeting places for the exchange of ideas without regard for whether they come from local, state, or federal officers. Such meetings produce a camaraderie that transcends allegiances to a particular "level" of government. The range of such contacts is enormous. Federal officers will take a prominent role in the horseshoe pitching match at the annual fish fry sponsored by the local Fraternal Order of Police in a small midwestern town. Communion breakfasts provide a different sort of tie in a large New England city. The Attorney General's occasional Crime Control Conference and other meetings sponsored by federal agencies bring together leaders of all police systems for sociability as well as the consideration of professional problems.

The evidence suggests that professional contacts often lead to personal ones. Despite inevitable points of tension, the very character of police work leads police officers of all governments to regard themselves generally as friends, as well as colleagues. Local and federal officers may habitually lunch or dine with each other. They may play bridge and poker and go fishing together. They and their wives may see each other at parties. In this milieu collaboration in professional matters is easy and natural, not even subject to special consideration. Local officers, on matters of particular federal interest, and federal officers, even where no national laws are involved, work together because, as one former FBI agent said, "We all work on the same side of the street, and we all know and like each other pretty well."

[73]It should be noted that a number of private and quasi-public police forces and civic crime control groups also share, and contribute to, national standards for police work. These include a number of Crime Control Commissions in the larger cities, often led by former special agents of the FBI. The Thoroughbred Racing Association's Thoroughbred Racing Protective Bureau, established in 1946 to insure honesty in racing and at race tracks, is also under the direction of a one-time FBI employee and enjoys close working relationships with FBI personnel in Washington and elsewhere.

Chapter 5

SHARING OF FUNCTIONS:
THE "NATIONAL" RECREATION SYSTEM*

I. THE CHAOS OF ACTIVITY

Recreation in the United States is a chaos of activity. It is no less a chaos of private and public responsibilities.

Consider first what people do for recreation. They swim in and under water. They walk, dig for archaeological relics, descend into caves, ascend in gliders and planes. They shoot (with camera or gun) birds and game. They seek the fresh air of mountains and the smoky atmosphere of boxing and wrestling arenas. They bowl and booze, separately or simultaneously. They build in wood, plastic, and metal everything from model aircraft to summer homes. They play musical instruments in jazz combos, chamber music quartets, and business men's symphonies. They play baseball, football, basketball, soccer, volleyball, croquet, tennis, table tennis, badminton, and shuffleboard. They participate in horse shows, dog shows, cat shows, bird shows, and flower shows as well as horse racing, dog racing, auto racing, turtle racing, and people racing. They manipulate dolls in puppet shows and toss each other around in judo. Americans trade stamps, coins, seashells, post cards, matchboxes, clocks, rocks, and color slides. They sing together (there are more than 28,000 members in the Society for the Preservation and Encouragement of Barber Shop Quartet Singing in America), and they search for silence in the solitude of wilderness areas. Some 68 million people—more than half of all Americans 12 years of age and older—"drive for pleasure," and each of these spends more than 11 days a year at it. Those who don't drive, and a large fraction of those who do,

*Editor's note: This chapter originally appeared as part of Study Report 22, *Trends in American Living and Outdoor Recreation*, of the Outdoor Recreation Resources Review Commission, 1962.

hike, bicycle, ride horses, canoe, sail, water ski, climb, skate, or ski. Or they stalk prairie chickens, encouraged by a national committee formally organized for preserving that bird. The only recreation activity more popular than driving is picnicking, and picnicking is also enjoyed under the widest range of circumstances. It includes the family roasting hamburgers in the backyard and more than 10,000 citizens of Polish extraction eating and otherwise celebrating in one of Chicago's parks.

For many, paid hours of work may be more joyful than the unpaid ones more usually regarded as recreation time. Here one finds those who work at play, whether it be the sort of work that improves homes or demonstrates wealth or muscular power. Others view recreation as absolute rest: just plain loafing. Still a third related view of recreation is the acquisition of new vigor, a literal re-creation of mind and body. This may be sought in many ways—studying the mating habits of reptiles and scaling near-vertical rocks, among others. And a fourth meaning is represented by those who use nonworking hours as a catharsis, letting off steam in weekend wenching, drag racing, rock fighting, or beer busting.

Even this list barely suggests what Americans do for recreation. There must be added a vast range of more or less unacknowledeged activities and purposes. We know from novels, if not more precisely, that an important aim of "two weeks in the country" for young urban workers is not recreation in any ordinary sense, but marriage. White slacks and blue jackets for men and artfully wired bathing suits for girls effectively camouflage ordinary indications of occupation, income, and physique. So prepared, young people use their two weeks of nonwork in looking for mates. Some resort hotels in the Catskills advertise themselves as propitious sites for this ritual, but few participants would admit even to themselves that they attend for any reason except enjoyment of the lake, trees, dancing, drama, and bigtime basketball, also provided by the management. This is the least well hidden of many covert recreation activities. The backwoods hunter or fisherman may seek not sport but the joys of not washing, or of all-masculine companionship, or of a three-day poker game. The awesome first sight of the Grand Canyon is completely lost upon the foursome who skid their car to an abrupt stop, quickly unload golf paraphernalia, and spend their time at the gorge hitting balls into it. Their only joy is that of smacking a golf ball for a mile, a joy undimininished by the fact that the National Park Service prohibits such practices. The traveler to exotic places may be interested chiefly in the slides or post cards he can bring home to show his neighbors. The motor-launch owner may be terrified of water but enthusiastic over the idea of meeting his social betters at the yacht club.

II. THE CHAOS OF RESPONSIBILITY

Facilities and services for this infinite variety of recreation activities are provided by an equally inchoate collection of private, semipublic, and public bodies. The industrial society begets industrialized recreation. Just as the automobile culture produces driving as a favorite "outdoor recreation," so the development and promotion of outboard motors have produced a new impetus to boating, and so the technical development of portable oxygen-supplying equipment has spawned a new and rapidly growing breed of underwater creatures. Television has taken people out of movies; aircraft have made skiing in Aspen (or Kitzbühel) easy.

The recreation industry is big business. Dollar estimates of exactly how big it is vary enormously. Using a restricted definition (excluding such items as liquor, soft drinks, tobacco, sports clothes, and recreation transportation), an authoritative study for 1952 showed recreation costs of $11 billion.[1] Adding vaction travel would bring this figure (in 1960) to well over $23 billion, almost twice as much as Americans spent that year for clothing, accessories, and jewelry. If such items as liquor consumption are added, the figure easily exceeds $48 billion, roughly double all public costs for primary, secondary, and higher education.[2] The principal suppliers of recreation commodities and services are the vast complex called American business enterprise, which consists of everything from a multimillion dollar business, manufacturing guns or fishing rods or outboard motors, to a family fishing camp. It meets and stimulates demand by its advertising, its products, and its services. It provides swimmers with ear plugs and hunters with shooting preserves for pheasant and elk, complete with guide and a guarantee of success. Private beaches, woodlands, and swimming places, open to the public for a fee and operated as investment properties, complete with government-operated areas and in some sections of the country serve more people than do public facilities. As in other aspects of commerce, one recreation business begets others. Traveling stimulates picture taking and vice versa. Motorboats boom water skis, camping equipment goes along with a canoe.

There is great overlap of the private and public in the American culture, including the recreation sector. One facet is reciprocal dependence: the

[1] Comparable figures for 1960 total $19.5 billion. U.S. Department of Commerce, Bureau of the Census, *Statistical Abstract of the United States, 1964*, p. 208.

[2] J. Frederick Dewhurst and Associates, "America's Needs and Resources, A New Survey" (New York: *The Twentieth Century Fund*, 1955), Ch. 2. See also Marion Clawson, "The Crisis in Outdoor Recreation," *American Forests* (March, 1959), p. 5, Resources for the Future, Reprint No. 13.

sale of fishing gear—almost $160 million in 1959[3]—is largely dependent upon public waters, not only the oceans, the Great Lakes, and the Gulf of Mexico, but also the streams (81,000 miles) and lakes (2.7 million arcres) of the Forest Service and the reservoirs built by the Tennessee Valley Authority, the Army Corps of Engineers, and the Bureau of Reclamation, not to mention the seeding of streams and other waters by federal and state agencies. (In the spring of 1961, Colorado put 2,515,926 fish into its streams.[4]) Most private recreation camps are adjacent to public parks or water, and many operate on public land, as at TVA reservoirs and in national forests. There would be far fewer horses rented, and a corresponding decrease in the sale of riding boots and clothes, without public bridle paths. The boating industry is similary dependent upon public waters, docks, and launching areas.

A second aspect of the public-private overlap results from enlightened self-interest. Most of the nation's large timber growers allow their lands to be used for some forms of public recreation. At least 60 million acres are involved.[5] Hunting, fishing, hiking, picknicking, among other activities, are invited. Some companies have full-fledged park and recreation programs.

A third manifestation of the overlap is the familiar group pressure on public policy. The boating industry participated in drawing up the Federal Boating Act of 1958 and a complementary draft statute, recommended for passage by the states. The Izaak Walton League, the motorboat industry, wilderness adherents, and fishing buffs (not always without conflict among themselves or without opposition from mining, grazing, and lumbering interests) attempt to mold public policy at innumerable points in the process of administrative-legislative decision making. The chains of influence are often circular. The U.S. Fish and Wildlife Service, for example, seeks support for its program from state fish and game commissions, which in turn depend on business and sportsmen's groups organized to promote hunting, fishing, and wildlife management. It is difficult in such cases to determine who is influencing whom. Federal and state programs could not exist without the legislative lobbying of private groups; but the success and implementation of those lobbying activities are in turn dependent upon federal administrative officers and their counterparts. Influence is symbiotic, and the result is a typical confusion of public and private spheres of responsibility.

[3] Laurence I. Hewes, Jr., "The Demand for Outdoor Recreation—Implications for Natural Resource Allocation," speech presented August 24, 1960, before the Western Resources Conference, Boulder, Colorado.
[4] Personal communication from Colorado Game and Fish Department.
[5] "Public Recreation in Private Forests," *American Forests* (April, 1958), p. 72.

The confusion becomes extreme when private groups perform what *a priori* appear to be public services. This is a final manifestation of the public-private overlap. The Trustees of Reservations in Massachusetts (an organization that receives no financial support from any government) spend privately donated funds for parks and forests or acquire such lands by gift. As a public agency might, the trustees base their acquisition program on a statewide survey of scenic sites. Land once acquired is either maintained for public use or, the more usual practice, given to the state or a local government for recreation purposes. A number of states have similar organizations, one of the oldest being The Society for the Protection of New Hampshire Forests. California's Save-the-Redwoods League has had an important role in establishing the state park system, not least of all through its purchase by private subscription of prime parkland. Even where formal groups for land purchase do not exist, an analogous function is performed in many states by community trusts and private philanthropies. They purchase parkland that may come on the market at a time when governmental funds for this purpose are not available. The land is subsequently resold to public agencies, thus freeing the private funds for another cycle of land purchase and transfer.

Land purchases are only one sample of private organizations doing the public's business. Often a community park will be improved by action of private groups. The Rotary Club will install lighting and picnic benches, and the Lions will provide funds for community swimming pools. In larger communities, the private contribution to public recreation is more likely to take the form of camps for the underprivileged operated by civic, church, and other welfare-oriented organizations. Thousands of such programs exist. If only they did not, public programs would almost certainly take their place.

The substitution of private for public programs is found in other areas of recreation work. The National Recreation Association, a private organization, carries on an extensive consultation service, aiding local governments and other public bodies to establish and improve programs. The association has also assisted state boards of education in the development of school recreation programs and has supervised the training of state and local recreation workers. Very similar services are offered by a number of state governments as well as by the National Park Service.

The welter of private and semipublic sources of recreation facilities and services is matched by a diverse group of governmental units. As a task force of the Second Hoover Commission noted, the concern of the federal government with recreation resources and activities has been incidental to other functions. Recreation has been a by-product of the objectives of conserving forest, water, and land resources and of effectively utilizing man-power during wartime. Nevertheless, the federal government now operates an extensive network of recreation programs. No fewer than ten agencies (see Table 6) are represented in the Federal Inter-Agency Committee on Recreation. All of these, except the Public Housing Administration, have important responsibilities for providing facilities for outdoor recreation. But

TABLE 6

AGENCIES REPRESENTED IN THE FEDERAL INTER-AGENCY COMMITTEE
ON RECREATION

National Park Service, U.S. Department of the Interior.
Administration of the national parks, monuments, historical sites and other areas which comprise the national park system and national recreation areas; planning of recreation facilities at Bureau of Reclamation reservoir sites; cooperation with federal and state and local agencies in planning for their park, parkway, and recreation area programs.

Forest Service, U.S. Department of Agriculture.
Recreation on the 186 million acres of national forest system, including national grasslands. Also research in forest recreation.

Fish and Wildlife Service, U.S. Department of the Interior.
Recreation in national wildlife refuges and federal fish culture stations. Administers program of grants to state agencies for conservation and fish and game management.

Corps of Engineers, U.S. Department of the Army.
Recreation in navigation and flood control project areas under jurisdiction of the corps. Other aids to recreation through beach erosion control and related programs.

Bureau of Reclamation, U.S. Department of the Interior.
Recreation at reservoir sites of the Bureau. For most reclamation reservoirs a master and development plan for recreation is prepared by the National Park Service.

Bureau of Land Management, U.S. Department of the Interior.
Recreation in the public lands of United States. Conveys land to state and local governments for recreation purposes.

Federal Extension Service, U.S. Department of Agriculture.
Rural community recreation through state agricultural college and county extension services.

Public Health Service, U.S. Department of Health, Education, and Welfare.
Public health, including environmental sanitation and control of stream pollution, in recreation areas.

Office of Education, U.S. Department of Health, Education, and Welfare.
School and community recreation: outdoor education and school camping.

Public Housing Administration, Housing and Home Finance Agency.
Concerned that local housing authorities which own projects in federally assisted low-rent housing programs obtain the same community services (including recreation) for their tenants as are available to other residents in the community. Indoor community activities, space and outdoor play areas may be provided on the project.

Source: Release (undated) of Federal Inter-Agency Committee on Recreation, supplemented by data from agencies.

the members of the Inter-Agency Committee on Recreation by no means exhaust the list of federal bureaus concerned with recreation. For example, the General Services Administration has a key role in the final transfer of surplus federal properties to states and localities for recreation purposes. In the nation's newest outdoor recreation program, the Urban Renewal Administration (Housing and Home Finance Agency) is charged with carrying out provisions of Title VII of the Housing Act of 1961, which provides grants to assist in the acquisition of open-space land in urban areas. The extensive system of dams constructed by the Tennessee Valley Authority provides the major source of recreation opportunities in what was previously a lake-poor region of the nation. The Soil Conservation Service (U.S. Department of Agriculture) has developed a number of recreation areas as a part of its land utilization projects (in 1954 these areas were transferred to the Forest Service). The SCS has also made important contributions to the preservation of wildlife in agricultural lands and privately owned forests, through its 2,900 soil conservation districts of the country, and to the development of facilities for recreation through its small watersheds program. The Coast and Geodetic Survey provides maps, charts, and tidetables to boaters, among other recreation services. Even the Department of State, through the Under-secretary's Special Assistant for Fisheries and Wildlife, contributes to recreation. These are only samples of a very long list.

The Federal Inter-Agency Committee on Recreation works under a general policy statement that declares "recreation is a human need which is essential at all times to the well being of the people," and "the national welfare is promoted by providing opportunities for wholesome and adequate recreation." Legislative authorizations are often far less clear-cut, and administrative practices have often subordinated recreation to other purposes.

The Corps of Engineers, for example, constructs reservoirs primarily for flood control, navigation, and power development. No authorization existed at all for the development of recreation activities at reservoirs until 1944. Even under that authorization, recreation became, at best, a secondary or tertiary purpose of the reservoirs. Recreation specialists have often criticized the Corps of Engineers (as well as the Bureau of Reclamation) for their failure to provide sufficient land at reservoir sites.[6] The Bureau of

[6] The Corps of Engineers has since evolved new policies placing "major emphasis on comprehensive planning . . . . Recreation is . . . dealt with in the same manner as any other use of water resources." In addition, "steps have been taken . . . to assure that adequate lands are acquired to meet the needs of future recreation use and development in accordance with the policy of the administration . . . " Personal communication from the office of Assistant Secretary of the Army, Financial Management, August 25, 1961.

Land Management, the federal government's largest landholder, similarly recognizes recreation as only one of a number of purposes it must fulfill. The Bureau's large-scale disposal of the public domain for commercial purposes has been opposed in recent years by many recreation and conservation leaders. Soon after assuming office in 1961, Secretary of the Interior Udall declared a moratorium on BLM land disposals for commercial use, awaiting completion of a classification study and, presumably, the allocation of prime land for recreation.[7] Substantially all of the national forests and grassland (186 million acres) are open to the public and used for hunting, fishing, and hiking. Wilderness areas, comprising more than 14 million acres, are operated to preserve their primitive condition, and in these areas all other uses are subordinate. Wilderness areas aside, a relatively tiny fraction of the national forests are set aside for exclusive recreation use (estimates range from one-tenth of 1 per cent to 2.5 per cent). Management of the rest of the national forests is based on multiple-use principles. Certain types of recreation use are compatible with some types of commercial use on a given area of forest land. But full development for one purpose must, in most cases, result in decreased utilization of the other. The sharpness of the conflict has tended to increase with the upsurge of both recreation and commercial lumbering on forest lands during the postwar years. The difficulty was by no means solved by the 1960 congressional legislation which established outdoor recreation on the same plane as "range, timber, watershed, and wildlife and fish purposes" in the Forest Service program. Such legislation simply transfers the struggle for actual land-use priority (in the large number of cases where equal intensity of commercial and recreation use is not possible) from the legislative to the administrative arena. Commercial pressures on the Forest Service are immense and well organized. Large gains in recreation use of the national forests depend upon concerted public efforts in support of that use. Steps in that direction are the Forest Service's "Operation Outdoors," a five-year program of recreation development begun in 1957, and a program for the national forests which lays great stress on recreation.[8]

The Fish and Wildlife Service is primarily concerned with increasing and

[7] The text of Secretary Udall's moratorium notice is given in the *Federal Register,* February 16, 1961, p. 1382.

[8] For discussion of actual and potential conflicts in multiple-use administration of national forests, see Evan W. Kelley, "Problems of Land Management and Administration Arising from Associated Use of Land for the Various Services which the Public Seeks from the National Forests," *Proceedings of the Western Farm Economics Association,* 1938; Marion Clawson and R. Burnell Held, *The Federal Lands: Their Use and Magnagement* (Baltimore: The Johns Hopkins Press, 1957), Chs. 2 and 3. I have also profited from reading an unpublished paper by Professor Michael McCloskey of the University of Oregon.

protecting fish and wildlife resources and enforcing federal game laws. "Incident to these responsibilities," according to an official policy statement, "the Service has recognized the necessity and desirability of providing, when not inconsistent with these primary objectives, the optimum of its facilities and services for recreation use."[9] Again recreation is not the primary legislated function. The several hundred national wildlife refuges make a direct contribution to recreation through the production and protection of wildlife, particularly migratory waterfowl. Facilities in the refuges are also provided for fishing, camping, boating, picnicking, and nature study. Furthermore, in this case the powerful, well-organized citizens' groups devoted to hunting, fishing, and wildlife preservation have produced an overall fish and wildlife program that substantially serves recreation purposes. The task has been easier because of the long-run compatibility between hunting and fishing, on the one hand, and production and management of fish and game, on the other. A powerful lever for sportsmen is the fact that their hunting and fishing license fees (plus taxes on their equipment) substantially pay for state fish and wildlife programs.

Of all federal agencies related to recreation, the National Park Service is most clearly focused on recreation. But even its mission contains ambiguities. It is charged with the conservation of "scenery and . . . natural and historical objects and wildlife," as well as with providing them "unimpaired for the enjoyment of future generations." Park areas must be preserved if they are to be enjoyed. Yet at any particular moment enjoyment of resources can conflict with their conservation, as when very large numbers of those coming to enjoy may, by their very overuse, threaten the natural scene with destruction. The Park Service in 1956 moved to solve this dilemma by its Mission 66 program, a ten-year effort to meet rising demand for park use by increased facilities and staffs and, in the process, to provide for the protection of natural and historic areas. The Park Service has been actively supported through the years by a large number of citizen groups, including the National Parks Association.

The states and localities present equally complicated patterns of organization for recreation purposes. Each state has at least one park agency (Massachusetts has ten). Agencies charged with park and recreation responsibilities range from rudimentary, part-time custodial commissions to highly professional, large-scale staffs doing specialized tasks, as in Cali-

---

[9] Federal Inter-Agency Committee on Recreation, "The Role of the Federal Government in the Field of Public Recreation" (mimeographed rev. ed.; Washington, D.C., 1956), p. 21. (This report is hereafter cited as "The Role of Federal Government.") The Fish and Wildlife Service also has important responsibilities in recreation planning for reservoirs of the Bureau of Reclamation and the Corps of Engineers.

fornia, New York, Pennsylvania, Michigan, and Indiana. Only about 12 states have unified recreation agencies whose responsibilities include both wildlife management (essentially programs for hunting and fishing) and park management for general recreation purposes. The largest number of states have separate administrative organizations for these purposes, each usually with its own governing commission, and almost uniformly the fish and wildlife program is supported by larger budgets, larger and more professional staffs, and better organized citizen support. Other independent agencies in most states perform peripheral recreation services. The maintenance of state forests is undertaken by a forestry commission in almost every state. Roadside parks are usually the responsibility of the highway department. Historical landmarks are frequently administered by private or semipublic historical societies. A water resources bureau in some states controls lakes or reservoirs which are the source of water for communities, agriculture, and industry.[10]

Competition and cross-purposes sometimes exist among public bodies as they do among private suppliers of recreation. Roads for tourists are the enemy of wilderness areas. The management of fish and game for sportsmen may conflict with the development of intensive-use park areas. Demands for water purity for household use may limit or prohibit recreation use of lakes and reservoirs. And private business may of course interfere with public pleasure. The lumbering industry has often opposed significant increases in the exclusive recreation use of national forest land (as in the designation of new wilderness areas). In Arizona a state park system was opposed for many years by livestock interests which feared reduction of grazing areas. When a State Parks Board was finally established in 1957, the livestock industry effectively curtailed its scope of action through two provisions in the law: no fewer than two of the seven board members must represent the livestock industry, and no park of more than 100 acres can be established without special legislative action.[11] In its first three years of operation, the State Parks Board acquired 14 acres of parkland.

On the local plane, virtually every city with 10,000 people or more, and many smaller ones, have park and recreation departments. The largest cities almost uniformly have well developed recreation programs, and city facilities may include parks, golf courses, tennis courts, amphitheaters, bridle paths, zoos, museums, arboreta, outside-the-city camps, stadia, scenic drives, and beaches and boat harbors. Special programs are offered for the

[10] "Directory of State Outdoor Recreation Administration," a Commission staff project based on an American Political Science Association study, ORRRC Study Report 14.
[11] *Ibid.*

young, old, indigent, potentially delinquent, and non-English speaking, as well as for special skill groups in areas ranging from archery and bowling to boat building and flying high-powered model airplanes. The smaller the city, the more private groups (Boy Scouts, YMCA, Rotary) are likely to be chiefly responsible for public recreation, and the more certain, too, that facilities will be fewer in number, the bare minimum being a picnic area, a Little League ball park, or a swimming pool.

County recreation programs vary even more widely, from none at all in perhaps one-half the nation's 3,000 counties to elaborate undertakings in a few places such as Kern County, California, Westchester County, New York, and Douglas County, Oregon. Where programs are rudimentary, they are likely to be operated by nonprofit groups, financed in some cases through community chests or united funds. The trend almost everywhere is toward formal, publicly financed agencies. Twenty-four of Oregon's 36 counties, for example, have some type of recreation program.[12] Many counties have developed recreation facilities jointly with schools or with schools and cities. Counties in highly urbanized areas have been especially active in recreation, and some urban counties have taken the lead in establishing joint programs with cities or adjoining counties. The Huron-Clinton Metropolitan Authority, for example, is a five-county, special tax-levying government, providing a wide range of park and recreation facilities for the Detroit metropolitan area. The Metropolitan Park District of Boston, the East Bay Regional Park District of California (serving Oakland, Berkeley, and other cities in two counties), and Cleveland's Metropolitan Park District are other examples of cross-county and county-city recreation areas.

Still other public agencies and facilities for recreation abound. Data on municipal and county forests are inexact, but holdings are extensive and growing. The town forest is common in Europe, and the first such forest in the United States was planted in Newington, New Hampshire, in 1710. There are today at least 3,600 community forests in 40 states, most of them in the Northeast (especially New York, Pennsylvania, and New England), in the Great Lakes region, and on the Pacific Coast. Michigan, New York, and Wisconsin have the most community forests. Over the country, the forests range in size from an acre or two to the 83,000 acres owned by Seattle. Ownership is vested variously in towns, townships, cities, counties, schools, hospitals, and churches. Many community forests are used to produce income, but recreation is an important function in most states. An important recreation resource of Chicago, for example, is the land of the Forest Preserve District of Cook County. The district owns more than

---

[12] Clayton E. Anderson, "Cooperation Helps to Build Parks in Oregon Counties," *The County Officer* (May, 1961), p. 146.

55,000 acres, principally strung out in irregular strips along major water courses on the outskirts of Chicago. Facilities include golf courses, swimming pools, and picnic areas, as well as large wildlife areas. A half-million people use the Forest Preserves on a peak summer day. In Wisconsin, more than 350 county and town forests include over 2.2 million acres, an area greater than the state's combined acreage of national and state recreation land.

III. THE SHARING OF RECREATION FUNCTIONS

North of San Francisco, near the entrance to Muir Woods, a park of giant redwoods in a wilderness setting, a visitor meets the following sign:

> Muir Woods is a geographic
> part of a unified public
> recreational area reaching over
> and beyond Mount Tamalpais.
>
> Muir Woods National Monument
> is administered by the National
> Park Service of the United States
> Department of the Interior.
>
> Adjoining to the North is Mount
> Tamalpais State Park. This, and
> the Samuel P. Taylor State Park,
> are administered by the California
> Division of Beaches and Parks.
>
> Between and connecting
> these two state parks are the
> lands of the Marin Municipal
> Water District.
>
> Trails open to the public
> link the entire area. Only fire
> precautions and plant and
> wildlife protection are required.

These lines reveal what the multiplicity of public recreation bodies easily obscures: the cooperative sharing of the recreation function by governments. This sharing of functions does not prevent different governments from doing the same thing. It does prevent them from working at cross-purposes through ignorance of what each is doing. Frequently, in fact, efforts can be dovetailed, and what appears to be duplication of effort turns out to be an attempt to increase the total resources for recreation. In some areas of activity a rough division of labor among governments has been achieved.

One small measure of this division of labor is found in the types of park land held by federal, state, and local governments. The National Park Service, for the most part, holds land of outstanding natural beauty or historical interest. Accessibility to nearby population has counted only slightly in the establishment of national parks. At the opposite extreme, city and county parks are use- rather than resource-oriented (the terminology is Marion Clawson's): they are open spaces chosen because they are convenient to the people nearby. If they possess no national beauty, developers add trees, grass, lakes, and other amenities. State holdings follow an intermedate principle. In the early years of the state park movement, parks were chosen on the same basis as national parks without regard for thir proximity to population but rather for their scenic, scientific, or historical significance. In the last 30 years state parks have largely been selected to provide recreation opportunities accessible to large population concentrates. Total state holdings reflect these dual purposes.

Exceptions of all sorts of course exist. Some locally operated facilities are a considerable distance from the population which supports them. (San Francisco operates a summer camp in the High Sierras, several hundred miles from the city.) On the other hand, nearby populations are the heaviest users of some national parks, Yosemite constituting a prime example. Some state parks (California's Point Lobos and Michigan's Porcupine Mountain State Park) possess natural attractions comparable to many sites of the national park system. Many state parks have more out-of-state than in-state visitors.

The distinctions in purpose and acquisition-principle become obliterated when other holdings used, or potentially usable, for recreation are considered. National forests, the residual public domain, revested railroad lands, and reservoirs of the Bureau of Reclamation and the Corps of Engineers were not chosen for recreation purposes at all. TVA reservoirs and most state forests were selected with recreation as only the most minor consideration. Recreation on all these properties is lagniappe: an added use of land secured for other purposes. On some of these properties, however, recreation has now become a major use. And these lands, because of their very size, will provide a major fraction of the future recreation resources in the United States. The disparities in acreage between parks and other public lands make this clear. Though the latter category contains large areas relatively unsuited for recreation purposes, comparisions are nevertheless illuminating. For example, state forests contain almost four times the acreage of state parks, and lands of the Forest Service and Bureau of Land Management (excluding large holdings in Alaska) together constitute an area 24 times the size of all national parks.

Although there are genuine differences in the character of state, local, and national park lands, those differences are relatively unimportant when one views the broader field of outdoor recreation. On the one hand, parks, as such, are only a small fraction of the nation's present, and needed, outdoor recreation resources. On the other, as park holdings increase, their national-state-local differences will inevitably tend to become less important. So-called level distinctions in type of parkland are, therefore, not the principal basis of cooperative sharing among the governments of the federal system. And no differences in park character can be used to justify the fact that all planes of government are in the recreation business. That justification exists, as we have seen, only in the need for recreation space, the impossibility of providing enough such space in the hands of "pure" recreation agencies, and the virtues of preserving multiple points of policy and administration in this continentwide nation.

More genuine evidences of collaboration among governments in recreation activities are grants of work, money, and land given by the federal government to states and localities, and similar grants given by states to localities. In addition, there is a widespread exchange of professional services among all workers in the field.

The first substantial federal aid to state and local recreation programs came during the depression through the Works Progress Administration, Civil Works Administration, and Federal Emergency Relief Adminstration, among other federal agencies. The contribution of the Civilian Conservation Corps was particularly important. From 1933 to 1943 the National Park Service operated camps for the CCC at a total cost of more than $130 million. By far the largest fraction of this manpower was used for long range planning and immediate physical improvement of state and local parks. General planning studies were made in 46 states, 18 states were given help in rewriting their conservation and recreation laws, and an influential series of technical publications was made available to state and local officers. More than 550 parks were developed by CCC workers. In Virginia, for example, a state park system was created where virtually none had existed before. Eleven areas (19,000 acres) were developed, the six principal parks were provided with roads systems, water supply, sewage disposal systems, telephone and power lines, and utility and administration buildings. Three recreation dams, a swimming pool, bathhouses, beach facilities, trails, and other amenities were provided. Smaller contributions to recreation facilities of the states were made by the CCC through the Fish and Wildlife Service and the Bureau of Reclamation, Department of the Interior, as well as through the Department of Agriculture.[13]

"GRANTS OF CASH"

The end of the depression was only the beginning of substantial aid by the federal government to states and localities. Cash grants have been the least important item. The Fish and Wildlife Service makes direct cash grants for recreation purposes. Under the Pittman-Robertson and Dingell-Johnson Acts, the grants are made to state fish and game (or conservation) departments to pay up to 75 per cent of the total cost of state programs designed to conserve wildlife and improve hunting and fishing opportunities. Federal outlays for these purposes have been between $19 million and $20 million during each of the past several years.[14] Until 1961, grants of the Fish and Wildlife Service were the only direct, cash aids for recreation purposes by the federal government. In that year, Congress recognized the special recreation needs of urban areas and authorized an appropriation of $50 million "to encourage and assist (urban areas) in the timely acquisition of land to be used as permanent open-space land." The chief purpose of the legislation is to help provide "necessary recreation, conservation, and scenic areas. . . ." Grants can be made up to 30 per cent of the cost of the land.†

There also exists a wide variety of federal grants that aid recreation more or less indirectly. Grants to states for forest fire prevention (in state forests and on privately owned lands), for the procurement and distri-

[13] Data about CCC work administered by the National Park Service are from "Civilian Conservation Corps Program of the U.S. Department of the Interior" (January, 1944), the final report of Conrad L. Wirth, departmental representative on the CCC Advisory Council, to Secretary Harold L. Ickes. The report states (p. 27), "It is believed that the work accomplished in the park conservation field, in the ten years of the CCC was equal to what might have been expected in 50 years without its assistance."

[14] Bureau of Census, U.S. Department of Commerce, *Statistical Abstract of the United States, 1960*, p. 405. Because the funds involved are derived from the sale of federal duck stamps and the payment of excise taxes on sporting arms and ammunition and on some types of fishing equipment, these payments are often considered shared revenues, rather than grants-in-aid. But the federal money is allocated as if it were a regular grant, and states must meet federal standards before they are eligible to receive it.

† Editor's note: In 1964, Congress passed the Outdoor Recreational Facilities Act (P.L. 88–578) which provides for federal grants to the states of up to 50 per cent of the cost for planning, acquisition, and development of needed land and water area and facilities, the federal funds to come from a permanent land and water conservation fund based on proceeds from certain recreation-related activities involving the federal government.

bution of forest planting stock, and for forestry extension work among farmers are not designed to be federal contributions to recreation. They nevertheless are important for the conservation of game and fish as well as for the preservation of recreation areas. Similarly, the public works planning grants of the Community Facilities Administration make possible interest-free advances of federal funds to states and localities for detailed planning of public works. The planning for recreation land and other facilities is thus stimulated. Grants of the Public Health Service (Department of Health, Education, and Welfare) for the control of water pollution are aimed, in part, at protecting recreation uses of streams and other public waters. The beach erosion program of the Army Corps of Engineers makes available substantial sums for engineering surveys and the construction of breakwaters, jetties, or other structures. This federal aid is of great benefit to shoreline parks, harbors, and swimming areas, as well as commercial shipping interests.[15]

Most states make no specific grants to localities for recreation purposes. Some states, however, preceded the national government in giving grants for open space. New York and Massachusetts, for example, provide funds for local park acquisitions, Wisconsin for the purchase of county forests. And other states go beyond any federal programs in the field. California has a liberal grant and loan program enabling local governments to establish small boat harbors. New Mexico and other states return portions of specified tax levies to cities and counties for support of recreation programs.

Federal grants of land and land use to state and local bodies have been far more significant than cash grants in creating a national program. Though the Bureau of Reclamation has no general authority from Congress to spend money for recreation purposes, recent legislation concerning specific reservoir projects has made provision for recreation development. In fact, virtually every one of the more than 170 dams and reservoirs built by the Bureau is used in some way for recreation. Existing reservoirs and those under construction have a shoreline of more than 9,000 miles, approximately three times the distance form northern Maine to southern California. By interbureau agreement, the National Park Service plans what, if any, recreation use should be made of reclamation projects. The Bureau itself administers some recreation facilities, but its policy is to transfer reservoir recreation areas under its jurisdiction to state and local governments for development and administration. (Areas "deter-

[15] The California State program for aiding local governments in the construction of small boat harbors has been greatly aided by the building of breakwaters by the Army Corps of Engineers. Interview with Lachlan M. Richards, Chief, Division of Small Boat Harbors.

mined to be of national significance" are transferred to the National Park Service, and, when the reservoir shoreline is in a national forest, to the Forest Service.) Under this program, almost 100 facilities are being operated by state and local governments in the 17 western states. Many intricate arrangements have been worked out, local or state governments sometimes purchasing additional land adjacent to the reclamation areas, and in a few cases sharing recreation responsibility with the Park Service. The smaller governments, in all cases where they assume administrative tasks, contribute to the cost of recreation structures and other facilities.[16] The limited development of recreation facilities by local and state bodies has subjected the Bureau to considerable criticism in a number of areas. On the other hand, state and local leaders have strongly criticized the Bureau for its policy of providing only "minimum basic facilities" for recreation and, indeed, less than minimum facilities at older reservoirs.

The Army Corps of Engineers has even greater holdings of reservoir properties than the Bureau of Reclamation. In 1960 the corps reported some 185 projects in 38 states, providing more than 20,000 miles of shoreline. Built basically for river regulation, these projects nevertheless constitute an important recreation resource, one that is put principally at the disposal of state and local governments. A policy statement of the corps that "since the benefits to be derived from public park developments in the reservoir areas(s) are largely local, the development and management of public parks and recreation facilities should be the responsibility . . . of state and local government agencies." States, counties, cities, towns, county boards of education, teachers colleges, and a number of quasi-public organizations, such as 4-H Clubs, Boy Scouts and Optimist Clubs, have contracted with the corps for recreation development of reservoir areas. The corps itself up to 1960 had spent some $12 million in reservoir recreation development. In the same areas, it was estimated that state and local governments and private entrepreneurs had spent more than ten times that amount.[17]

The Federal Bureau of Land Management operates under legislation that generally provides free ingress and egress to the public in the several million acres that it administers. Hunting and fishing and other recreation activities are generally encouraged on this public domain, though businessmen using the land (under mineral leases, for example) have frequently been less than cooperative. States, localities, and nonprofit organizations

[16] Charles C. Butler, Chief, Land Branch, Division of Irrigation and Land Use, Bureau of Reclamation, Department of the Interior, in *Planning and Civic Comment* (December, 1960), pp. 21–26.

[17] Carter Page, Chief of Planning Division, Civil Works Division, U.S. Army Corps of Engineers, "The Role of the Federal Government" in *ibid.*, p. 27.

can obtain use or ownership of Bureau land under many different kinds of arrangements. Lands classified by the Bureau as most suitable for recreation purposes may be directly purchased at greatly reduced prices. (If a development program is not maintained, the lands revert to federal ownership.) States and local units may also develop prime recreation acreages under long-term leases. In lands retained under BLM management for multiple-use purposes, management responsibilities for recreation are characteristically transferred by contract to state and local agencies. The Bureau also attempts to aid states and localities in their use of public lands by arranging for access roads with private landowners whose holdings often completely surround public tracts. Several hundred land parcels have been transferred by the Bureau for development as state and local parks, beaches, boat landings, picnic sites, campgrounds, highway waysides, wildlife refuges, and historical monuments.[18]

This catalog by no means exhausts the list of federal grants in land, by lease or reduced-price purchase, to state and local institutions. One of the most active agents in this process is the General Services Administration, whose responsibility includes custody of all property declared excess by other federal agencies. Since 1948, legislation has made it possible for such property to be conveyed to the states and their political subdivisions for park development, wildlife preservation, and historical monuments. Business has been active, especially for land declared excess by the Coast Guard, the military services, and the Veterans Administration. Between 1948 and 1960, more than 250 tracts, ranging in size from less than one acre to more than 7,000 acres, have been conveyed to state and local agencies. The National Park Service reviews all such transactions and enforces compliance with the terms of the transfer.

The Forest Service also gives permits to smaller governments for the construction of recreation facilities on national forest lands. The TVA to even greater extent has encouraged state and local government agencies to develop and operate its properties for recreation use, and it has conveyed to valley states relatively large tracts of land and water for wildlife management areas. A number of demonstration parks, initially constructed by TVA, have been transferred to state and local management. The National Park Service prior to 1942 developed 46 recreation demonstration projects (covering almost 40,000 acres in 24 states) and subsequently conveyed most of them to the states. (One was transferred to the city of Louisville.)

[18] Bureau of Land Management, "Scope and Interest of Federal Government in Recreation," a statement prepared for Eighth Annual Conference of State Inter-Agency Committees on Recreation, Washington, D.C., May 25–27, 1960, mimeographed.

IV. RECIPROCAL GRANTS OF SERVICES

No review of formal programs can catch the manner in which the federal government, states, and localities do their job in recreation. The overriding impression is of neither antagonism, confusion, nor duplication of effort. It is that of professionals working together on a single, multifaceted task. Interlevel difficulties of course exist. Some are the consequence of genuine points of difference among experts; some result from the relatively low level of professional development among park personnel in several states; some flow from the parochialism of citizen governing bodies of state recreation agencies. But such conflicts also exist within a single governmental plane: in the federal government coolness, if not outright enmity, has characterized the relationships between upper echelons of the Park and Forest Services for many years. (The 1961 appointees, Secretaries Udall of Interior and Freeman of Agriculture, have attempted to dissipate this ill will.) In the states, park personnel may find their greatest differences with fish and wildlife officials. The most frequent conflicts have nothing to do with federalism, as such. They are between the more or less "pure" recreation workers and those whose definition of the job includes other objectives. Complaints about long-prevalent (but now changing) minimum recreation land and facilities policies of the Army Corps of Engineers and the Bureau of Reclamation are expressed alike by federal, state, and local park officials. But even these sore points are not characteristic. Issues of conflict, including interlevel conflict, are subordinate to issues of common mission.

There are many factors making for identical purpose. The workers in given fields—federal, state, and local—are, above all, professional colleagues. They share common definitions of program goal and program excellence. They are also friends. Their personal contacts are fostered by many meetings on the job and conferences of their professional associations. Field officers of national agencies may have more face-to-face meetings with state and local officers than with their own colleagues in central headquarters. There is also considerable shifting of employment from one plane of government to another. Many federal officials were once employed by states and localities. The flow also goes in the other direction: because state and city salaries are not infrequently higher than federal ones in the recreation field, leading state and municipal officials are recruited from federal ranks. (For example, DeWitt Nelson, Director of the California Department of Conservation, spent 19 years in the U.S. Forest Service.) All these circumstances minimize warfare between the so-called levels of the federal system and maximize the characteristic easy-working-together of recreation specialists, whoever happens to pay their salaries.

The range of interlevel collaboration generated by the colleagueship of workers is enormous. Some of it is specified by law, but most has developed in the interstices of the law's unspecified permissiveness. Collaborative efforts spontaneously emerge as the simple result of professional friends aiding each other.

There is a Branch of State Cooperation in the National Park Service's Division of Recreation and Resources Planning, and at least one worker represents this branch in each of the five park service regional offices. The branch funnels to state park officers a number of technical publications and comparative statistics. It aids the states—and particularly park directors—in all aspects of planning, site selection, and operation, including the establishment of scientific and historical interpretive programs. In more than one-half of the states, the state cooperation branch has given substantial assistance in the drafting of legislation to establish or improve park programs and practices. The branch publishes some of the most important periodical professional literature in the field in collaboration with the National Conference on State Parks, the principal organization of state park officials. This includes the serial publications issued under the park practices program: *Design, Guideline,* and the widely read *Grist.*

All offices of the Park Service, in fact, are involved at some level of formal or informal collaboration with state and local officers. When the Park Service plans the recreation use of a Reclamation Bureau reservoir, or when it surveys the historical and archaeological antiquities of a state in order to make recommendations for their preservation, a wide range of Park Service officials are brought into working relationships with their state and local counterparts. A national park ranger gives and receives suggestions about safety regulations in meetings with state field personnel. The Secetary of the Interior and the Director of the Park Service concert their efforts with those of leading state officials when important new national legislation is being planned.

What is true for the Park Service is also true for other federal agencies involved in recreation. The cash grant programs of the Forest and Fish and Wildlife Services mean, in effect, that a substantial fraction of the mission of those bureaus cannot be fulfilled without the close, day-to-day collaboration of state officials. The conservation, fish propagation, regulatory, and research functions of state fish and wildlife agencies are largely paid for with federal funds. The definition of specific tasks is the product of friendly negotiation between federal and state leaders. Forest Service grants extend only to items peripheral to recreation, such as fire control and forest management. Yet even in areas of apparent exclusive federal concern, such as the management of the national forests, the states are in fact heavily involved. State forestry agencies, for example, are responsible for fire control adjacent to national forests and in some cases within them. (Reciprocally, the Forest Service assumes responsibility for fire control in some state areas outside the national forests and for private or state-owned acreages within the forests.) In the national forests as a whole, a principal recreation activity is hunting and fishing. State regulations and license laws are applicable to these activities, and state wardens operate within national forests. State forestry departments act as formal agents for the Forest Service in federal programs for small watershed and flood protection projects and for programs involving private woodlot owners. State foresters are designated as Forest Service "collaborators."

Interlevel collaboration of a different sort has emerged from the National Conservation Needs Inventory of the Soil Conservation Service (authorized by Public Law 566). Under this program more than 13,000 small watersheds have been identified for development. In more than 2,000 cases the need for recreation facilities was specifically recognized. State and local utilization of this technical assistance by a federal agency can produce significant additions to recreation resources in many parts of the country.

The SCS small watershed program brings the federal officials into contact with local, as well as state, officials. Other agencies also often extend their services to the local plane, as in the depression programs, TVA-aided local parks and Park Service planning in the establishment of local parks, the preservation of antiquities, and the development of Reclamation Bureau reservoir areas for local administration.

State aid in services to local units varies (again) widely. In some states, technical assistance is nonexistent; at the other extreme, it is highly developed indeed. In Tennessee (through the State Planning Commission and Division of State Parks), California (Department of Parks and Recreation), Michigan (Inter-Agency Council for Recreation), New York (Department of Conservation), and a few other states, relatively comprehensive aid is given local governments in all aspects of park planning, acquisition, development, and operation. In at least seven states interagency committees operate for this purpose. Michigan's committee puts the resources of 19 state bureaus and 13 professional organizations and state-supported colleges and universities at the disposal of cities and counties (and private organizations) through a single point of contact. (Organization of the council was first financed by a private foundation, and the system as a whole provides a good incidental illustration of the public-private mixture of responsibilities.) California's aid program extends to recommendations for local personnel programs, the provision of training materials, plans and surveys for park acquisition, and encouragement to communities in the establishment of regional parks. It also includes technical (as well as financial) aid in the construction of small boat harbors, an activity which involves both the Coast Guard and the Army Corps of Engineers.[19]

The larger point is the unity of the recreation field. A professional worker doing a job looks for aid from other professional workers without much concern for what bureau or what level of government employs them. When the California Public Outdoor Recreation Plan Committee was given the task of surveying California's future needs in the field, it consulted with officials of no fewer than 21 federal agencies, as well as 150 private organizations. Some of its more important conclusions concerned the need for federal action. When state officials administering a motorboat registration law (the statute itself being the product of federal-state collaboration) wished to offer a training program to local enforcement officials, they turned as a matter of course to specialists in the U.S. Coast Guard to teach the necessary classes. The collaborative dependence goes also in the other direction. When the National Park Service considered a general expansion of the nation's park facilities, it responded to, and depended on, park officials of cities, counties, and states. When the Forest Service faces an acute problem of fire danger in a given area, solutions of the problem are sought in common by a federal official and a state forester.

V. THE ROLE OF PROFESSIONAL ORGANIZATIONS

Professional organizations in the recreation field clearly reveal the extent to which federal, state, and local lines are obscured in common function. The principal organization of state park officials is the National Conference on State Parks. Its committees and officers include many federal and local employees. Its most important publications, the several series on park practice, are prepared (under committee supervision) and distributed by the National Park Service. A Park Service official serves on the three-man editorial board of the conference's quarterly journal, *Planning and Civic Comment* (also the journal of the American Planning and Civic Association). A large fraction of this journal is written by workers in federal agencies.

[19] For Michigan see "The Michigan Inter-Agency Council for Recreation" (East Lansing, Michigan, 1953); Julian W. Smith, "Michigan's Inter-Agency Council on Recreation," *State Government* (September, 1950), pp. 192–194. On California aid to localities, see California Public Resources Code, sec. 8701; also "Standards for Professional Recreation Personnel," State of California Recreation Commission, Publication No. 5, January, 1950.

Other leading professional organizations in the recreation fields show the same mixture of interlevel personnel and the same similarity of purpose and outlook among federal, state, and local agencies. Both the Society of American Foresters and the Wildlife Society publish journals to which federal officials contribute heavily. Indeed, the *Journal of Forestry* has at times been charged with following too closely the policy views of the U.S. Forest Service. The American Institute of Park Executives, a leading professional organization for municipal and county park administrators, has many state and federal officials among its members. Virtually every issue of its journal, *Parks and Recreation,* contains articles by nonlocal officers. Even the many state organizations of park and forest officials usually have a number of federal officials who contribute to conferences and in other ways participate in organization activities.

At one time it could be said that the national bureaus were the source of leading professional ideas, and that national officials in professional organizations were related to state and local officials as teachers to students. This is no longer true. Some states are fully equal, if not superior, to federal agencies in standards of professional conduct and positions of professional leadership. The most impressive government publications on recreation of the last decade include the two-volume *California Public Outdoor Recreation Plan* and the several publications on "Parks, Recreation and Open Space in the Tri-State New York Metropolitan Region," prepared under the joint auspices of the Metropolitan Region Council and the Regional Plan Association. Recreation planning for reservoirs is more advanced in California than in Washington, D.C., and New York leads rather than follows in boldness of park acquisition and development. Officials of these and other states (among them Indiana, Michigan, and Pennsylvania) rank as high in professional councils as do federal officers.

The professional groups are often the source of new programs and always the arena for mediating conflicts of policy. The strongest lines of political force run from state and local groups to Washington, not between Washington bureaus and Capitol Hill. A federal department, developing a new policy, as a matter of course "preclears" it to whatever extent possible. Professional organizations present an ideal place for this process of preclearance. Objections of various interests can be met, compromises achieved, and support of the back-home constituencies solicited. In the absence of such a process, national programs are likely to fail, as the National Park Service discovered in unsuccessful attempts (in 1936, 1947, and 1949) to encourage a national grant-in-aid program for parkland purchases. As one close observer of the scene remarked, "The state park boys were not sold."

The preclearance function of the national organization does not represent manipulation of state and local interests by federal interests. National programs are not generated spontaneously in Washington. Rather they often represent responses of national offices to the demands of interest groups. And state and local administrators are often closer to such groups —and closer to centers of congressional power—than those in Washington. This gives state and local representatives a strong position in the bargaining process that takes place within the professional organization. National bureaus are more politically dependent on state and local agencies than vice versa.

In fact, however, political considerations are rarely the principal terms of reference. For one thing, the same constituency groups are shared by federal, state, and local bureaus. For another, discussion is based upon— and agreements are achievable because of—a body of shared goals and shared, preferred methods for achieving them. This is the essence of professionalization. It makes possible the very existence of organizations whose membership includes federal, state, and local officials. Without this community of outlook on general principle, the important functions of program origination and preclearance could not exist. Ideas are exchanged and compromises reached by friends talking a common language and agreeing on a common, larger goal.

The process of policy formulation is far more complex than this discussion of professional organizations would indicate. Legislators have ideas of their own, sometimes influenced by powerful commodity-based groups or other business organizations whose ideas about the use of public land may conflict with those of recreationists and conservationists. A recommendation of the Wilderness Society for additional wilderness areas in national forests is not likely to be approved by lumbering interests or the Natural Resources Department of the U.S. Chamber of Commerce. In addition, there are frequent disagreements among many recreation interests, themselves. Yet the significant conflicts are not on federal-state-local lines. And professional workers in recreation usually compose their differences and join together in support of programs that they bring before state and national legislative bodies. Only one example need be given. At the end of 1960, in response to a growing public demand for greater recreation facilities (in part inspired by the professional workers' own activities), a new "Parks for America" program was announced. Formal drafting of the plan and of implementing legislation was accomplished in the offices of the National Park Service. Private consultation with a large number of state and local workers preceded public announcement. The first open discussions were held only after substantial agreement was achieved. The actual announcement of "Parks for America" was made jointly by officers of the American Institute of Park Executives (local) and the National Conference of State Parks (state). The steering committee appointed to implement the plan was composed of 15 members, five from each plane in the federal system, who pledged to work together in a "crusade for more parks for Americans everywhere."[20] The new park, recreation, and wilderness preservation programs that have emerged in Washington, the states, and the localities in the five years since then are testimony to the possibilities inherent in the national recreation system.

EDITOR'S NOTE:
SOME ADDITIONAL CHARACTERISTICS
OF THE MARBLE CAKE

The author distinguished three other basic elements of the "marble cake"; the sharing of functions entrusted to the national government on a formally unilateral basis, either by constitutional design or legislation; "federalism without Washington," a phrase he invented to describe cooperative relations among the states; and sharing in its fiscal and economic aspects. His notes are here summarized or excerpted, to indicate the way in which the first two function in the American system. For the third factor, see Jacob Cohen and Morton Grodzins, "How Much Economic Sharing in American Federalism," American Political Science Review Vol. LVII, No. 1 (March, 1963), pp. 5–23.

THE SHARING OF "NATIONAL" FUNCTIONS

The formalized cooperative programs, usually cited as the major channels of sharing represent, no more than part of the picture and not necessarily the largest part. Of equal interest is the manner in which apparently unilateral federal functions such as the administration of federal laws, agricultural price supports, veterans' benefits, old age and survivors insurance, labor regulation, and defense spending are brought into the sharing system. In light of the continuing expansion of such functions, their assimilation into the system is particularly important for its maintenance. In general, they are assimilated into the over-all pattern through politics.

Sharing through politics in the administrative and judicial realms is indeed traditional. To give only one example, "senatorial courtesy" makes federal patronage appointments in the various states (postmasters, federal law enforcement officials, and federal judges) subject to the desires of the

[20] See "Parks for America," *Parks and Recreation,* Journal of the American Institute of Park Executives (December, 1960), pp. 528–29, 541–43.

state's senators in Washington and ultimately to the state party organization connected with the incumbent President's party, insuring that ostensibly federal officials will be drawn from and be part of each state's political order.

The very pervasiveness of sharing is responsible for the interjection of the states and localities into areas considered to be the exclusive domain of the national government. Consider the two great national functions specified in the Constitution: foreign affairs and national defense, plus a new national function developed through technical breakthrough in our age: atomic energy.

There is considerable evidence of state and local involvement in matters attending the nation's foreign relations dating back to the early days of the republic.[21] The states and localities have acted in matters of their internal concern that have involved foreign governments by using constitutionally legitimate state police powers. At the turn of the century, California segregated Japanese school children, causing a crisis in dealing with Japan that contributed to the long-range deterioration of American-Japanese relations despite President Theodore Roosevelt's efforts to force the state to heel. More recently, New York applied its laws forbidding racial or religious discrimination in employment to the New York-based Arabian American Oil Company (ARAMCO) which refused to employ Jews because Saudi Arabia would not allow them to enter its borders. Despite State Department pressures to exempt ARAMCO from the state's law for the sake of American oil interests in the Middle East, the New York courts successfully held the state's interest to be paramount. States or localities have applied pressure on Washington regarding specific problems of foreign relations. State legislatures and congressional delegations have been active on behalf of Irish independence and the creation of the state of Israel, to name only two outstanding examples. More recently, such pressures have been directed to the support of movements opposing Russian domination of the countries of eastern Europe or discrimination against certain groups in those countries.

State and local influence in the national defense field is felt in all the major areas of defense preparedness: the distribution of defense contracts, the location of military installations, and the organization of the nation's reserve forces. In all three cases, state and local interests are obvious— their economies stand to benefit from defense contracts and military payrolls, and the maintenance of the National Guard (and even local reserve

---

[21] See, especially, Dennis J. Palumbo, "The States and American Foreign Relations," unpublished Ph.D dissertation, Department of Political Science, University of Chicago, 1960.

units) affects their pride as well. In times of local emergency, National Guard units form the first line of civil defense and relief, enhancing their importance to the states. The influence of the states and localities in all three areas is continuing, pervasive, and powerful.

The harnessing of the atom was stimulated and paid for by Washington. If ever there were a function likely to remain in federal hands, management and control of atomic energy development should have been it. Yet, since the early 1950's, atomic energy regulation and development has been transformed into a shared function through the conscious efforts of Congress and the Atomic Energy Commission. Under congressional authorization, the states have been given the opportunity to acquire the authority to supervise and regulate most uses of atomic energy within their limits and foster the development of peaceful uses of atomic power. The Atomic Energy acts of 1954 and 1959 progressively extended the states' potential role, and by 1964 at least two-fifths of the states were involved.

FEDERALISM WITHOUT WASHINGTON

Grodzins' discussion of interstate relations for the Hoover Commission report, while necessarily excluding recent developments, points up an accelerating trend. It also indicates how even such cooperation is part of the over-all sharing system.

Recent years have seen an increasing effort among the states, acting on their own, to coordinate common activities. Many of these efforts also signify an increasing appreciation of the flexibility of state-to-state relations in the federal structure. No cooperation between state and state is barred by the Constitution. There is no practical limit to interstate cooperation save the will of the states themselves.

Historically, joint state action has taken four forms: (1) interstate compacts and agreements, (2) uniform state laws, (3) reciprocal or contigent legislation, and (4) interstate administrative cooperation.

There were nine intercolonial pacts and four under the Articles of Confederation. From 1789 to 1913, twenty-seven interstate compacts received congressional approval and eleven others were put into effect without such approval. In recent years, the number of cooperative compacts has increased rapidly: thirty-seven were adopted in the fourteen years from 1934 to 1947.

Compacts have been utilized to compose boundary disputes, to solve jurisdictional conflicts, to help construction of interstate public works, to conserve natural resources, to reduce interstate tax differences, to regulate interstate water resources, to provide continuous supervision of parolees and probationers, and to meet various other social and economic needs.

The strength of compacts has ranged from that of mere definitions of policy among the signers to firm statutory pacts establishing continuing administrative machinery. In recent years, especially following recognition of the success of the Port of New York Authority, a noticeable interest has arisen in the possibilities of the interstate compact as a means of creating corporate instruments capable of administering continuing interstate programs.

Problems shared by the states have led to greater emphasis on uniform, concurrent, and reciprocal or contingent state laws. Such recasting of the laws has been sponsored, at different times, by a variety of public and private agencies interested in particular fields of governmental activity. The organization of the National Conference of Commissioners on Uniform State Laws in 1892 was an important development in the history of model legislation. Ninety-six statutory proposals have been drawn and recommended to the states by the conference since then. Many of these model laws have been adopted. The Council of State Governments and the Commissions on Interstate Cooperation have made machinery available to the states to carry on continuous study of governmental functions and public needs and to formulate legislative and administrative proposals for interstate cooperation.

Administrative cooperation among the states has supplemented legislative coordination. Such cooperation takes various forms: adoption of uniform or contingent rules, regulations, and procedures to govern interstate dealings; adoption of uniform rules for the interpretation of related statutes; negotiation and arbitration of interstate differences; acceptance of findings of the agency of one state by other states concerned; interstate conferences and associations of officers; and exchange of information and reports.

Other moves to coordinate interstate and national-state activities include the unsuccessful National Emergency Council of the National Government (1933), which later was incorporated into the Office of Facts and Figures but afterward dropped from the budget. An officer of the national government was maintained in each state to channel information and reports between Washington agencies and the state government and between national field agencies and the states. The effort was not systematic, thorough, or powerfully supported, and the results proved disappointing to both levels of government.

The Council of State Governments proposed a Joint Federal-State Committee on Intergovernmental Relations in 1940 before the Temporary National Economic Committee, but no action resulted. The committee was to consist of congressmen and administrative officers working with the council. The suggestion sprang from the success of the council's conferences on such matters as interstate trade barriers, where meetings of national and state officers produced tangible successes.

During World War II, the national government utilized the Council of State Governments as the joint instrumentality of the states for the purpose of maintaining continuous contact in regard to many emergency programs. With respect to programs requiring state legislative action, a cooperative pattern was developed between the Federal-State Relations Section of the United States Department of Justice and the Council of State Governments. Proposals involving both the national and state levels of government were transmitted by national or state agencies to the appropriate liaison agency, and these, in turn, were submitted to the drafting committee of the council to be drawn up in form suitable for submission to the states for appropriate action. The machinery has continued into the postwar period.

Part III

PARTICIPANT PERSPECTIVES

Chapter 6

THE BUNDLE OF
GOVERNMENTAL SERVICES

I. INTRODUCTION

At the local level, as at other points of the American system, all planes of government collaborate in virtually all activities of government. Local governments are not responsible for all "local" services; indeed it is difficult to find any service performed, or regulation imposed, that does not involve the federal and state governments in important responsibilities.

The state-local mixture of functions is easy to demonstrate and needs little detailed attention.[1] Less obvious and less well understood are federal-local contacts at the local level. It is easy to demonstrate even these contacts in the great cities of the nation. The great urban problems are also great national problems, and the relationship of federal programs to the government of the largest cities needs little documentation.[2] Furthermore, one can have complete confidence that if extensive federal-local contacts exist in small cities, they exist to an even larger degree in the great ones. The discussion that follows is therefore concentrated on the "bundles" of governmental services offered in small towns and, to the extent that the data allow, in rural areas. The "easy" case for demonstrating the unity of American governments at the local level would be to focus attention on state-local or federal-local relationships in big cities; the decision to look

[1] For a discussion of this mixture, see Charles R. Adrian, *State and Local Governments: A Study in the Political Process* (New York: McGraw-Hill Book Company, 1960).

[2] For discussion of housing and urban redevelopment, see Edward C. Banfield and Morton Grodzins, *Government and Housing in Metropolitan Areas* (New York: McGraw-Hill Book Company, 1958); for a discussion of other urban problems in this context, see Robert H. Connery and Richard H. Leach, *The Federal Government and Metropolitan Areas* (Cambridge, Mass.: Harvard University Press, 1960).

primarily at federal-local contacts in small towns represents the now-familiar choice of the "hard case."*

II. ARIZONA COTTON TOWN

Casa Grande, Arizona, sits athwart one of two principal highways that run through the hot country from Phoenix to Tucson. Casa Grande was for many years nothing but a desert stop-off. Deep wells and irrigation have brought long-staple cotton to the Salt River Valley, and farming, wherever water is available, is intensive and profitable. The town is a shopping and marketing center for Pinal County, and to some degree a dormitory for the adjacent farm areas. Its population of 1,545 in 1940 almost tripled by 1950 when the census showed 4,181 residents. In 1958, according to unofficial estimates, Casa Grande with a population approaching 9,000, had become even larger than the county seat of Coolidge.

The bundle of governmental services delivered to the citizens of Casa Grande is a considerable one. Some of these services are not carried on by the city government at all, and for others, local officials have only peripheral responsibilities.

Public welfare activities in Arizona, for example, are administered by the counties under state supervision, and no item for welfare appears in the Casa Grande city budget. The case load within the city limits is nevertheless considerable: in the winter of 1958 some 300 residents of the city were receiving welfare aid, not counting recipients of child welfare services. By far the largest fraction of those receiving aid were under programs defined by national legislation and partially paid for with federal funds. For example, there were 159 persons in Casa Grande receiving old age assistance and 97 benefited from aid under the program for dependent

---

* Editor's note: Interviews were initially carried out in six scattered places in addition to Casa Grande: Allegan, Michigan; Ashtabula, Ohio; Brockton, Massachusetts; Borger, Texas; La Fayette, Georgia; and DuBois County, Indiana. For reasons given in the text Benton, Arkansas, was added. In addition, directly relevant data are contained in Paul N. Ylvisaker's detailed monograph on Blue Earth County, Minnesota, *Intergovernmental Relations at the Grass Roots, op. cit.,* and the scattered publications of the Councils on Intergovernmental Relations that operated during the early and middle 1940's in Blue Earth County; Henry County, Indiana; Colquitt County, Georgia; Santa Clara County, California; and Skagit County, Washington.

The San Francisco study provided convincing evidence that (1) big cities were equally involved in the sharing system, and (2) their ability to bring greater material resources and expertise to bear on their own problems made them less dependent on unqualified federal assistance. Neither conclusion affects the validity of the description in this chapter.

children. A substantial, if uncertain, number of Casa Grande residents received Old Age and Survivors Insurance payments, a program wholly administered by the federal government.

In a similar fashion public health services for the residents of the city are largely carried on through programs of county, state, and federal governments. The city has a small item in its budget for health and sanitation activities, the local government's activity in this "local" field being largely confined to milk inspection and to sanitation control in restaurants and other places handling food. The county public health office operates a diverse program. Federal funds in 1958 were being utilized for the treatment of tuberculosis, for the investigation and control of venereal diseases, and for the reimbursement of nurses under the maternal and child care program. Polio vaccine provided at no cost by the United States Public Health Service was available. Federal aid was responsible for a contemplated study of mental health. County and state officers were also at this time planning a county health center; they were confident that 30 per cent of the cost of the building would be paid by the federal government under the Hill-Burton Act. These are but samples of the national government's role in activities carried out in the city of Casa Grande by officers of Pinal County under the supervision of, and with funds partially supplied by, the State of Arizona.

Federal-state collaboration supplies citizens of Casa Grande with unemployment insurance and employment placement services. The local office of the Arizona Employment Security Commission is a particularly busy place because of the seasonal nature of a large fraction of Casa Grande's employment needs. Standards of compensation, financing, and administration are regulated by the intricate system of federal-state law and administration.

Education in Casa Grande is not a responsibility of city officers. Separate districts for the high school and elementary schools are maintained, each with its own elected governing board and taxing power. Schools operate under the customary state legal and administrative standards. Arizona schools receive state financial aid to a degree roughly parallel to the national average. In 1957–58 the Casa Grande schools collected slightly more than 60 per cent of their total revenues from local taxes, the remainder ($400,000) coming from state and county aid calculated on a per capita basis.

Federal contributions to the schools were peripheral but considerable. All schools participated in the federally sponsored free lunch and milk program. The high school received funds under the Smith-Hughes Act for special classes in vocational agriculture and homemaking. A portion of the salary of four teachers, out of a total of 36, was paid from this federal contribution. Direct supervision of these teachers was given by state officers who themselves were paid with federal funds and worked by federal standards. Several teachers have received summer training fellowships from the National Science Foundation. Technical aids to all parts of the schools come from publications of the United States Office of Education and the Department of Agriculture.

The proximity of Indian reservations to Casa Grande provided a relatively unusual point of national contact for the schools. Indian children for the most part attended reservation grammar schools, but in 1958 almost 10 per cent of the high school students were reservation residents. The Bureau of Indian Affairs compensated the school on a per-student per-day basis.

Finally, the Casa Grande schools have benefited materially from the distribution of federal surplus property. The State Department of Public Instruction operated an office to facilitate the flow of federal surplus materials to local schools. This flow in the past has on occasion been too active, and several criminal indictments were at one time returned against some Arizona local school administrators who were acquiring federal surplus equipment in large quantities, including such items as B-21 bombers, and trading it to private businessmen, not always for the exclusive benefit of the schools. Casa Grande was not touched by this scandal, and the schools have received at virtually no cost an impressive quantity of surplus materials. These include for the high school such items as a truck; radios for classrooms; tools for the automobile mechanics and woodworking classes; and stoves, refrigerators, dishes, and dishwashers for the lunchroom. Surplus goods utilized by the school range from scrap paper to an outmoded Link Trainer for airplane pilots and several dismantled aircraft.

The Casa Grande Community Hospital, like the schools, is operated by a special local government. The hospital was the product of several acts of intergovernmental collaboration, initiated by a civic group and abetted by senatorial "casework."[3] The local Lions Club was concerned with the community's need for a modern hospital facility, but little progress was made until a new city attorney for Casa Grande drafted a law, readily passed by the Arizona legislature as a state statute, which authorized creation of special hospital districts that could issue bonds and, under certain circumstances, levy taxes. The statute also provided that a certification of need had to be issued by the State Department of Health before the local district could be formed. Once initiated through this typical process of private-local-state collaboration, the Casa Grande Community Hospital

[3] See Chapter Nine.

soon received federal assistance. A grant of approximately $30,000 was made to the hospital by the Department of Health, Education, and Welfare under the Hill-Burton Act. These funds were used primarily for supplies and equipment. In addition, city officials succeeded in having an unused federal hospital, constructed during the depression by the Rural Resettlement Administration, declared surplus and given to the new community hospital. The surplus facility was then completely razed, and the new Casa Grande Community Hospital was able to salvage a substantial amount of building materials as well as a large number of beds, carts, stretchers, sickroom supplies, and other equipment.

A full quota of federally engineered local governments for agricultural purposes existed in Pinal County, providing important services to Casa Grande citizens. The County Agricultural Conservation and Stabilization Committee, whose offices were in the city, was responsible for administration of the soil bank (which provided payments to farmers for not growing certain crops and using the land set aside for rebuilding its fertility); the cotton marketing quota (which guaranteed cotton prices under a program limiting production); and the conservation practices program (which provided grants and loans for soil conservation).[4] There were some 1,000 farms in the county of which more than 800 participated in one or more of the ASC programs. Perhaps 10 per cent of the farmowners—estimates run from 50 to 100 of the participating farmers—were residents of Casa Grande itself. The funds distributed through ASC programs represented the largest single expenditure by any government within the county, and of course had the most profound effect on the economy of the city.

The Soil Conservation Service operating its characteristic local government, the Farmer's Home Administration, the Federal Land Bank, and the Agricultural Extension Service also provided significant services to the residents of the city, both directly and indirectly. For example, the Extension Service (whose offices incidentally were in the Casa Grande City Hall) operated a program in home economics administered through homemakers' clubs: three of the ten clubs in the county were in Casa Grande. Work with 4-H clubs also spilled over into the city, and the agent estimated that of the 560 farmers in the county who participated in technical meetings and demonstration programs, approximately 100 were city residents. A state program operating with funds supplied by the federal, state, and county governments (concerted through the University of Arizona), the extension service reflected more than the mixture of governments. It also illustrated, through the range of its activities and the clientele it served, the disappearing frontier between farm and city life. Finally, its sponsorship underscored

[4] For fuller discussion of these programs, see Chapter Fourteen.

the thin line separating public and private activities: as in other states, agricultural extension services of Pinal County were sponsored by the County Farm Bureau, a private organization.

The list of services, supplied by governments other than the government of Casa Grande, having direct and immediate local impact cannot be a complete one. The statute books are fat, and the vagaries of classification could spin the list out unendingly. The regulatory functions have so far been ignored. They were largely functions of the federal government and the state, alone or in combination, and included inspections for industrial safety and the purity of food and drugs, regulation of labor relations, licensing of the professions and vocations, examination of banks and the provision of deposit insurance. One important service, that of delivering the mail, had its purely federal administrative apparatus leavened by political influence of the states and localities. Finally, one function also touching the whole population, that of selective service, was operated jointly by the federal government and the state, making use of a state-appointed board of local citizens.

The services of government described thus far are carried on within the boundaries, and directly affect the residents, of Casa Grande. They can be considered local services of government, but they are not carried out by what is normally considered "the" local government, the municipality of Casa Grande. Indeed, these are services for which the municipality has little or no responsibility; they are the responsibility of the federal and state governments, the county, the school districts, and the several species of federally sponsored local governments for agriculture.

The streets of Casa Grande provide an avenue of approach to functions in which city officials have a more direct responsibility. The main street of the city is a federally aided state highway; it was constructed and maintained by the state highway department, utilizing standards of the federal government and paid for in part with federal funds. In an earlier period the federal government's Works Progress Administration was responsible for a good share of all the paving done on the city's own streets. Now this is a state-local activity. The city spent more on its street program (some $55,000 in 1957) than for any other single function. By far the largest fraction of this money, almost $46,000, was collected by the state in automobile and gasoline taxes and returned to the city. Very few controls were exercised by state officers over expenditures for city streets. But technical standards for street construction, made available by both the state and federal governments, were an indispensable guide for the city's construction and maintenance program.

Police activities loom second largest in the city's budget. What has already been described as the national police system operated effectively in Casa Grande.[5] The most notable objects in the office of the Chief of Police were a diploma signifying his graduation from the FBI's National Police Academy and an autographed photograph of J. Edgar Hoover. Contacts between field agents of the FBI, headquartered at Phoenix, and the local police department were frequent and cordial; an office in the city hall, also usd occasionally by the state's game warden, was made available to the FBI representative during his weekly visits. FBI laboratory facilities in Washington, D.C., were utilized by the local police as a matter of course on difficult cases. Casa Grande police have also worked closely with the Narcotics and Alcoholic Control divisions of the Treasury Department. Training schools established throughout the state by the Arizona Chiefs of Police Association were for the most part staffed by FBI instructors. A special federal-local linkage in police work resulted from the city's south-western location and the need of nearby farms for inexpensive seasonal labor supplied from Mexico. Control over the use of aliens in farm work was partially vested in the United States Border Patrol. An office of the Border Patrol was maintained in the Casa Grande City Hall, close to the local Chief of Police. The officers were friends, as well as close collabora-tors, although the patrol's duties only infrequently demanded services from local police.

One connection leads to another, and the Border Patrol's work in Casa Grande often led to the use of the city jail for federal prisoners who were awaiting transportation to other places. This was the source of a small city income and a larger city pride. When the jail was rebuilt and enlarged in 1957, city officers called upon the U.S. Bureau of Prisons for assistance. Consultations were held even before the blueprint stage, and a specialist from Washington, D.C., visited the city several times during actual con-struction. So it was that persons suspected of crimes against the laws of Arizona were lodged in the Casa Grande city jail, which was constructed under the *de facto* supervision of the federal Bureau of Prisons.

Federal-local collaboration was demonstrated daily in the local adminis-tration of justice. Arizona police magistrates were appointed to their part-time duties by city councils. (Casa Grande's magistrate sold insurance as his principal occupation.) Jurisdiction of the courts was limited to the most minor offenses: traffic violations, vagrancy, and the like. Yet the federal government's impact on this most local of local courts was felt in a number of ways. For one thing the magistrate did everything within his power to assist the Border Patrol. If the Patrol suspected that a drunk or vagrant was an alien who had entered the country illegally, the magistrate would

[5] See above, Chapter Four.

try to keep him in jail long enough for reports to come from Washington. A person who ordinarily would have been fined or given a suspended sentence was, at the request of the Border Patrol, kept the maximum period in jail. A similar service was performed for the local chief if he suspected that a person before the magistrate's court was wanted in other jurisdictions for more serious crimes. Finally, in cases where records from the FBI were already available on a person brought before his court, the magistrate found this information controlling. "When a man tells me that he has never been in trouble before but when the police department then gives me a record sheet from the FBI showing convictions in ten states running back for 20 years, then I know I have a person in front of me who deserves all the punishment I can give him."

The first city planning in Casa Grande was made possible by federal grants. These grants were administered by the Community Facilities Service of the General Services Administration under Public Law 352 of the 81st Congress. No local matching was required, and the city received $19,200 in all. Plans were made for a citywide drainage system and for sanitary sewers, curbs, gutters, and sidewalks for substantial portions of the city—improvements that were of the first importance to the rapidly growing community.

Two side effects were also significant. For one thing, the planning grants provided the first occasion on which city officials worked with the private engineering firm, *Jones and Gore*,[6] a company that subsequently became the city's principal agent in negotiations with federal agencies. *Jones and Gore* was responsible for calling to the attention of city officials the availability of the planning grants. It undertook the work of soliciting a grant for the city on the understanding that no fee would be paid if the grant were not received and the subsequent planning not approved. The entire negotiation with the federal agency, aided by the city officers and by Arizona's United States senators, was carried on by the private firm. In subsequent years, the same firm played a similar role in the city's efforts to take advantage of other federal grants.[7]

A second by-product of the planning grants was unexpected and the source of one of the few points of friction between the city and the federal government. The grants provided for repayment without interest to the federal government of the money advanced "when the construction of the public works planned with the aid of the government's advance is undertaken or started." This proved to be a point of embarrassment for the city

[6] Names of private firms are pseudonyms and printed in italics.
[7] For discussion of the significance of the role of private firms in the American governmental system, see Chapter Eight.

when it wanted to construct a drainage system covering only a part of the city. The federal advance for the street drainage plans had amounted to $8,000. Federal officials insisted that the total advance (rather than a fraction proportional to the construction contemplated) be repaid. Casa Grande officials in turn insisted that they were unable to repay the entire $8,000. The loggerhead had the effect of postponing construction of even the partial drainage system. So the federal planning grant, designed to encourage public works, in this case had the opposite effect. City officers were still somewhat wrathful concerning this point in 1958, but they were confident that federal rules would soon be changed to conform to their own more "reasonable" position.

Public health measures, although principally in the domain of federal-state-county services, do not completely escape the attention of city officers. Dysentery and infant diarrhea are particularly serious problems in the desert community, and the infant death rate has been a high one historically. To combat one important source of these difficulties, the city was aided, from 1950 through 1953, by a team of specialists from the United States Public Health Service (working through state and county health offices). The federal team made studies of the number and sources of flies, supplied spray trucks and insecticides, and began a systematic program to control flies in the city. Instructions for continuing this work were given by federal specialists to city workers, and the city has maintained the spraying program with what it believes to be considerable success.

One source of flies difficult to control was the city's raw sewage, which was dumped untreated in an open field at the outskirts of the city. This disposal system created health hazards and constituted, moreover, a considerable odoriferous nuisance. A better method of sewage disposal became one of Casa Grande's most pressing needs, especially if it wished to continue to grow. The federal government met this need, first, through a grant of $107,000 for the construction of a modern sewage disposal system; and, second, through a loan of $250,000 to enable the city to pay its share of the costs.[8]

Application for the grant was formally made through the Arizona Department of Health, but city officials and their representatives carried out direct negotiations in 1956 and 1957 with the United States Public Health Service. City representatives in this matter included not only the engineering firm, *Jones and Gore,* but also a group of bond attorneys, and an investment securities company. Legislation limited the outright federal grant for the sewage disposal system to one-third of the total cost, and it

[8] The direct grant was made under terms of the Federal Water Pollution Control Act of 1956 (Public Law 660, 84th Congress).

was necessary for the city to raise an additional $250,000. A bond issue was clearly necessary, but private sources for the loan were not available at a reasonable interest rate. Consequently the city called upon still another federal department, the Housing and Home Finance Agency, which authorized the city to obtain the needed loan from that agency. The first bonds were ready to be issued when a private bonding house indicated its willingness to assume the lender's role at the already fixed rate of interest. The bonds were accordingly sold to the private company and the loan authorization was never utilized, cutting off this Casa Grande-federal contact. But it had well served its purpose. The interest rate paid on the bonds by the city would undoubtedly have been higher if federal loan funds had not been available.

The sewage disposal plant, made possible by federal grants and federal loan facilities, was under construction during the winter of 1958. But it was not the federal government's most valuable capital contribution to Casa Grande. City officials believed that in the long run even greater returns would come to the community from an airfield and a mountain park, the first an outright gift from the federal government, the second a virtual gift.

The airfield had been constructed on public lands during the war as a training facility and auxiliary landing area, and was declared surplus after the war by the Department of Defense. Casa Grande's interest in acquiring the field began in 1954 when the local Chamber of Commerce, in a report to the city council, urged the desirability of city ownership. Almost three years of negotiations were necessary before the field was transferred, the biggest stumbling block being the need for all other federal agencies to certify that the facility was not needed by them. Senators Hayden and Goldwater were active on behalf of Casa Grande at every step of the process. The facility is an impressive one, a complete square mile of perfectly flat table land. Land of this sort in the vicinity of Casa Grande was being sold in 1958 for building lots at approximately $1,000 an acre. Since the airport consisted of exactly 640 acres, city officers believed that in placing a valuation of $500,000 on it they were being conservative.

Improvements were needed on the airport when it was acquired. Its facilities consisted only of four paved runways. Even before the transfer of the airport title, city officials (again assisted by *Jones and Gore*) applied to the Federal Civil Aeronautics Administration for funds to improve the field. Aid was asked for the construction of an administration building, a water system, telephone and power lines, and runway lights. The original application had to be scaled down because of lack of funds available to the CAA, but the federal agency did give the city $5,000 of the $8,000 needed to bring water to the field. With the advice of the CAA district engineer, the city in 1958 resubmitted plans for additional improvement grants. City officers, confident that at least $30,000 in CAA funds would ultimately be made available for the airport, contemplated an investment of some $19,000 from the city's own funds. They considered this a good investment in a "$549,000 piece of useful property," especially since some of the airport land could be leased for industrial purposes. Once improvements have been completed, the field is expected to be completely self-supporting.[9]

A parcel of federal land, even larger than the airfield, was being transferred in 1958 to Casa Grande. It consisted of no fewer than 1,400 acres and was named the Casa Grande Mountain Park. The land itself was less valuable than the airfield, being in a mountainous area, but the city assumed no financial obligation whatsoever in acquiring the park. The parkland was being acquired from the Bureau of Land Management of the Department of the Interior under federal statutes by which surplus portions of the public domain may be sold to public bodies for recreational purposes. The sale price was nominal—some three cents an acre—and the actual cash payments were assumed by the local Rotary Club which initiated the project. The Rotary also paid for initial improvements of the land. City officials believed the park would be of inestimable value in the years ahead. Senators Hayden and Goldwater again gave active aid to both city officials and Rotary Club members as negotiations for the land transfer were carried on.

Housing in Casa Grande has been affected by a number of federal programs. In 1946 a federal public housing agency built 20 low-cost housing units in the city, primarily for veterans. This project was given to the city in 1950, and in 1958 the units were still being rented. A more significant federal-local relationship in housing was a less direct one. The largest fraction of home construction in the area was financed by loans from the Federal Housing Authority and the Veterans' Administration. Under the FHA program individual loans were not approved unless an entire site met federal standards. The city supplied information regularly to the FHA on new subdivision sites, certifying to the width of streets, and to the provision of sewers, water, and other amenities. Further, the FHA would not

---

[9] Acceptance of the airfield as a gift involved Casa Grande in a continuing federal relationship. The federal government, for example, retained the right to make use of the landing strips, subject to regulations of the CAA, and during periods of national emergency to take (but pay for) exclusive use of the field. The contract deed imposed the obligation on the city to maintain the field at all times. It cannot grant exclusive rights to the field or exclusive franchises (except for the sale of gasoline and oil) to service and sales agencies. Furthermore, the use of the field and its facilities cannot be limited "on the grounds of race, creed or color."

approve building loans in unzoned subdivisions, and consequently the city had to bring up to date, and in some cases to alter, zoning requirements. The pressure on the city council to provide this kind of zoning—as well as to build streets and sewers—came from local builders and not from the federal agency. But the latter's demands were freely cited by the builders as compelling reasons for taking action, and the city council did what was demanded because the builders were important members of the community and because the city badly needed new housing. Thus FHA policies led to an extension and updating of zoning and in some cases to the annexation of new areas in order to bring them under the city's zoning authority. A final federal-local contact with respect to housing resulted from the appointment of the city building inspector as inspector for the FHA and for the VA. The local official received extra compensation for these services. In his capacity as a local officer, he inspected each new home five times during the construction period. The VA required four inspections. In this case he discharged his local and federal duties simultaneously. For the FHA, additional site inspections were required.

Officials of Casa Grande, in common with local leaders throughout the country, participated in federal civil defense programs. Two Casa Grande officers, their expenses paid by the federal government, have attended civil defense training courses. Federal funds have furnished visual aid equipment for the training of local citizens in civil defense work. Local leaders in 1958 were completing a disaster relief plan under the supervision of federal and state officials. At that time, Casa Grande, unlike many other cities, had not taken advantage of the civil defense contributions program which made possible the acquisition of two-way radios for police and fire departments. The city officials were well informed about what was available to them under this program, however, and their plans included making application for this equipment.

This extensive list of programs involving many governments is not an exhaustive one. The federal contribution to the bundle of services in Casa Grande includes a considerable miscellany. The larger and better equipped of the city's two fire trucks was purchased at exceedingly low cost from the surplus property division of the federal General Services Administration. A principal building in the city was the National Guard Armory, used not only for training purposes but also as a facility for dances and other civic events. A rent-free office in the City Hall was provided the local officer of the Treasury Department's Bureau of Internal Revenue. The National Park Service maintained the Casa Grande Indian Ruins, a national monument closer to Coolidge than to Casa Grande, but which Casa Grande officials believed could be an important tourist attraction provided the Park Service did a more energetic job of publicizing and maintaining the ruins. Cordial relationships were maintained with officers of the nearby Gila, Pima, and Papago Indian Reservations. The city was an official weather reporting station for the United States Weather Bureau, supplying information twice daily to a central station in Phoenix. Similarly, the city provided a monthly report to the Department of Labor on building in progress. A brass plaque on the older portion of the City Hall, long forgotten by even the inhabitants of the offices, made known the fact that this focal point for the many activities of many governments was, appropriately enough, constructed in 1936 with federal funds through the Works Progress Administration.

TABLE 7

THE BUNDLE OF GOVERNMENTAL SERVICES PROVIDED THE
RESIDENTS OF CASA GRANDE, ARIZONA,
1958

Service	City of Casa Grande	Special District	County of Pinal	Special Local Government Engineered by U.S.	State of Arizona	United States
1. Activities for which city government has little or no responsibility.[a]						
Agricultural conservation and stabilization				**	*	**
Agricultural extension			**		**	**
Bank examination and deposit insurance					**	**
Education	**		**		**	*
Employment security					**	**
Farmers Home Administration				*		**
Hospital	**				*	**
Industrial safety					**	*
Inspection of boilers, weights and measures; other commercial inspection	*				**	
Inspection of food and drugs	*		**		**	**
Labor relations					**	**
National Guard					**	**
Postal service						**
Professional licensing and examinations					**	*
Public health	*		**		**	**

TABLE 7

THE BUNDLE OF GOVERNMENTAL SERVICES PROVIDED THE
RESIDENTS OF CASA GRANDE, ARIZONA,
1958 (CONTINUED)

Service	City of Casa Grande	Special District	County of Pinal	Special Local Government Engineered by U.S.	State of Arizona	United States
Public welfare			**		**	**
Selective Service				**	**	**
Soil Conservation Service			*	**	*	**
2. Activities for which city government has important responsibilities.[b]						
Airport	**				*	**
City planning	**				*	**
Civil Defense	**				**	**
Courts	**		**		**	**
Fire protection	**				**	*
Garbage disposal	**				*	
Library	**				*	
Parks	**					**
Police	**		**		**	**
Recreation	**					
Sewage and sanitation	**				*	**
Streets and highways	**		*		**	**
Zoning and housing	**				*	**

[a] This section of the table is abbreviated and is meant only to be illustrative.
[b] All lines in the official city budget are included in this section of the table.
** Major role.
* Minor role.

Table 7 summarizes the responsibilities of the various governments for services provided the citizens of Casa Grande. The table attempts to take account only of formal spheres of authority, and if informal lines of influence were charted there would be many more indications of shared functions. The distinction between important and unimportant responsibilities is, of course, not an exact one. Judgments on this score were made after on-the-spot observations and after consultation with appropriate officials. Other observers might in some cases have judged differently: for example, they might not have given the Casa Grande city government a major role in civil defense. Yet the chart can be taken as a generally accurate map of which governments do what within the borders of Casa Grande. What does this sort of mapping reveal?

First, it is notable how many and how important are the functions provided to the local citizens by governments other than the municipality. Of the range of services in the top half of the table, the city formally participates in only two, public health and inspection of commercial establishments, and in these only to a relatively minor degree.

Second, the activities for which Casa Grande has no formal responsibility are nevertheless shared functions. Only two federal activities—the postal service and the loans of the Farmers Home Administration—do not involve the state and *some* local government, or both. In even these two cases, state-local influence is not inconsiderable.[10] One state function, inspection of boilers and weights and measures, does not involve the federal government, but this is more the result of the classification scheme than of any real separation of functions: the federal government is heavily involved in the closely related and overlapping functions of providing for industrial safety and the purity of food and drugs.

Third, still focusing attention on the top portion of the table, in those functions which are not the responsibility of the city of Casa Grande, other local governments have important roles. These include the county, the special governments for education and for the hospital, and the federally sponsored or stimulated local governments in the large-spending agricultural programs and in Selective Service.

Fourth, without discounting the importance of the nonmunicipal local governments in the functions listed in Part 1 of the table, it can be said that the county is assigned its functions largely as an administrative arm of the state, and that the local governments for agricultural programs and for Selective Service are created specifically to administer federal programs. It is therefore obvious that, with the important exceptions of education and the hospital, the top half of the table represents a range of functions in which the federal and state governments take the leading role in providing services to the local community.

Fifth, the activities in which Casa Grande plays an important role (Part 2 of the table) are also activities to which the federal government makes a major contribution. No function of the municipality, as recorded in its own budget, is omitted from this listing. With only three exceptions, the budgeted local functions are also federal functions. And again the exceptions result largely from accidents of the classificatory scheme. Without doing violence to common sense, for example, it could be said that the

---

[10] The Farmers Home Administration does not make loans directly but guarantees the payment of loans made by private local banks; services to farmers who make loans involve the local representative of the Farmers Home Administration in a multitude of ties with local and state officers.

federal government has markedly influenced garbage disposal in Casa Grande through its aid in the fly control program and the sewage system. No direct federal participation was noted in recreation. Yet the federal government's virtual gift of the Mountain Park is probably the most important single factor in the future of the city's recreation program. Since recreation is carried as an item separate from parks in the city budget, however, it is shown in the table as not including a federal linkage. Finally, the city library has so far not profited from federal contributions. But the library is eligible for assistance under the federal Library Services Act and undoubtedly will take advantage of the program in the relatively near future.

In sum, then, the federal government supplies more services to the citizens of Casa Grande without the participation of the city of Casa Grande than the city provides without the participation of the federal government. Local services are not exclusively or principally the province of local governments. All governments in the American system provide local services. And the characteristic means of providing any given service is through the collaboration of several governments.

III. ARKANSAS SMALL TOWN IN THE
YEAR OF LITTLE ROCK

The mixture of governments at the local level is not unique to Casa Grande, Arizona. On the contrary. What exists in Casa Grande also appears to exist throughout the country. Yet the universality of the fact is matched by an almost equally universal nonrecognition of it. Slogans and sentiments of home rule are strong, and many state and federal services in the local community are unobtrusive or, if obtrusive, are looked upon as aberrations. The local citizen frequently has his eyes focused on other matters. Even the local official is a poor witness to the facts of his own day-to-day existence.

So it is that the city manager of a small midwestern town emphatically told an interviewer that he had nothing whatever to do with federal programs or federal agencies and never wanted to. He was interrupted by a message from a radio receiver at his back; and in the next ten minutes he gave radio messages to a street maintenance crew, the chief of police, and a member of the fire department. He turned away from his business with the remark that he could never get his day's work done without the convenience of the short-wave two-way radio. The interviewer ventured the opinion that the system looked expensive as well as efficient. The manager said it was, but added with satisfaction: "Of course the Civil Defense Administration paid for most of it." The discovery of this federal contact soon led to many others. Similar initial blank spots were frequently encountered. As fish in water have little occasion to consider the fact of wetness, so those most involved may be insensitive to the intermeshing of governments.

There are, of course, variations in the impact of the federal and state governments on the local scene. The more significant fact, however, is the apparent universality of governmental sharing. No completely conclusive test of universality has been made. But studies carried out in randomly chosen smaller towns and cities all showed remarkably similar results, as typified by the extensive mixture of federal-state-local responsibilities in Casa Grande. As a further, if still not conclusive, test it was decided to investigate sharing—and especially federal contributions—in what, *a priori,* seemed to be a least likely place for it to flourish.

The year 1958 was a period of bitter controversy over the school desegregation decision of the Supreme Court. The center of controversy was Little Rock, Arkansas. On September 24, 1957, President Eisenhower sent federal troops to Little Rock following Governor Orval Faubus' use of the National Guard to enforce segregation in the Little Rock high school. Tempers in the city and in the state ran high. Jokes about the "military occupation in Little Rock" did not efface the seriousness of the clash between national and state officers. The city's population was divided in a number of ways, large fractions experiencing bitterness against both the Governor and the President. Little Rock itself would have been a good "hard-case" test for the prevalence of federal-local relationships during a period of intergovernmental crisis. But for practical and technical reasons, it was decided to examine the city closest to Little Rock (a) that had a population of more than 5,000 and less than 10,000 and (b) that did not appear to have any particular dependence upon the federal government.[11] The town so chosen was Benton, some 24 miles southwest of Little Rock, with a 1950 population of 6,500 grown, according to a special 1957 census, to 10,148.

Our field worker soon discovered that, far from being minimally affected by the federal government, Benton booms because of federal interest in the nation's largest deposits of bauxite (the raw material from which

[11] The smaller place was chosen in order to provide data comparable to that about other places studied intensively. In addition, it was believed that Little Rock, like other large cities, would inevitably have a far larger number of important federal contacts than nearby smaller places. Finally, a complete case study of a city so large (102,213 in 1950) was prohibitively expensive.

aluminum is made) which are nearby. In 1941, under the pressure of international emergency, factories for the processing of bauxite were opened near Benton by the Reynolds Aluminum Company and the Aluminum Company of America. These plants were built under authority of the War Production Board and financed by the Reconstruction Finance Corporation. A number of other possible sites were under consideration. Benton and Arkansas officials and businessmen, including an official Arkansas lobbyist then resident in Washington, fought hard and successfully to have the plants located in Benton. The 1941 action of the national government, steered by local lobbying and cheered by the entire population, accounts in largest measure for the growth of the city.[12] Benton had more children in school in 1958 than its total population in 1941.

Still, the extensive network of national-local relationships existing in Benton in 1958 (see Table 8) was only to a minor degree the consequence of the location of the alumina plants. Benton schools have profited greatly from federal grants because it has been possible to demonstrate the impact of the federally financed plants upon the school population.[13] The city's only high school was largely paid for with $506,000 of federal funds. One of the four elementary schools was similarly aided. These federal funds came to the community as the direct result of the federally sponsored expansion of the bauxite industry during the Korean War. But other forms of federal assistance to the schools have not been the consequence of this unique circumstance. Still a third school, for example, has added to its plant two large buildings declared surplus by an army camp a short distance away. A steady stream of other surplus property also reached the schools, very much as it did in Arizona. The schools participated in the school lunch and milk program, and the high school received federal aid for vocational and agricultural education.

At a time when federal troops were guarding the nearby Little Rock high school, the school superintendent of Benton chose not to speak at all about segregation and described in terms of high praise the entire range of federal services to his schools. Without them, he said, education would

[12] There is an instructive irony in trying at a distance to choose a place that was not particularly affected by federal programs and selecting in the process a city whose prosperity depends upon a plant built 17 years previously with federal funds. This unexpected result of the selecting process is itself testimony to another anomaly: the widespread nature of the "unique federal contact," discussed below.

[13] An act of September 23, 1950, subsequently amended, provides federal contributions for schools in "federally-affected" areas. The legislation authorizes financial grants for planning school construction as well as for construction itself. Financial aid for general school purposes is also provided in compensation for local tax losses as the consequence of property acquisitions by the federal government. Definitions of "affected" areas are detailed and complex. See 64 *U.S. Stat.* 967–978, c. 995.

have suffered greatly in Benton. Federal aid had stimulated greater local effort. He hoped that new legislation would make possible additional federal funds for the construction of still another school. Federal assistance had led to no interference of any sort.

The location of alumina plants in Benton by the federal government led indirectly to another important federal contribution to the city: a dam and reservoir. This facility, used principally as a reserve water supply, and for simple recreation purposes, was obtained when civic and business leaders, as a result of the city's industrial expansion, saw the need for developing new water resources. They attempted to have the dam constructed with federal funds under then-existing legislation. When their project failed to qualify for federal aid as a standard rivers and harbors project, they utilized the data gathered by the Corps of Engineers to secure federal funds under the newly enacted Community Facilities Act. Indeed, the community leaders of Benton firmly believe that they were instrumental in having new legislation passed that made possible the use of federal funds for their purposes.[14] The principal argument before Congress was that the federal industrial plants justified the use of federal funds for insuring a continued ample supply of water to the city.

School aid and water supply were the only two items in Benton's bundle of governmental services produced by the city's "unique" federal contact, the bauxite field development. Other services were also delivered to residents of the city by a *mélange* of collaborative governments. Of the functions for which the city had little responsibility (see Table 8), there were four points of particular interest.

1. The county health officer, or "sanitarian" as he was officially titled, exemplified in his person the whole idea of the marble cake of government. His particular case has already been described in Chapter One.

2. As in Casa Grande there were in Benton many urban consumers of the agricultural services of the federal government, the state, and the federally engineered local governments. To take but a single example, the county agricultural extension agent estimated that at least 10 per cent of his time was spent serving the citizens of Benton on matters relating to gardens, trees, livestock, and insect control. One of the county's home demonstration clubs was composed exclusively of women from the city, and a number of other Benton residents were members of nearby rural home demonstration groups. Landscape gardening was an important emerging "urban agricultural" activity of the extension service.

[14] The case discussed more fully below, pp. 246–48, neatly illustrates how even small towns can shape federal legislation.

TABLE 8

THE BUNDLE OF GOVERNMENTAL SERVICES PROVIDED THE RESIDENTS OF
BENTON, ARKANSAS, 1958

Service	City of Benton	Special District	County of Saline	Special Local Government Engineered by U.S.	State of Arkansas	United States
1. Activities for which city government has little or no responsibility.[a]						
Agricultural conservation and stabilization				**	*	**
Agricultural extension			**		**	**
Bank examinations and deposit insurance					**	**
Education		**	**		**	**
Employment security					**	**
Farmers Home Administration						**
Industrial safety					**	*
Inspecting boilers, weights and measures, other commercial inspection	**		*		**	
Inspecting food and drugs			**		**	**
Labor relations					**	**
Postal service						**
Public health	*		**		**	**
Public welfare			**		**	**
Selective Service				*	**	**
Soil Conservation Service			*	**	*	**
2. Activities for which city government has important responsibilities.						
City planning and zoning	**				**	(b)
Civil Defense	**		*		**	**
Fire protection	**				**	
Garbage disposal	**				*	
Library	**				**	(c)
Parks	**					
Police	**		**		**	**
Public utilities	**d	**			*	**
Recreation	**				*	**
Sewage disposal	**				**	(b)
Streets and highways	**		*		**	**

** Major role, * Minor role.
[a] This section of the table is abbreviated and is only meant to be illustrative.
[b] Federal aid pending.
[c] Federal aid under discussion.
[d] Utilities are operated under a three-man commission appointed for life by city council.

3. The national Bureau of the Census has been an unexpected source of assistance to the city. State financial aid in Arkansas, as in many other states, is based upon national census data. The more people officially counted, the more state aid received. A growing city can profit from special interdecennial censuses, and Benton has done just that. It has contracted with the Census Bureau on several occasions for up-to-date enumerations of its population. Each time, the special federal count produced new income for the city from the state. The city paid the federal government $1,900 for its last special census. Under the state-aid formula that gives four dollars per capita to the city, Benton gained $5,000 of extra income annually from this enumeration. The city fathers consider this a profitable transaction, and they are duly grateful to the federal government for making the special enumerations both possible and inexpensive.

4. As in Casa Grande, welfare services were provided through the collaboration of federal, state, and county governments. The welfare program of Saline County included the distribution to needy persons of surplus commodities provided by the United States Department of Agriculture. The county welfare department, utilizing state standards, determined eligibility. Federal officers regularly visited the county department to be certain that federal regulations were satisfied. Actual distribution of the commodities was undertaken under the supervision of the county judge. A majority of those in the county who received surplus food were residents of Benton.

The activities for which city officials have major responsibilities (Part 2 of the Table) were for the most part also activities of other governments. Both the city and county police departments, for example, had the usual contacts with federal law enforcement agencies. One unusually important relationship was with the alcohol control division of the Treasury Department: moonshining and bootlegging constituted a major source of rural Arkansas crime. Consultation between local and federal officers was continuous with respect to these problems, and occasionally they joined forces in staging a raid. On the other hand the local police departments had not yet profited, unlike many other local police systems, from federal Civil Defense aid for the purchase of radio equipment. This partly reflected the underdeveloped state of civil defense activity in Benton and the county, local officers generally having a poor opinion of both the federal and state programs.

The city government, which received substantial aid from the state for street maintenance, was confronted with an unusual street problem as the consequence of federal action. A link of the federal-aid interstate highway system was built through Benton, separating the western third of the city (its area of greatest growth) from the remaining two-thirds, which contained most of the city's public facilities. This new highway replaced the old route through the heart of Benton, which had brought numerous benefits to the city. Federal-state funds had built and maintained its principal street, and the highway had brought tourist and other traffic to the local merchants. This combination of dislocations provoked the major conflict between the city fathers and the federal and state highway agencies. The expanding city was faced in 1958 with planning a new network of streets that would efficiently link local traffic to the limited number of access points of the new highway. Characteristically (for the governmental system of shared functions), the city of Benton proposed to solve the local problems created by a highway built by the state with federal assistance, by turning (with state assistance) to the federal government.

Benton had profited from neither city planning nor zoning. In 1958 the city council appointed a planning commission under the chairmanship of a former employee of the U.S. Bureau of Internal Revenue. This act was stimulated by problems emerging from the new highway, as well as by other difficulties consequent to rapid growth, and it made clear the city's need and desire for federal aid in planning. The state statute that authorized cities to accept federal funds for planning purposes established the University of Arkansas as the official state intermediary.[15] The University's Planning Division was prepared to process Benton's application for the federal grant, draw up the city's master plan once the grant was made, and train local personnel in planning and zoning techniques so that efforts at achieving effective land use would be continuous.

Officers of Benton were confident in the summer of 1958 that their planning grant would soon be forthcoming from the Housing and Home Finance Agency. They were also looking forward to the successful conclusion of negotiations with the U.S. Public Health Service that would bring financial aid for a new sewage system. State legislation here, as with planning, required the participation of a state agency (the Public Health Service); but in this case actual negotiations with federal officials were being carried on directly by city officers and by a private engineering firm action on behalf of the city.

Benton, like Casa Grande and other cities, carried on a few functions unaffected, or affected minimally, by federal contacts. In this category were

---

[15] This is in nice contrast to the situation in Arizona where the state's role was purely a formal one and where the actual work for Casa Grande's federal planning grant, including the processing of applications, was undertaken by a private engineering firm.

recreation, fire protection, garbage disposal, and library services. Except for fire protection, definitions would not have to be strained greatly to establish federal-local relationships. The Benton Library, to consider only one case, was greatly aided during the depression when its operations were assumed by the Public Works Administration. During this time the entire book collection was reconditioned. Benton's congressman supplied the library with materials from the government printing office. And most importantly, Benton librarians in 1958 were making active plans to transform their library into a regional facility so that it would qualify for financial aid under the federal Library Services Act. The state had already profited considerably from this act, receiving in 1957–58 more than $107,000 in federal funds. Some of this money had trickled down to Benton. But federal aid would become direct and substantial only when a number of local citizens, who were responsible for the development of the library, became convinced of the desirability of having it serve the entire county, thus making it eligible to receive federal funds.

Benton, even in embattled Arkansas in 1958, presented no exception to the important general characteristic of the American system at the local level: many governments, through processes of amiable collaboration, supplied most local services. As in other places, more governmental services were provided the citizens of Benton by the federal and state governments, without the substantial participation of the city government, than by the city government without the participation of the others. And virtually all programs of city government were shared with the federal government. Casa Grande and Benton were far more similar than dissimilar in these respects. Local officers of the Arizona town were more rapid in taking advantage of federal aid for planning and sewage than Benton officials.[16] But this was only a difference in timing and reflected no basic difference in posture towards the federal government: Benton in the summer of 1958 was awaiting favorable federal action for these very purposes. Casa Grande's "'unique'" federal contracts resulted from the existence of huge acreages of public domain in the nearby desert, and the city airfield and mountain park represented the city's ability to bring about public land transfers from federal to local ownership. The Benton analogue was the city's success in locating the alumina plants and its subsequent ability to capitalize on the federal school construction program and to alter national legislation to make possible a reserve water supply. In both cities,

[16] This was more a reflection of the energies of Casa Grande's full-time city manager than anything else. Benton had no chief executive officer as such, the part-time mayor taking responsibility for some major problems, a clerk handling routine matters, and the manager of the utilities department (established under state law as a quasi-independent government) supplying leadership in most areas of local government.

activities carried on without actual or forthcoming federal participation are relatively unimportant. In both cities the sharing of functions is the characteristic mode of providing local services.

Benton's schools were still segregated in 1958, and this represents an exception to the general picture of aimable intergovernmental collaboration.[17] The significance of the exception can be easily overestimated. Of more than 40 officials and civic leaders interviewed in Benton, only one broached the issue of school segregation. He did so apologetically. No defense of Governor Faubus' actions in Little Rock was offered in Benton. Little Rock, on the contrary, seemed to make Benton officials anxious to demonstrate their greater moderation. Whatever covert hostilities may have existed, one fact is clear: neither school desegregation in general nor the Little Rock situation in particular disturbed in any way the widespread, easy quality of federal-local relationships, including federal-local relationships with respect to education.

Casa Grande also has experienced, in the not too distant past, points of tension with the federal government. Its officers and citizens were implacably opposed during the depression to the location nearby of a Rural Resettlement Project. The collapse of this venture, still referred to with some bitterness as "little Russia," was hailed with glee. And even more recently the community displayed intense hostility to the wartime Gila River Japanese Relocation Center, established on Indian reservation land just north of the city. These situations, as well as the failure of Benton to desegregate its schools, were evidence of antagonisms within a general climate of cooperation. They demonstrate that institutions and communites, like individuals, have many facets of personality. Cordial and abrasive relationships can exist simultaneously. For both Benton and Casa Grande, the larger drift is clearly in the direction of cooperation and cordiality.

Benton was founded as a way station on a major military road when Arkansas was still a national territory. Its schools were provided by a federal land grant. Its first period of growth in the nineteenth century followed the coming of a railroad (now the Missouri Pacific), made possible by land grants from both the federal and the state governments. A period of relative stagnation followed, broken by the bauxite boom under federal auspices.

The periods during which the city neither grew nor prospered were periods of relative federal inactivity. This is not to say that the federal government has been responsible for what has happened in Benton. For recent years, at least, the initiative of local officers, businessmen, and civic leaders has been the controlling factor. Federal programs have made the

[17] A discussion of federalism and desegregation is contained in Chapter Eleven.

opportunities, and local people have capitalized upon them. Expansion of the city and federal-local cooperation have gone hand in hand. The state has played an important role, too, providing the necessary legal sanctions, considerable technical assistance, and assuming many new administrative burdens. Local people do not look upon federal programs as largesse. They feel that they must justify them in national as well as in local terms. Despite the existence of strain with respect to segregation, and other less important annoyances (over civil defense, for example), local officers think of federal officers as "fine, friendly, and cooperative" people. Federal rules are not considered onerous. The federal-local relationship is looked upon as a necessity for the further development of the community, good for city and nation alike.

IV. VARIATIONS IN STATE AND FEDERAL IMPACT ON THE LOCAL SCENE

State-by-state differences in the impact of the state government on the local scene are differences in degree, not in kind. State constitutional provisions vary with respect to the extent to which the state legislature is allowed to concern itself with local affairs. Legislative ingenuity and judicial interpretation have, in effect, reduced these variations, and no constitutional provisions have anywhere effectively protected local governments from special legislative enactments. The protection, where it exists, is political, not legal. Classification devices have made it possible to legislate for specific localities despite constitutional prohibitions against special, local legislation. Each of California's 58 counties has been classified, for example, so that a law for all counties in a given classification may apply to only one county. General classification laws in at least nine states place only one city in a given class: Indianapolis is the only first-class city in Indiana, Louisville the only one in Kentucky, Philadelphia the only one in Pennsylvania. Finally, many laws set forth their own classification, a process by which state legislatures are able to group cities in one law, to separate them in another, to separate them in different ways in a third, and to isolate them in a fourth. Legislative inventiveness is sometimes great. A law in Minnesota refers to "counties now or hereafter having 24 organized townships and a population of not less than 23,500 and not more than 24,000, and a land area of not less than 795 and not more than 805 square miles." Such laws are almost always deemed legal by the state courts.[18]

[18] If a classification is "reasonable," the state court will ordinarily sustain it. The courts have considered it their duty, in the words of an Alabama decision, "not to

They are also considered necessary by the localities concerned. Although no exact calculation is available, there can be no doubt that the preponderant portion of special legislation applicable to local governments is legislation requested by those localities. The attempt to separate state-local spheres of action by prohibitions against special legislation doesn't work. If it does work, as experience for short periods in Ohio and other states has indicated, it proves cumbersome and embarrassing to the localities themselves.

In constitutional home-rule states as well as in states where no home rule exists, a short rope may tie city affairs to the state legislature. In North Carolina a town was forced to have the legislature pass a special law in order that the council might declare it a misdemeanor to use roller skates, bicycles, or scooters on the sidewalks. In Maryland a special statute was needed to increase the annual salary of a local government stenographer by $300. In Kentucky, Louisville found it necessary to secure a special law giving it authority to condemn property for off-street parking purposes; when city officials decided they wished to lease the property to private operators, a second law had to be secured.

The question and answer columns of a single issue of the publication of the Iowa Municipal League illustrates the extent to which local governments are dependent upon state legislature authorization. An official of one small town inquired if the town council might purchase uniforms for the members of its police force; an officer of a second municipality wanted to know if the city could assess property owners for the cost of paving a sidewalk which extended from the benefited property to the corner curb; a third town asked if it would be possible to raise the salaries of underpaid council members; and a fourth official inquired if city funds might be used to erect a civic plaque, listing the names of local men and women serving in the armed forces. It would be difficult to find four spheres of governmental activity that would seem to be more "purely local" in character than police officers' uniforms, special assessments for sidewalks, the salary of city councilmen, and the erection of a war memerial. In each case, nevertheless, the city was advised that no state law existed under which the proposed project might be achieved.[19]

construe a law as local when it is so *worded* as to be interpreted as a general one . . . ." If an act is general in language, its validity is not affected by the fact that it applies only to a single locality. Thus, state legislatures are freed by the courts to legislate for specific localities under the fiction of general (classified) laws. This discussion, and the paragraphs that follow, are derived from *State-Local Relations* (Chicago: Council of State Governments, 1946), Parts 2 and 5.

[19] *American Municipalities* (Marshalltown, Iowa: Municipal Publishing Company). Vol. LXIX, No. 12 (September, 1945), pp. 28, 30–31.

State involvement of this sort is by no means confined to small or medium-sized cities. Chicago's charter is a vast document, containing more than 600,000 words. It details many functions which the city can, and cannot, perform. Its very length constitutes an impediment to local discretion. As the late Ernest Freund remarked, "Since practically every charter, being a binding state law, constitutes in the absence of saving clauses a limitation, it follows that the volume of a charter is generally in an inverse proportion to the home rule which it bestows."[20] Thus, in the absence of a specific statute, Chicago was powerless to regulate the maintenance of refrigeration systems employing deadly gases. The city was likewise without the discretionary power to require the examination and licensing of automobile drivers. It was necessary for the city to secure legislative sanction when it desired to consolidate its 22 park districts, all of which were located within the city's boundaries; and still another legislative act was necessary to consolidate the park and city police forces. In the municipal tax crisis of the 1930's, the city's Advisory Committee and Recovery Administration discovered that statutory enactments or constitutional amendments were required for each of their detailed recommendations for relieving the city's financial distress.[21] At the other extreme the city also needed special legislative authorization when it wished to regulate peanut vendors on the municipal pier.

Chicago's situation is not markedly different from that of other cities. In Boston the state-local mixture reaches its extreme. The state legislature (General Court) considers approximately 100 bills in each annual session with respect to special Boston problems. In addition, the city's police commissioner is appointed by, and responsible to, the governor of the Commonwealth. The Boston Finance Committee, which sets taxes, is appointed by the governor and reports to the legislature. And the Boston Licensing Board and Arena Authority are also appointed by the governor.[22]

The general dependence of localities on state legislation does not erase state-to-state differences with respect to legislative involvement in day-to-day local affairs. Colorado municipal home rule is established in the constitution and is maintained by political tradition. Cities have great leeway in determining taxes and functions with little reference to the state leg-

---

[20] Quoted in Barnet Hodes, *Law in the Modern City* (Chicago: Reilly and Lee, 1937), p. 36. Albert Lepawsky has said that the law of municipal corporations amounts to "the law of municipal limitations" (*Home Rule for Metropolitan Chicago* [Chicago: University of Chicago Press, 1935], p. 121).

[21] With respect to the limitations on Chicago's power, see Hodes, *op. cit.*, pp. 36–39; Lepawsky, *op. cit.*, pp. xiii, xv.

[22] League of Women Voters of Massachusetts, *Massachusetts State Government* (Cambridge, Mass.: Harvard University Press, 1956), p. 357.

islature. In Wisconsin, general permissive legislation, combined with home rule, is also effective in allowing localities a relatively large scope of discretionary action. But even in such states the absence of state involvement in local affairs is only a relative matter. The legal and financial dependence of localities upon states, the almost complete overlapping of functional responsibilities, and the unity of their politics make these two "levels" of government a single enterprise.

This conclusion is strengthened if one examines the administrative supervision by states over local units of government. Again variation exists. For example, in a majority of states there are no general merit systems covering local personnel. But ten states provide such supervision, and in some cases it is extensive. Massachusetts, for example, exercises direct control over merit examinations and general personnel policies of all cities. The service is optional for towns, and, when a town becomes a city, its entire service becomes classified under close state supervision. Similarly, variations exist in state administrative supervision over education, welfare, highways, public health, conservation, police, recreation, licensing, taxing, and other fiscal and nonfiscal operations. Whatever the variations, the trend is nevertheless clearly in the direction of greater state administrative supervision. This infrequently takes the form of state orders or state coercion. Supervision, rather, is largely a matter of local reporting to state offices, state auditing of local financial transactions, and state professional workers consulting with their local counterparts. States and local units everywhere have become more and more involved in the same activities and to an ever-increasing degree have had to work out collaborative working arrangements. The development has been hastened directly by federal grants to states that require statewide standards for services often performed by local units, and indirectly by the increasing tempo of federal-local contacts, as when states establish supervisory airport or housing agencies following federal grants to cities for these purposes.

Variations in the federal impact upon the local scene are greater than variations in state impact. But, again, the larger fact is the universality of federal involvement.

State laws produce some differences in federal-local relationships. Legislation in some states, for example, does not allow municipalities, or only allows those of specified population, to participate in federal low-cost housing and urban development programs. Some states (Indiana is an example) do not participate fully in vocational education and welfare programs, thus altering federal activity at the local level. Even where states participate fully in federal programs, differences in the controlling legislation establish different federal-local patterns. For example, in approximately half of the states, negotiations for national airport aid by even the largest cities must be channeled through a state agency; but in the other states direct federal-local negotiations may be carried on. The difference in some cases is a difference of form rather than substance. Even where "channeling" of local applications and national funds through state agencies is required, the locality itself may carry on the detailed negotiation, the state's role remaining *pro forma*.

Where federal grant programs exist, insistent local pressures have the effect of bringing state laws into a rough approximation of each other. The development is not completely uniform, and state situations differ. It is no accident, for example, that the four states which have not (1959) authorized their localities to participate in nationally aided low-cost housing programs are Iowa, Oklahoma, Utah, and Wyoming, states in which urbanization is not highly developed and in which the state legislatures have a high degree of immunity from urban population groups. The last factor is probably the controlling one. The general overrepresentation of rural interests in state legislatures undoubtedly accounts for the near-uniform state legislation that takes fullest possible advantage of federal aid to agriculture.

To say that state laws, with relatively small variation, have implemented federal grant legislature is only to say that the grant legislation has achieved its purpose. The intent of the national grant, after all, is to utilize the national spending power to create nationwide programs. Federal grant programs further erase differences between states (and between localities in given states) by allocating funds according to formulae that spread funds among the states. Though some grants vary according to rough criteria of need and fiscal capacity, they are nevertheless made to encourage every state to partcipate in all programs. The allocation process, reflecting the strong localism of the national legislature, has never been designed for any program so as to eliminate federal funds for certain states, though there is no doubt that this would occur if the criteria of need were the only ones utilized. Despite varying allocation formulae, therefore, the grant-in-aid device has the effect of making federal-local relationships more uniform throughout the country.

The very multiplicity of available federal services also reduces variations in federal-local contracts. The task of simply enumerating federal functions on the local scene is a bewildering one, and the description of federal activities in Casa Grande and Benton only suggests the full range of the local activities of the federal government. A bare listing of "federal services to cities and towns" covers 74 pages and ranges from "abbatoirs" and "adminstrative management" to "zoning" and "zoo administration."[23] If a city officer wants aid and technical information on how to combat hazards from gas explosions—sewer gas, methane, carbon monoxide, and others—the Bureau of Mines of the Department of the Interior will investigate causes, advise on methods of conservation, and recommend safe practices. If a city is having difficulties in tracing a water distribution or sewage disposal route, the Geological Survey (also in the Department of the Interior) has available a whole set of technical aids including topographic maps and aerial photographs. If local health authorities wish to consider the use of sodium fluoride in dental health programs, they can get full information from the Division of Dental Public Health, Public Health Service, Department of Health, Education, and Welfare.

The Library of Congress provides many aids to municipal libraries and the United States Office of Education many services to local schools. The National Bureau of Standards, Department of Commerce, has for perplexed local officers model codes covering building, fire prevention, plumbing, electrical and masonry work, elevators, industrial safety, and other matters. A model milk ordinance is available from the Public Health Service. The city may be beautified by advice on grass suitable for the local climate and soil from the Bureau of Plant Industry, Soils, and Agricultural Engineering of the Department of Agriculture; it can receive consultation on beach erosion from the Corps of Engineers of the Army; it can be given free fish for its reservoir or lake—and free buffalo, deer, elk, and other animals for its zoo—from the Fish and Wildlife Service of the Department of the Interior; and if it has a surplus of such animals, it may exchange them for more exotic kinds (assuming equal value) with the National Zoological Garden of the Smithsonian Institution. In the event of disaster, federal emergency funds of the President and loans of federal property are available. The military services or the Coast Guard, or both, will supply emergency equipment to open roads, clear debris, and transport food and medical supplies; will make available standby generators, emergency water supplies, fire-fighting and heavy construction equipment, communication facilities, medical personnel, and policing; and will give

[23] Robert H. Blundred and Donoh W. Hanks, Jr., *Federal Services to Cities and Towns* (Chicago: American Municipal Association, 1950). The pioneer listing is Paul V. Betters, *Federal Services to Municipal Governments* (New York: Municipal Administration Service, 1931). See also Wylie Kilpatrick and Staff, "Federal Relations to Urban Governments," in the Supplementary Report of the Urbanism Committee to the National Resources Committee, *Urban Government* (Washington, D.C.: Government Printing Office, 1939), Vol. I, Part II; Office of Area Development, U.S. Department of Commerce, *Federal Activities Helpful to Communities* (Washington, D.C.: Government Printing Office, 1958).

free use of an aerial ambulance service. The Public Health Service will give aid in combating epidemics. If the event is a civic celebration rather than a disaster, it may be enlivened through federal participation by air shows (consult Civic Aeronautics Administration, Department of Commerce); troops, bands, "fly-overs," and mechanical vehicles (consult Department of Defense or Coast Guard, Treasury Department); and art or library exhibits (consult National Gallery of Art, Smithsonian Institution, and Library of Congress).

The smorgasbord of federal services is thus one of infinite variety. It extends to those fields that, in Casa Grande and Benton, were relatively untouched by federal contracts: fire protection, for example. Federal aids in this area exist and have been widely used, though private insurance and equipment associations have assumed many of the "federal" functions in this field.[24] As for the federal government itself, the National Bureau of Standards, Department of Commerce, will supply information to municipalities on the regulation and inspection of fire hazards and advice on the use and installation of fire alarm equipment. The Forest Service of the Department of Agriculture will give technical aid for the establishment of special fire districts, and the Service also contracts with municipal governments for protecting municipal forests and watersheds; it also trains local personnel in a special Forest Service fire school. The Bureau of Mines, Department of the Interior, will investigate causes and recommend corrections for fire hazards resulting from gas, petroleum products, mineral dusts, and other mineral substances. A President's Conference on Fire Prevention (1949) issued a widely used *Manual of Fire Loss Prevention* as well as model inspection and fire report forms. Federal aid has also been supplied for vocational education to municipal firemen. Teacher training institutes, the holding of conferences, and the preparation of instructional material have been paid for with federal funds. In 1935 fire training courses in 15 states had more than 5,500 local firemen in attendance.[25] The increasing responsibility of the federal government in civil

[24] See below, pp. 232–36.

[25] Blundred and Hanks, *op. cit.,* p. 25; Kilpatrick and Staff, *loc. cit.,* p. 88. Federal participation in recreation programs of local governments is also not inconsiderable. Ignoring the primary role of the quasi-federal American Red Cross, federal contributions to local recreational programs include advice and assistance from the extension service of the Department of Agriculture; use of federal surplus land for recreational purposes, through the Departments of Agriculture and the Interior and the General Services Administration; development of river bank recreational areas through the Army Corps of Engineers of the Department of the Defense; and development of recreational facilities on national forest land through the Forest Service of the Department of Agriculture. In addition, influential demonstration programs in recreation have been worked out cooperatively between local governments and a

defense activities will undoubtedly lead to its playing a larger role in local fire prevention and fire-fighting training as well as increase the federal contribution to the equipment of local fire departments.

One type of federal program does produce important variations in federal-local contracts. These result from legislation granting funds to local governments because of the special impact of federal activities. An important program of this sort supplies educational aid (school construction and general support) to school districts whose student body is materially affected by nearby federal installations or federal contractors. The Benton schools, as we have seen, profited greatly from this sort of assistance. A different sort of "impact" law provides federal payments "in lieu of" taxes to local governments on property held for national purposes. There are more than 50 statutory provisions for such payments.[26] Variations in local-federal contracts of another sort result from local ownership of street-car and bus lines, airports, radio stations, and power projects. Municipal owners, like private ones, are subject to the regulations of the Interstate Commerce Commission, Civil Aeronautics Administration, Federal Communications Commission, and Federal Power Commission. Finally, the proximity of a city to a national forest may produce a special federal relationship for the purchase of water or for recreation purposes; localities in the TVA area have many special contacts with that agency, especially for the purchase of power; and other federal installations, whether a research laboratory, munitions depot, or federal prison, basically affect the economic and social life of a given locality.

Federal "impact" laws, the location of federal industrial plants, federal ownership of land, and other such factors produce what might appear to be unique federal-local relationships. But the unique relationship is paradoxically quite general. It does not produce the variation in federal impact on the local scene that one might expect. National government activities are vast in scope. And the ingenuity of local officials to tap federal resources is also not negligible. Localities, large and small, in all parts of the country, whether or not in areas affected directly by federal programs, evolve their own unique relationships with the federal government.

number of federal agencies, notably the Children's Bureau of the Department of Health, Education, and Welfare. For evidence of the considerable impact of federal assistance on the recreational program of a single city, see Ellis McCune, *Inter-Governmental Co-operation in Recreation Administration in the Los Angeles Area* (Los Angeles: Bureau of Governmental Research, University of California, Los Angeles, 1954), pp. 26–27.

[26] *Federal Land Ownership and the Public Land Laws,* a Report on Taxes and Other In-Lieu Payments on Federal Property, prepared by Legislative Reference Service, Library of Congress, for the Committee on Interior and Insular Affairs, House of Representatives, Committee Print No. 23, 83rd Congress, 1954.

In Casa Grande, the great civic achievements of the past years were all the result of federal collaboration. The sewage plant was the result of the city officials taking advantage of a nationwide federal program. But the city's airport and the mountain park were possible by the availability of nearby federally owned land. The "uniqueness" of Casa Grande's relationship to the federal government, it then can be said, was based upon the existence of large tracts of the public domain adjacent to the city. In Benton, Arkansas, and Borger, Texas, striking expansion was the result of successful civic efforts to have federal plants located nearby. Borger's proudest acquisition, its community hotel, was again the consequence of combined city-civic pressure that produced a Reconstruction Finance Corporation loan to cover the major fraction of the hotel's construction costs. In Allegan, Michigan, the fact that the city's biggest source of income, its electrical generating plant, was situated on a navigable stream resulted in important, special relationships between the city officials and the Federal Power Commission. In Ashtabula, Ohio (and the case is duplicated in many other localities), civic and business leaders saw that opportunities for future growth—specifically, the development of the city as a major port on the St. Lawrence waterway—depended upon the United States Corps of Engineers.

One can conclude that the generality of the federal government's importance in local affairs is far more significant than the variation. Even unique federal contacts are general.

A second conclusion is that the variations that do exist are products of local energy and political organization. They are not the result of design or accident so far as the federal government is concerned. Federal legislation cannot require state or local participation in any activity, but the availability of federal funds, as we have seen, produces virtually unanimous state participation at least in the great grant programs and, in turn, a general local impact of those programs. Within the grant programs— and just as importantly outside of them—there are wide areas for the play of local energies and the local mobilization of political forces (see Chapter Eight). Substantive federal programs and federal technical skills to aid localities are available in a multitude of areas; and the federal purse can be opened for local advantage in a multitude of ways. How localities moblize themselves to take advantage of what the federal government offers becomes the crucial factor in the extent to which the federal government affects the local unit.

Influence potentials and influence skills of local leaders vary, thus producing the chief variations in federal impact on the local scene. But the distribution of influence is widespread, and so is sensitivity among local leaders concerning the importance of federal contributions to their communities. So, again (and this is the third conclusion), the similarities in local influence efforts are more important than the differences. Ideas or theories about the proper role of the government at the local level have very little to do with the extent to which localities attempt to direct federal programs to local ends. Nether party nor regional difference seem to affect the local desire to take full advantage, and frequently more than full advantage, of federal funds and federal assistance. Texans who speak strongly of home rule and the dangers of Washington encroachment are as anxious, and as successful, in capitalizing upon federal programs for local purposes as those from Illinois who believe firmly in the need to increase the scope of national activities.

The extension of free enterprise to local-federal relationships produces some communities which profit handsomely and some which get less than an equitable share. But the distribution as a whole seems remarkably uniform. Federal grant-in-aid programs that blanket the nation; the anomalous generality of the unique federal-local contact; the great variety of federal services to choose from; the widespread mobilization of local influence efforts; the general informal collaboration of professional workers in many fields—all of these factors produce federal participation on the local scene that is, as far as such things ever are, universal and universally important.

Chapter 7

LOCAL IS AS LOCAL DOES

The view of the federal system as a three-layer cake invariably sees the national and state governments as separate layers stacked neatly above local government. Close under the bottom layer, as the platter on which the cake rests, is the mass of citizens. In less image-laden terms, it is almost universally stated that local governments are "closest" to the people.

The layer-cake view, and the vocabulary that goes with it, are inadequate for understanding the operation of the American system. Utilizing the concept of shared function, rather than that of separated and layered governments, this chapter analyzes the variety of state and federal impacts upon the local scene. It becomes apparent that there is no consistent correspondence between local units of government and "closeness" to the people, however closeness is defined.

I. A PARADIGM OF FEDERAL AND STATE IMPACTS ON THE LOCAL SCENE

Table 9 provides a convenient method of summarizing the variety of ways in which the federal government supplies services at the local level. One route is the direct one. No other government intervenes between agency and citizen when the national government delivers mail, or imposes an income tax, or prohibits use of channels of interstate commerce to manufacturers who do not comply with nationally defined "fair" labor standards. Similarly, disability payments for veterans and checks for those insured under the Old Age and Survivors program are mailed directly from federal offices. Contracts are negotiated directly between federal administrators and local businessmen. An FBI man may arrest you if you drive a stolen car across a state border. Where such direct federal-citizen contacts exist, it should not be assumed that the central government alone

190

TABLE 9

CHANNELS OF FEDERAL ACTIVITY ON THE LOCAL SCENE

Mode of Activity	Examples
1. Federal direct-to-people activities	Old Age and Survivors Insurance Veterans' benefits Mail delivery Taxation Licensing
2. Federally engineered local governments, relatively independent of state or local governments	Soil Conservation Agricultural Stabilization and Conservation Grazing Service Advisory Board
3. Federally engineered local governments, relatively dependent on state or local governments	Selective Service Civil Defense Rationing during World War II Public housing and urban re-development (in some states)
4. Federal grants channeled through states	Welfare, highways, employment security, forestry, vocational education, public health, etc.
5. Federal grants and other aid directly to local governments	Airports (in some states) Public housing and urban re-development (in some states) Flood control School construction (in some states) Disaster relief (in some cases) Technical assistance in many fields Services by contract

occupies a field of service or regulation. Significant sharing of functions exists in these endeavors, as in others.

A second federal avenue for local activity is through what we have called "federally engineered local governments." These are special governmental units created by the states to meet specific federal demands in order to participate in certain federal programs, whose structures and responsibilities follow precise patterns established by federal law. The United States Department of Agriculture has been primarily responsible for the proliferation of these little governments. During the 1940's it seemed to some that "the federal government was on the way to establishing its own system of local government to match that of the state."[1] In 1940, according to one estimate, almost 893,000 people were serving in one capacity or another in local governments sponsored by the Department

[1] Ylvisaker, *op. cit.*, p. 42.

of Agriculture: as directors or advisors of committees, operating personnel, or in other capacities.[2] Some of the enthusiasm disappeared from this program with the end of the New Deal and the retirement of M. L. Wilson, Undersecretary of Agriculture and chief apostle of the new "agricultural democracy." But many aspects of the system still flourish. The country is blanketed by Agricultural Stabilization and Conservation Committees, Soil Conservation Districts, Extension Service sponsoring groups, Rural Electrification Cooperatives, farm-loan associations, advisory boards for the Grazing Service, and similar instrumentalities of local government in agriculture.

Local elections are the customary way of organizing these governments. In Indiana, for example, the local ASC committee is selected by the votes of all eligible farmers in a given township, the nominees being put forward by a county selection board consisting of the County Farm Agent, the Soil Conservation Service Officer, a representative of the Farmers Home Administration, the president of the County Farm Bureau, and the president of the local Farmers Union. Township chairmen, elected by the local committee, serve as delegates to a county ASC convention which in turn elects a county committee. There is a state committee selected through similar mechanisms. Full-time local officers are appointed by both county and state committees. They work closely with the local citizens' groups and with federal employees in programs that provide federal payments under the soil bank, crop price-support, and conservation programs. State laws are of course necessary to establish this elaborate edifice of local governments for the implementation, and partial local control, of federal programs in agriculture. The federally sponsored governments work collaboratively with the regularly constituted local units, as well as with state agencies. But their mission and the scope of their action is essentially defined by federal legislative and administrative action. They are local governments under direct federal supervision.

A third channel of federal activity at the local level may also be characterized as a federally engineered local government. But here the federally engineered units are directly related to, and more immediately under the supervision of, the states or the regularly constituted local governments. These federally engineered local governments, unlike those described above, are not merely permissibly authorized by state law; they are relatively dependent upon state or local administrative offices for their day-to-day operations. The prototype of this sort of federal activity is supplied by the national Selective Service system. This program is, of course, defined

[2] Carleton R. Ball, "Citizens Help Plan and Operate Action Programs," *Land Policy Review*, Vol. III, No. 2 (March-April, 1940), pp. 19–27.

by national legislation. But it is administered through the states. State Selective Service directors are appointed by recommendation of the Governors and members of local boards, and are effectively chosen at state headquarters. Within guidelines defined in Washington, the choice of particular individuals for induction into the armed services is made by the local committees, and appeals go initially to state committees. Rationing of scarce commodities was similarly handled during World War II, and the postwar Civil Defense organization follows the same general lines, the latter becoming increasingly a state-local program that receives federal assistance. In other programs of this sort cities and counties, rather than states, play the principal intermediary role. For example, federal legislation encourages the establishment of independent or quasi-independent public housing and urban redevelopment boards.[3] Appointments to a city public housing board are usually made by the mayor, sometimes with council approval and always with state legislative authorization. The board then becomes responsible for the administration of the federally aided programs. Extensive direct local-federal contacts are maintained. The "independence" of the local housing and urban renewal boards still leaves them in most cases financially dependent upon city budgets and politically dependent upon city political leaders.

A fourth type of federal involvement at the local level is widely believed to illustrate the proper federal-local relationship and is often falsely assumed to be the only one. This is the grant-in-aid device of channeling federal funds through state offices for the provision of services at the local level. Grants of land were made by the federal government to both states and localities from the very first days of union and indeed before the Union was established. The modern cash grant began in 1884 with the Hatch Act, providing each state with funds for the establishment of agricultural experiment stations at the land-grant colleges. As with earlier land and later cash grants, regulations accompanied the federal contribution. The federal grant-in-aid to the states, now a characteristic feature of the American system, is the major device for fulfilling national programs for highways, employment security, agricultural extension, forestry, vocational education and rehabilitation, and public health.[4] Some programs by their very nature—employment security, for example—are administered at the

[3] The legislation in fact authorizes federal aid to any public housing agencies: state, county, municipality, or other government entity or public body authorized to engage in low-rent housing or slum clearance or urban renewal. In practice, quasi-independent agencies have been established to operate most of these programs on the local scene.

[4] For discussion of the grant system see Chapter Three; for fiscal problems of grants, see Chapter Fifteen.

local level through state offices. Within broad federal standards, state-by-state variations characterize other grant activities. Public assistance programs, for example, are administered directly from state offices in some states, by counties in others, and by municipalities in still others. And examples can be found of both state and local administration with and without local financial participation.

Most grant programs to states involve local officials in one way or another. Involvement ranges from the city whose main street is a federally aided highway to a county whose federally aided welfare department accounts for the major fraction of the budget. In a number of federal programs that formally channel funds for local purposes through state agencies, these agencies in fact play a minor and *pro forma* role. This was the case, for example, in the grants to Casa Grande and Benton for sewage disposal systems. But whether the state's role is *pro forma* or not is a matter of state—not federal or local—choice. When states choose to become active participants in any program carried on within their borders that directly affects their citizens, they are invariably able to do so.

This is true even in another group of grant programs that does not involve the states at all, except for passing the necessary enabling legislation. The consequent direct federal grants to local units of government are thus a fifth mode of federal activity on the local scene. Direct federal grants to localities are made for a number of programs, including watershed protection and flood control, disaster relief, school construction in "'federally-affected" areas, certain health grants, and, in some states, public housing, urban renewal, and airport construction.[5] New York, however, is actively involved in the public housing programs conducted by its local subdivisions because the state government provides financial and technical assistance alongside similar federal aids and its plans are often superior to those prepared under the aegis of Washington. No new federal-local "starts" in Arkansas were possible without the governor's approval simply because he chose to exercise his prerogatives to assign priorities for political reasons.

[5] The Federal Airport Act of 1946 authorizes the Federal Aeronautics Administration to deal directly with any airport "sponsor": state, city, county, village, or other governmental entity. The Act, however, gives states the opportunity to require localities to channel applications through state agencies. Roughly half the states allow direct local-federal relationships. In some, state grants may supplement federal money. For fuller discussion of the formulation of this act, see Chapter Ten. Though not involving grants of funds, a very large range of additional federal aids are also made directly available to local governments. These include technical advice in many fields, contractual arrangements for federal services (school curriculum surveys, for example) and contributions of many other sorts, all available on request of local officers (see above, Chapter Six).

This fivefold paradigm of federal impacts on the local scene cannot be taken as anything more than a convenient device for furthering analysis and understanding. Like all such schemes, whatever clarity it may provide is partially offset by what it hides. On the one hand it does not take into account national activities that are not "carried out" on the local scene but that may nevertheless have the greatest "local impact" of all: for example, foreign policy and military programs which may include the "local" consequence of complete destruction. On the other hand some of the distinctions established among the various avenues of federal impact on local affairs may be clearer in statement than they are in actuality. There are important technical differences, for example, between situations in which (a) the federal government channels funds through the states for local sewage disposal systems and (b) the federal government deals directly with municipalities in the planning and construction of airports. Actual operations may in fact be quite similar. In the sewage disposal program, local officers or their representatives may deal directly with federal officials, keeping the state agency informed but not expecting or receiving from it any active assistance. Thus, the channeling requirement may be practically quite meaningless. From the other direction, the states are not left out of consideration even when the federal government deals directly with local governments. Where state laws allow direct federal aid to localities for airport development, local officers are nevertheless obliged to consult state officials in order to relate their own airport plans to those of other municipalities or of the state itself. Even if this direct local-state contact with respect to airports does not take place, there are inevitable indirect contacts. State legislation is necessary in the first place to enable municipalities to construct and operate an airport. Important airport zoning regulations are dependent upon state legislation, and state police powers are directly involved in airport regulations for health and safety. Finally, localities are dependent upon state action, or lack of action, for their revenue, and no local expenditures, including airport expenditures, are possible without continuous reference to the state executive and legislature.[6]

This discussion of what the paradigm conceals has one incidental by-product: an underscoring of the point previously made that states and local units of government must perforce work together on all activities. No alterations in federal legislation with respect to the channeling of funds alters this absolute, if sometimes antagonistic, union between states and local units. The very indivisibility of state-local activities means that in some degree all local functions are also state functions. It is nevertheless

[6] See Report of the Committee on Federal Grants-in-Aid, *Federal Grants-in-Aid* (Chicago: Council of State Governments, 1949), pp. 239–40.

convenient to distinguish for states, as for the federal government, the several ways that states contribute to the bundle of local services.

All local functions must rest upon state authorizations of one sort or another. This purely permissive state role aside, the fivefold table of channels of federal activity on the local scene may be compared with three categories of local action by the states (Table 10). State governments (1)

TABLE 10

CHANNELS OF STATE ACTIVITY ON THE LOCAL SCENE[a]

Mode of Activity	Examples
1. State direct-to-people activities	Highways Higher education Health and hospitals Welfare Recreation Courts and correctional institutions
2. State aid to local units for specified activities	Education Highways Welfare Safety Health and hospitals
3. Local activities made mandatory by state law	Local elections School standards Fire and police protection Courts and jails Tax assessment and collection standards Health program Sewage standards

[a] The table intentionally does not take account of the fact that all local government activities rest upon state law. A notable demonstration of the singleness of state and local governments is the fact that it is difficult to find any direct state activity (category 1) that does not overlap state-aided or state-ordered local activities or both (categories 2 and 3).

directly supply services to the local community; and they do so indirectly (2) by providing financial aid to local units for specified programs as well as (3) by making mandatory certain local functions even though no specific financial aid is supplied.

No two states do the same things in the same way. But all states directly do some of their own highway building, providing funds to local units for other aspects of the highway program, and all states, without exception, provide directly for higher education, although funds and forms vary dramatically. Every state also provides some direct-to-citizen health, welfare, and hospital services; all license the major and certain minor professions; all maintain parks and other recreational facilities; all provide correctional institutions; and all have some sort of program for the development and conservation of natural resources. Some states give direct benefits to veterans, and some operate alcoholic beverage distribution systems. A few are responsible for housing programs. And some states have more or less uncommon direct functions, for example, the system of Savings Bank Life Insurance in Massachusetts, New York, and Connecticut. These are only samples of the wide range of direct-to-citizen functions carried on by the states.

A very large fraction of all state expenditures is in the form of fund transfers to local units of government. And the largest part of these sums is for state-specified purposes, notably education, highways, and public welfare. (In 1957, $7.3 billion, or 30 per cent, of state general expenditures were payments to local units, of which $6.2 billion, or 85 per cent, was for the three specified functions.) This method of fulfilling state-defined programs is indirect only in the sense that locally selected officers are in actual supervision although they work, of course, under state, and in many cases federal, standards. Functions that in one state are carried out directly, in other states are carried out indirectly (welfare and health services are particularly diverse in this respect). There are also state-by-state variations in the local government through which state aid is channeled for specific purposes. Educational aid may, for example, be given to municipalities, to counties, or to special school districts; hospital funds are also diversely channeled to local governments with many states in addition operating hospitals directly.

The other indirect channel for fulfilling state functions on the local scene involves no specific cash grants. Here are found virtually endless obligations imposed upon local units by state constitutions, laws, and administrative regulations. They vary widely from state to state and no less widely by area of activity. Minnesota laws, for example, provide a complicated and detailed calendar controlling local authorities with respect to such matters as the timing of tax levies, the holding of elections, the filing of reports and accounts of all sorts, the dates of town meetings, schedules for reviewing tax assessments, *ad infinitum*. The same sort of specifications cover substantive fields. Tax and debt limits and rules for tax assessment and collection are fixed; requirements for various local units to operate courts and jails are detailed; standards for fire and health protection are set forth; police units and their organization are made mandatory; rules for school construction and curricula are established. The state statute books are in large part a record of local obligations.

II. WHICH GOVERNMENT IS "CLOSEST"
TO THE PEOPLE?

This overview of federal and state impacts on the local scene throws light on the statement that local governments are "closest" to the people. "Closeness" when applied to governments means many things. One meaning is the provision of services directly to the people. Another meaning is public participation in governmental affairs. A third is control: to say that local governments are closer to the people than the federal government is to say that citizens can control the former more easily and more completely than the latter. A fourth meaning is understanding, a fifth communication, a sixth identification. Thorough analysis of "closeness" would have to compare local, state, and federal governments with respect to all these, as well as other, meanings of the term. The most important differences in closeness are not between local governments and the federal or state governments. The differences are rather between rural and urban areas. Rural residents are "closer" than urban ones to both federal and local governments in significant, but not in all, ways.

"CLOSENESS" AND THE PROVISION OF SERVICES

Local governments are clearly not closer to the people if the statement means that only local governments provide services at the local site. All governments in the American governmental system operate in direct contact with people at their places of residence and work, and in most important areas the units operate collaboratively. It cannot even be said that the local units provide the most important local services. The important services are those of shared responsibility. Where it is possible to distinguish primary responsibilities, the greater importance of local government does not at all emerge. All this has been made clear in the previous discussion.

Least of all can local units be considered "closest" in fiscal affairs. The federal government, in any area, collects far more taxes than localities and states combined, and the presence of the federal Internal Revenue Service is more clearly felt than that of any other tax gatherer. The federal government dwarfs the states as a lender and insurer, and the localities are far behind the states in these areas.[7] Even in direct governmental expenditures

[7] Federal loan programs range widely and include crop loans to farmers; Reconstruction Finance Corporation loans to businessmen; Veterans Administration loans for housing and business purposes; Federal Housing Authority loans over a wide area; and a large number of rural cooperative loans, typified by those for rural electrification. Federal insurance activities include crop insurance, deposit insurance, and especially Old Age and Survivors Insurance. The states participate in unemployment insurance and, in many cases, operate teachers' and public employees' insurance and annuity funds.

(omitting debt service, capital expenditures, and commercial transactions), it is likely that federal outlays equal or exceed those of all but the largest local units in most of the country (although, in the last decade, the share of federal expenditures may actually have decreased). This is certainly true for virtually all agricultural areas where local government services are relatively underdeveloped and where federal farm programs are extensive. Ylvisaker computed that the state and federal governments finance one-third of the cost of local government in Blue Earth County (1945), in addition to which they spend as much within the community as do all local units combined.[8] Indeed his data show that the federal government alone probably spent more in the county than all local units combined if the calculation is made for expenditures from own sources, i.e., if expenditures are allocated before, rather than after, intergovernmental transfers. This clear federal fiscal primacy probably does not exist within the great cities, where expenditures per capita by local units are highest. But it is improbable that combined local-unit expenditures anywhere exceed combined federal-state outlays.

One can ask this question about closeness in another way: Where in the American system is government closest to the people as a provider of services? The answer is clearly in the rural areas, and there it is the federal government that provides more services to the people it serves than any other governments provide for the people they serve. As a consumer of services, the farmer has more governmental wares to choose from than any other consumer. They are largely federal or federally sponsored wares, and they cover virtually all aspects of his personal and economic life.

If he wished to take full advantage of what was offered, an individual farmer could assemble a veritable convention of government helpers in his home and fields. He could have a soil conservation technician make a soil survey, prepare plans for conservation practices and watershed protection, and give advice on crops, growing practices, wood-lot plantings, and wild-life maintenance. A Forest Service officer collaboratively with a state forester would provide low-cost tree stock. Extension workers would aid the farmer's wife on all aspects of home management, including gardening, cooking, and sewing; instruct the children with respect to a whole range of health, recreational, and agricultural problems; provide the farmer himself with demonstrations and information aimed at reducing costs, increasing income, and adjusting production to market demands; and give the entire family instruction with respect to "social relations, adjustments and cultural values." An officer of the Agricultural Conservation Program

[8] *Op. cit.,* p. 135.

would arrange federal grants for part of the costs of his soil conservation practices, including ditching and building ponds. (Another official would provide a supply of fish at little or no cost with which to stock the pond.) A Commodity Stabilization Service worker would arrange for loans on some crops, for government purchase of others, and for special incentive payments in still a third category; he would also pay the farmer for constructing crop-storage facilities. Another officer from the same agency would arrange cash payments to the farmer under the soil bank program, if he took out of production acres devoted to designated basic crops (the "acreage reserve") or put general cropland to conservation use (the "conservation reserve"). An official of the Farmers Home Administration, if credit is not elsewhere available, will make loans to the farmer for the operation, improvement, and enlargement of his property, and (to maximize repayment possibilities) will "service" the farmer-borrower by providing him with comprehensive and continuous technical advice on how to make his operation as profitable as possible.

These potentially available on-site services are merely the beginning of a list of federal help available to a farmer. He is supplied with the results of special research of all kinds (through the facilities of the Department of Agriculture, sometimes collaboratively with the experiment stations of the land grant colleges). The younger members of his family are given instruction in vocational agricultural work (through the National Vocational Education Acts). He can profit from federal inspection services covering all sorts of produce and meats. He can borrow money, personally or through one of his federally sponsored cooperatives, from any of a whole series of lending agencies, including the Farm Credit Administration (operating through the National Farm Loan Association), and the Federal Intermediate Credit Bank. He can insure his crops through the Federal Crop Insurance Corporation.

Probably no single farmer has ever attempted to take advantage of all this federal assistance, and to a certain extent the various programs are geared to different strata of the farm population. Furthermore, virtually all federal agriculture services are carried out through mechanisms of federal-state-local collaboration (the Extension Service, for example) or of federally engineered local governments (the Soil Conservation Service, for example). Despite qualifications of this sort, two important points can be made. First, the farm sector of the population receives a wider range of governmental services than any other population group, partly because the farmers represent an economic unit, something more than a specific population group of the kind found in the contemporary urban setting. Second, these services are largely inspired by federal legislation and largely financed with federal funds. From the point of view of services received, the federal government is clearly "closest" to the farm population and closer to it than any other American government is to the population it serves. Outside of institutionalized persons and those dependent upon relief, the American farmer is more immediately dependent upon more governmental services than any other American. And while he is dependent upon the collaboration of all governments, the federal government plays the key role.

The reality of government services in the rural areas contradicts the myths about self-reliant yeoman farmers. At the same time, the decline of the farm population also makes the rural case increasingly atypical. To date, the urban resident does not find the federal government "closest" to him in terms of services rendered. Most of the governmental services benefitting him directly are conducted by state and local authorities even as they are beneficiaries of federal aid in its various forms. But the very intermixture of functions, coupled with the direct federal services that do exist, means that the federal government is at least as close as local government even in the urban areas.

"CLOSENESS" AS PARTICIPATION

When it is said that local governments, rather than states or the federal government, are closest to the people, perhaps the most important meaning of the statement is that local governments maximize citizen participation in governmental affairs. The Kestnbaum Commission stated that it was only at "the lowest level of government" that "every citizen has the opportunity to participate actively and directly."[9]

The greater closeness of local governments to the people, when closeness is taken as participation, also has dubious validity. If citizen participation, for example, means eligible voters voting, then participation in local governments is low. It is lower in rural than urban areas. And elections for national officers everywhere attract the largest number of voters. The exceptions are extremely rare.

Participation in ways other than voting presents a more complicated picture. Variations exist in the degree to which citizens take part in local, state, and federal affairs. The most important variations, however, are not between "levels"; they are rather between urban and rural areas. Participation is greater in the latter, and it is greater with respect to both local and federal governments.

The participation of citizens in the affairs of local governments is greater

[9] The Commission on Intergovernmental Relations, *A Report to the President* (Washington, D.C.: Government Printing Office, 1955), p. 47.

in rural than in urban centers partly as the consequence of the simple arithmetic of governmental units. In areas of low population density, there are far more governments (and far more government officials) per unit of population than in areas of great population density. Increasing population almost everywhere produces an increasing number of local governments, but nowhere does the growth of governments match the growth of people. Table 11 provides one of many possible demonstrations of this relationship. In 38 of the 48 mainland states, the most populous county has more general local governments than the least populous county; but in every state without exception there are far fewer people per unit of local government in the least heavily populated county. The most populous counties as a whole, compared to the least populous ones, have 20 times the number of people per local government. In the highly urban counties, each local government serves 27,866 people; in the rural counties, 1,298.* Many other indexes show the same relationship between local government units and people. For example, more than 55 per cent of the population in 1950 lived in the nation's metropolitan areas, but those areas contained only 14 per cent of the total number of local governments (including special purpose governments). The greater the population concentration the more people per government: the five largest metropolitan areas, with 14 per cent of the nation's population, had only 0.6 per cent of the local units of government.

Where relatively many governments serve relatively few people, participation of citizens in some ways must increase. A basic fact is that the very ratio of people to governments in rural areas makes it statistically more probable, in a given population group, that one will hold an official position (as distinct from nongovernmental employment or employment by government in a technical or clerical capacity). Consider a single rural county of Indiana, with a 1950 population of 23,785 of whom 9,075 were employed.[10] In 1958 the county, municipal, and township governments provided no fewer than 393 appointed jobs, of which 210 were on a full-time basis. One of every 28 employed people in the county worked in 1958 for one of the local governments. In addition there were 87 elected office-

---

* Editor's Note: The 1962 Census of Governments indicates that this general trend has been maintained even though governments in the nation's metropolitan areas are proliferating, dropping the average number of people per local government; and school district consolidations are decreasing the number of rural local governments. The latter trend is outstripped by the decline in population in most rural counties.

[10] The county is DuBois, studied by Douglas St. Angelo, a member of the Federalism Workshop of the University of Chicago. See his unpublished master's thesis, "Patronage in a Rural County," Department of Political Science, University of Chicago, 1957.

TABLE 11

The Number of Local Governments Related to the Number of People

(population per local government for the counties of largest and smallest population of each state, Excluding Alaska and Hawaii)

County	Population	Number of Local Governments	Population Per Local Government	County	Population	Number of Local Governments	Population Per Local Government
Alabama				*Georgia*			
Jefferson	558,928	25	22,357	Fulton	473,572	11	43,052
Coosa	11,766	3	3,922	Quitman	3,015	1	3,015
Arizona				*Idaho*			
Maricopa	331,770	14	23,698	Ada	70,649	5	14,130
Mohave	8,510	2	4,255	Clark	918	3	306
Arkansas				*Illinois*			
Pulaski	196,685	7	28,098	Cook	4,508,792	130	34,683
Perry	5,978	8	747	Putnam	4,746	10	475
California				*Indiana*			
Los Angeles	4,151,687	46	90,254	Marion	551,777	34	16,229
Alpine	241	1	241	Ohio	4,223	6	704
Colorado				*Iowa*			
Denver	415,786	1	415,786	Polk	226,010	14	16,144
Hinsdale	263	2	132	Adams	8,753	5	1,751
Connecticut				*Kansas*			
New Haven	545,784	30	18,193	Sedgwick	222,290	43	5,170
Tolland	44,709	16	2,794	Greeley	2,010	6	335
Delaware				*Kentucky*			
New Castle	218,879	10	21,888	Jefferson	484,615	25	19,385
Kent	37,870	20	1,894	Robertson	2,881	2	1,441
Florida				*Louisiana*			
Dade	495,084	27	18,336	Orleans[a]	570,445	1	570,445
Glades	2,199	2	1,100	Cameron	6,244	1	6,244

(continued on next page)

TABLE 11 (continued)

County	Population	Number of Local Governments	Population Per Local Government	County	Population	Number of Local Governments	Population Per Local Government
Maine				*Nevada*			
Cumberland	169,201	30	5,640	Washoe	50,205	3	16,735
Lincoln	18,004	22	818	Esmeralda	614	1	614
Maryland				*New Hampshire*			
Baltimore city[a]	949,708	1	949,708	Hillsborough	156,987	32	4,906
Calvert	12,100	3	4,033	Carroll	15,868	19	835
Massachusetts				*New Jersey*			
Middlesex	1,064,569	55	19,356	Essex	905,949	23	39,389
Nantucket[a]	3,484	1	3,484	Sussex	34,423	25	1,377
Michigan				*New Mexico*			
Wayne	2,435,235	44	55,346	Bernalillo	145,673	2	72,836
Keweenaw	2,918	7	417	Harding	3,013	3	1,004
Minnesota				*New York*			
Hennepin	676,579	46	14,708	Erie[b]	899,238	122	7,371
Cook	2,900	2	1,450	Hamilton	4,105	11	373
Mississippi				*North Carolina*			
Hinds	142,164	9	15,796	Mecklenburg	197,052	7	28,150
Issaquena	4,966	1	4,966	Tyrrell	5,048	2	2,524
Missouri				*North Dakota*			
St. Louis city[a]	856,796	1	856,796	Cass	58,877	71	829
Carter	4,777	4	1,194	Billings	1,777	3	592
Montana				*Ohio*			
Yellowstone	55,875	4	13,969	Cuyahoga	1,389,532	65	21,377
Golden Valley	1,337	3	446	Vinton	10,759	17	633
Nebraska				*Oklahoma*			
Douglas	281,020	8	35,128	Oklahoma	325,352	12	27,113
Arthur	803	2	402	Cimarron	4,589	3	1,530

TABLE 11 (continued)

County	Population	Number of Local Governments	Population Per Local Government	County	Population	Number of Local Governments	Population Per Local Government
Oregon				*Vermont*			
Multnomah	471,537	6	78,590	Chittenden	62,570	21	2,980
Sherman	2,271	5	454	Grand Isle	3,406	7	487
Pennsylvania				*Virginia*			
Philadelphia[a]	2,071,605	1	2,071,605	Arlington	135,449	1	135,449
Forest	4,944	10	494	Craig	3,452	2	1,726
Rhode Island				*Washington*			
Providence[a]	574,973	16	35,936	King	732,992	18	40,722
Bristol[a]	29,079	3	9,693	Garfield	3,204	2	1,602
South Carolina				*West Virginia*			
Greenville	168,152	7	24,022	Kanawha	239,629	13	18,433
McCormick	9,577	5	1,915	Wirt	5,119	2	2,560
South Dakota				*Wisconsin*			
Minnehaha	70,910	35	2,026	Milwaukee	871,047	22	39,593
Washabaugh[a]	1,551	0		Florence	3,756	9	417
Tennessee				*Wyoming*			
Shelby	482,393	7	68,913	Sweetwater	22,017	8	2,752
Moore	3,948	2	1,947	Sublette	2,481	3	827
Texas							
Harris	806,701	17	47,453	All smallest counties	349,190	269	1,298
Loving	227	1	227	All largest counties	31,767,635	1,140	27,866
Utah							
Salt Lake	274,895	10	27,490				
Daggett	364	1	364				

Source: U.S. Census of Governments, 1957.
[a] County government not counted.
[b] Borough counties of New York City omitted.

holders in the local governments, all of whom received some compensation but few of whom worked full-time.

A total of 470 appointed and elected local government positions thus existed in the county.[11] Taking account of the fact that some people held more than one position, it is a conservative estimate that one in every 15 families in the county included a member with an appointed or elected governmental position. Rural government is not only a government by neighbors, it is a government by members of one's own family. This is a form of "participation" unmatched by either the federal or state governments in rural areas and unmatched as well by any government in the urban centers.

Another aspect of participation in government flows from the rural situation in which virtually every officeholder is known—as neighbor or as family member—by virtually every citizen: recipients of governmental services personally share in the decisions of government, and the services themselves are personalized. A father delivers his son to jail, explaining to his neighbor, the chief of police, that the lad has been drinking again and the family would appreciate the courtesy of allowing him to spend a few days behind bars. Poor relief is granted through the mechanism of phone calls from a doctor to a county supervisor to a welfare officer. A local businessman comes before the school board to complain that not enough food for the school lunchroom is being purchased through local shops. A farmer appears before both the township and county board to argue that an old road near his place should be scraped or that a new one must be constructed because the present road creates drainage problems in his pasture. This intimate characteristic of rural government extends to those who govern. A township meeting is adjourned so that the members can do their chores before dark. The part-time mayor must be consulted in his plumbing shop, and the part-time justice of the peace in his blueberry patch, where, in minor cases, he may even hold court. Many local jobs are apportioned to those who are maimed or blind; or they are held more or less permanently by the incumbent, not infrequently being handed on from father to son, or from husband to widow.

Larger governments seek to duplicate the personal service aspects of rural governments by a variety of devices, ranging from the "case work" of national congressmen and senators, to the neighborhood office-hours of a big city alderman, to the welfare operations of political leaders among immigrant groups in a large city. But these are palliatives for the inevitable impersonality of governments that have more to do, more people to serve,

[11] This does not include 80 elected and 72 appointed *party* officials, nor does it include teachers in the schools.

and more specialized workers on the payroll. No attempt to personalize bureaucracy can fully replicate the nonbureaucratic situation in which nonspecialized work is carried out by friends and family members.

In the affairs of the federal government, just as in the affairs of local government, rural citizens play a greater participant role than urban dwellers. The wide range of federal services to rural residents is largely administered through the several nationwide grids of federally engineered local governments. With services touching virtually every farmer in the United States, these governments directly involve a significant number of rural dwellers: as members and managers of soil conservation districts, extension service groups, agricultural conservation and commodity stabilization programs, and electric and telephone cooperatives, to give but a sample.

Consultative and participating groups of all sorts exist in the nonagricultural sectors of federal activity.[12] But these groups do not compare with the agricultural governments in the scope of their impact on the life of those served; and they do not involve in participant roles as large a fraction of the people concerned.

One can conclude that if closeness to government is defined as citizen participation in government, those in rural areas are closer to both the local and the federal governments. The important partial exception is in voting. Here participation is lowest with respect to rural local governments, and highest (in both rural and urban areas) with respect to the federal government.

"CLOSENESS" AS CONTROL

Closeness as participation should not be confused with closeness as control. Residents of rural areas do not necessarily direct the affairs of either the local or federal governments to a greater extent than the big city dweller. Where control is greater, it is not the consequence of greater participation.

With respect to local rural governments, widely shared citizen control is in many cases difficult despite widely shared citizen participation. In fact, such governments are probably more frequently boss-controlled than other American governments. Roscoe Martin has said flatly that local rural government is "too small to be truly democratic."[13] He referred particularly to the fact that these governments did not excite or stimulate citizens and

[12] Avery Leiserson, *Administrative Regulation* (Chicago: University of Chicago Press, 1942).

[13] Roscoe C. Martin, *Grass Roots* (University: University of Alabama Press, 1957), p. 92.

that the scope of rural governments was "too picayune, too narrow in outlook, too limited in horizon, too self-centered in interests . . . ." Beyond such considerations, in small communities homogeneity of outlook is combined with inequality of power. A small group of farmers or businessmen, a single politician, or a rich family of old settlers can frequently control the entire politics of a rural community. The control may contain attributes of beneficence, and it may be wielded silently and skillfully. It nevertheless represents an effective monopolization of power over those things which the rural government does and refuses to do. The small size of the community means that dissenters find difficulty in organizing opposition, a difficulty that is compounded because of the wide range of personal, social, and economic penalties that may be exacted by the ruling group. It may not be true that the widespread sharing of influence is impossible in the small community; but possibilities of clique and one-man rule are maximized, ideal images of small town democracy notwithstanding.[14]

A system of shared governmental functions, by its nature, rarely allows a single government to exercise complete control over a given activity. All officers of government in the United States consequently experience what may be called "frustration of scope of action." This is the frustration produced by the inability of decision-makers in one government to produce action at their own discretion: other governments must also be moved. Limited scope of discretion is felt universally, by the largest as well as the smallest governments; but it is felt most keenly by the rural local governments.

A big city example is provided by the difficulty experienced by Chicago in gaining permission to divert Lake Michigan water through the Chicago River in order to facilitate disposal of the city's sewage. Other cities and several states objected; the federal government was involved because of its

---

[14] A prime example of a rural boss emerges from the pages of Arthur J. Vidich and Joseph Bensman, *Small Town in Mass Society* (Princeton: Princeton University Press, 1958). The small town in question is in upstate New York. Jones, the leader of the invisible government in both the village and the township, is from an old family and the head of the area's most prosperous business. He is shy, quiet, kindly, and unassuming. He does not take stands on public issues and holds no public office. But "everyone in the community knows that Jones is the most powerful man in town and that he is the political boss." He influences all aspects of local government. "No official can be nominated to the village, town or school boards without his approval." The village is overwhelmingly Republican and village offices are not contested by Democratic candidates. By controlling the nominations, Jones controls the offices. Rarely do more than 30 people of the 350–450 eligible voters cast ballots in village elections.

Vidich and Bensman seem to the present writer excessively ethnocentric in evaluating the rural community. The big city perspective in the small town can be as distorting an eyepiece as the "civilized view" in a "savage" environment. But their portrait of the boss is factual and convincing. See also Martin, *op. cit.,* pp. 64–66.

jurisdiction over the Great Lakes; and the issue even extended to the international plane, Canada's stake in Great Lakes water being involved. Suburban frustration over the scope of control is illustrated by the difficulties faced in building a railroad underpass in the town of Mountain View, south of San Francisco. The city officers needed state aid for the project, and the state was dependent on federal aid. They needed to persuade the Southern Pacific Railroad to contribute a share of the costs, the state's share being contingent upon the railroad's share. And they needed cooperation of other suburbs. One side of the road to be altered was in Mountain View; the other side was in the city of Palo Alto; the street itself was in unincorporated territory; and, to complete the picture, Mountain View officials believed the town of Los Altos should also contribute to the underpass since it would serve Los Altos residents as a principal artery to transportation.[15]

The smaller the government, the more limited the span of control. Hardly any function of the small rural government fails to involve other governments. A farmer may gain full support from local officers about where a road should go through his land, but he sees the road go elsewhere because the basic decisions are not made by his friends in the local government but by the combined efforts of local, county, state, and federal officials. Decisions of rural governments with respect to most other matters are similarly conditioned by decision-makers elsewhere. Frustration of scope of control, if a universal of the American system, is nevertheless felt most acutely in the small local governments of rural America.

Channels exist, as we shall see, by which local populations can bring effective pressure to bear upon officers of the state and federal governments. Sharing by local groups in the decisions of those governments is characteristic. But it is not the consequence of the opportunity of citizens at "lowest level . . . to participate actively and directly," as the Kestnbaum Commission wrote. Rather it is basically the consequence of the manner in which the American party system operates.[16] Similarly, as we shall see, the very genuine rural control of federal agricultural programs is not the result of farmer participation in the many federally sponsored local governments.[17] Direct participation at the grass roots may be only a surrogate for genuine power and may indeed be the device of others to implement their own programs. Unremitting civic participation is more characteristic of totalitarianism than of democracy, and the greater participation of rural. than urban citizens in the affairs of both local and federal governments cannot be equated with the citizen control of those governments.

[15] *Palo Alto Times,* December 30, 1958.
[16] See Chapter Ten.
[17] See Chapter Fourteen.

In sum, citizen participation in local government affairs, described by the Kestnbaum Commission, does not lead to control of those affairs, as implied by the Commission. Even the factual assertion is partially in error: in no sense can it be said that citizens participate in the affairs of local urban governments to a greater extent than they do in other American governments. In rural local governments, participation (except for voting) is maximized. But this participation is easily and frequently combined with boss or clique rule. Even where the local rural government is controlled through wide citizen participation, control may be frustrated. Limitations in the scope of action are faced by all American governments, but they tend to be greatest for those small governments where participation, in the sense of "taking part," is greatest.

CONCLUSION: THE ISSUE OF CLOSENESS TO GOVERNMENT

Many other meanings of "closeness" could be analyzed. "Closeness" may mean understanding, or communication between officeholder and citizen, or the process by which citizens identify themselves with institutions. In none of these meanings is it true that local governments are closer to the people. With respect to understanding, for example, the structure of the federal government, and that of most state governments, is infinitely less complex, and therefore far easier to comprehend, than that of most local governments, rural governments not always providing the exception. For the great metropolitan areas, including the suburban fringes, the overlapping of governments and the splintering of functions is extreme, and citizen comprehension of local government affairs is at its lowest. And it is worth remembering that most Americans live in these areas. Similarly, most citizens identify themselves in national rather than in state or local terms. They are more likely and more intensely apt to think of themselves as Americans than as Illinoisians, Little Rockians, Casa Grandians, New Yorkers, or even Texans.[18]

The issue of "closeness" to government has not been well defined. The scales of measurement are at best crude, but at least some precision in meaning can be given the concept: (a) Local governments are not closer to the people than is the federal government (or the relevant state government for that matter) as the provider of services. They supply neither all nor the most important local services; nor are they the chief collectors or spenders of public funds. (b) In rural areas the federal government is primarily responsible for supplying local services that for range and impact

---

[18] But it is also easy for the double or triple identification to be held simultaneously. The identifications are not contradictory and, where they seem to clash, easy modes of reconciliation are possible.

have no counterpart in the services of any other government anywhere in the nation. (c) If closeness means electoral participation, local governments are further from, not closer to, the people than the federal government. (d) The same statement is true for all localities if closeness means identification. (e) It is almost certainly true in the great metropolitan areas if closeness means understanding of who does what. (f) On the other hand, closeness as directly "taking part" is greatest for rural local governments (largely the result of the high ratio of elected and appointed officers to population), and probably least in the local governments of the great metropolitan areas, with rural participation in federal affairs here occupying some intermediate point. (g) This sort of closeness—i.e., participation— also leads to the personal touch of rural local governments and a hand tooling of service for the recipients, a type of closeness that federally sponsored rural governments also supply to a lesser measure. (h) In many meanings of closeness the differences between urban and rural governments (local and federal) are thus more important than differences between local and federal governments. (i) But in no sense does closeness mean control, and (j) in no sense is closeness exclusively or principally the attribute of local (as opposed to state or federal) governments.

The traditionally described three-level American government is in fact telescoped on the community. From the point of view of the local consumer of governmental products, the American system of government is not a pyramid, but a range of sometimes-supplementary and sometimes-duplicating (but rarely alternative) services. Accidents of history, politics, and place have produced bundles of governmental services. No logic can distinguish between the "local character" of one government's services and the "nonlocal" character of another's. The federal government has built city halls for many cities and has paid for tearing down slums in others. It pays insurance directly to the aged and indirectly provides for the health of new mothers. It draws plans for the best land use for a poor farmer and supplies funds for the construction of a vast manufacturing plant to a multimillion-dollar corporation. It constructs schools here and libraries there. It aids one community in drawing up a city plan, supplies a second community with funds to build a sewer, gives a park to a third, and provides expert advice to the police chief of a fourth when the hardware store is robbed. By any standard, federal activities of this sort are as "close" to the citizen as any activities of the states and localities. To deny the local character of federal activities one would be forced to deny the local character of local governments. Closeness to the citizen is an attribute of all American governments. Local is as local does.

Chapter 8

LOCAL STRENGTH IN THE
AMERICAN SYSTEM:
PATTERNS OF REPRESENTATION

The true measure of the "localness" of given functions is not which government performs them. Rather it is the extent to which local citizens are able to influence governmental activities, regardless of which government is involved. The localities are substantial participants in the making of important federal and state decisions. It will be seen in subsequent chapters how the mechanism of participation operates—in national and state legislation, and in a number of national administrative programs. Here the focus is on the way localities influence and direct governmental activities which affect the local scene. There is no absolute local direction of the activities of nonlocal governments. But substantial participation and influence are everywhere apparent.

In the most general sense, the primary control mechanisms available to localities are (a) their formal representation in the state and federal legislatures and (b) the ability of their residents to participate in the election of state and national officials. It is important to understand that every system of representation is structured to favor certain interests more than others. This means that different local communities or kinds of localities have different degrees of influence over federal and state programs in the various systems in which they are represented. Since the American system is composed of a number of different systems of representation, the end result is to offer every kind of locality some formal channel of access to the state and federal governments that is particularly favorable to its interests.

I. ISSUES OF LOCAL REPRESENTATION IN
STATE LEGISLATURES

The greater numerical strength of rural areas in the legislatures of both the federal government and the states has been an important general factor maximizing the influence of the smaller and less populated places.* Urban areas have been almost everywhere underrepresented in state legislatures. The largest cities and the smaller metropolitan areas are often accurately represented in proportion to their populations but are still underrepresented in proportion to the seats accorded the rural counties and small towns. The suburbs in the great metropolitan areas tend to be underrepresented absolutely and proportionately. A number of state constitutions provide either minimum or maximum representation for given counties or other districts and so prevent corrections of the imbalance. Even where constitutions specify regular reapportionment of at least one house, this seldom takes place on schedule. Without reapportionment, the rural advantage consequently tends to become greater as population increasingly moves to the metropolitan centers.

The payoff by the legislature can be measured in fiscal terms. Two-thirds of the revenue of the village and town comes from state aid, not counting direct state investment in local facilities, such as roads. The county receives approximately 20 dollars in state aid for every dollar it pays in taxes of all kinds, including state taxes. Ninety-five per cent of the state taxes from which aid is derived, according to the calculation made by Vidich and Bensman, "is levied in the metropolitan-urban centers of the state." No less than 80 per cent of the school budget, not counting construction aid, is derived from state sources.[1] The editor of the community newspaper, the principal of the school, the leading lawyer in the city, and other citizens are fully aware of the favorable position their community enjoys as a consequence of the rural domination of the state legislature. The principal political effort is made in state politics. Elections for statewide offices bring out a far larger vote than local elections or national elections unaccom-

*Editor's note: In 1962 the Supreme Court decision in *Baker* v. *Carr* inaugurated a period of extensive federal and state court intervention in the field of legislative apportionment and consequent upheavals in the structure of representation. Since 1962 additional Supreme Court decisions culminating in *Reynolds* v. *Sims* (1964), which held that the apportionment of either house of the legislature using criteria other than population is unconstitutional, have further accelerated the changes in this field. This chapter is based on the situation that prevailed before 1962. Since the total national picture has not yet crystallized despite widespread reapportionment activity, and the issues discussed in it remain valid, it is presented here virtually as written, with certain specific passages updated. For comprehensive data on state legislative apportionment prior to 1962, see Advisory Commission on Intergovernmental Relations, *Apportionment of State Legislatures* (Washington, D.C., 1962).

[1] Vidich and Bensman, *op. cit.,* pp. 201–6. New York school laws make it impossible for the rural schools to receive greater state assistance by the simple expedient of keeping their own real estate assessments at a low level. The rural schools, in addition to the flat "attendance aid" which is available to all public schools in the state, also receive added state stipends, one for the special purpose of financing central schools, another for transportation, and still a third for the construction of buildings in rural areas.

panied by state contests."The increased political acivity at the local level in state elections represents an exchange of rural votes for favorable state Republican policies in reference to rural areas."[2]

In marked contrast, the average city of over 25,000 in New York receives only 17.3 per cent of its revenue from intergovernmental sources, including federal ones.[3] But economic data of this sort overlook justifications for proportionately larger state aid to rural areas—justifications based upon their relative lack of wealth. Compared to urban areas, rural local governments have both a smaller tax base and a greater cost per unit of services rendered (though also less demand for certain services). Some reallocation of wealth within a given state can therefore be defended in the same terms that justify reallocations among the states by the federal government.

No justification in legal or political theory accounts for the regional representation in the upper houses of many state legislatures. Here the analogue to the federal system is unpersuasive. The geographical units— usually counties—represented in the state senates are without independent legal status, and are not cultural, economic, or geographic entities. Consequently the states cannot be considered "little federal" systems; in law and fact they are unitary institutions. The only principle justifying upper-house representation by geographic units is political. This is the same principle that justifies rural overrepresentation in the lower houses—the advantage of control it gives to rural areas.

If the present imbalance in state legislatures gives an advantage of influence to rural populations, it gives the same advantage to some urban populations. Urban interests are by no means unitary, particularly when urban places by definition range in population size from 2,500 to nearly 8 million and even standard metropolitan statistical areas as defined range in population from 50,000 upward to 11 million. They are far less homogeneous than rural interests. To say that the "urban plight" is the result of underrepresentation in the state legislatures is falsely to assume a unity of urban interests and to hide a general alliance between some urban and nonurban groups. Aside from questions of size, urban members of the alliance are those of the wealthier classes, generally Protestant, generally white, generally more conservative, and, in the two-party states, generally Republican. This fraction of the urban population is not at all underrepresented in the state legislatures; rather it is overrepresented along with its nonurban allies. This is because suburbs often make common cause with rural areas against the central cities, and on certain issues it would be

[2] *Ibid.,* pp. 205–6.
[3] Calculated from U.S. Bureau of the Census, *City and County Data Book,* 1957.

accurate to speak of rural-suburban control of the state legislatures. Even within central cities, the rural-suburban axis finds many friends because the conflicts of intracity politics are carried over into the state legislatures. When Republicans introduced and supported a bill to reimpose a tax limit on Chicago, *The Chicago Daily News*—an independent paper with a Republican preference—supported the bill. "It seems to us," an editorial said, "more important to preserve it [the tax limit] than to get beguiled by the phrase 'home rule' into a position where our pocketbooks are too easily vulnerable to a council controlled by the city administration."[4] Similarly, a substantial minority of the residents of New York City voted against a proposal that would have opened the way for reapportionment of the New York legislature, with greater opposition to the referendum apparent in the wealthier residential areas of the city.[5] Even more relevantly, several chambers of commerce, especially that of Los Angeles, vigorously led the opposition when an initiative election proposed giving cities more equitable representation in the California senate. Principal support for the proposal came from the State Federation of Labor. But business opposition led to defeat of the plan even in the cities that would have gained representation.

Urbanites who are exceptionally underrepresented in the state legislature are those of lower income, those not of the white race, those without suburban or rural allies.[6]

Simple statistics to the contrary, greater initial strength is not tantamount to control, nor is underrepresentation the single cause of big city failures to gain state support. An intensive study of roll call votes in two legislatures, those of Illinois and Missouri, demonstrated that by far the most effective opposition to legislation on behalf of big cities comes from the cities themselves. Conflicting groups in the big cities are almost always at odds within the legislatures. There are hardly any occasions when the legislatures are presented with a clean division of metropolitan versus nonmetropolitan members because metropolitan legislators seldom stand together. When

[4] May 20, 1957.

[5] *New York Times,* November 7 and 8, 1957.

[6] Patrick Healy, Jr., Executive Director of the American Municipal Association, told the Fountain Subcommittee that legislative reapportionment was no cure-all for urban problems. ". . . in many states the cities appear to get a more favorable consideration of their problems from legislators residing in small towns and rural areas than they do from some living in larger cities." He attributed this to the low quality of state legislators and suggested the need for bringing them up to the competence of national congressmen by giving them "adequate personal . . . and . . . committee staffs." (Fountain Subcommittee, *Hearings,* [Volume not numbered], July 29, 30, 31, 1957, p. 107). Mr. Healy's prescription for improving the caliber of state legislators may be accepted; but it would do little, if anything, with respect to the nonsupport of big city representatives for big-city problems. That problem is a problem of the disunity of interests within the big cities.

they do, the legislation they support is, in fact, almost aways passed. "The city's bitterest opponents in the legislature are political enemies from within its own walls, and those camped in the adjoining suburban areas."[7]

Disunity and underrepresentation account for big city disadvantage in the state legislatures, but the consequences are not as serious as one might imagine. They are, in fact, somewhat diminished by the importance of the large metropolitan areas in the election of the governor. In 12 states (generally those with the biggest cities) a majority of the voters live in metropolitan areas of 500,000 population and above. While divided by intra-urban problems, the sheer size of these areas creates special difficulties that make for more of a big city outlook. Future population trends will increasingly make the governor's electoral base a metropolitan one. Political disagreement, based on central city-suburban differences in race, class, and party identification, will continue to be an obstacle to big city influence. Nevertheless, the big city Democratic vote is already far more effective against the "upstate" or "downstate" Republican power in shifting the governor's office than it is in shifting the balance of power in the legislatures.[8] This big city influence over the governors will grow, especially if urban-suburban differences decrease with time, as they are likely to do.

[7] David R. Derge, "Metropolitan and Outstate Alignments in Illinois and Missouri Legislative Delegations," *American Political Science Review,* Vol. LII, No. 4 (December, 1958), pp. 1051–65. The following table, taken from this article, shows how infrequently metropolitan delegations voted together for the period and in the states studied:

VOTING COHESION OF METROPOLITAN DELEGATIONS ON CONTESTED ROLL-CALLS:
1949–57 SESSIONS

Metropolitan cohesion %	Illinois				Missouri House			
	House		Senate		St. Louis		Kansas City	
	N	%	N	%	N	%	N	%
91 or more	12	1	20	3	60	3	23	1
67–90	234	24	216	34	451	22	538	26
Less than 67	738	75	395	63	1,536	75	1,486	73
Totals	984	100	631	100	2,047	100	2,047	100

"Metropolitan cohesion" in the table means simply the percentage of the full membership of the metropolitan delegation which voted together in contested roll calls. (A contested roll call in Illinois was one in which at least 15 per cent of the total House voted on the other side; at least 10 per cent in Missouri.) Thus the Illinois House figures at the top of the first two columns say that on 12 occasions during the period 91 per cent or more of the metropolitan delegation voted together on contested roll calls; this constituted only 1 per cent of the total number of contested roll calls.

[8] V. O. Key, Jr., *American State Politics: An Introduction* (New York: Alfred A. Knopf, 1956), Ch. 3.

Even within the legislatures, big city influence is considerable, especially where lobbying is vigorous and where political leaders of the cities are capable of wielding influence over substantial numbers of their own legislative representatives. "Downstate" and "upstate" legislators are not insensitive to the pressing nature of many urban problems; indeed, they frequently seem to be more receptive to big city requests than suburban and dissident big city legislators. As a consequence of such factors, most state legislatures in recent years have considerably widened the areas of discretion for city governments. Constitutional home rule has not made significant headway for good reasons.[9] But permissive legislation has increased in scope, and in many cases where a city turns to the legislature for permission to inaugurate a service or to expand its taxing power, some results are usually achieved, even if they are not completely satisfactory to the city concerned.

Housing and urban redevelopment,[10] relatively recent problems, provide a convenient example of the situation that confronts cities. A good case can be made for states to allow cities complete freedom in this field. Yet, in fact, all sorts of restrictions are imposed. At the beginning of 1958 Wyoming and Utah did not allow their cities to participate at all in federal programs for redevelopment, urban renewal, or public housing; and Idaho, Iowa, Mississippi, Montana, and New Mexico did not allow cities to receive federal aid for redevelopment or urban renewal programs. Aside from such blanket restrictions, states hedge their cities in other ways. Indiana's redevelopment laws may be limiting or crippling. Despite the popularity of urban redevelopment in Milwaukee, the Wisconsin legislature passed a law permitting the sale of housing projects before their completion; city officials predicted that this measure would promote so many lawsuits that slum clearance would be delayed indefinitely. California requires that a local referendum be held for *every* proposed public housing project. An Ohio statute specifies that all local bond issues for redevelopment projects be approved by 55 per cent of those voting (a 1954 bond issue in Columbus failed although it received 53 per cent of the vote). North Carolina's redevelopment law prohibits the use of eminent domain powers for acquiring standard structures, a provision that forced at least four cities to abandon their programs when the legislature refused to change the law.

While this catalogue of restrictive acts could be readily enlarged, the positive side of the situation is also impressive. Forty-five states have

[9] See Chapter Ten.
[10] Federal and state legislation of 1937 marks the beginning of continuous active public housing interest by American governments on a nationwide scale, but the significant developments in urban redevelopment have all been since World War II.

enacted legislation permitting cities and other local governments to participate, completely or partially, in federal housing and urban redevelopment
programs, opening doors for the latter within a decade of the program's
inauguration. At least ten states, New York being the outstanding example,
have actively aided in the planning and financing of housing programs.
Furthermore, as studies in Baltimore and elsewhere have indicated, a
number of cities have discovered that they have relatively comprehensive
power with which to carry out urban renewal programs, much of it in legislation not specifically related to urban renewal.[11] Where such powers do
not already exist, many legislatures (Illinois is a good example) have been
willing to grant them. Cities have clearly been given many tools by the
states for carrying out housing and urban renewal programs; just as clearly
they have not been granted all the powers their leaders think they need.

Political leaders of big cities are more wrathful about what they have
failed to receive from the states than grateful for what they have received. How facts are viewed is as important as the facts themselves. Big
city mayors perceive largely their disadvantaged position, and they express
deep resentment. Mayor Dilworth of Philadelphia has complained that
"rural legislators pretty completely dominate the state, and they take an
almost perverse delight in walloping both Pittsburgh and particularly
Philadelphia.[12] A member of the Hartford city council charged that the
"rotten boroughs system" of Connecticut vested control over state government "in a minority of the people of the state, and, as a consequence, in
every field unique to the municipality, the cities say, of 40,000 and up, are
ignored or taken very lightly, and great consideration is given to . . . a
minority of the people who do not live in the cities."[13] Mayor Ben West
of Nashville, speaking as President of the American Municipal Association
(representing 12,532 municipalities), commented bitterly on urban underrepresentation in state legislatures throughout the country. He said that
"24 per cent of the population controls the state legislature" in Tennessee
and that "pigs in some of our rural counties have more direct representation in the General Assembly of the State of Tennessee than human beings
in the city."[14]

---

[11] *Report of the Urban Renewal Study Board,* Baltimore, September, 1956, pp.
76–77. See also Banfield and Grodzins, *op. cit.,* Ch. 6.

[12] (Fountain) Subcommittee of the Committee on Government Operations, House
of Representatives, 85th Congress, 1st Session, *Hearings,* Part 1, p. 348. For a similar
statement by Mayor David L. Lawrence of Pittsburgh (". . . representation is lopsided
. . . we get the worst of it in Pittsburgh all the time."), see *ibid.,* p. 114.

[13] *Ibid.,* p. 90.

[14] *Ibid.,* Part 2, pp. 584, 589. The quotations are from Mayor West's formal statement. Later in his testimony he revealed the calculation was made "by actual

Complaints of this sort have come from all areas of the country. The United States Conference of Mayors has pointed to the issue of under-representation as the major source of the cities' plight and has protested against the status of urban residents as "second class citizens" and as victims of "taxation without representation." The mayors of most cities, said the mayor of Boston, feel that the cities "are sort of ugly stepchildren."[15] Yet the very vehemence with which big cities' leaders express their discontent, combined with their willingness to turn from the states to the national government for aid, in itself puts considerable pressure on state legislators and administrators. Mayor Wagner of New York, when asked if he thought that states would be left "mere administrative shells" in twenty-five years or so, did not answer in general terms. He only said, "Not yet. I think even in 20 or 25 years from now the mayor of New York will have a lot of headaches."[16]

One can conclude that the overrepresentation of rural areas in the state legislatures gives those areas some degree of disproportionate influence over state programs. This control, in many cases, is made more secure by the greater social and political homogeneity of rural areas, especially in contrast to urban ones. More important, certain urban groups ally themselves with rural interests, often forming real as well as legislative majorities, to the disadvantage of other urban groups. Small and medium-size cities and metropolitan areas, along with groups in the larger metropolitan areas whose interests are close to theirs, form the urban segment of this alliance. As the rural population has declined, this urban segment has become the dominant force in opposing so called urban interests which are really "big city" and "megalopolitan" interests. Today the old urban-rural conflict is rapidly becoming—if it has not already become—a conflict between dif-

count," the census of pigs being derived "from Department of Agriculture figures." Congressman Reuss (Dem., Wisconsin), a member of the subcommittee, thereupon volunteered the following observation: "We in Wisconsin had a somewhat similar problem . . . . There the suggestion used to be made . . . that the so-called areacrat group, which believed in representation other than on the basis of one voter, one vote, were willing to apportion the state on the basis of butterfat or lily pads. In fact, some poet went so far as to say [that] *if* they had their way, namely, the area-crat group . . . they [would] base the vote on outdoor plumbing, and every farmer with a three holer could cast three votes . . . . That was before the last reapportionment." It should be added that the 1954 reapportionment in Wisconsin, coming after 30 years of inaction, gave cities an equitable share of legislative places.

[15] *Ibid.*, Part 1, p. 67. The Fountain Subcommittee *Hearings* contain a rich mine of urban views with respect to underrepresentation. For critical views by the mayor of Bloomington, Indiana, see *ibid.*, Part 2, p. 495; the mayor of St. Paul, Minnesota, Part 2, p. 413; the mayor of Santa Fe, New Mexico, Part 3, pp. 856–67; the mayor of Salt Lake City, Utah, Part 3, pp. 924–46; the mayor of Denver, Colorado, Part 3, pp. 911–22.

[16] *Ibid.*, Part 1, p. 231.

fering urban interests whose main, but not exclusive, point of division is population size. In Illinois, Chicago is opposed by five of the state's eight medium-size metropolitan areas (with populations ranging from 100,000 to over 250,000) on most "urban-rural" issues as well as in partisan politics.

Detroiters believe themselves hemmed in by "rural" outstate interests, yet much of the strength of those interests is located in such places as metropolitan Bay City (population 107,000), metropolitan Flint (population 416,000), metropolitan Lansing (population 299,000) and, particularly, metropolitan Grand Rapids (462,000).

The very existence of an alliance that unites established rural power-holders and those burgeoning—if relatively small—metropolitan centers increases the difficulty of correcting the legislative imbalance. New apportionments can help little, particularly since the big cities are losing population. On the other hand, the increasing importance of the large metropolitan areas as gubernatorial constituencies, among other factors, has produced a more receptive audience for big city voices at the state capitals. The net results make for a degree of big city influence but a far lesser degree of big city satisfaction.

II. ISSUES OF NATIONAL REPRESENTATION

Because of what they conceive to be an underprivileged position in state governments, big city leaders have turned to the national government. Mayor Zeidler of Milwaukee has written, ". . . there is an intense struggle going on . . . between the central cities and the state governments," and ". . . the central cities now look to the federal government as their protector and defender from the arbitrary or negligent attitude of the state government."[17] Mayor Dilworth of Philadelphia has been equally specific. He did not have "any great confidence in a state government." The federal Congress was "a much more responsible body than the state legislatures," the latter being "pretty irresponsible." Congress possessed "a much broader point of view toward the overall needs of the nation." Consequently the mayors of large cities believed that "the logical place for the cities to turn is to the federal government and not to the states on those kinds of big programs that require a great deal of money, like airports, housing, and particularly highways and public health."[18] Mayor Dillon of St. Paul, Minnesota, put the matter thus: "The only way the major cities are going

[17] Quoted in Banfield and Grodzins, op. cit., p. 54.
[18] Fountain Subcommittee Hearings, Part 1, pp. 356, 360.

to get the fair representation they are entitled to is in the Congress of the United States. . . . Our experience in working with the state legislature is very poor. . . . That is why I . . . go to Washington."[19] Convictions such as these, widely shared throughout the country, have led both the American Municipal Association and the United States Conference of Mayors to establish headquarters in Washington, D.C.

In terms of simple representation, the big cities are more favorably situated in Congress than they are in most state legislations. But this does not mean that they have representation equal to their numbers. The Senate, of course, discriminates against the most populous, and therefore the most urbanized, states by virtue of the great constitutional compromise that made union possible in the first place. Today ten states contain more than half the nation's total population; yet these states are represented by only 20 per cent of the Senate. Each senator from New York represents 7,400,000 people; each senator from Nevada, 80,000.

The Constitution provides that the House shall be apportioned among the several states "according to their respective numbers" with a minimum of one for each state. It is stipulated that enumeration of the population will take place every ten years. While the "times, places, and manner" of electing members of Congress are left to the state legislatures, "Congress may at any time by law make or alter such regulations." Congress has thus far failed to do so.

Nineteenth-century statutes set standards for congressional districts in terms of compactness, contiguous territory, and—"as near as practicable"— equal number of inhabitants. An "automatic" reapportionment law of 1929 empowered the President to allot congressional seats among the states according to each decennial census, but the then-existing provisions for "fair districting" were omitted. Subsequent attempts to establish such standards have failed. As a consequence the rurally dominated state legislatures are free—within the state's allocation of total seats—to establish congressional districts as they see fit. They see fit to discriminate against urban areas.

The state legislatures accomplish this by failing to draw new district lines if decennial censuses do not alter their total number of congressmen. This is the silent gerrymander: inequitable representation produced by population changes unaccompanied by changes in district boundaries. The metropolitan areas are victims of this gerrymander because they have gained, while the rural areas have lost, population. If a state wins new seats, old districts may be preserved by providing that new members be elected at large; or the redistricted state may gerrymander to the advant-

[19] *Ibid.*, Part 2, pp. 441, 443.

age of rural areas, a practice that is also possible if a state loses seats as a consequence of the presidental allocation. Failure to redistrict thus produces in a number of states urban constituencies that are double the size of rural ones—in some cases even more.

When rurally dominated legislatures are moved to draw new district boundaries, they do so to the disadvantage of cities. Urban constituencies were involved in fifteen of the seventeen states that were redistricted between 1950 and 1959. In 14 such instances, the drawing of new boundaries produced urban congressional districts with far more population than the rural ones. The Ohio legislature, for example, constructed one constituency in Dayton with 545,644 population, another in a rural area with 226,341. A new Detroit-Dearborn district in Michigan has 525,334 people while the same redistricting produced a rural constituency of 178,251. (The national average, assuming districts of equal population, approximated 345,000.) The combined result of silent and active gerrymanders is to produce a serious imbalance in the congressional representation of urban areas. Baker calculated that in 1955 the 13 most populous congressional districts (all of them in big cities and each containing more than 500,000 people) should by equitable standards have 22, not 13 congressmen, and that "a computation of all large city districts in the nation would [probably] show a shortage of at least two dozen seats."[20]

The total effect of congressional malrepresentation is not merely fewer congressmen per unit of city population; it is also a tipping of the congressional advantage (especially in close elections) to the Republican side outside the South and to the more conservative, rural-based Dem-

---

[20] Gordon E. Baker, *Rural versus Urban Political Power* (New York: Doubleday & Company, 1955), p. 44. Baker also demonstrates, pp. 45–46, that even where state legislatures allocate a proportional number of congressional seats to large cities, they can nevertheless discriminate in favor of the majority party of the legislature. Thus in the 1951 California redistricting, the Republican legislature gave Los Angeles its equitable number of seats, but gerrymandered the seats within the city to produce five underrepresented and four overrepresented districts as follows:

Overrepresented		Underrepresented	
District	Population	District	Population
16	223,703	17	431,254
18	286,505	19	453,942
20	226,679	23	421,623
22	219,018	26	480,827
24	287,325		
Totals:	1,243,230		1,787,646

In the 1952 elections, every one of the overpopulated (underrepresented) districts voted Democratic and every one of the underpopulated (overrepresented) ones voted Republican.

ocratic factions in the South. Why do the cities nevertheless look increasingly to the national government for the solution of their major problems?

The cities suffer disadvantages in the legislatures of both states and nation, but the lesser disadvantage is on the national side. The combined power of all cities in Congress is probably greater than the power of the cities of any single state in that state's legislature. The national Senate, which might seem to be a natural point of urban discrimination, is consistently becoming the center of urban influence in the legislature as statewide constituencies become increasingly urban constituencies.[21] The cities' power, moreover, is especially important in the election of the President. And finally, the federal budget has a degree of elasticity unknown to most state budgets. Horizons of the possible are less limited, and fiscal views less restricted. Rural groups controlling a state legislature are likely to regard an urban advantage as a rural disadvantage, if for no other reason than the limitations in total budget size. The relative ease with which the federal budget can be expanded makes such views far less prevalent on the national scene, and allows room for simultaneous rural and urban advantage. Well recognized log-rolling techniques, in fact, often make one contingent upon the other. The wealth of the nation, and the way in which that wealth is regarded and utilized by members of the national executive and legislature, are important factors in the tendency of cities to turn toward the national government.

Political factors unrelated to issues of representation also affect the influence potential of urban and rural interests. International tensions, the popularity of a national leader, and rapidly shifting political tempers produced in 1958, for example, a holdover Republican President and a dominantly Democratic Congress. The President advocated economies on matters of first concern to the largest cities, including housing and urban renewal. Such situations are testimony to the dynamics of a party system in which the urban-rural distinction may be cross-cut by more powerful forces. Yet it does not alter the basic point concerning the greater long-run influence of the urban centers on the office of the President than on the Congress.

[21] In 1960, only 11 states, or hardly more than one-fifth of the Senate, had larger proportions of their populations in rural, rather than urban, areas. More important, the urban population of 19 states, or close to two-fifths of the Senate, represented more than two-thirds of the total state population. Those states were spread over seven of the nine census regions. Even allowing for the inclusion of not very "urban," populations in the Census Bureau's definition of "urban," this reflects the emergence of the Senate as the legislative representative of variegated urban (though not always big city) interests.

The total political configuration is one which has led to a number of big city problems being attacked through national-local arrangements rather than state-local ones. Since the war, this has clearly been the case with respect to public housing and urban renewal, and, to a lesser extent, airport development and a few public health programs. Cities have also been successful in their efforts to make sure that a portion of federal highway funds is specifically allocated to urban areas. All this has had an important, but not a decisive, impact on the cities' most pressing problem: their inability within relatively small areas to tax mobile wealth effectively. State tax and debt limits, other state-imposed restrictions, the generally ineffective state system, and the distribution of state subventions in ways that penalize the larger cities, have added to the difficulty of closing the gap between income and expenditure. Still, even the new national-local arrangements are limited to a few select areas of activity. It is not beyond constitutional or political possibility for the federal government to aid the larger cities with general subventions. But such a proposal has never been seriously considered. In its absence, major efforts to solve big city problems must remain largely state-local efforts.

The rural areas can effectively play both the state and national sides of the street. Their national advantage, as within individual states, is the advantage of overrepresentation, both in absolute terms and through alliances. The seniority system of the national Congress assigns key roles to rural members, whose tenure is far more secure than those from more keenly contested urban areas. The homogeneity of rural interest, often found within a single state, does not exist equally across the nation. But conflicts of rural interests that hinge on geographical or crop differences are effectively mediated through powerful agricultural associations. In the context of readily expansible federal budgets, the advantage of one rural group—rather than denying privilege to others—can be traded to their equal advantage.

III. REPRESENTATION BY GROUPS OF OFFICIALS

A different sort of representation is provided to local governments by interest groups. An important role is played legislatively and administratively, in both the state and federal governments, by associations of local and state officers. The American Public Welfare Association, for example, is a powerful representative of the local and state point of view in the establishment of administrative standards for national public assistance programs. The American Municipal Association (composed of state leagues of municipalities) and the United States Conference of Mayors have been in the forefront of lobbying for increased federal programs to benefit urban populations. Within the states similar groups efforts are carried on. State municipal leagues, organizations of firemen, policemen, judges, clerks, and other associations of public officials work to make their views effective.

These groups frequently take contrary stands on a given issue. A representative of the Michigan Institute of Local Government, for example, testified before a congressional committee on behalf of the following groups:

> Michigan Sheriff's Association
> Michigan Association of County Clerks
> Michigan Association of County Treasurers
> Michigan Association of Registers of Deeds
> Prosecuting Attorneys' Association of Michigan
> Michigan Association of County School Administrators
> Michigan Association of County Drain Commissioners
> County Road Association of Michigan
> Michigan Probate and Juvenile County Judges Association
> Michigan Circuit Judges Association
> Michigan State Association of Supervisors.

He said that his group also represented 49 counties of Michigan, and his argument was against any and all federal programs that might "encroach . . . upon the sovereignty of the states" because such programs also weakened local governments. A subsequent witness before the same committee represented the city of Detroit. He stated flatly that "the previous speaker . . . does not represent the municipal governments of Michigan. Municipal government in Michigan is represented by the Michigan Municipal League. . . ." He argued in favor of the joint federal-state-local programs that the previous witness had condemned.[22] This conflict roughly represents the opposition between the smaller, rural communities and the larger urban ones. But unanimity, even among groups representing officials within a given government, does not always exist. For example, associations of police and fire officers have been successful in establishing pension funds and minimum wage scales through state legislation. City councils, mayors, city managers, and others have objected strenuously on the grounds that such legislation shifts control of local affairs from local to state hands.

The power of group efforts by local officials varies with time, place, and the political milieu. Rural, small-town, suburban, and smaller city groups

[22] Fountain Subcommittee *Hearings,* Part 2, pp. 424–36, 449–58.

are generally more effective within the states than those representing the larger cities; this is mostly because, as we have seen, the formal institutions are more receptive to their views.[23] Big city organizations are more effective on the national than on the state plane. But this is not to say the other groups are any less effective there. If organizations of rural officials have less to do with congressional and national administrative matters, it is because they can get what they want through channels of official representation and through the activities of private groups, such as the American Farm Bureau Federation. Furthermore, the local cause of all but the biggest cities vis-à-vis the national government is also most frequently the state cause. Organizations such as the Council of State Governments (for general issues) and the American Association of State Highway Officials (which establishes standards of construction officially promulgated by the Federal Bureau of Public Roads) effectively substitute for groups of local officials representing constituencies outside the metropolis.

IV. LOCAL ORGANIZATION OF INFLUENCE

Almost every large city maintains a full-time legislative representative in the state capital. Philadelphia does. In addition, the mayor himself makes a lobbying journey to Harrisburg during legislative sessions on an average of once or twice a week; and the city annually invites all members of the legislature to come to Philadelphia to view big city problems on the scene.[24] San Francisco has two full-time representatives in Sacramento, where they work "12 months a year."[25] Los Angeles has a larger delegation. These are typical cases. No technique of persuasion is left untried. A St. Louis mayor made an 1,800-mile tour of Missouri's hinterland; his mission was to convince rural members of the legislature of the necessity for maintaining the big city's tax on earnings.[26] Efforts such as these supplement the close political and personal relations that may exist between local and state

[23] Even when unreceptive, state officials must respond to simple power. A midwestern governor was asked why he did not join the movement to abolish townships in his state—townships, according to the questioner, being vestigial governments of no utility. The governor might have replied that townships served more purposes than they were given credit for, but instead he only said: "Sir, the township officers are too damned well organized in my state."

[24] See Mayor Dilworth's testimony before the Fountain Subcommittee, *Hearings,* Part 1, pp. 336–66.

[25] *Ibid.,* Part 2, p. 1049.

[26] Baker, *op. cit.,* p. 29. In many states, efforts of the larger cities are augmented by work of the Municipal League, while the latter may be the sole legislative representative of the smaller cities.

leaders. A member of the state legislature is frequently identified as the "spokesman" of his locality. A phone call or visit by a mayor to the governor or legislative leader may be the most effective channel of local influence on state programs. An Illinois legislator told an interviewer that "a telephone call from Mayor Daley [of Chicago] can control 40 of the 42 Chicago Democratic votes in the House."[27]

The larger cities also have many resources for exerting strength in Washington and in the field offices of Washington agencies. Cities from San Francisco to Philadelphia maintain full-time representatives in Washington. Some congressmen regard this as criticism of their own efficiency in giving service,[28] and not all large cities keep their own employees in the capital. In any case, local officers are in daily contact, by telephone and actual visits, with one or more members of the congressional delegation. Cities turn to their congressmen and senators for administrative aid as well as for legislative purposes. Congressional offices are even used to influence state programs. Mayor Dilworth has revealed how this may be done. He was bitterly critical of the Pennsylvania Highway Department for neglecting Philadelphia interests. He thought that federal legislation should be amended so that larger cities "could directly appeal" to the federal agency concerned. Even without such legislation, he had arranged, "through the intercession of the two senators," meetings with members of the national Bureau of Public Roads. "Of course, it causes some bad feelings back in your own state highway department when you go over their heads, there is no doubt about that, but it reached the point where we felt we had no other recourse."[29]

Officials of all big cities, in Mayor Dilworth's words, "know our way around fairly well down in Washington." So do many leaders of smaller localities. The congressman representing a (usually small) district composed of smaller towns has less "case work" to do and therefore more time for the affairs of municipalities and other local units. The desires of local leaders are less likely to be contested by dissenting minority voices from the same area. For the smaller places, therefore, influence over national programs is often simply the result of local initiative and organization. Where there is local administrative readiness, federal action at the local

[27] Derge, loc. cit., p. 1064.
[28] Philadelphia in 1957 appointed a professional lobbying firm (as opposed to one of its own employees) to represent it in Washington. Mayor Dilworth said that the six congressmen from the city were initially completely favorable to the move but the "newspapers began raising the devil with them on the ground of what were [the congressmen] for, why couldn't they do this. . . ." Consequently, at the request of the congressmen, the contact with the professional lobbying firm was broken off. See Fountain Subcommittee Hearings, Part 1, pp. 360–61.
[29] Fountain Subcommittee Hearings, Part 1, pp. 357–58.

level, in forms prescribed by local leaders, is likely to follow. Local mobilization for such matters is greater where there are full-time professional workers operating the local government, a city manager, for example rather than an old-resident clerk who holds her job because her mother once did or because she is a widow with an epileptic child. But the local forces may also be effectively mobilized by civic groups, such as the Rotary, or by business groups like the Chamber of Commerce, or by community-wide, county-wide, or regional development associations. The source of local organization may be either inside or outside the formal local government, and the fact of mobilization is far more important than its source.

For both large and small local governments, relationships between local leaders and members of the national legislature are crucial in determining the scope of local influence. Party labels frequently do not reveal political postures, and it is not always true that federal-local relationships are closest where the mayor of a city, or the supervisors of a county, are members of the same party as the local congressman or one of the state's senators. Furthermore, a well established rule of congressional "case work" is to aid all constituents, whatever their party. The Democratic senator from a given state will perform services for Republicans, including Republican mayors, if it becomes known that he is more diligent in such matters than his Republican colleague. A member's committee assignment is often of crucial importance in determining the extent of his services, while the simple matter of his personal efforts and energy can make all the difference in the world. It nevertheless remains true that a congruence of party labels, and especially a congruence of factions within the party, maximizes local opportunities for molding national programs to local desires.

The simplest illustrative case is one in which there is not only a congruence of party labels but also a solid consensus on political matters and no troublesome organized minority. From an agricultural Michigan county or an upstate New York area, for example, voters periodically elect Republican local officers and Republican national congressmen who share a common view of the world, including the world of politics. Under such circumstances, any program of the locality becomes *ipso facto* the program of the congressmen.

In contrast, it is easy to find situations in which elected local leaders and congressmen are on opposite sides of the fence. Local influence over a federal act is particularly impaired if the congressional representative is allied with competing groups on the local scene—a most frequent source of this kind of friction. Thus the elected officers of a Democratic city in a Republican county may find a new post office placed where they do not want it. From one perspective this represents the failure of local leaders to control a federal action. Closer scrutiny reveals, however, that an alternate group of local leaders, working closely with the congressional representative, is doing the controlling. Their steering of programs in opposition to the elected officers may represent a genuine divergence of values. It may also represent a way of embarrassing the formal local leaders, thus increasing the possibility of replacing them. This embarrassment is less likely to occur in rural than in urbanized areas, but when it does occur in rural areas its effect is likely to be all the greater. Local leaders of larger communities always have a number of congressmen to whom to turn, and support may be expected from at least one of them. But if the rural local leader is at odds with his congressman, he may find no one else to whom to turn.

In rural and urban areas alike, skilful mobilization of local interests—especially divesting local programs of partisan or factional overtones by making them community programs—does much to overcome the penalties of local-national political discord. Partisanship and factionalism give way before community programs that cut across party and faction lines. The looseness of the American party system makes such cross-cutting pressures easy to mobilize effectively. From the local point of view this is accomplished by taking full advantage of the concerted strength of public and private action.

In general, then, variations in local influence over state and federal programs reflect basic variations in the patterns of representation. Rural overrepresentation in the legislative bodies of states and nation would be expected to give greater influence to rural populations and to rural governments. And it does. The basic unity of interests in rural areas, compared to urban diversity, also gives an influence advantage to the less populated localities. The scales are, however, somewhat balanced by the sheer weight of growing urban populations, a weight particularly effective in the constituencies of governors and the President. Vigorous representation by organizations of local officials, as well as by quasi-public and private interest groups, also gives strength to the urban view, though not to any rural disadvantage.

Differences in representation are not the only factors that determine the influence of urban and rural areas over state and federal programs. We have seen that big cities turn to the national government for solution of many of their pressing problems, and the very appeal to national agencies is a potent weapon against state ones. Big city mayors perceive their disadvantages in a manner not entirely consistent with the facts, overlooking the disunity of their own populations as a source of their cities' relative ineffectiveness in the state legislatures. Nevertheless, this perception itself provides a moral justification for federal-local programs, and it attracts political support for the urban point of view. Further, major political events and personalities can upset the expected greater influence of cities over the office of the presidency than over the national Congress. Finally, how a particular locality at a given time mobilizes community influence is a matter of first importance in determining the degree to which local control is exercised over programs of the state and national goverments.

Chapter 9

LOCAL MOBILIZATION OF
PUBLIC-PRIVATE INFLUENCE

Factors considered up to this point establish the most general boundaries within which localities, as groups, are able to influence state and federal programs. They include: (1) formal representation in legislative bodies, (2) representation in the constituencies of chief executives (in the states, minor executives, too), (3) representation by organizations of public officers, and (4) local organization of influence brought to bear at higher levels of government. These modes of representation constitute a series of partially concentric, partially overlapping, circles within which specific cities attempt to exercise influence over particular state and federal programs. They define the limits of the possible. More purely local considerations determine whether the possible is made actual.

The foremost local consideration relates to point four in the previous paragraph—the ability of the civil community to organize influence and bring it to bear at higher levels of government. The key to that ability lies in the mixture of the public and private spheres which is characteristic of the civil community and, to a slightly lesser degree, of the American system generally.

I. THE MIXTURE OF PUBLIC AND PRIVATE

The mixture of public and private spheres can be seen with great clarity on the local scene. Local influence on national programs is exercised by bringing to bear on national officers the combined weight of the public and private sectors. Where the public-private linkage is strong and where its strength is utilized, local influence over federal activities on the local scene is maximized.

It should occasion no surprise that public and private purposes easily

231

merge; or that a public function in one place may be private in another; or that in a given community there may be easy substitution of public and private responsibilities. Not more than four centuries ago in Europe even tax collecting and the armed forces were in private hands. Within the memory of living men aid for the indigent in the United States was conceived to be charity: a private virtue and a private responsibility.

Some confusion exists in distinguishing the public from the private sphere even for central portions of both. But a determination is in most cases possible. The manufacturer of steel who has important government contracts, for example, convinces both himself and others that his first concern is the national defense. In some larger sense, especially at moments which threaten the fate of the nation, the public concern of the industrialist can be taken as true. For most of the group, however, in noncrisis periods (and for some even in crisis), private ends are primary responsibilities. Profits, dividends to stockholders, responsibilities to employees are paramount values. Similary, officers of the Department of Defense have many obligations to the private sector of the economy. Their programs are carried out with the advice of many business advisory groups, and they must always be sensitive, for economic as well as political reasons, to the need for distributing defense purchases among large and small businesses and among the various regions of the nation. But their primary business is the public business of maintaining the nation's armed strength. The mixture of the public and private in these "pure" cases suggests that the distinction becomes greatly blurred in cases that are not so pure. This is so. At the local level, private groups perform public functions, and public offices are used for private purposes.

PRIVATE GROUPS DOING PUBLIC BUSINESS

Private groups are involved, and often play a dominant role, in a wide assortment of public, local activities. Private schools, including the parochial schools, are an obvious near-universal example of the substitutability of private for public services. Here public and private facilities exist in parallel fashion for common purposes. In other cases, private contributions are used to initiate, or enrich the public program. The recreation program of Casa Grande exemplifies this relationship. The Rotary Club was the principal force behind the drive to secure federal land for the large mountain park, and Rotary funds were used in payment for the land conveyed to the city. The city swimming pool was secured through the joint efforts of the Lions, Rotary, and other civic groups, and the same cooperation was responsible for building a Scout Lodge on city-owned land.[1]

[1] Examples could be multiplied indefinitely. In many places individual businessmen play an important role in recreational programs. In La Fayette, Georgia, the basket-

In still other cases there are complete amalgams of the public and private spheres. They retain their separate identities but become institutionalized as a unified arm of the government. Many health and welfare departments take this form. To cite only one example, Washtenaw County, Michigan, operates public health services through a city-county, visiting nurses' association department. The visiting nurses' association is a private organization deriving its income from private donations and the community chest. It maintains its private character, but it has become an integral part of the official health department. Similar amalgamations can be found over a wide range of activities: from fire departments in small towns that are operated by private volunteer organizations with equipment frequently furnished from public funds, to hospitals in the largest cities in which services to indigent patients are provided through a combination of public funds, medical association cooperation, private university staffing, aid from women's clubs, and donations of time and skill by private practitioners. Local libraries, museums and parks often represent the same combination of public and private resources.

In many cases the private groups make important public decisions, later ratified by public bodies. An observer in Benton, Arkansas, remarked that the local Chamber of Commerce handled "virtually all new projects" for the city. "Anything that must be tested before the city council will formally risk committing itself is handled through the Chamber." Once a program is proved worthy of official city acceptance, it is taken off the Chamber's hands. Ylvisaker has said that in Blue Earth County's largest community, Mankato, the Chamber of Commerce, the Junior Chamber, the Builders' Exchange, and the Manufacturers and Wholesalers Association constituted an "economic legislature." "Here are staged the preliminary, and in many cases the decisive, debates on such issues as whether the commercial zone of the city is to extend more than a block and a half up from Front Street, whether and at what expense the state's postwar planning council should be invited to conduct a local economic survey, whether certain business practices are to be condoned. . . ."[2]

In a number of areas private organizations performing public services directly assume important intergovernmental responsibilities. Welfare activities of the veterans' organizations provide a case in point. Each of the

ball leagues were sponsored by one of the largest businesses; Little League baseball groups by the local bank, a mill, and the Rotary Club; teen-age baseball by the Veterans of Foreign Wars, and teen-age dances by the Womens' Club, utilizing the American Legion clubhouse. The town stadium was built by an *ad hoc* group drawing membership from many civic and business groups. The town square and the courthouse yard were landscaped and maintained by the Women's Club, and plans for new parks in the city were being made in 1958 by a private utility company.

[2] Ylvisaker, *op. cit.*, p. 49.

veterans' groups maintains a nationwide network of "service officers" whose function is to aid veterans in qualifying for federal and state benefits. Where the veterans' groups are strongly organized, their service officers are very active indeed. Under these circumstances an officer of a private club in effect acts as the local representative of a vast federal (and a more modest state) welfare program, and simultaneously represents local constituents in pressing their claims before federal and state administrators. This is an important adjunct to the more widely publicized lobbying activities of the veterans' groups.

In a small town in DuBois County, Indiana, for example, the American Legion service officer has done this work for 12 years. He is a specialist in veterans' benefits, a private public servant of experience and competence. His aim is to be certain that veterans in his community make maximum use of the special services available to them. These have included a state bonus and federal pensions, disability compensation, aid to widows and orphans, hospitalization and medical appliances, educational training, insurance and burial allowances. The officer does not consider it desirable to forward claims for every veteran who comes to him for aid. He feels free on the basis of his experience to tell inquirers that their claims will not be allowed and to advise them not to prepare formal applications. In so doing he exercises greater discretion than many government field officials usually do.

The service officer estimates that he spends a minimum of ten hours a week on his social welfare activities. The breakdown of his work load by his own estimate (Table 12) is an impressive record of services rendered. A considerable private bureaucracy at central points is needed to handle business of this volume, and the Indiana Department of the American Legion has 15 full-time people in the Indianapolis office working on veterans' benefit problems. Moreover, the Legion places its own personnel in the Washington office of the Veterans Administration to act as expediters and as liaison officers between the public and the private bureaucracies.

The other veterans' organizations maintain parallel national networks for the private administration of public welfare services. In DuBois County the Veterans of Foreign Wars and the Disabled American Veterans are active. The very effectiveness of American Legion service officers in the county has led to the practice by the other groups of referring their "cases" to the Legion. In difficult matters, nevertheless, the VFW service officer will take an active role in soliciting aid from the local congressman. In other places the rivalry of the service organizations in the public welfare field precludes this sort of cooperation.

The collaboration in DuBois County among the private organizations

TABLE 12[a]

THE WORK LOAD OF A PRIVATE PUBLIC SERVANT

(breakdown by types of cases of a small town American Legion service officer's function)

Service	Approximate Number of Cases
Indiana bonus applications	250
Pension claims	150
Hospitalization cases	100
Miscellaneous affidavits	1,200
Welfare cases	20
Medical and dental outpatient treatment	50
Insurance matters	50
Guardianship cases involving direct reports to Veterans Administration	10
Annual Income Questionnaires to Veterans Administration with respect to nonservice compensation cases, widows, etc.	500
Back pensions and mustering-out pay	50
Interviews with veterans, widows, guardians, and others	3,000
Letters received on veterans' claims	2,500
Letters written on veterans' claims	3,000

[a] Adapted from the service officer's own record of service rendered over a ten-year period. The table does not include the considerable load of work that involves no direct government contact, e.g., counselling the widows of every deceased veteran in the community and working with ministers and priests on problems of divorce and the care of orphans. Also excluded are (1) services with respect to educational aid because, by a division of labor, the Legion officer for the county handles these "cases"; and (2) services with respect to burials because local undertakers, informed that a deceased person is a veteran, make their own applications for funds.

engaged in veterans' welfare work is matched by collaboration between private and public officers. No local government in the county has any official responsibility for veterans' affairs despite the fact that Indiana, like many other states, makes it possible to spend county funds for a veterans' service officer. The post has not been filled in DuBois County, partially because of the efficiency of the Legion services, and partially because cooperation between the private veterans' groups does not extend to an agreement on who should be named to the official post. The county therefore does not duplicate Legion veterans' welfare activities. But the Legion service officer and county welfare workers nevertheless find themselves working on many common problems. The exchange of information, and referral of persons by one service to the other, is continuous, easy, and informal. The cooperative circle extends beyond the specialized boundaries of welfare activities. For example, the mayor of one of the towns in the county, acting as municipal judge, became irked at the continued necessity of sending a mentally deficient veteran to the county jail (usually at the request of the veteran's wife). The mayor-judge requested that the veterans' service office find some solution. When an application to the Veterans Administration was filed by the service officer on behalf of the veteran, the mayor continued his good offices by writing to the local congressman to insure, as he said, that the application receive "fast and fair treatment."[3]

PUBLIC BUSINESS FOR PRIVATE GAIN

In many cases where private groups perform public business, private advantage is apparent. The service functions of the American Legion are clearly aimed at bringing advantages to Legion members and, by no means incidentally, at strengthening the Legion itself. Sponsorship by the Farm Bureau of extension service activities is a well-known example of a similar amalgamation of public and private purposes. And when a Chamber of Commerce assumes leadership for a local function, it is often possible to see, in the short or long run, some special advantage to the business groups concerned. Nevertheless it is important to distinguish these cases from those in which private business firms perform public services directly for private gain. Here the profit is immediate and the result of contractual obligations assumed by the local government in return for service received.

All localities at one time or another must take advantage of the special skills and competences of engineering and legal firms, planning and survey organizations, and private specialists in public financing and other fields. In the larger local governments—New York and Chicago, for example—the scale of operations is large, specialization is possible, and experts are employed within the government on a full-time basis. Specialists under contract are utilized as an adjunct to the official administrative group. For the smaller local governments, however, many special competences are not available within the official staffs at all. This personnel gap is often filled by professional associations of government workers. Organizations such as the American Municipal Association, the International Association of City Managers, and the Federation of Tax Administrators are an important source of technical assistance and advice over a wide range of activities. Private nationwide organizations, such as the National Bureau of Fire Underwriters, may play the same role. And in all states, official state agencies supply technical aid over a variety of fields, from local borrowing to

[3] Discussion of the welfare activities of the veterans' organization in DuBois County is based upon the field notes of Douglas St. Angelo. See his unpublished Ph.D. dissertation, "Local Influence on Federal Programs," Department of Political Science, University of Chicago, 1959.

school construction, from personnel standards to assessment procedures. We have seen, for example, how the University of Arkansas served as the technical arm of Benton in making an application to the federal government for an urban planning grant and in providing personnel for utilizing that grant once it was received. No state has established a single office to give general assistance of this sort to local units, mostly because the range of aids offered runs the gamut of states agencies, but a number of states have specialized agencies offering local governments a considerable range of services.[4] In a very large number of cases, localities turn to private organizations for this technical service, another incidental demonstration of the easy substitution of the private for the public. Frequently private firms do not simply act as an adjunct to local skills; rather they constitute the local government's total specialized staff.

Casa Grande, Arizona, again provides a convenient example. There a private engineering firm has in effect become the city's planning and construction agency and simultaneously one of its chief avenues of influence in shaping national and state programs to local purposes. The process by which Casa Grande secured its sewage treatment plant illustrates how this relationship operates. It will be recalled that Casa Grande received a construction grant from the United States Public Health Service as well as a loan authorization to cover a special bond issue, from the Housing and Home Finance Agency. The private engineering firm was responsible for negotiating both.

The possibility in the first place that Casa Grande was eligible for this federal aid was made known to city officials by the engineering firm of *Jones and Gore*.[5] In an original letter of contract the engineering company agreed to perform necessary field surveys; prepare plans, specifications, bidding and contract documents; provide a complete inspection for all work done under the project; and, most important, "prepare a project application for the proposed work for submittal to the State Department of Health and the United States Public Health Service." Once the contract was approved by the mayor and the city council of Casa Grande, the entire task of securing the sewage disposal plant for the city was in the hands of the private engineering company, though city officers were kept fully informed and were called upon occasionally for aid.

The engineering firm was in direct contact with the state and federal agencies concerned. It submitted directly to the state Department of Health the elaborate federal form justifying the grant-in-aid to the city. The state

[4] Good examples are New Jersey, New York, North Carolina, and Tennessee.
[5] The firm name given here, as well as other private groups named, are pseudonyms and are printed in italics.

agency had only to certify that the project was "constructed in accordance with state approved plans and specifications," and transmit the application to the regional office of the United States Public Health Service. After state approval of the application, the engineering firm continued direct negotiation with the officers of the Public Health Service. Well before official word concerning the grant was received by the city, an officer of *Jones and Gore* had informed the city manager that he had been "advised unofficially" that the federal grant had been approved.[6]

The Public Health Service grant could not be completed until arrangements were made for financing the city's share of the sewage plant's cost. While managing the grant application for the sewage plant itself, officers of *Jones and Gore* simultaneously steered the local money-raising effort. They did this by looking to another federal program, administered by the Housing and Home Finance Agency, and by mobilizing further private assistance for the city. This assistance was provided by a Phoenix investment securities firm (*Ray, Estes, and Barr*), which acted as fiscal agents of the city in the issuance of the sewage approvement bonds, and a law firm (*Gary, George, Dorfman, and Rust*), which gave the necessary legal advice for the proposed bond elections. The engineering company recommended both the legal and the investment companies to city officers.

Just as *Jones and Gore* had previously taken full responsibility for justifying the Public Health grant, so it supplied all technical information to the Housing and Home Finance Agency. The city's only role was to have the mayor fix his signature to the loan application form. A technical assessment of the city's financial ability to service the loan was at the same time provided the federal agency by the investment securities firm. Once the preliminary loan application had been approved by the Housing and Home Finance Agency, the engineering firm completed the final application and sent it directly to the federal agency, and a copy was sent to Casa Grande. This was a technical document, more than 40 pages in length. Officers of *Jones and Gore* and *Ray, Estes and Barr* visited the Housing and Home Finance Agency in order to work out an arrangement for the bond purchase. And when officers of *Jones and Gore* were informally given notice that the Public Health Service had approved the basic grant, they pushed

---

[6] Federal officials were scrupulous in dealing with the city through the State Department of Health. When a medical officer of the Public Health Service, for example, desired further information on the sewage disposal plant, he sent his inquiry to the state Health Department, which submitted it to the city manager of Casa Grande, who in turn transmitted the inquiry to *Jones and Gore*. The engineering firm was less formal. It replied directly to the state, keeping the city informed through a carbon copy of the response. Officers of the engineering firm followed this up by a direct visit to the field office of the federal agency.

hard by wire and telephone for quick approval of the bond arrangement to avoid the possibility of losing the grant because of delays in the bond financing.

The private firms were also active on the local scene, managing all arrangements for the necessary special bond election. For example, the investment securities firm supplied the city with all the needed forms, including poll lists, tally lists, challenge lists, and signs warning that electioneering could not take place within 50 feet of the polling place. The attorneys supplied the city council with the actual text of the bond resolution and the mayor with the text for his official announcement of the bond election. And when the special election was won, the bond attorneys in cooperation with the engineering firm provided all the technical information needed to support the offering and call for bids; and the engineering firm, in cooperation with the investment company, drafted the city ordinance establishing a sewer-rate schedule to provide income for the repayment of the bonds. Finally, the investment security firm supplied the Housing and Home Finance Agency with all the relevant technical information the agency needed to approve purchase of the city's bonds; then the private firms collaboratively produced for the housing agency an exceedingly long list of documents that were required before the actual purchase of the bonds could take place.[7]

This sort of service to localities by private firms is exceedingly widespread, although existing data do not make it possible to provide exact calculations of its importance in comparison with projects managed by the localities themselves. *Jones and Gore,* which handled Casa Grande's affairs, was the largest engineering firm in Arizona, and a major fraction of its business was with state and local governments. Similar firms exist in other states, some highly specialized in school or road matters, some covering wide areas of work. In Arkansas, private organizations gave Benton the same sort of services that have been described for Casa Grande in Arizona. A number of private engineering and construction firms have departments whose sole responsibility is to encourage local governments to take advantage of existing state and national programs. In some places this service

---

[7] In effect, the Housing and Home Finance Agency asked the city (through its private consultants) to supply justification for the sewage disposal plant very much like the original justification that was necessary for the Public Health Service. In addition there was required a list of classification of laborers and mechanics, their minimum hourly rates, certification by trade unions that the prevailing wage rates were being met, complete plans and contract documents for construction, and the actual forms for contract advertisements, instruction to bidders, forms of the contract, forms of the bid bond, forms of performance and payment bond, and a long list of additional technical data.

extends to bringing together citizens for the formation of special *ad hoc* governments to improve electrical, road, drainage, irrigation, or other services. The private firms are then able to solicit funds and perform work for the very governments they helped to establish.

PUBLIC OFFICERS AND THE PUBLIC-PRIVATE MIXTURE

Private, quasi-governmental, and governmental areas fuse so imperceptably with each other that even public officials cannot distinguish among them. Local officers believe they are serving public purposes while promoting private interests. At least they find it convenient to act as if they do; and in many cases they would not remain public officers if they tried to draw clear lines of separation.

Simple cases of public support for private and quasi-public activities are those in which public funds are involved. The budget of a county or a city, for example, may contain appropriations for a humane society, a children's aid group, a tourist association, a Chamber of Commerce, a 4-H Club, a soldiers' burial fund, a family-operated museum, a poultry society, and an agricultural fair.[8] A step removed from cases of outright donations are those in which departments of the local government (or officers of those departments) are enrolled as active members of private or quasi-private organizations. Chambers of Commerce benefit frequently from this type of relationship.

The activities of locally elected officers, like the "case work" of congressmen and senators, often illustrate the public-private mixture. The mayor of Chicago traveled to Washington in February, 1958, with a pocketful of problems to present to federal officers. He wanted increased aid for public housing, and he wanted the federal government to provide insurance on home mortgages for persons displaced by slum clearance projects. But his primary aim was to seek from defense department officials "top priority for new defense contracts for the Ford Motor Company's aircraft engine factory in Chicago." The mayor explained that he wanted to obtain additional work for the Ford plant because recent layoffs there were the result of cutbacks in defense spending.[9] His concern was not with what the cutbacks were doing to the nation's defense, over which he could have no comprehensive view, but rather with the unfortunate effects they were having on employment in Chicago.

Similarly, local prosperity and not national defense was the primary issue when Mayor George Christopher of San Francisco was charged by

[8] State budgets, as well as the federal government's, are used for analagous purposes.
[9] *Chicago Sun Times*, February 4, 1959.

a political rival with having lost a valuable naval installation for the city. The mayor, his critic said, was "at fault for not sending a lobbyist to Washington, D.C., as we asked him to do. . . ." The mayor's response was to indicate that he would be his own lobbyist. He released a letter he had written to the senior senator from California in which he asked for a conference with "the highest officials of the Department of Defense" to discuss the city's future as a defense center. He said he would try to work out "a formula for the equitable distribution of shipbuilding and ship repair, along with other defense facilities, in this highly-important strategic area."[10]

These are typical examples of public officers laboring for mixed public-private purposes. In such circumstances, of course, the private interests concerned cooperate. Energies are merged for a common end that can be designated public or private depending only upon the perspective from which it is viewed. For example, when it became known in Borger, Texas, shortly before World War II, that the federal government was expanding facilities to produce synthetic rubber, city officials and the managers of the city's largest industries were as one in believing that it would be wholly desirable to locate a new rubber manufacturing plant near Borger. The city was in an advantageous position because it was located close to a deposit of natural gas, a principal ingredient of synthetic rubber, and because a basic industrial complex, including large refineries, was already located nearby. Yet a number of other oil and natural gas centers were competing for the synthetic rubber factories, and it was by no means certain that one would be located in or near Borger. Officials of the city, civic leaders, and businessmen joined forces to fight for the plant. In the words of the then city manager, "all of us worked like the devil, and [Senator] Tom Connally worked right along with us." The city manager, in company with officers of the petroleum corporation which would operate the plant, made a number of trips to Washington, D.C. City officials realized that their work benefited the petroleum company. Then and afterward, they were also sure that success in locating the plant near their town was of first civic importance. "It brought us some problems, but it also brought us a lot of new residences and a lot of our prosperity."

The extreme case of the public-private mixture occurs when a single person cannot tell at a given moment whether he performs a public or a private service. In Texas a number of cities have official Boards of City Development. Board members in Borger were appointed automatically by the city council on the nomination of the local Chamber of Commerce, and the secretary of the Chamber was automatically named manager of the

[10] *San Francisco Chronicle,* January 13, 1959. But on February 4, 1959, it was announced that San Francisco was sending a full-time lobbyist to Washington, D.C.

Board of City Development. Fifteen leading businessmen of the city were thus given official advisory posts in the city government. Moreover, the Chamber of Commerce in 1958 received half of its total budget by a direct subvention from the city in the guise of an appropriation to the official Board of Development. Functionally it was hard to say whether the city paid the Chamber to do the city's work, or whether the city paid for the private activities of the Chamber, or whether the Chamber made a contribution of labor and time to the city for public purposes. All three statements were true, and they were true for many individual actions by many persons. The Chamber, for example, was responsible through its paid staff for developing the sidewalk and sewer programs of the city. Sidewalks were built only if 50 per cent of the homeowners on a given block agreed to pay the cost, at which time all owners could be assessed. Chamber staff members drummed up the needed support.

Even more significantly, a given individual simultaneously represented the private Chamber of Commerce and the public Development Board in matters involving the state and federal governments. Representations in 1957–58 were made (before federal agencies) to increase postal services and to extend airline services and (before state agencies) to build a colosseum just outside the city limits. In all such matters, a community spokesman truthfully could say that he represented both the Chamber and the city. Nor, if pressed, could he distinguish one role from the other. It was even impossible to determine at any given moment whether a representative of Borger was spending private or public funds. The Chamber secretary and Development Board manager explained: "I go to Washington to testify before the Civil Aeronautics Board, for example, as a representative of this city. I don't know until I come back whether my trip will be charged to [private] Chamber or [public] Development Board funds. What difference does it make? They are used for the same purpose. I see which of the funds has more liquid cash in it. Then I charge my trip to the one that can take the item most easily."

II. ANALYSIS OF FUNCTION:
THE PUBLIC ROLE OF PRIVATE GROUPS

The dependence of local governments upon civic organizations for the performance of public functions is in some cases the simple result of official caution or official ineptitude.[11] And the incentive of private firms is clear:

[11] This accounts for the important role played by the Community Club in the upstate New York community of Springdale, according to Vidich and Bensman, *op. cit.,* pp. 130–31.

profit. The less simple and less clear aspects are, nevertheless, the more important ones for understanding the operation of the American system of government.

First, the sponsorship of public activities by civic and social groups gives the local community the opportunity of trying out politically what otherwise might not be tried at all. If private sponsorship proves successful, the public body often assumes responsibility without political penalty. Second, private civic sponsorship also gives the people of a community a sense of molding activities to their own specifications. This is particularly true in large national programs like that of veterans' welfare services: one can go to his friend at the grocery store or the freight office and there find personal aid in matters involving complicated forms and distant Washington offices. The services of government are thus translated into very human and very personal terms.[12]

In addition, the network of public services maintained by private groups represents in some measure savings for public treasuries. This is seen directly in the failure of DuBois County to appoint an official veterans' service officer. It is true for many other private-public services. The Community Chest budget of any large city, for example, may include lagniappe items such as summer camps that might be considered inappropriate for public treasuries in some local communities. But such private budgets also contain many items—hospital and welfare services, for example—that would undoubtedly become charges against a public budget if they were not supported by privately collected funds.[13]

Third, the firms for profit supply the expertise and sophistication needed for the planning and execution of large and complex governmental programs. They serve as a supplementary arm of local governments—like state agencies in some programs, like professional associations in others—

[12] Whether the same services would be, or actually are, performed by official local governments or by the Veterans Administration itself—or whether the special privileges available to veterans are themselves desirable—are questions seldom raised at the local level.

[13] It may be true that the total social cost would be less for the same services if they were entirely supported by public funds and entirely administered by public officials. This might, for example, reduce costs of duplicating personnel for both fund raising and administration. Assuming this to be true does not negate the point made in the text. Year-to-year budgetary savings for public bodies are not inconsistent with larger total public-private costs.

From the private side, the public-private mixture plays an important legitimating role. For civic groups it provides purpose and status. For individuals it rectifies what might in other circumstances be deemed improper. A businessman seeking special consideration from a federal agency may have less need for aggressiveness when he can in truth say he is also performing a public service. But if he must be demanding, he can be so with relative impunity when accompanied by city officials who argue that what the businessman wants is what the city needs.

that make it possible for localities to deal expertly and aggressively with the state and federal governments. "What the engineering firm did for us on the sewage disposal system," said the city manager of Casa Grande, "we could not possibly have done for ourselves." From this point of view, private firms are substitutes for civil servants and other professional workers of larger governments. They aid in balancing the scale of power, particularly the power of knowledge and of specialization, between small and large local governments and especially between units of the federal system.

Fourth, the specialized knowledge is also utilized as a means of communication. The *Federal Contributions* manual of the Civil Defense Administration is a large and cumbersome set of regulations, resembling a big city phone book in size and reading partly like a legal, and partly like an engineering, text. City officials, especially those in smaller places, have neither the time nor skill to make full use of it. Salesmen for electronics manufacturing firms are of first importance in bringing possible federal contributions to the notice of local officers.[14] The engineering firm of *Jones and Gore* was similarly assiduous in pointing out possibilities for other forms of federal aid to local officers in Arizona. Officials of Casa Grande were informed in the first place by the engineering firm of the existence and availability of most of the grants from which the city has profited. Other firms in other fields in other states perform the same communications function.

Fifth, knowledge and specialization, given impetus by the desire for profit, are powers of persuasion. The typical contract is received, the bonds are sold, or the facility is built. Considerable investments, especially investments of time, are made in the early stages of any federal contact, and these investments have to be protected by a high percentage of successes. This is a strong spur to the private firm to render rapid and professionally competent work that will stand the scrutiny of federal inspection. More relevantly here, it also enlists the private firms in campaigns for winning approval of local proposals. The process is a simple and natural one. It is abetted by the easy professional ties that exist between federal and private lawyers, engineers, school specialists, and financial experts. They talk the

[14] A city manager of a small midwestern town told an interviewer that he had received a two-way radio system from the CAA "by courtesy of the General Electric Company." The manager said that "the GE salesman told me about the program and filled in all the forms." The interviewer noticed that the radio was made by the Motorola Company. "Sure," said the manager, "that poor GE fellow did all the work and was then underbid by Motorola. But it was still his idea." During World War II the Office of Price Administration carried on an elaborate program to keep butchers informed of rationing and price changes. But a study revealed that butchers hardly ever utilized the official publications. They acted upon information received from their wholesalers.

same language. A phone call or a cocktail conversation can settle in a few moments a problem that might go unsolved for months if it followed the official channel from federal to state to local officer to private consultant and then back up the chain.

Finally and most importantly, the civic groups, local officials and firms-for-profit come together at this point of persuasion. Working as a single unit for a single purpose they utilize all possible avenues for fostering the local program. They can speak with the voice of the Chamber of Commerce at one moment, the Rotary at another, the City Council at a third, the expert engineer at a fourth. They can present their cause at a congressional hearing, a public meeting, or an administrative conference; and though the cause is one, the local voices are varied for maximum effectiveness. If a phone call or wire to a congressman is deemed helpful, it will be sent by a person or group close to the congressman. If a conference in a senator's office will expedite matters, someone in the nexus of public-civic-private relationships can be found to make such a conference possible and effective.

In sum, the public activities of civic groups and business firms strengthen the position of local governments, especially small local governments, *vis-à-vis* the state and federal governments. As the local government's equivalent of a professional, specialized civil service, the firms-for-profit play the principal role. As a powerful lobbying aid at all administrative and legislative points, the civic and social groups are most prominent.

III. THE STRENGTH OF THE MOBILIZED PUBLIC-PRIVATE FRONT

The mobilized locality is very strong indeed. It operates through diverse channels and hits many points of the legislative-administrative process, making use of what we will call the "multiple crack."[15] It capitalizes on the regard of the legislative member for the local constituency, a regard that must be maintained if the legislator is to remain in office. It can be obdurate and badger an administrative official, knowing that the local congressman and state legislator are watchdogs in any administrative affront to local interests.

A single small city can thus win significant concessions from both state and federal officials in establishing personnel standards for the administration of public assistance programs. Local insistence not only maintained in office a person formally without qualifications for his job; it also led to the alteration of state merit standards in order to qualify the unqualified local

[15] See below, Chapter Ten.

incumbent; and to the approval of this change by federal officials.[16] When a federal agency decided for economy reasons to close a field office in a city of 49,000, local officials and businessmen mobilized in protest. They were capable of bringing together for a final conference an assistant secretary of one of the great federal departments, four congressmen, representatives of three others, and representatives of three senators. The decisions was made to keep the office open.[17]

When it was announced that a link of the national highway system was to run through Hillcrest, an unincorporated suburb of Binghamton in upper New York State, residents of the community first asked themselves in despair: What chance do we have against the State Department of Public Works and the United States Bureau of Public Roads? They discovered that their chances were very good indeed. The local citizens established a protest group that included representatives of the Rotary and the Kiwanis; a number of churches and the American Legion; the PTA and the Town Board; the Board of Education and the Children's Home; several garden clubs and a general community association. Leaders of the group were soon in touch with the local congressmen, the state senator, the state and district engineering officers concerned, civil defense authorities, local planning boards, and other officials. "We kept Albany and the Washington Bureau of Public Roads and our legislators at all levels apprised of what we were doing." When their request that the highway be built at another place was initially rejected, the group simply redoubled its efforts. An impartial expert was employed, the local congressmen and both New York senators were again contacted, and over a thousand signatures, telegrams, and letters "appealed to Governor Harriman." The state senator arranged a meeting between community leaders and the superintendent of the state Board of Public Works. Subsequently, a new routing of the highway was established.[18]

A final example of the power of community mobilization comes from the small city of Benton, Arkansas. The Chamber of Commerce, other civic groups, and city officials have worked for a number of years in collaboration with a regional organization, the Ouachita River Valley Association (organized in 1893), for the development of the entire Ouachita River basin, from its mouth, south of Natchez on the Mississippi River, to Camden, Arkansas, a distance of some 610 miles. Congressional authorization

[16] See Paul N. Ylvisaker, "The Battle of Blue Earth County," in Harold Stein (ed.), *Public Administration and Policy Development* (New York: Harcourt, Brace, and Company, 1952), pp. 89–106.

[17] Field notes of Kenneth Gray, Washington, D.C., February, 1958.

[18] Polly Traeger, "Extinction by Thruway: The Fight to Save a Town," *Harper's Magazine* (December, 1958), pp. 61–71.

for a comprehensive plan of development for the river basin was received in 1950. The River Valley Association continued its efforts to implement this plan through actual appropriations. Several dams of particular importance to Benton were included in the original development plan.

In 1950–51 the Benton group and the association worked hard to secure a dam and reservoir to supply reserve water for the city and its growing industry. No existing federal legislation justified federal aid for that type of construction. Strong local support was nevertheless mobilized, with the Chamber of Commerce taking the lead. The cooperation of both Arkansas senators and the local congressmen was assured. Fifteen years earlier, the Benton people had requested a dam for flood control on the Saline River near the city. The ensuing preliminary study undertaken by the Corps of Engineers at the request of the Senate Public Works Committee had revealed the project to be unjustified economically under the then-established benefit-cost ratio formula. The Benton group knew that it would no doubt still lack justification, but requested another study in order to get data for use in obtaining federal assistance under other legislation that would allow the construction of some type of storage reservoir. The second study was made by the Corps of Engineers, and part of it produced evidence of widespread public support from the entire county. (Since there were three times as many people in the county as in the city, city leaders believed county support was of particular value.) With this information, the Arkansas senators steered an appropriation through Congress for a complete engineering survey for the proposed dam.

While the survey was being made, Benton's elected and civic club leaders, with technical aid from the Ouachita Association, were working with their congressional delegation, particularly Senator McClellan, in order to draft a new statute that would justify federal aid for the then unjustified dam. This was not difficult. Legislation was prepared extending federal aid (1) to dams supplying water to "federally impacted" areas, i.e., places affected by national defense efforts, when (2) the local government concerned contributed substantially to the project.[19] Benton, of course, qualified under the first specification; the second was completely acceptable. The proposed bill had the advantage of being attractive to other areas of the country, and, therefore, attractive to other members of the Congress. Introduced by Senator McClellan, the bill was duly passed by Congress as the Community Facilities Act. Benton received $225,000 of federal aid under the law and the city's contribution came to $81,000. Benton's application for aid was submitted before the law was passed, and consequently became the first city in the country to obtain a grant under

[19] Field notes, Federalism Workshop.

the new legislation. Local leaders took satisfaction in the speed with which they qualified for aid. But after all, they reasoned, wasn't it justice for them to benefit first from national legislation for which they were responsible?[20]

IV. ALLIANCES WITH NATIONAL INTEREST GROUPS

In efforts to shape state and federal programs to local purposes, officials are frequently abetted by private interest groups operating on the state and national levels. The linkage of public and private operates at many levels in the American system of government. The point made here is a limited one: private (and quasi-public) organizations may represent the localities in state and federal programs very much in the manner that organizations of local officials do.

On the plane of federal legislation, for example, the strong support of the CIO Political Action Committee for liberalized public housing and urban renewal programs has complemented efforts for these programs by the Conference of Mayors. The national Rivers and Harbors Congress, whose officers are nominally members of Congress and whose membership is composed of a mélange of public, quasi-public and private groups, has wielded a potent influence on behalf of localities over the numerous projects of the United States Army Corps of Engineers. The National Association of Home Builders has opposed some city-sponsored legislation (public housing) and supported others (more liberal financing for home mortgages). Professional groups like the American Library Association have given important assistance to some localities, as in the successful lobby to establish federal support for rural libraries.

Official and private espousal of a common cause may of course conceal divergent purposes. When the National Association of Manufacturers, for example, argues against federal contributions for public education on the grounds that local control might thus be prejudiced, it is fairly clear that another purpose, perhaps even more important than the announced one, is to prevent expanded federal expenditures and to maintain the decisional

---

[20] The data on the Benton dam are from the field notes of Daniel J. Elazar, June, 1958. Benton has, as a consequence of the dam construction, a full year's reserve water supply (with attendant recreational advantages) in a lake less than 16 miles from the city. In 1958 the city and the Ouachita River Valley Association were still working to achieve their large general-purpose dam, and in that year it appeared that they were on the verge of success because local interests from all over the country had succeeded in persuading congress to expand the list of "benefits" used to compute the benefit-cost ratio.

point at the state and local level, where the Association feels its influence is more certain. That the covert purpose is congenial to some localities—those smaller in size and in the South—and antagonistic to others—the more populated places outside of the South—is evidence again of divergencies in the local view. This issue aside, when a given group of localities can work congenially with a private interest group, the chance of success in influencing action is increased. Forestalling opposition from private groups is an equally important element in the strategy of local influence. These rules are equally true for the federal and state governments, for legislative and administrative decisions.

V. THE BUNDLE OF LOCAL SERVICES: PATTERNS OF LOCAL INFLUENCE

Evidence of the strength of the mobilized locality in influencing state and federal programs is not evidence of absolute local control over those programs. All localities do not pursue the same objectives. The influence of localities, as we have seen, varies according to differences in several modes of representation, differences in the degree of community solidarity, differences in the relationships between local and other political leaders, and differences in the extent to which local causes are linked to public and private interest groups. Local influence also varies markedly from program to program. Local control over the many projects of the United States Army Corps of Engineers is maximized by virtue of the Corp's definition of its mission, its relationship to Congress, and its procedures for determining what to do. While local influence is not inconsiderable regarding certain aspects of foreign policy, the nature and extent of that influence is of a different and lesser order than is true with respect to the Corps of Engineers.[21] Even apparent "victories" of local interests in national programs conceal processes of compromise and mutual adjustment. Despite the success of Blue Earth County in altering social security personnel regulations to suit local purposes, the county in the years of altercation developed a program of public assistance in conformity with state and national standards, standards that were initially opposed by local leaders. Despite Benton's victory in securing federal funds that gave the city a small dam and reservoir it would not otherwise have qualified for, many localities, including Benton, have worked unsuccessfully to meet national standards for Rivers and

[21] For discussion of shared functions in foreign policy matters, see Dennis Palumbo, "The States in American Foreign Policy," unpublished Ph.D. dissertation, Department of Political Science, University of Chicago, 1960.

Harbors aid. Despite Hillcrest's success in altering the course of a federal-state highway, many communities have found that even well-organized protests have not been sufficient to reroute such highways.

The correct conclusion to be drawn from considerations of local influence on federal and state programs is not that the local view is controlling. It is rather that the localities can be full and powerful participants in the process of decision-making. A civil community with the ability to organize and marshall local sentiment on a specific issue will not be overlooked or ignored in the decision-making process. Not every civil community is always or everywhere decisive: some have unrealistic demands, some face insurmountable internal or external opposition, some make demands that are inescapably unconstitutional; but in most programs at most times some group of localities (or a single one) exercises a substantial influence. Most erstwhile federal domestic programs have been locally initiated, often simultaneously, in many civil communities across the country. Their proposals are transformed by Congress into concrete programs, not in response to any "federal power grab," but because congressmen respond to local pressures. Once established, the local operations of those federal programs can often be locally controlled, again because of local ability to mobilize influence from the courthouse to the White House. It is the locality's ability to initiate and control the bundle of government programs affecting its destiny regardless of the source of such programs which makes it a civil community—with a large measure of internal cohesiveness despite the seeming chaos of governments that serve it. The local leaders concerned understand this intuitively, and local influence generally has more meaning for them than the fact of federal or state administration and financing. From this perspective many federal or state programs may be considered local programs.

The discussion of local influence in national programs raises the question of how the general or national interest is expressed when local and other special interests are so powerful. The problem is dealt with earlier in this volume (see Chapter One), but two points must be made here.

First, the power of the mobilized community (or group of communities) is the power of those who feel strongly about a given matter when the majority is uninterested or indifferent. Yet the widespread understanding among localities (and other groups) of how the system may operate to their special advantage is a two-edged sword. On the one hand, acting upon that understanding often gives them what they want. On the other hand, it sets up numerous competing influence sources. If every individual locality, and every group of localities, and every group of officers serving localities were well organized to exercise influence, the influence of any single place or group would thereby be diminished. Special privileges are readily available only if the knowledge and skill necessary to achieve them are relatively limited. Widespread sensitivity to what localities may accomplish with respect to federal programs means, in effect, that the special influence of one locality or one group of localities is continuously checked by the influence of others. The wealth of the nation is such that accommodations to many special requests are possible. At the very least, however, it can be said that attempts to satisfy competing special interests have the effect of freeing the hands of those who have broader views. The competition of special interests may make it easier to assert and implement the general interest.

Second, the rhetoric of local influence in national policy becomes easily and falsely a rhetoric of conflict. It erroneously conceives localities, on one side, and the central government, on the other, as being in the position of adversaries. There are undoubtedly occasions when the advantage of one locality, or group of localities, or region becomes a disadvantage to the nation as a whole. But in most circumstances at most times compatibility rather than conflict of interests is characteristic. There are simple and sufficient, if often overlooked, reasons for this compatibility, rooted in the character and values of the United States as a civil society. Voters at local and national elections are the same voters. A congressman in one role is a local citizen in another. Professional workers in education, welfare, health, road building, and other fields adhere to the same standards of achievement, regardless of which government pays their salaries. Federal and local governments serve the same people. These facts contradict the concept of localities and the federal government as adversaries. So do actual operations. "Victory" for the locality is not national "defeat." The Public Health Service did not grant funds grudgingly to Casa Grande for a sewage disposal plant. The Reconstruction Finance Corporation believed it served national purposes when Benton, Arkansas, was chosen as the site of an alumina plant. National and local officers celebrated in common when Chicago's application for a large urban renewal program was approved by the Housing and Home Finance Agency.

The process we have described—of localities sharing responsibilities in state and federal programs—extends from formal decision-making on the most important issues to informal cooperation in the everyday tasks of government. A single incident can sometimes encapsulate the entire system. A congressional subcommittee, headed by Congressman Fountain of North Carolina, held its San Francisco hearing in an auditorium of the San Francisco Health Center. Motor noises from a nearby roof at times were disturbing. The city director of public health, when it came his turn to testify, volunteered the information that the noises were made by three pumps that were owned by the Public Health Service of the national Department of Health, Education, and Welfare. They pumped air through filters, and the filters were sent daily by city health workers to federal laboratories as a contribution to a national cancer research program. The committee council inquired whether this was a direct federal-local relationship. The following colloquy took place:

> *City Health Director:* It is a direct relationship . . . but the [six-county Bay Area] air pollution-control district receives copies of all the correspondence between the Public Health Service and our office, in both directions. [Earlier the local health director had revealed that the State Department of Health also received full information and that the state and Territorial Health Officers Association, acting in an advisory capacity to the United States Surgeon General, had aided in establishing this local-federal relationship.]
>
> *Committee Council:* Where did the initiative come in starting this particular project?
>
> *City Health Director:* From the Public Health Service. . . . However, we did have a project operating here, and we still have it operating for oxygen determination, in which we cooperate with the State Department of Public Health on that particular aspect of it, and we do our own laboratory work with our own money. The state does a certain amount of laboratory work, and the equipment which the state loaned us has been loaned to the state by the Public Health Service. Does that make it complicated enough?[22]

Complicated it is; complicated because cooperative.

[22] Fountain Subcommittee *Hearings,* Part 3, p. 1042.

Part IV

THE DYNAMICS OF THE SYSTEM

Chapter 10

AMERICAN PARTIES AND
THE AMERICAN SYSTEM

It is easy to overlook the uniqueness of American political parties. They represent something alien to what foreign students understand by the term. A distinguished Indian scholar recently told an interviewer that he thought it was a fraud and a mockery to call American parties by that name. They had no program, they had no internal solidarity. The reasoning is familiar and easy to follow. A foreign student does not wish to designate as a "party" a political group that controls a majority of the Congress but cannot formulate and by its own votes pass a program; that stands together only, and not always then, for national elections, for matters of patronage, and for the organization of the legislative business; that in convention chooses a leader and presidential candidate by unanimous vote and then, in Congress, forces that leader as President to depend upon defections from the other side.

The argument, in a single sentence, is that the nature of American political parties accounts in largest part for the nature of the American governmental system. The specific point is that the parties are responsible for both the existence and form of the considerable measure of decentralization that exists in the United States. The focus of attention is, therefore, upon the classic problem of a federal government: the distribution of power between the central and peripheral units. Yet there is little in what follows concerning formal, or constitutional, power relationships. The word "sovereignty" does not appear. No decision of the Supreme Court is cited. Our concern here is not with juridical concepts but with social reality; not with the sporadic umpiring of the courts but with the day-to-day pattern of who does what under whose influence; not with the theoretical locus of supreme powers but with the actual extent of the sharing of decision-making in legislation and administration between the central, state, and local governments.

To say that the parties function as decentralizers is not to say that they cause decentralization. The two statements are of a different character. Saving until later a discussion of the difference between *function* and *cause*, we ask: How, then, do the American parties contribute to the operation of the American system?

I. THE BASIC SHARING IN LEGISLATION

They do so, first of all, by determining in legislation the basic sharing of functions between the federal government, on the one hand, and state and local governments, on the other. Today—given the great increase in the velocity of government in the twentieth century—the parties play a role of first importance in determining the manner of sharing of federal programs by the other levels of government. Now, as in the first days of the republic, the local as opposed to the national orientation of most members of the national Congress leads to legislation that gives important responsibilities to states and localities.

The point is supported generally by the entire development of grant-in-aid programs. The grant device from this perspective allows the federal government to utilize its purse powers while sharing with the states important responsibilities. Two specific examples will demonstrate the process. The National Airport Act of 1946 and the unemployment insurance provisions of the Social Security Act of 1935 are both "hard cases" with respect to the sharing hypothesis because there seemed to be compelling reasons for establishing each program without state participation.

The issue that vexed Congress with respect to the postwar airport bill was a direct sharing question: Should local governments, particularly large cities, deal directly with the Civil Aeronautics Administration or should the flow of applications and funds between large cities and the CAA be "channeled" through state agencies? The cities, as represented by Mayor Fiorello LaGuardia of New York and the United States Conference of Mayors, supported direct negotiations; the states, through the Governors' Conference, demanded channeling. An impartial observer, if one could be found, would almost certainly have concluded that the cities had the better case. The states had few and rudimentary airport authorities and contributed from 1933 through 1945 less than 1 per cent of total national airport expenditures. Federal funds were preponderant (75 per cent), the federal-local pattern then existing had proved successful, and federal administrative officers testified that, for larger airports, they preferred to deal directly with local authorities.

The Governors' Conference took a strong stand in favor of channeling,[1] and the Senate version of the bill was amended so as to channel all federal aid to airports through state agencies. The amendment was proposed, by no means incidentally, by Republican Senator Owen Brewster of Maine, a former governor and former chairman of the executive committee of the Governors' Conference. The roll call vote on the Brewster mandatory channeling amendment was as follows:

	Republicans	Democrats	Progressive	Total
Yea	24	15	1	40
Nay	7	26		33

Party influence is apparent, but party control plainly is not: the Republicans, a clear minority in the Senate of the 79th Congress, could not have won without the 15 Democratic defectors and the 13 Democratic nonvoters. The crucial factor that brought victory to the states was not party affiliation. It was the conduct of senators who had once served as state governors. Sixteen ex-governors voted. Twelve were in favor of the amendment. Party identification made little difference: five of six Republican ex-governors and seven of ten Democratic ones supported the channeling amendment. Fifty-two per cent of the senators who were not ex-governors approved it. If the ex-governors had divided their votes in the same way as their fellow senators did, the amendment would have been defeated by one vote rather than winning by seven.

The Brewster amendment represented an extreme victory for the states and the principle of shared functions. Later in the debate it was pointed out that some states had no airport programs or indeed no legislative authorization at all to concern themselves with airport development. A further amendment, passed without discussion and by voice vote, authorized the CAA to carry out airport projects directly with localities in states which could not themselves participate for lack of the necessary legislation. The states could share in airport development, said the Senate, if they were in the slightest way prepared to do so. The choice was the states': only if they failed to provide enabling legislation for their own executives would the federal agency deal directly with local governments.

The House version of the bill was originally reported out by the Committee on Interstate and Foreign Commerce with no channeling provision whatsoever. It was amended on the floor with virtually no discussion and by voice vote to provide that:

[1] In addition to the several resolutions of the Conference, telegrams from 46 governors endorsing channeling were read into the record.

Nothing in this act shall authorize the submission of a project application by any municipality or other public agency which is subject to the law of any state if the submission of such project application by such municipality or other public agency is prohibited by the law of such state.[2]

The bill was easily passed by the House in this form. The Conference Committee was presented in the two versions of the bill with what would seem to be a distinction without a difference. The Senate version provided for channeling of all funds through state agencies, but if states did not have appropriate agencies, then direct federal-local relationships were authorized. The House version said nothing about channeling, but any state by its own initiative could make channeling mandatory and thus prohibit direct federal-local negotiations. In both cases, the states could control the administrative handling of the federal program. Nevertheless, the state governors and the ex-governors who were senators, tried hard to have the Senate version of the bill adopted. For a time Republican Senate members of the Conference Committee held fast as a group. The Conference Committee remained deadlocked for four months. The bill finally reported and passed was substantially the House bill: affirmative state action was required if federal airport funds were to be channeled through state agencies.

The history of the 1946 National Airport Bill is notable for the clear view it gives of the cross-cutting of party by other lines of influence. It is equally significant for the opposite views taken by the states, on the one hand, and the larger cities, on the other, in this case competing for participation in the sharing process. The role of Congress was in many ways that of mediator, seeking in Senator McCarran's words "to effect a compromise" between state and local views.[3] The strength of the idea of shared functions was perhaps most marked in the unstated assumption by all concerned that the federal government would not do the airport construction job alone. Constitutional authority, fiscal predominance, administrative ease, and military necessity might have justified this course of action. There is no evidence to indicate that any responsible group or agency seriously considered it. The states did not get all they wanted in the bill. But their failure to achieve full victory carried no sting. The power to compel channeling—which was the power to insure their full sharing in the airport program—

[2] A subsequent attempt to require channeling was initially defeated, then passed by teller vote, and finally shelved by a roll call. The final defeat was by a vote of 185–170, 164 Democrats and 20 Republicans opposing the mandatory channeling, 133 Republicans and 36 Democrats favoring it.

[3] U.S. Congress, Senate, Subcommittee on Aviation of the Committee on Commerce, *Hearings, Federal Aid for Airports,* 79th Congress, 1st session (March 13–23, 1945), p. 114.

remained exclusively a state power. Approximately half of the states have subsequently taken action to require both the channeling of applications by local units to the federal government and of funds from the federal government to the localities. That more states have not taken this action is evidence that the states' political power to bring about their participation in federal programs is sometimes greater than their energy or desire to effectuate their participant role. The political strength of the states on the national scene may not correspond to intrastate political unity or administrative readiness.

The social security legislation of early New Deal days is a more important case, illustrating the political process by which the states insure their basic sharing in national programs. The legislation may indeed have marked a turning point in the federal system. If the social security program had been established as an all-federal one, as it very nearly was, the American government might look very different today. In a revealing aside in a book review on another matter, Rexford Guy Tugwell described how close he and Harry Hopkins came to establishing social security as a program administered completely by the national government:

> As an historical matter it was not hard to see that the states had declined in importance as responsibilities had gravitated to Washington. . . . It was not a mistake to think that the states were obsolete and ought to be superseded by regions; the mistake was in thinking that it would be the policy of President Roosevelt to enhance the federal power (of which he was talking a good deal in those days of crisis) at the expense of that of the states. He seemed to conclude finally that both powers could be enhanced at the same time. The evidence that he still clung to the Brandeis-Frankfurter view was not supplied within the Committee on Social Security. In this struggle Harry Hopkins and the writer [Tugwell] put up what seemed to them to be a sound argument against decentralization to the states. Miss Perkins' advisers were determined to use the social security system to bolster up the states. This appeared to be so costly an undertaking that it might jeopardize the system and, anyway, it would artificially interrupt the natural desuetude of the states. On an historic occasion Mr. Hopkins and the writer asked the President if it was wrong to go on objecting. The answer was not clear; but it was plain that the objections were not going to win his support. The objectors then withdrew from the committee and from then on neither had any contact with the formulation of the report, the shaping of the law, or its subsequent administration. Both regarded it as perhaps their worst defeat.[4]

[4] Rexford Guy Tugwell and Edward C. Banfield, "Grass Roots Democracy—Myth or Reality?" *Public Administration Review,* Vol. X, No. 1 (Winter, 1950), pp. 48, 50.

There existed, as a matter of fact, several solid justifications for joint federal-state programs. The sharing-of-functions controversy raged most hotly over the administration of unemployment compensation. For one thing, the 1933 Wagner-Peyser Act had established employment offices on a federal-state basis (replacing an older all-federal program). This clearly helped "to fix the world into which the unemployment insurance system was to be cast."[5] For another, many states had existing systems of unemployment insurance and argued that a new federal-state program would be less damaging to ongoing activities than an all-federal one. Wisconsin had a system, and a former Wisconsin official, Edwin Witte, was executive director of the Cabinet Committee on Economic Security which was drafting the new federal legislation. Thirdly, it was believed that a federal-state system would have greater constitutional security than an all-federal one. Miss Perkins put great weight on this point.[6] Finally there were many arguments put forward with respect to the desirability of state experimentation, decentralization, and local participation.

Nevertheless, none of these factors or any combination of them was controlling. Mr. Tugwell is completely accurate in his recollection that the unemployment compensation program came very close to being established as an all-federal one. In addition to the general argument with respect to the "natural desuetude" of the states, there were other good technical reasons for establishing an all-federal unemployment compensation program. The movement of workers and the consequences of unemployment were clearly national in scope. A nationally uniform unemployment insurance scheme seemed highly desirable. Many relief and other depression programs had been administered directly from Washington. The states, administratively and financially, were in poor condition.

In the eyes of those directly concerned, the weight of the argument was in favor of the all-federal unemployment compensation program. Miss Perkins has revealed that the Cabinet Committee in fact made, relatively late in their deliberations, a formal decision to recommend such a program. But the decision was reversed in favor of the collaborative federal-state programs. The final decision was made not for technical reasons, but rather for purely political ones. Miss Perkins has written:

> After long discussion we [the Cabinet Committee] agreed to recommend a federal system. We went back and informed colleagues in our own Departments. Within the day I had telephone calls from members of the Committee saying that perhaps we had better meet again.

[5] Paul Douglas, *Social Security in the United States* (New York: McGraw-Hill Book Company, 1936), p. 32.

[6] Francis Perkins, *The Roosevelt I Knew* (New York: Viking Press, 1946), p. 291.

There was grave doubt, our latest interviews with members of Congress had shown, that Congress would pass a law for a purely federal system. State jealousies and aspirations were involved. So we met again, and after three or four hours of debate we switched back to a federal-state system.[7]

The entire depression crisis, plus the powerful personal leadership of President Roosevelt, plus the proclivities of Tugwell and Hopkins, Wallace and Morgenthau, plus the overwhelming congressional majorities possessed by the Democrats—all provided the opportunity *par excellence* for a basic reordering of the federal system. Yet it was not achieved even under these ideal conditions. It was not achieved because of decisive political considerations. The distribution of power within the majority party made an all-federal system impossible. Virtually the whole debate on the unemployment compensation bill, as introduced in its federal-state collaborative form, revolved around criticism of the power given to federal administrators. Amendments to the bill, proposed by Democrats and passed with Democratic votes, drastically curtailed even the limited power initially provided federal agencies. When the Cabinet Committee was making a following for its proposal and when the proposal itself was altered by the Congress, the localism of the legislator was the controlling factor. If party solidarity had been effective, if it had been believed that the most powerful President since Lincoln could have held on to his majority, the unemployment compensation program would have been an all-federal one. The lack of party solidarity fundamentally establishes the marble cake of shared functions that characterizes the American federal system.

II. LEGISLATIVE INVOLVEMENT IN THE ADMINISTRATIVE PROCESS[8]

The second manner in which undisciplined political parties establish the character of the American system is through the impact of congressmen and senators on national administrative agencies. The congressional interference is constant, effective, and institutionalized; and it is almost uniformly exercised in behalf of local interests, individual, group, and governmental.

Some aspects of the process of legislative involvement in administrative affairs are formalized and well known. Administrative justifications before

[7] *Ibid.*, pp. 291–92. Miss Perkins does not mention Tugwell's or Hopkins' views, but notes that Henry Wallace and Secretary of the Treasury Morgenthau argued for the all-federal system.

[8] I am indebted to Kenneth E. Gray, a member of the Federalism Workshop, for aid at many points in this section.

subcommittees on appropriations or the routine hearings before permanent legislative committees provide natural access points for members of the Congress to press constituency interests upon administrative officials. The Legislative Reorganization Act of 1946 made explicit the responsibility of the standing committees: each "shall exercise continuous watchfulness of the execution by the administrative agencies concerned of any laws, the subject matter of which is within the jurisdiction of such committee."[9] Both houses also have a Committee on Government Operations, each spawning a number of subcommittees. The House of Representatives has founded the (Moss) Subcommittee on Government Information, another potent tool for looking into all sorts of administrative processes on behalf of local constituents. The Congressional Committee on Printing has assumed a number of direct administrative responsibilities. Joint committees of the Congress and the executive have for many years made decisions concerning the purchase of land for wildlife refuges and national forests.[10] The General Accounting Office is a creature of Congress with important and pervasive executive functions.

The legislative involvement with executive business has been aided by a number of statutes in recent years that require administrators to report either past actions or future plans to committees of Congress or to Congress as a whole. The 1955 Defense Appropriations Bill, for example, required the Secretary of Defense to secure prior consent of the House and Senate Appropriations Committees before turning over departmental functions to private industry.[11] The Secretary of the Air Force, by a 1949 statute, was required to "come to agreement with" the House and Senate Armed Forces Committee before acquiring land for a guided missile proving ground.[12] Sometimes the statutes provide merely for "consultation" between congressional committees and administrative agencies; sometimes for reports; sometimes for a suspensive veto that Congress can exercise over administrative actions.[13] The Joint Tax Committee maintains a "branch office" in

[9] 79th Congress, 2nd session, 60 *U.S. Stats.* I, 832.

[10] See Paul H. Appleby, *Policy and Administration* (University: University of Alabama Press, 1949), pp. 8–10.

[11] Department of Defense Appropriations Act of July, 1955, Section 683. 69 *U.S. Stats.*, p. 231. The President strenuously opposed this provision, and it was eliminated in 1956.

[12] 63 *U.S. Stats.,* I, 66.

[13] Lease purchase agreements are subject to direct committee supervision. Public Law 519, 83rd Congress, 2nd Session (1954), amending the Public Buildings Act of 1949, reads (Title I, sec. 411 (e) and Title II, sec. 202 (g)): "No appropriation shall be made for purchase contract projects which have not been approved by resolutions adopted by the Committee on Public Works of the Senate and House of Representatives respectively. . . ." Identical statements are included in legislation relating to the Post Office and General Services Administration. See the review of such statutes in

the Bureau of Internal Revenue where members of the Committee's legal staff review administrative recommendations for tax refunds and credits and do not cavil at recommending that the legislative committee reverse administrative determinations.[14]

A general scrutiny of administrative stewardship is of course made possible by this elaborate formal network of legislative-administrative relationships. The very nature of the reporting and consultation statutes, as well as the local propensities of the members of Congress, substantially turn the system into one in which, for better or worse, the legislator serves as the watchdog of national administrative actions on behalf of local constituents. The system formally provides very extensively for joint responsibilities by congressional committees and administrative officers in the making of administrative decisions. Administrators in effect must "preclear" their actions with the appropriate subcommittee, in some cases with individual members. At the very least, an opportunity is provided congressmen and senators to register protests—in many cases having the effect of a veto—with respect to problems affecting their constituencies. At its worst, the system makes it possible for an individual member to bludgeon an entire department on behalf of local causes.

The formal and legally specified overviews of administrative action by legislative committees frequently encounter strenuous opposition by executive officers and are in some cases subject to constitutional inspection. In any case informal understandings are far more important than the provisions of law for producing continuous legislative involvement in administrative affairs. Rivers and harbors legislation caricatures the process. Members of Congress nominally serve as officers of the leading interest group (the Rivers and Harbors Congress), and the Corps of Engineers has established procedures for entertaining local viewpoints in the field and for implementing them in Congress, subject only to whatever measures of control can be mustered by the Bureau of the Budget and the President. Institutional caricatures, like others, make overt what elsewhere may be hidden.

J. Malcolm Smith and Cornelius P. Cotter, "Administrative Accountability: Reporting to Congress," *Western Political Quarterly,* Vol. X (June, 1957), pp. 405–15. Concurrent resolutions by Congress, as well as statutes, are used to terminate administrative powers, require administrative actions, and veto administrative acts. See Cornelius P. Cotter and J. Malcolm Smith, "Administrative Accountability to Congress: the Concurrent Resolution," *Western Political Quarterly,* Vol. IX (December, 1956), pp. 955–66. See also Kenneth T. Kofmehl, "Congressional Staffing: With Emphasis on the Professional Staff," unpublished Ph.D. dissertation, Department of Political Science, Columbia University, 1956.

[14] See sec. 3777 of the Internal Revenue code. In 1949–50, almost 1,000 cases involving $766 million were reviewed in this fashion.

Thus the Committee on Interstate and Foreign Commerce instructs the Department of Commerce and the regulatory agencies with respect to the imposition of licensing fees.[15] A House subcommittee prevents the Department of Defense from closing military hospitals that, according to defense officials, are no longer necessary.[16] The House Armed Services Committee, in an effort to keep military post exchanges from competing with local retailers, works out detailed, informal agreements with each of the services concerning what may and may not be sold at post exchanges. Regulations of the services implement these legislative-administrative settlements.[17] Appropriations hearings provide the stage for securing many commitments of this sort.

The most important and pervasive method of legislative participation in the administrative process is through activities of individual legislatures on behalf of local constituents. Workers on the Hill call this their "case work." Alben Barkley had a story illustrating both the range of services rendered and the occasional ingratitude of the recipients:

> . . . I called on a certain rural constituent and was shocked to hear him say he was thinking of voting for my opponent. I reminded him of the many things I had done for him as prosecuting attorney, as county judge, as congressman, and senator. ҉ recalled how I had helped get an access road built to his farm, how I had visited him in a military hospital in France when he was wounded in World War I, how I had assisted him in securing his veteran's benefits, how I had arranged his loan from the Farm Credit Administration, how I got him a disaster loan when the flood destroyed his home, etc., etc.
>
> "How can you think of voting for my opponent?" I exhorted at the end of this long recital. "Surely you remember all these thing I have done for you?"
>
> "Yeah," he said, "I remember. But what in hell have you done for me lately?"[18]

Barkley's joke is a form of caricature, and again it reveals what is widespread but frequently unrecognized. The joke in fact may be documented. Its exact counterpart may be found in a letter to a constituent written by

[15] *Congressional Record,* Daily Digest, 83rd Congress, 2nd Session (March 30, 1954), pp. 239–40.

[16] *Chicago Daily News,* May 3, 1957.

[17] Field notes, Washington, D.C., February 11, 1958. Consultation on what may be sold in commissary stores has a statutory base. See H.R. 12738, sec. 613, Department of Defense Appropriations Bill, 85th Congress, 2nd Session.

[18] From *That Reminds Me,* by Alben W. Barkley. Copyright 1954 by The Curtis Publishing Company. Reprinted by permission of Doubleday & Company, Inc.

Texas Congressman Wright Patman. Mr. Patman was angry when he wrote his letter because he had heard that the constituent was supporting another candidate for the congressman's seat. The congressman reviewed his relationships with his constituent over a period of 20 years. On no fewer than 20 occasions Mr. Patman had interposed himself in administrative matters on behalf of this single voter and his family. Ten of Mr. Patman's acts concerned the Post Office Department (the congressman not only secured jobs for his constituent and members of his family, but saved them from being dismissed when they misappropriated funds); two concerned part-time jobs with the Bureau of the Census; one involved an authorization of veterans' payments to students in a school founded by his constituent; three concerned loans from the Reconstruction Finance Corporation, the Small Defense Plants Administration, and the Public Housing Administration; and three concerned War Department matters involving the names of ROTC officers who might make good candidates for insurance sold by the congressman's constituent.[19]

The very tone of Mr. Patman's letter indicated his belief that all this activity was perfectly normal and proper. He was doing what congressmen naturally do. Senator Lehman of New York spent considerable personal sums to augment his staff, the largest fraction of which devoted itself to constituent problems. Not that senatorial staffs are picayune. Senator Douglas revealed in 1957 that his offices in Washington and Chicago had 21 employees whose total salaries amounted to $119,222.[20] A good fraction of these people were involved in the simple process of opening the senator's mail and finding an easy way of handling it—a form response, a stereotyped referral slip, or a request for a pamphlet from one of the departments. These processes involve little direct contact with the administration, though in more than a few instances the proper response, even if a canned one, is dependent upon a phone call to a bureau or a corridor conversation with a bureau representative.

Aside from clerical workers, Senator Douglas' personal staff in 1958 included three full-time persons in a Chicago office and five in Washington. Some of their work was concerned with publicity, party and campaign relations, and the Senator's obligations in legislation. But their principal task was to place problems of the senator's constituents before the appropriate administrative office in the way best calculated to achieve the con-

[19] The letter was placed on March 23, 1956, into the record of the Subcommittee for Special Investigations of the House Committee on Armed Services investigating the sale of life insurance to prospective members of the military service. It was reprinted in *The Reporter*, July 12, 1956, pp. 19–22.

[20] *Chicago Sun Times*, March 27, 1957, p. 10.

stituent's satisfaction—and, it goes without saying, the constituent's vote for the senator. Their very areas of specialization say a good deal about the nature of the senator's constituency.[21]

The examples of Senators Lehman and Douglas are good ones because they should remove any doubts concerning the propriety of such acts of involvement by the legislator in administrative matters. In these matters, as in others, Messrs. Lehman and Douglas provide models of the ideal senator. There is no hint of venality or impropriety. Their activities are a normal part of a senator's business. Senator Douglas' complaint is only that the government does not provide him with enough money to maintain an office staff large enough to do all the things he thinks ought to be done in response to the needs of his large constituency.

The looseness of the party system makes all of this activity possible. It also makes it nonpartisan. Congressional and senatorial administrative assistants form a pool of expertise, not least of all in case work problems, and a member of one party may have an assistant from another. Congressional delegations often join forces without regard to party for city, state, or regional issues. For example, the California congressional group for a number of years has been formally organized for such purposes, and the entire West Coast delegation also works as a single unit in pursuit of mutual interests. When it becomes known that the Republican senator from a given state is less efficient than his Democratic colleague in case work matters, Republican voters (including mayors and state legislators) find their way to the Democratic senator's office. They receive service all the

[21] The essential difference in the roles of American and English legislators in this respect is made clear when one compares their respective office staffs. Unless the M.P. holds a ministerial post, the government does not even provide him with an office. Since M.P.'s usually can't afford to pay for their own office accommodations in the neighborhood of the Parliament, most of them have no office at all. And the idea that 21 people at an expenditure of more than $100,000 a year would not be sufficient for an M.P. to do his job properly would only arouse the utmost mirth. Again, unless he holds an official post, the M.P. is not even supplied with a personal secretary from government funds. This does not mean that a British M.P. neglects to nurse his constituency. "Holding surgery" to listen to constituent complaints and proposals is a well-established part of a member's routine. But his course of action is not a demanding one with respect to the departments. Except for matters of information, the M.P. must take up his constituent problems with the ministers concerned, themselves controlled by party decisions, and on no issue may he transgress party policy or embarrass party stewardship or, as American legislators do as a matter of course, join with opposing members contra party pro locality. An opposition member has greater latitude, but still not that of successfully badgering bureaucrats up and down the line in behalf of local interests. At least if he tries this course of action, he is politely referred to the appropriate ministerial officer who, as a member of the majority party, has a powerful platform from which to respond.

more prompt and energetic because of the delight that the Democratic member and his staff have in building fences where none existed before. Even this minor partisan pin-pricking may be absent. For example, Colorado Senators Millikin (Rep.) and Johnson (Dem.) maintained a common office, jointly staffed, to give service to those with general state problems. Correspondence from the office carried the signatures of both senators. This cooperation continued for 12 years without a major disagreement.[22]

Although no exact calculation of the magnitude of the case work is possible, one can be sure it is very large indeed. The Office of Price Administration during the calendar year 1944 averaged 1,397 congressional "contacts" (phone calls, letters, and visits) a week, or more than two for each five working days from each member of the Congress. Peak periods were higher. In one 20-week period of 1943, for example, congressional letters alone averaged 842 weekly.[23] Data for less vulnerable agencies during less intense periods are also available. In the ten working days between May 21 and June 4, 1958, the Department of the Interior received by actual count 553 pieces of congressional mail, plus an estimated 200 phone calls—an average of 75 congressional contacts per day.[24] The Office of Legislative Liaison of the Air Force averaged 3,000 "monitored" congressional contacts a month (as of the winter of 1958), and this did not count the personal contacts of the three Senate and four House liaison officers who were on full-time duty in the Capitol and House and Senate office buildings. (The Army, Navy, and Department of Defense each have separate liaison staffs.) The congressional liaison office of the Department of Health, Edu-

[22] Field notes, February, 1958. The relationship was apparently a unique one. See *Roll Call* ("The Newspaper of Capitol Hill," published weekly by Capitol employees), February 12, 1958.

[23] Tabulated from "OPA and Congress," and "Report of Congressional Mail," Office of Price Administration, National Archives, Record Group 188. For technical reasons, all of these tabulations are underestimates. A report by an OPA official, Frank Ketcham, estimated (and probably overestimated) that from 1943 through 1946, the agency received 150,000 letters and telegrams and 300,000 telephone calls from members of Congress. See "Legislative Supervision of the Office of Price Administration" (typescript, 1947), National Archives, Office of Price Administration, Record Group 188.

OPA kept a separate record of *public* criticisms made of its operations by members of Congress. This recounts a lengthy list of bitter attacks in committee hearings, in public speeches, and on the floor of both houses. The March 1, 1944, entry is more meaningful than most others. It says simply: "No Congressional criticism this day." *OPA and Congress* (a duplicated intraoffice information sheet), March 6, 1944.

[24] The count was of mail processed by the Correspondence Control Office in the Secretary's office. Many bureaus in the department, for example the highly decentralized Bureau of Land Management, undoubtedly handle congressional mail directly. The number given, therefore, is an underestimate. The phone calls are similarly underestimated.

cation, and Welfare, according to an official estimate, responds to 500 congressional phone calls a month, and this, one can be sure, is only a fraction of the total number of calls to the many bureaus and field offices of the Department. An official tally by the Department of Agriculture recorded 5,564 letters from Congress during 35 working days, a daily average of 159.[25]

A very large fraction of work on behalf of constituents is implemented through personal contacts between a senator or congressman's staff members on one side, and permanent administrative officials, on the other. Through trial and error a congressional assistant will discover those officials who "get things done." The assistant expedites his case work by phoning (or bucking a letter) to those with whom he has established good relations in this fashion. The administrative agencies seek to service congressional requests more effectively by establishing special liaison staffs and by institutionalizing procedures for congressional contacts. The Air Force in 1958 had, under the command of a major general, 137 people (55 officers and 82 civilians) working in its Office of Legislative Liaison.[26] Every congressional contact, except those made directly by Air Force officers who worked in the House and Senate office buildings, was "controlled" (the word was used to indicate the desire to render more rapid service), no fewer than nine copies of a route slip being distributed strategically to the personnel concerned. Many agencies have rules that require congressional requests to be answered within a limited time (24 or 36 hours), and many others require all but the most routine responses to carry the Secretary's signature.

A similar institutionalization occurs within the congressional offices. We have already noted the specialization of function within the staffs. In addition, a given staff develops systems of priorities in handling cases; there are so many that all cannot be given an equal amount of time. Priority ratings are influenced by the source of the request (an old friend, a heavy

[25] U.S. Congress, House, Subcommittee of the Committee on Appropriations, *Department of Agriculture Appropriations for 1959, Hearings,* 85th Congress, 2nd Session (1958), p. 865. Magnitudes of interference are also impressive when measured from the side of the individual congressman or senator. In a single week, for example, one midwestern senator received 122 constituent letters which required 100 separate contacts with administrative agencies, involving 30 different bureaus or offices in 12 departments as well as 12 additional federal agencies.

[26] Field notes, January, 1958. For analysis of liaison offices, their numbers, functions, and costs, see U.S. Congress, House, Committee on Government Operations, H.R. No. 2947, *Availability of Information from Federal Departments and Agencies,* 84th Congress, 2nd Session (1956). For questionnaire and responses, see U.S. Congress, House, Committee on Government Operations, *Replies from Federal Agencies to Questionnaire Submitted by the Special Subcommittee on Government Information of the Committee on Government Operations.* 84th Congress, 1st Session (1955).

campaign contributor, or a city mayor get special attention), but they are sufficiently flexible to bring out full effort when a "good case"—in terms of injustices done, or publicity potential, or constituency reaction—comes from an unknown and uninfluential constituent. In many cases priorities are established in terms of staff interest and competence. Priority values determine whether a request is handled with a perfunctory phone call or routine reference—"just to get it from our desk to theirs"—or with a full-scale assault upon administrative offices.[27] The latter may start with a staff assistant making a casual inquiry and end with the congressman or senator meeting personally with a cabinet secretary or attacking an agency on the floor. The institutionalization of interference also includes establishment of standards for ignoring or rejecting constituent requests, based upon considerations of decency and propriety, as well as of defining acceptable and unacceptable modes of dealing with administrative officers. Both sets of standards vary from member to member and from staff to staff. It is not difficult to find examples of the abusive congressman demanding, as the price of his support, that an inordinate fraction of funds for a particular agency be spent in his district or that normal procedures for rotation of military assignments be abrogated for the son of an important constituent. (By the same token, there exist administrators who promote their bureau, their project, or themselves by encouraging congressmen to expect such special considerations.) More generally, congressional involvement is amiable. It is directed at producing rapid and full consideration for constituent and district interests. It expects impartial treatment without favoritism,[28] but it also demands special consideration for hardship cases and other special circumstances. It assumes an adversary quality only when the normal give and take between legislative requests and administrative adjustment breaks down.

The legislator's ability to command information from the administrative agency, on the one hand, and his access to press, television and radio, on

[27] Even with respect to the most perfunctory inquiries, a member of Congress usually wants it to appear to the constituent that a special and "justifiably privileged" service has been rendered, whether that is the case or not. Staff members and administrators play this game knowingly with each other. When a service is rendered to a constituent that an administrative agency was going to do in any case and it only appears that congressional interference had something to do with it, full credit is likely to be publicly accorded the congressman by all hands. Staff members call this a "fall in" case. A special kind of "fall in" case is the practice of administrative agencies to inform congressmen and senators in advance of the decisions to spend money or build public works in their areas, thus allowing the members of Congress to make the announcements in the local newspapers.

[28] But all congressional inquiries lead to two forms of favoritism. They hasten the consideration of the particular problem raised; and they move the decision from lower to higher levels of the administrative hierarchy.

the other, produce a double sanction. Administrators know that any failure to satisfy congressional requests may result not only in congressional penalties, ranging from criticism to new legislation, but also in adverse publicity. Both sorts of penalties are avoided whenever possible, although where congressional requests are immoderate, administrative officers have recourse to both legislative and public means of defense. The typical means of avoiding clashes and of promoting the continuous executive-legislative collaboration necessary for administrative action is through the mechanism of "preclearance." Preclearance works in both directions. Legislators informally work out in advance with administrators what they later formally request. More relevantly here, administrative officers clear contemplated actions in advance with strategic subcommittees and members of Congress. The clearance is sought not only for new legislative and budget requests but also for contemplated administrative actions. Important clearance activities of this sort are those that seek advance approval of the congressmen and senators who represent localities to be affected by what a national agency is planning to do. Mechanisms of clearance range from phoning a congressman to full-scale conferences between bureau chiefs and committee chairmen with staff members from both sides in attendance. The informal periodic reporting of agencies to subcommittees is a particularly effective means of preclearing administrative acts.

The widespread, consistent, and in many ways unpredictable character of legislative interference in administrative affairs has many consequences for the tone and character of American administrative behavior. From the perspective of this study, the important consequence is the comprehensive, day-to-day—even hour-by-hour—impact of local and state views on national programs. No point of substance or procedure is immune from congressional scrutiny. No point of access is neglected: from phone calls to regional offices to conferences with chiefs of the Bureau of the Budget; from cocktail conversations to full committee investigations. A very large portion of the entire weight of this impact is on behalf of individual constituents, group interests, and state and local governments. It is a weight that can alter procedures for screening immigration applications, divert the course of a national highway, and amend a social security or flood control law to accommodate local practices or fulfill local desires.

The larger point is that virtually the whole process of legislative participation in administrative affairs would be impossible if the American party system were more tightly controlled from the top. With disciplined parties, the freewheeling interference of individual members on behalf of local constituents could not take place. It would not be tolerated. If members of the parties were responsive to their leadership, if they were committed to a program, if they were subject to discipline in the event of defection from that program, the administration of policy, like the making of policy in legislation, would be unified and controlled. The individual legislator would have less access to the administrator and less influence in altering administrative direction in terms of nonparty interests. To a corresponding degree there would be diminished the leavening of national administrative programs by state, local, and other group interests, interests that are so energetically represented by members of the Congress.[29]

III. THE ADMINISTRATOR AS POLITICIAN

Bluntly put, it can be said that the failure of national political leaders to control the legislative members of the party accounts, *ipso facto*, for their failure to control the national administration. Stated positively, the undisciplined party system impels administrators to seek political support for their programs. The parties do not supply this support, and administrators and their programs cannot survive without it. This leads to the third important manner in which the parties affect the operation of the American system: they make the administrator play a political role.

The previous discussion makes clear why some administrative officers walk in fear of the telephone. A bureau chief in the Department of the Interior once told an interviewer that half of his fellow chiefs intoned a daily morning prayer: "Oh Lord, let not the chairman of my appropriations subcommittee call me this day." But if a bureau chief is craven before a

---

[29] The discovery that pressure groups in Great Britain are vastly influential does not in any way alter this point. Indeed, it strengthens it. As Samuel H. Beer has pointed out, the relationships between interest groups and government in Britain are "quasi-corporative." The "individual legislator, and the legislature generally, under cabinet government occupy a less important position." The American legislative committees have no British counterparts. Interest groups in Britain are agglomerated in large associations, and they must focus on winning the support of the minister and the Chancellor of the Exchequer. In the United States there are more points at which pressure can and must be applied. The Cabinet control of the party and government means precisely that pressure upon that government can be effective only if approved by the Cabinet. The American contrast—where, in Beer's words "pressure is so much noisier and less tidy"—rests upon the lack of party control. See Beer's two excellent articles, "Pressure Groups and Parties in Britain" and "Representation of Interests in British Government," *American Political Science Review* Vol. L, No. 1 (March, 1956), pp. 1–23; Vol. LI, No. 3 (September, 1957), pp. 613–50. See also W. J. M. MacKenzie, "Pressure Groups in British Government," *British Journal of Sociology* Vol. VI, No. 3 (June, 1955), pp. 133–48; S. E. Finer, *Anonymous Empire* (London: The Pall Mall Press, 1958); J. D. Stuart, *British Pressure Groups* (Oxford: Clarendon Press, 1958).

congressman, how then can he follow the directives of his own administrative superior? If a legislator can substantially interfere with the operation of an administrative office, how can a series of administrative offices concert their efforts into a unified program?

Administrators need not be craven. Some welcome conflict with congressmen; some are polite but unresponsive; some just plain hide; some can find protection by appealing to other legislators; some serve other masters who themselves may be influential with significant congressional blocs; some are successful in protecting their own views and their own agency program by deftly juggling the opposing views of congressmen, constituent groups, administrative superiors, and others. The very multiplicity of pressures upon administrators provides opportunities for discretion, independence, and invention.

These activities of the administrator do not sound significantly different from the activities of many congressmen. And they are not. As Paul Appleby and others have made clear, the higher administrator performs an intrinsically political role.[30] The reason such a role is possible for the administrator is the same reason that accounts for the interference in administration on the part of the legislator. The administrator can play politician, just as the politician can play administrator, only because the parties are without program and without discipline.

The administrator's response to the unprotected position in which the party situation places him is a natural one: he seeks support where he can find it. One ever-present task is that of nursing the Congress of the United States, that crucial constituency which ultimately controls his agency's budget and program. For this task he may partially depend on the clients his agency serves. To take an easy example, the Veterans Administration can rely to some degree upon the veterans' organizations to reward the supporters and punish the opponents of VA programs. But this is neither a quick nor a certain process. And it is necessary for the administrator to lubricate the continuous interaction of his agency with Congress and individual congressmen by a sympathetic consideration of, if not downright accommodation to, congressional requests. This is the administrative basis of the successful congressional case work we have already considered. An additional point can now be made clear. The case work relationship goes

[30] Appleby, *op. cit.*, and *Big Democracy* (New York: Alfred A. Knopf, 1945); Norton E. Long, "Power and Administration," *Public Administration Review* Vol. IX, No. 4 (Autumn, 1949), pp. 257–64; Herbert Simon, Donald Smithburg, and Victor Thompson, *Public Administration* (New York: Alfred A. Knopf, 1950), pp. 381–401; Harlan Cleveland, "The Executive and the Public Interest," *The Annals*, Vol. CCCVII (September, 1956), pp. 37–54.

both ways. Not only is the congressman dependent upon administrative accommodation. A more fundamental truth is the administrator's dependence upon the congressman.

From the administrator's side, the servicing of congressional requests is to build the political support without which the administrative job could not continue. The servicing role sometimes takes an extreme form. "We try to consider ourselves part of the senators' staffs," an agency liaison officer recently told an interviewer. This posture is sometimes assumed to offset the attitudes of those bureau workers who view congressional interference with something less than receptivity. But even the completely task-oriented administrator must be sensitive to the relationship between case work requests, on the one side, and budgetary and legislative support, on the other. "You do a good job handling the personal problems and requests of a Congressman," a White House officer said, "and you have an easier time convincing him to back your program."[31] Thus there is an important linkage between the nursing of congressional requests on local matters and the most comprehensive national programs. The administrator must accommodate to the former as a means of gaining support for administrative programs. But the importance of administrative service to members of Congress is evident at every hand, particularly in the size and cost of the liaison staffs themselves. At least five staffs—Army, Navy, Air Force, Veterans Administration, and Civil Service Commission—maintain quick-service offices on Capitol Hill. Other liaison officers headquarter themselves in the offices of friendly congressmen or senators. Liaison with the highest executive officers is close and continuous. "Preclearance" of administrative acts works at every level, a cabinet officer consulting a subcommittee chairman on important points, a liaison clerk calling a freshman congressman on others.

The need for executive offices to build their own political support is the principal cause of that conflict which characterizes American administrative life—among departments and among bureaus within departments. It accounts for the relative immunity of some agencies from presidential control; and the stronger the source of independent support, the more immune the agency is. It explains why an act of legislation may not at all define the real power of an administrative office.[32] The necessity put upon administrators to build political support also provides the sociological base for

---

[31] Quoted in *Wall Street Journal,* June 16, 1959.

[32] "A price control law wrung from a reluctant Congress by an amorphous and unstable combination of consumer and labor groups is formally the same as a law enacting a price support program for agriculture backed by the disciplined organizations of farmers and their congressmen. [But] the differences for the scope and effectiveness of administration are obvious." Long, *loc. cit.,* p. 257.

Charles G. Dawes' otherwise enigmatic statement that "every member of the Cabinet is the natural enemy of the President."[33]

One result of administrative politics is that the administrative agency may become the captive of the nationwide interest groups it serves or presumably regulates. In such cases no government may come out with effective authority: the winners are the interest groups themselves. But in a very large number of cases, states and localities are also influence winners. The politics of administration is often a process of making peace with legislators who for the most part consider themselves the guardians of local interests.[34] It is politics that makes possible decisive influence roles by states and localities, as well as by other power groups.

The position of states and localities may be directly tied to nationwide interest groups: the United States Conference of Mayors has been at one with the Congress of Industrial Organizations, for example, in urging federal urban renewal programs. In other cases, the state or local view (frequently opposed to each other) may be represented on its own: as when a congressman hastens the transfer of a defense airport to a municipality, or a group of congressmen aids state welfare officers in bringing about changes in federal public assistance rules, or a bureau chief, under pressure from city lobbyists and the state delegation (one of whom is a key figure in the bureau's appropriations subcommittee), orders the establishment of a field office where it otherwise would not have been.[35] The complete mobilization of a state or locality—when elected officers, community and business leaders, and congressional delegations act in concert—produces maximum potency. A group of state legislators and administrators will travel to Washington with the governor's blessing, accompanied by leading businessmen and several administrative specialists from state offices. They will convene a meeting which is attended by both of the state's senators and a majority of the state's congressmen. The federal administrators summoned

[33] I am indebted to Louis Brownlow for the Dawes quotation. Richard F. Fenno, Jr., supplies an overview of the literature on presidential-cabinet relationships and an illuminating case study of the divisive effects of independent sources of support in "President-Cabinet Relations: A Pattern and a Case Study," *American Political Science Review,* Vol. LII, No. 2 (June, 1958), pp. 388–405.

[34] Even those legislators who define their roles as national statesmen—Senators Douglas, Mansfield, and Fulbright, for example—cannot neglect constituency interests responsible for their officeholding. Such men occasionally must draw a thin line between national and local interests, sacrificing the latter where it clearly conflicts with the former in their definitions. For the majority of both houses, however, the potential conflict is not even discerned. What is good for the 24th District is *ipso facto* good for the nation. Many election statements make this explicit.

[35] The localities even attempt to use this process to alter *state* policies. See the testimony of Mayor Richardson Dilworth of Philadelphia before the Fountain Subcommittee, *Hearings,* Part 1, pp. 357–58.

to this meeting perforce pay careful heed to the requests of such a group.

Bureaucrats and the bureaucratic system in the United States do not at all follow the model classically set forth by Max Weber. The system is not described by his term "monocratic control," control by one from the top. Such control must be predicated upon the existence of a program—defined, administered, and policed by an organized majority. The United States majority is unorganized. It has no single program, no single leader or cadre of leaders, no effective means for political punishment, and therefore no easy mechanism for controlling the political activity of the bureaucrat. Lack of political program and control not only leaves room for, it compels, political activities on the part of the administrator. Without this activity he will have no program to administer. And the political activity of the administrator, like the administrative activity of the legislator, is often turned to representing in national programs the concern of state and local interests, as well as of other interest-group constituencies. The total impact of the political role of the bureaucrat is not unmixed. He may use his political power to aggrandize his own position and his own agency, thus shifting the power focus to the center. He may produce, or be forced into, a situation in which no government is in effective control. But always he must find support from legislators tied closely to state and local constituencies and state and local governments. The administrator at the center cannot succeed in his fundamental political role unless he shares power with these peripheral groups.

IV. THE MULTIPLE CRACK

Those who have discovered the politics of the administrator have not made sufficiently clear that his political attributes are not unique or privileged. His role in politics is matched by that of other individual citizens and other professional and vocational groups. The administrator is in politics not because he is an administrator; but because the political system gives all groups the privilege of playing politics. The administrator is in a somewhat privileged position. But his position differs in degree, not in kind.

This suggests a fourth manner in which the parties are crucial in establishing the way the American system operates. Weber predicted that "the living machine which is bureaucracy, in cooperation with the inorganic-physical-machine, is bringing about the structure of super- and subordination which will characterize the future. In that structure human beings will be forced into impotent obedience—like fellaheen in the ancient Egyptian state." What a misreading of the current American situation this is! The picture is not one of obedience at all. It is one in which individuals and groups attempt to influence governmental policy at every step of the legislative-administrative process. We call this the "multiple crack" attribute of American government.[36]

If the parties were more disciplined, the result would of course not be a cessation of the process by which individuals and groups impinge upon the central government. But the present state of the American parties clearly allows for a far greater operation of the multiple crack than would be possible under the conditions of centralized party control. Local and other interests make themselves felt in the British system. But it would be difficult to adduce any cases in which British interests act as American ones characteristically do: finding and attempting to exploit cracks at literally innumerable points in the legislative-administrative process. If legislative lobbying (from the committee stages to the conference committee) does not produce results, the cabinet secretary is contacted. His immediate associates are petitioned. Bureau chiefs and their aides are hit. Field officers are put under pressure. Campaigns are instituted by which friends of the agency apply a secondary influence on behalf of the interested party. A conference with the President may be urged. Attempts may be made to activate the wife of the President or other members of his immediate family.

To these multiple points for bringing influence must be added the multiple voices of the influencers. Consider, for example, those persons in a small town who wish to have a federal action taken, whether it be to amend a flood control law, or to secure a sewage disposal grant, or to have a surplus plant sold to a local businessman. The easy merging of public and private interests at the local level means that at selected points in the decision-making chain the local Chamber of Commerce speaks; at other points it is the Rotary Club; at still others the mayor or city manager, and at still others an engineering consultant or fiscal specialist. In many matters the state or national professional organizations of local officials can be enlisted. In almost every case individual congressmen and senators, and not infrequently whole state delegations, will make the local cause their own. Federal field officers who service localities frequently assume local views. So may elected and appointed state officers. Friendships are exploited, and political mortgages called due. The voices are many, but the cause is one. Many people and groups may accumulate pressures at a single point, and, according to rough criteria of efficiency, forces are allocated where they will do the most good. If a phone call to a congressman is deemed helpful, it will be made by a person or group close to the congressman. If a conference in a senator's office will expedite matters, someone in

[36] See above, Chapter One, p. 14.

the local scene can be found to make such a conference possible and effective. If technical information is needed, technicians will supply it.

All local causes, of course, need not be so energetically or efficiently pursued, and even if the need exists the skill and energy may not. The competition of interests—within single localities, between them, between localities and other interests, and between localities and states—complicates the process. Acceptance of a given locality's view is dependent upon the defeat, or more typically the acquiescence, of other interested groups. Despite all qualifications, two facts are indisputable. The lack of central discipline within in the party system makes the multiple crack possible and profitable for those who exploit it. The effect of the multiple crack is further to disperse decision-making power within the institutions of the central government and between the central and peripheral governments.

V. DIVERSE FUNCTIONS AND THE DISTINCTION BETWEEN FUNCTION AND CAUSE

The discussion thus far has attempted to demonstrate how the party system is reflected in the governmental system and particularly how the undisciplined parties function to produce governmental decentralization. It should be made clear that this view (a) does not preclude the parties from functioning in other fashions, and (b) does not involve any simple causal relationship between party and governmental processes.

The first point can be briefly disposed of. The literature abounds in analyses that see the party system as having quite different consequences for government. One such consequence, for example, is alleged to be the difficulty of setting a general course of policy for the government as a whole. A second, related result is said to be that special interests gain undeserved governmental privileges. A third is that disunited parties deprive voters of clear choices and make it impossible to tell who is responsible for particular acts of government. Still a fourth alleged consequence is that the parochialism of party members makes parties "meaningless and even dishonest in the mind of the public."[37] And so the list could be continued. No attempt can be made here to assess the validity of such analyses. It can

---

[37] See a report of the Committee on Political Parties of the American Political Science Association, "Toward a More Responsible Two-Party System," published as a supplement to *The American Political Science Review*, Vol. XLIV (September, 1950). The quotation is from James MacGregor Burns, *Congress on Trial* (New York: Harper & Brothers, 1949), p. 46. See also E. E. Schattschneider, *Party Government* (New York: Rinehart & Company, 1942). This literature is critically reviewed in Austin Ranney, *The Doctrine of Responsible Party Government* (Urbana: University of Illinois Press, 1954).

only be said that the functional consequences of party arrangements are undoubtedly numerous and include many consequences not related to the issue of decentralization. The decentralizing functions of parties and their consequences for political life may be highly valued; and other functional consequences may be considered disadvantageous to particular purposes at particular times and occasionally threatening to the nation as a whole. One task of political analysis is to delineate such contrary consequences (and contrary evaluations) of political institutions and processes.

The principal theme here is that the party system acts primarily to foster decentralization in government. Yet it is easy to show that on occasion it has done the opposite, as when, for example, demands for action by the central government follow the failure of parties to organize effective programs under the auspices of state governments. Thus, even with respect to decentralization, the consequences of parties for government are not simple and do not always move in one direction. Again, political analysis must separate the functional strands and decide in which direction the more important truths lie.

The distinction between function and cause is a more complicated matter. In tracing party functions in terms of governmental decentralization, there is no implication that the parties alone cause decentralization. In fact, parties in the United States do stand in an immediate causal relationship to governmental processes and specifically to governmental decentralization. But it would be a great error to ignore other, more general, causal factors.

In the first place, it can easily be shown that the causal relationship between party and government is a reciprocal one. While the constitutional mechanisms may not be controlling in the perpetuation of decentralized government in the United States, the formal structure remains an important bulwark, offering a framework which acts to shape the party structure in numerous ways. The ways are well known:

1. Under the Constitution, the states have important responsibilities for conducting the election of the President and Vice President—from establishing the mode of choosing electors to managing the electoral machinery. The national government's role is limited to apportioning the elector allotment among the states after every decennial census and assuring that the right to vote in each state is not denied on grounds of race, color, sex, previous condition of servitude, or failure to pay a poll tax.

2. Congress is elected through the states. House districts are apportioned among them on the basis of population after each census, while each state is represented by two senators in the upper chamber. The requirement that congressmen must be residents of the states from which they are elected militates against the English system of a national party with power to

secure the election of certain people by assigning them to safe districts. Since a state's representation in the Senate cannot be reduced without its consent, every state is assured an equal voice in that chamber. The time, place, and manner of electing members of Congress is left to the states (subject to Fifteenth, Seventeenth, and Nineteenth Amendment restrictions), but Congress can act to set basic standards if it so chooses. In fact, it has only chosen to do so in such a way as to increase local control by requiring that representatives be elected from districts ("contiguous and compact" from 1842 to 1929). If all the Representatives in each state were chosen on the basis of which party wins the state, more centralized party organization would be possible. Of course the decision to maintain districts is more influenced by the party system than by constitutional provisions.

3. Members of Congress are constitutionally forbidden to hold any other civil office. This not only enforces the separation of powers but prevents the situation which prevails in parliamentary systems whereby leading legislators are made responsible for administrative functions and are thus tied to the national administration. Approximately one-third of the M.P.'s in the United Kingdom hold administrative posts in the government and are thus tied to their national party for their very jobs.

4. The electoral college system has offered a means for strengthening the state party organizations because it is state-based. The national congressional party caucus that was used to select presidential candidates between 1796 and 1824 represented a nationalizing trend by putting the selection of future Presidents into the hands of national figures. Its overthrow by the convention system restored this power to the state party organizations. Thus a great decentralizing force was made possible because the states are constitutionally responsible for choosing the electors.

5. The fixed and staggered terms for the President and members of Congress lead to decentralization. National leaders do not have the power to call elections, a power which serves as a strong lever for national party organizations and discipline in parliamentary systems and one which allows the national party leadership to frame an issue and force the whole party to run on it.

6. Extraordinary majorities are needed in Congress and the states in order to amend the Constitution formally, adding a measure of stability to those decentralizing features dependent upon constitutional rules.[38]

---

[38] For relevant discussions see Herbert Wechsler, "The Political Safeguards of Federalism: The Role of the States in the Composition and Selection of the National Government," in Arthur W. Macmahon (ed.), *Federalism, Mature and Emergent* (New York: Doubleday, 1955), pp. 97–114; Austin Ranney and Willmoore Kendall, *Democracy and the American Party System* (New York: Harcourt, Brace and Company, 1956), especially Ch. 21.

Though it is true that any disciplined party acting legally and constitutionally could override most of these constitutional restrictive devices, the existence of the devices, when coupled with the socio-economic factors militating against party discipline, is a very potent deterrent to the development of disciplined parties. Thus constitutional impediments serve as sources of support for groups advantaged by undisciplined parties who want to keep the parties disunited.

Franklin D. Roosevelt's experience in his effort to "pack" the Supreme Court is a case in point. The Constitution required that he go to Congress for legislation authorizing the change in the Court's structure. In Congress, his party was at peak strength numerically, but that had no bearing on the outcome, since a sufficient number of Democrats deserted their President and nominal national party leader. FDR's plan failed because of their desertion; the locally-oriented party system made that desertion possible, but the constitutional requirements that put those forces into play must also be considered of importance.

No formal amendment procedure is needed to alter many constitutional practices. But it is clearly not true that the Constitution is no longer important in establishing the distribution of power between the federal government and the states. The latitude of interpretation that is possible with respect to the interstate commerce clause cannot equally be applied elsewhere. The simple, clearly stated, unambiguous phrases—for example, the President "shall hold his office during the term of four years"—are subject to change only through the formal amendment processes. And it is this sort of constitutional statement that is at once an impediment to the tight organization of both government and parties. If the terms of the President and members of Congress were not so firmly defined in the Constitution, the power of party leaders to enforce discipline would be immeasurably increased, as British experience positively, and French experience negatively, demonstrated. Similarly, state constitutional provisions, such as those providing for the independent election of state administrators and for the direct primaries in the nomination of candidates for the governor's office, have the effect of splintering state parties and, by extension, of impeding the development of structured national parties and national party government.[39] The parties become a chief avenue for the achievement of decentralized government. But governmental (here formal constitutional) factors are partially responsible for the manner in which parties are structured. So government "causes" the form of party; party "causes" the form of government.

Yet constitutional factors alone cannot account for the nature of the

[39] Key, *op. cit.*, especially Chs. 3, 4, and 7.

American party system. If a party were simultaneously to gain control of Presidency, Congress, and Court, there would be few limitations indeed on either the centralized power of the controlling party or of the government it controlled. The constitutional barriers to this sort of control are not in themselves sufficient to explain why it does not exist. Constitutional impediments serve as points of support for those who profit from parties without unity. They make disunity easier to maintain. The factors accounting for disunity lie outside, as well as inside, the Constitution.

A wide range of factors not directly related to the party-government interrelationship contributes to governmental decentralization. Moreover, as the next chapter indicates, it would be a mistake to view the parties as other than products of their social and political environment. One factor certainly is in the form of creed: the opinion of Americans as molded by tradition and history, that places a high value on the grass roots, local initiative, and vigorous local institutions. Another is pride in locality and state, and allegiance to them, fostered by the nation's size, the different speeds of cultural and industrial development, and the varieties of regional, if not state, histories. The sheer wealth of the nation can also be shown as a cause of governmental decentralization. It renders possible the sharing of governmental largesse by many groups, including the state and local governments, provides leeway for experimentation and even waste, and renders unnecessary the tight organization of political power that is found when the support of one cause necessarily means the deprivation of another.

Other social and economic forces are important for the decentralized structure of American government. All of them may variously make themselves felt (1) directly on government; (2) directly on parties; (3) through parties on government; and (4) through government on parties. To take only the most obvious sort of example, the lack of deep, divisive schisms with respect to basic economic issues in the American society makes possible a viable government in which the executive is controlled by one party, the legislature by another. So social structure directly affects government. The same basic unity on economic matters allows parties to be only marginally unlike and permits members of one party to support the other party on many issues. So social structure affects parties and through parties affects government. Even more elaborate causal chains could be constructed if they served any useful purpose. In fact, they rarely do. The only point here is to make clear that many cultural factors are causal for both undisciplined parties and decentralized government. Reciprocally, it can also be shown that party and government processes reflect back on the culture. The open government and the open society may be conceived as separate entities; but they markedly affect each other.

A cause of party disunity and governmental decentralization also exists in the mediating role that parties play between society, on the one hand, and government, on the other. This is a special case of the reciprocal influence of social factors and party organization. Norton Long has outlined, without providing the empirical evidence, the manner in which the present disunity of the parties serves significant social groups: businessmen and professional workers, farmers, ethnic groups, and state and local office-holders.[40]

Businessmen are, by and large, committed to decentralized government and, if they do not understand the role of the party system in maintaining local control, they are certainly used to utilizing the "cracks" it provides to reach government officials. The spokesmen for the business community are, of course, much more knowledgeable as to where their interest lies. Historically, the business view opposing centralized government has some justification inasmuch as big business has lost power at the hands of the central government.

Business and professional groups also tend to be satisfied with the measure of control they exercise within the present system. For example, with the licensing of professional persons resting in state hands, the professions themselves usually control the licensing boards, standards, and examinations.[41] Even if it can be shown that the railroads exercise what amounts to considerable self-regulation at the national level through the Interstate Commerce Commission, this would not contradict the beliefs of other groups that state-level regulations serve them well, nor would it account for the difference in power between the railroad companies and, say, the beauticians. The insurance industry, a very powerful one, is as satisfied with state regulation as the beauticians, and even the largest corporations are happy to be incorporated under state laws.

The commitment of business and professional groups to decentralized

[40] Norton E. Long, "Party Government and the United States," *Journal of Politics,* Vol. XIII (May, 1951), pp. 187–214. For historical evidence see Herbert Agar, *The Price of Union* (Boston: Houghton Mifflin Company, 1930).

[41] According to Walter Gellhorn, "By 1952 more than 80 separate occupations, exclusive of 'owner-businesses' like restaurants and taxicab companies, had been licensed by state law," *Individual Freedom and Governmental Restraints* (Baton Rouge: Louisiana State University Press, 1956), p. 106.

The list includes not only lawyers, pharmacists, and dentists but also threshing machine operators, dealers in scrap tobacco, guide-dog trainers, tree surgeons, and hypertrichologists (who remove excessive and unsightly hairs), to name only a few of the diverse professions covered.

government is tempered in fact by their inconsistency in seeking specific favors from the federal government. While this inconsistency may lead to a change in the system in the long run, it is not considered unnatural among those businessmen aware of it today.

Farmers have secured benefits from government out of proportion to their share of the population or even the voting population because they have been pivots for both parties, who compete actively for their votes. Programmatic party discipline could only hurt their cause by reducing their importance on the electoral scene.

Ethnic groups have been able to advance their status by gaining power in state and local politics. Only when they have no power in the states and localities do they look to national authorities to accomplish their ends. The Negro situation is a case in point. Negroes in the South who are disenfranchised look to Washington. Those who can vote direct their demonstrations against local officials because they can direct their votes against them as well.

State and local officeholders have a clear stake in the present system. Their basic myth is that of local self-government and they react unfavorably to any idea of really centralized government or a centralized party system. Either kind of centralization would seriously affect their power and prestige and—unlike the other groups—they know it. The governors, for example, have everything to lose by either kind of centralization: their influence at national conventions and their direct lines to the White House, to name only two possibilities. On the other side, those officeholders who profit from their offices not only through their salaries but through honest (and dishonest) graft feel very satisfied with the *status quo* and are quite unwilling to experiment with changes.

The argument, in brief, is that sizable population groups believe that they profit from the present organization of parties and that they might be deprived (or at least not equally indulged) if parties became more programmatic and unified. On the other hand, no easily organized, powerful groups are presently deprived, or believe they would be appreciably indulged, by greater unity. Some federal officeholders believe they would gain from centralization. So do some labor people and those who represent disadvantaged groups like the Negroes (the largest single group that would gain from a change). Some individuals exist here and there who feel they cannot get what they want under the present system and think their chances would be improved under unified programmatic parties, many of them "men of good will" who seek grand social improvements. Such groups are constantly being reduced in one of two ways. Either they remain too small to be influential or they grow stronger and secure an entrance into the system. Once a group is strong in some type of electoral district, it can gain a measure of power. Only if it is scattered is it deprived of a chance. And once a group becomes strong enough to have power in electoral districts and thus effectively work for centralization or party unity, there is no more need on their part to do so since they can begin achieving their demands on the local level and do not need reform.[42]

Proof of the argument involves one in difficult methodological problems. Yet it contains a fundamentally sound perception. If majority social groups in the country were convinced of the advantages of party unity, constitutional barriers might make the task of creating unified parties more difficult, but those barriers would hardly be controlling. Party disunity and governmental decentralization are partially the direct consequences of the rewards that they give to significant social groups.

Finally, it must be clear that the party function, if it is not the sole cause for governmental decentralization, must be considered one cause. The parties themselves are institutions of power and importance. They are not mere weather vanes moved by the shifting winds of law, ideology, wealth, and social structure. They supply breezes of their own. Members of Congress express their own will, as well as that of constituency groups, in their devotion to the seniority principle for committee assignments and the right of unlimited debate in the Senate. The state governors and other local party chiefs play roles that they would not play in a system of centralized parties, and it is to their personal and professional advantage to maintain those roles. Cash for careerists is one consequence of disunited parties.[43] Status and power are others. Issues of sociability, of personal ambition, of honest (and dishonest) graft, of the patronage of prestige, of intraparty institutional stability are all involved. In the view of those most concerned, these factors are inseparable from their view of the welfare of the nation, however narrow or exalted that view may be. The party-government relationship, in other words, can be understood as a closed system, with the parties standing as a relatively independent social force. Their undisciplined character is the product of their internal dynamics, as well as of other factors. When the parties function to encourage governmental decentralization, they also, therefore, are one cause of that decentralization.

This discussion barely touches the complexities involved in separating

[42] This is not to argue that some groups do not gain more from one level of government than from another, but that even groups like organized labor that turn to Washington with greater success have found a reasonably satisfactory place for themselves in the system.

[43] My colleague Lewis A. Dexter has emphasized this point.

functional from causal strands.[44] The causes of party disunity and governmental decentralization are numerous, overlapping, and reciprocal. Lack of unity in parties and the institutions of decentralized government (including constitutional factors) mutually support each other. A series of extra-governmental factors, ranging from social structure through ideology to national wealth, are in part responsible for the character of parties and government. Direct benefits accruing to defined social groupings act to support the disunity of party structure and decentralization in governmental operations. And the internal dynamics of parties—the diverse rewards they produce for those who operate them—can be considered as a cause of their own character as well as of their decentralizing impact on government. The larger point here is only to emphasize the difference between causes and functions. But once one sees the anthropological unity of society, government, and party—which is only another way of recognizing the seamless web of cause and effect—the problems involved in altering any single aspect of the design become more apparent. At the very least it is clear that changes at one point necessarily involve some changes at other points.

VI. AMERICAN ANTIPARTIES

Physicists have postulated the existence of subatomic antiparticles that exhibit characteristics opposite to those of particles. One is tempted to say that it would be appropriate to consider American political parties as anti-parties. The classical party functions are functions of gathering together segments of power and wielding them as one. The American parties, as we have seen, do the opposite: they are antiparties, not parties. Many responsible voices have urged that it would be in the national interest if the antiparties were transformed into parties, that is, given programs and discipline and the sort of leadership that would elevate centrally determined

[44] See Herbert A. Simon, *Models of Man* (New York: John Wiley & Sons, 1957), Part I, "Causation and Influence Relations"; Carl G. Hempel, "The Function of General Laws in History," in Herbert Feigl and Wilfrid Sellars (eds.) *Readings in Philosophical Analysis* (New York: Appleton-Century-Crofts, 1949), pp. 459–71; Ernest Nagel, "The Logic of Historical Analysis," in Herbert Feigl and May Brodbeck (eds.) *Readings in the Philosophy of Science* (New York: Appleton-Century-Crofts, 1953), pp. 688–700; Paul F. Lazarsfeld and Morris Rosenberg (eds.), *The Language of Social Research* (Glencoe, Ill.: Free Press, 1955), especially Section II, on "multivariate analysis." A basic paper on functional analysis is Robert K. Merton, "Manifest and Latent Functions," in *Social Theory and Social Structure* (Glencoe, Ill.: Free Press, 1949), pp. 21–81.

values to positions of greater relative importance. This argument is honorable with age; it was first made in 1879 by Woodrow Wilson.[45]

It is remarkable how many of those who believe in the desirability of disciplined parties see trends and social forces moving in that direction, while those who believe not, see not.[46] There is no room here for a detailed analysis of the evidence brought forward in support of the thesis that parties are, in fact, becoming significantly more centralized, disciplined, and programmatic. In general, this evidence is not persuasive. It suffers from imprecision as to what is allegedly being demonstrated. For example, centralization in the management of presidential campaigns becomes confused with the far more important, central leadership over congressional votes, although the former assuredly can grow without concomitant growth of the latter. Some of the evidence brought forward to demonstrate party centralization is indisputable: for example, that party membership is important in determining how a member of Congress votes. But such evidence is partial and overshadowed by other facts: there are no data to show any tendency towards the increasing importance of the party label in determining congressional votes. And, in any case, hardly any national legislation, not even legislation strongly supported by a popular President whose party controls both houses, is passed by the votes of a single party; defectors from the other party are almost invariably needed to offset defections from the majority. Other evidence advanced to support the thesis of growing party centralization is more difficult to assess. For example, Paul T. David has suggested that "centralization is . . . a product of the cohesion that is induced by competition."[47] He is here pointing to consequences that he sees in the disappearance of one-party states. There is some evidence that Congressmen who win in close elections are indeed more likely to agree with congressional leaders than are those from safe constituencies. But this relationship has been shown to be true *only* for Democrats when there was a Democratic President, and even then it does not hold for

[45] In a paper published while Wilson was still an undergraduate, and later elaborated by him in several major works. See Ranney, *op. cit.,* p. 25.

[46] See the several works by E. E. Schattschneider, and notably, with respect to the emergence of national, disciplined parties, his "United States: The Functional Approach to Party Government," in Sigmund Neumann (ed.) *Modern Political Parties* (Chicago: University of Chicago Press, 1956), pp. 194–215; also Part III of the Report of the Committee on Political Parties of the American Political Science Association, cited above; Paul T. David, "The Changing Party Pattern," *Antioch Review,* Vol. XVI (Fall, 1956), pp. 333–50.

[47] Paul T. David, "The Changing Political Parties," in Marian D. Irish (ed.), *Continuing Crisis in American Politics* (Englewood Cliffs, N.J.: Prentice-Hall, 1963), p. 54.

southern Democrats.[48] Fewer safe Democratic seats in the South might, in fact, produce fewer congressmen who buck the leadership as a matter of course. On the other hand, the consequence might simply be the further distribution of mavericks among *both* parties, it being plausible that a southern victor might retain his southernness whether elected under a Democratic or a Republican label. Without further evidence, which can come only with the passage of time, it is not possible to say what effect increased party competition in the South will have on congressional willingness to follow party leaders.

If it is true that the form and style of political parties reflect both constitutional arrangements and social structure, then it follows that a basic alteration in parties—their centralization—must be preceded by basic changes in constitutional practice and in the parties' social base. One would expect the constitutional changes to include some central control over congressional nominations, a decline in the importance of the Senate, and a desuetude in the functions of the Supreme Court. These are changes in constitutional practice which conceivably might not need formal constitutional amendment. Beyond them lie needed formal amendments, such as the one that would provide for the simultaneous election of the President and the Congress. As for required social changes, an intellectual commitment to unlimtied majority rule is less important than the conviction by large population groups that their basic situation would be improved by centralized and programmatic parties, a development that probably depends upon growing class-consciousness, greater regional differences, or other marks of divisiveness which efface the tendency of extensive republics, in Madison's words, "to break and control the violence of faction." If the turn towards party centralization takes place, it is not likely that theoreticians will have to debate the meaning of what is happening: the needed constitutional and social changes are so fundamental that, if they do occur, they will be unmistakable.

The most important predictable facts of America's political future are (1) the upsurge of population, (2) the urbanization of that population, and (3) within the great metropolitan areas the social and racial separation

---

[48] David B. Truman, *The Congressional Party* (New York: John Wiley & Sons, 1959), pp. 212 ff. Duncan MacRae, Jr., who studied the same Congress, shows that Republicans who won by narrow margins were more likely to be sensitive to constituency than those winning by wide margins, but that this relationship was not true for Democrats (*Dimensions of Congressional Voting* [Berkeley: University of California Press, 1958], pp. 294–98). The Truman and MacRae evidence together suggests that the election-margin data must be qualified by data on presidential leadership before they are useful for predicting adherence to party leadership.

of populations on urban-suburban lines. The details need not be set forth here. The first simple fact is that the nation's population will increase to something like 218 million people by 1975, a jump of 40 per cent from the 1950 census count. The second fact is that more than three-quarters of the total populations will reside in metropolitan areas by 1975, as compared with slightly more than half in 1950 and fewer than one-third in 1900. In these facts, one might believe, lies the basis of party metamorphosis, a change in which the urban masses will be enrolled behind a party of program and leaders of mass appeal. Thus would be fulfilled Professor Arthur Holcombe's prediction of the community of urban interests overcoming the disparate interests of section, if not fulfilling the Marxist's view that class consciousness will breed class revolutionary parties.[49]

Yet the third simple fact makes all of this most unlikely. For the "urban masses" are anything but an undifferentiated mass. The most striking trend *within* the metropolitan areas is one that finds the center cities becoming stabilized in (or losing) population, with the suburban fringes accounting almost wholly for the spectacular increases. Profound social and political differences exist within central cities and, especially, between central cities and suburban fringes. In time, the central cities will become increasingly lower class, Negro, and (as the parties now stand) Democratic; the suburban fringes middle and upper class, and increasingly (though not exclusively) Republican. The non-central-city residents will be a numerical majority in most metropolitan areas, considered separately, and in all of them, considered as a whole. The new style urbanism is in large part suburban, and the political signals once called for urban mass politics are no longer relevant.

Even within the core cities, themselves, social and, especially, racial differences will not be conducive to the building of a mass party. The largest single self-identifiable group will consist of Negroes. And though an increasing number of local and state conflicts on Negro-white lines can be safely predicted, it is hardly likely that the racial group, or the racial issue, can again polarize programmatic parties. The exact opposite may be true. Growing differentiation of income and status within the Negro communities will very likely decrease whatever political solidarity the communities possess for national political issues; at the same time, the Negro can expect to be increasingly wooed by both parties and, as a consequence, discover that his position as a balance weight in close constituencies will be far more productive than any long-term commitment to a single party.

[49] Arthur N. Holcombe, *Our More Perfect Union* (Cambridge, Mass.: Harvard University Press, 1950).

None of this analysis denies the weight of the metropolitan areas in presidential elections[50] nor of the possibility that Presidents of the future, like Presidents of the past, will build victories on urban majorities. It is also clear that Presidents, in time of crisis, will again attempt to beat recalcitrant legislators, when they fail to lead them, by direct appeals to the voters, utilizing in the future more refined methods in psychology and communications technology for that purpose. But this is not to say that the localism of the legislator will thereby give way, or that the presidential constituency will become coterminous with the legislative, or that legislative majorities can be built upon principle and program, or that the local party chiefs will give way to national leaders; or that the national legislator will accept as his principal role that of majority-maker in substitution for his present role of governor on behalf of constituency interests.

A political system cannot be designed to serve antithetical ends, and every system suffers the ills of its own virtues. We have seen that American political parties operate to maintain a division of strength between the central government and the geographical (and other) peripheries. This division of strength has many values; not the least of them are the widespread generation of energies and allocation of responsibilities, and the defenses erected against authoritarian rule. The defects of the system include, most importantly, the nation's occasional slowness in responding to national leadership in a period of crisis, especially when crisis is confused with the norm. It is difficult to cure the defect without debasing the virtue. Tightening party control at the top decreases strength at the base. Centralized parties would seriously attenuate the four characteristics of the American system discussed above. If control from the top were *strictly* applied, the characteristics might entirely disappear. To be specific, if disciplined and programmatic parties were achieved:

1. It would make far less likely legislation that takes heavily into account the desires and prejudices of the highly decentralized power groups and institutions of the country, including the state and local governments.

2. It would to a large extent prevent national legislators, individually and collectively, from intruding themselves on behalf of non-national interests in national administrative programs.

3. It would deprive administrative officers of a large part of their political weight, a weight often used to foster state, local, and other powers.

4. It would dampen the process by which individuals and groups, in-

[50] See Samuel J. Eldersveld, "The Influence of Metropolitan Party Pluralities in Presidential Elections since 1920," *American Political Science Review,* Vol. XLIII, No. 6 (December, 1949), pp. 1189–1205.

cluding state and local political leaders, take multiple cracks at the national government in order to steer legislation and administration in ways congenial to them and the institutions they represent.

The sharing of functions is, in fact, the sharing of power. This sharing is the hallmark of modern American federalism. To it can be traced in large part the continued important participation of state and localities in virtually all programs of government: the marble cake of administration. It accounts, with historical considerations added, for the fact that federal and state laws share, rather than exclusively occupy, areas of service and regulation. It provides the basis for states and localities to exercise an extraordinarily wide range of informal influence over federal legislation and administrative programs, an influence that is sometimes channeled through members of Congress but which is also manifest through the activities of professional organizations and direct "cracks" at federal agencies by state and local officers. It indicates, in sum, the existence of a substantial devolution of power in the American political system.

Chapter 11

SHARING AND
THE DISADVANTAGED:
THE CHANGING STATUS OF
THE NEGROES*

I. THE SPECIAL SITUATION OF THE NEGROES

Margaret Mead some years ago said of Americans, "We are all third generation." The phrase is figuratively if not statistically accurate. Immigrants, their children and grandchildren probably constitute less than half of the United States population today; the last great wave of European immigration came at the turn of the century. In New York, Boston, Philadelphia, Chicago, Detroit, and other cities the great ethnic islands of Italians, Germans, Irish, Poles, Czechs, and Swedes are shadows of their former size, distinctiveness, and foreign cast. Remnants of their neighborhoods, language, social customs, and political cohesion everywhere exist. But suburbia is the natural home of the third and fourth generations, and their mode of life is ethnically reminiscent but in no sense ethnically oriented. For them the melting pot has done its work.

The process of integration is never complete, and there is no lack of ethnic political problems in the United States. For example, the old ethnic populations, despite Americanization and dispersion, still maintain some degree of cohesion in voting. On the local plane, the Irish are still politically dominant in Chicago, the Italians strong beyond simple numbers in New York and Providence. On the national scene, as Samuel Lubell and

* Editor's Note: This chapter is based on a paper prepared for the 1961 meeting of The International Political Science Association, entitled "Politics of the Changing Negro Status in the United States." While much has happened to modify some of the specific comments in the original paper, its general thrust remains accurate, and its assessment of the Negro struggle in the light of American federalism raises important points of analysis.

others have demonstrated, ethnic cohesion can still turn a presidential election and still affect the posture of American foreign policy. One can hardly scratch a city or state without exposing an ethnic problem. Especially in the semi-arid regions of the West, but also in other areas, a native Indian population rapidly increases in size and rapidly sharpens its political skills. Mennonite and Brethren communities in Indiana, Scandinavians in the upper Midwest, French Canadians in New England, Mexicans in the Southwest, Chinese and Japanese in Los Angeles and San Francisco, and a large new group of 600,000 Puerto Ricans in New York City—each of these ethnic islands presents its own subtle and interesting problems for political analysis. And a literal island, Hawaii, the newest of the states, has a population that is a bewildering mixture of color, national origins, and language, with whites constituting less than a quarter of the whole. Hawaii, in its first national election, sent Americans of Chinese and Japanese parentage to the national Congress.

All of these groups fade to insignificance in comparison with the Negro population. Negroes are not only the most numerous ethnic group in the United States. They also crucially test American political institutions and political ideology.

Skin color is the single mark distinguishing Negroes from other Americans. On all other counts, Negroes do not even merit being considered as an ethnic group. They are not a new group in the nation; rather they are among the oldest settlers. Negroes as slaves were among the first arrivals in the New World, and their importation largely ended before the Civil War. Negroes are not distinguished from other Americans by barriers of language, religion, or lifeways, except those that are the consequence of region and economic class. Unlike ethnic groups in other countries, the responsible leaders of this group plead for integration and full citizenship, not for separate status, not for an autonomous state, not for political linkages with compatriots in other nations. There is no issue of loyalty to nation among Negroes. The Negro "problem" is a consequence not of disloyalty to American ideas but of full allegiance to them. There would be no Negro problem if the Negroes were satisfied with less than the complete fulfillment of American, not foreign, political principle.

Further to add to the complexity, the integration of Negroes is being carried out jointly by their own efforts, white sympathizers, the national executive, and the Supreme Court. The law is on the Negroes' side. It is law that speaks of equality, the most basic theme in American political life.

There are almost 19 million Negroes in the United States, a group only slightly smaller than the combined populations of Belgium and the Netherlands, almost nine times more numerous than the population of Israel.

What is badly understood, inside as well as outside the United States, is that this population is no longer a southern population. For more than 40 years Negroes have been leaving the South for the large cities of the Midwest and East. They have moved in search of better jobs, homes, and social acceptance. Jobs, the crucial impetus, have been supplied above all by the two great wars. Today there are more Negroes in the State of New York than in Louisiana, more in Illinois than in Mississippi. The five states of the Deep South (Louisiana, Mississippi, Alabama, Georgia, and South Carolina) together have only one-sixth of the nation's Negro population. Illinois, Pennsylvania, and New York together have a larger fraction.

On the other hand, Negroes still constitute a larger fraction of the population of southern than of northern states. In the Deep South, the fraction ranges from 28.6 per cent in Georgia to 42.3 per cent in Mississippi. In contrast, no midwestern or eastern state has more than 11 per cent. Illinois is at that figure, Michigan has 9.4 per cent nonwhites, New York 8.9 per cent, New Jersey and Pennsylvania are close behind. Negroes outside the South are heavily concentrated in the big cities, and in these cities the Negro population reaches proportions close to those of southern states and large southern cities. Washington, D.C., indeed, has proportionately more Negroes (54 per cent) than any state in the Deep South, or any large city there for that matter. Atlanta and Memphis, in the far South, with Baltimore, in the border state of Maryland, have more than 30 per cent Negro populations constituting more than one-fifth of the total.

The general picture, then, is a Negro population which is no longer predominantly a southern population. In the South, farm areas as well as cities have large fractions of Negroes. Outside the South, Negroes are most numerous in the big cities, but drastically underrepresented in the suburbs of those cities, in the middle-sized and smaller urban places, and in the rural areas.

II. THE "NEGRO PROBLEM" AND FEDERALISM

The largest aspect of the Negro problem in the United States can be stated bleakly: The American Constitution guarantees Negroes full rights of citizenship, but they are prevented from exercising those rights. The rights of citizenship include, basically, the vote and the equal use of publicly supported facilities, especially schools, but also such amenities as public transportation, libraries, parks, and swimming pools. These are the current issues at stake in the South. They have already been won in the

North, and there the salient issues are of a different category, involving principally the free choice of employment and places to live.

The pattern of national-local relationships in the United States, a pattern that has evolved in large measure as the consequence of American federalism, seems to me to be the most important *political* fact accounting for the underprivileged civic status of Negro citizens as well as for the manner by which that status is being changed. It is true, of course, that there are no serious movements to concentrate Negro citizens in a given area under their own state administration. This would indeed be a "purely federal" solution. But it would be antithetical to the dominant assimilationist tendencies in American life and unpalatable to Negro and white leaders alike. Separation via federalism aside, there is hardly any aspect of the Negro problem in the United States that is not in large measure affected by the fact of federalism.

Consider, first, the manner in which federalism accounts for the differential role of national institutions in bringing about greater equality for Negroes. In Congress there are virtually no direct constitutional impediments to legislation promoting the cause of racial equality. No act of Congress, legal on other grounds, is likely to be declared illegal because it transgresses constitutional definitions with respect to the federal-state division of powers. The expansion of the congressional power over interstate commerce and taxation, begun in the 1930's and extended since, means that the direct limits on congressional power are political, not legal. At first blush this seems to demonstrate the unimportance of federalism; in fact, it only makes the importance of federalism less apparent. The barriers to congressional action—which make politically infeasible what is constitutionally possible—are at base barriers of federalism.

Some of these barriers of course have a constitutional base. For example, the Constitution assigns two senators to each state, thus insuring the South a voice in Congress far greater than simple numbers would allow. Senators and congressmen serve fixed terms. They are relatively impervious to central direction, and their political careers are dependent upon satisfying local constituencies. The Constitution further vests the states with primary responsibility for administering national elections (subject to a congressional supremacy which has not been comprehensively exercised since post-Civil War days), and those with a stake in white supremacy are thus provided a crucial lever for insuring it at the polls.

These constitutional provisions, which make it difficult to get congressional action on racial problems, are buttressed by a whole series of practices which follow from, though they are not specified by, the Constitution.

The staggered and fixed terms of President, senators, and congressmen, for example, make organization of Congress by the chief executive a practical impossibility. The houses of Congress organize themselves. They have found no better way than a seniority system to choose all-important committee chairman. The effect is to elevate long-serving members from safe constituencies to leadership posts. Since the safest constituencies are in the South, the predominant congressional leadership is southern, producing the anomaly, so puzzling to Europeans, of Senate and House leaders from the President's own party consistently and as a matter of course voting contrary to the President. Legislative votes are not the most important aspect of the matter. Southern committee chairmen use their positions to block civil rights legislation, perhaps most effectively by using other needed statutes as hostages and thus preventing measures against racial discrimination from being introduced at all.

The total situation does not make Congress a likely source of action on behalf of Negro equality. In fact it has not been. In the field of voting, for example, post-Civil War legislation, enacted between 1866 and 1873, established a comprehensive program of civil rights and a detailed federal supervision of congressional elections. But this legislation was largely repealed in 1894, and other aspects of it have been nullified by Supreme Court decisions. Of the Reconstruction legislation protecting the franchise only a few provisions of limited application and difficult enforceability are still in existence. For 82 years following 1870 Congress was inactive with respect to protecting Negro voting rights. In 1957 the national legislature again took note of the position of Negroes and gave federal agencies new civil (but not criminal) powers to protect Negro voters. In 1960 (in the bill that Mr. Lyndon Johnson, then the Senate majority leader, steered through Congress in evidence of his *bona fides* as a presidential candidate), the 1957 act was strengthened by making provision for federally appointed referees in cases where qualified Negroes were denied the right to vote by local registrars. The ameliorative action made possible by this act is so slow and cumbersome that, like the 1957 act, it is for the most part ineffective. One can say, therefore, that the most far-reaching action taken by the Congress during the last eight decades to overcome discrimination against Negro voting was the establishment, also in 1957, of a Commission on Civil Rights. The chief accomplishment of this Commission was a meticulous documentation of the obvious. The record of Congress is hardly better with respect to issues of education, housing and employment.†

† Editor's Note: The original paper upon which this chapter is based was completed and delivered three years before the civil rights breakthrough of 1964 which brought a total collapse of the Southerner's veto power over civil rights legislation

National-local power relationships in the national legislature have thus promoted the primacy of localism, especially southern localism, and (until recently) produced relative congressional inaction with respect to ending racial discrimination. The case is quite different for the executive office and the Supreme Court.

Presidential candidates stand for office before a national constituency which is likely to be very closely divided. A candidate can win without the electoral votes of the South, but he cannot win without a substantial fraction of the heavily populated areas of the East, Midwest, and Far West. Those areas contain the great urban centers of the nation, and in those centers two groups of voters will not accept policies of racial discrimination. One such group is a substantial fraction of the liberally oriented middle classes who take seriously the constitutional statements of equality. The other group, even more important for the issue at hand, is composed of the Negro voters themselves. In a voting system that delivers the entire electoral vote of a state to the candidate with a simple numerical majority of the state's voters, the Negro voters in such cities as New York, Baltimore, Boston, Philadelphia, Detroit, and Chicago hold a crucial lever in presidential elections. Because they have the potential for swinging the large states into one electoral column or the other, they are nursed by both parties. In the 1960 election a solicitous telephone call by Mr. Kennedy to the wife of Martin Luther King, the then-jailed leader of southern Negroes, is believed by close observers to have been very important in keeping Illinois as a Democratic state. A shift of fewer than 3,000 votes would have produced a Republican victory in Illinois and probably thrown the election into the House of Representatives.

As southern power in the Congress produces inactivity there with respect to race relations, so Negro power in presidential elections produces action to end discrimination by the President himself and the executive offices that he (more or less) controls. Presidential regard for Negro rights can be

in Congress. The conditions which brought about the radical change conform in every detail to the Grodzins thesis: the admission of Alaska and Hawaii to statehood dropped the southern states' percentage of Senate seats below the 33 1/3 per cent necessary to prevent majority action on civil rights legislation or even to prevent cloture from being applied to stop a filibuster. Meanwhile civil rights senators from northern and western states had been gaining in seniority and power by virtue of their length of service. When public opinion in the North and West was sufficiently aroused, the midwestern Republicans, whose lack of interest in civil rights legislation had given the Southerners a virtual majority against such legislation in the past, came over to the civil rights camp. This gave the latter the extraordinary majority necessary to pass a strong civil rights bill and, a year later, a strong voting rights act as well. The nearly three-to-one majority backing both measures is indicative of the fact that only when an extraordinary majority in Congress, supported actively by the White House, was willing to support such legislation could it be passed.

traced easily as far back as Wilson's presidency and perhaps earlier. To take only the record of Mr. Kennedy, one can tick off a long list: appointment of many Negroes to high judicial and administrative posts (including the appointment of Mr. Robert Weaver as housing commissioner, a near-cabinet-level post); heightened activity of an administrative committee to end employment discrimination in the important sector of the economy supported by government contracts; further steps to end discrimination in the armed services (here integration even at southern bases has been carried further than any place else in the nation except perhaps in university communities); finishing touches to an already extensive program to give equality in lunch rooms and recreational activities; and renewed attempts by the Department of Justice to protect Negroes from legal discrimination of all sorts. In the last category are actions under the difficult-to-enforce 1956 and 1960 civil rights statutes to insure Negro voting rights in the deepest South, intervention to protect freedom riders (whites and Negroes travelling together in the South on interstate carriers), and to compel the reopening of schools in those few communities where local officials have chosen to stop public education rather than to face integration. This list of executive actions is by no means complete. But it serves to indicate the greater sensitivity of the executive than of the legislature to the issue of civil rights for Negroes.

Administrative action cannot be divorced from legislative authorization. There are many further administrative steps that might be taken to quicken the pace of integration. For example, federal funds for housing and urban redevelopment, or for agriculture, or for higher education could be withheld as long as segregation exists in a given state. Such steps have not been taken either because authorizing legislation does not exist, or, if it does (by design or by default), because of administrative fears of legislative reprisals.‡ The more interesting issue is why determined legislative opposition has not developed to the many desegregating administrative acts that have already been taken. The problem is a complex one, but one reason is surely that many southern legislators are less segregation-minded than their constituents. What his constituents cannot directly charge him with, a southern member of Congress is often willing to see undertaken. He has enormous formal and informal resources to harry administrators, even Cabinet members, whose acts are not to his liking.[1] His willingness not to use these resources is one important reason why the executive has gone as far as it has on the road to racial equality.

‡ Editor's Note: The 1964 Civil Rights Act contained comprehensive authorizing legislation which is now (1965) being implemented by the appropriate executive departments with "deliberate speed" and with half an eye on Congress.
[1] See Chapter Ten.

Little need be said in this context about the Supreme Court. Its 1954 decision striking down racial segregation in public schools was the last, natural step in a long list of decisions that attempted to protect Negroes against discrimination. These decisions concerned, among other things, housing, higher education, voting, and interstate transportation. The only revolutionary finding of the 1954 decision was that separate schools for Negroes, even if equal, were a form of discrimination and therefore unconstitutional. Even this conclusion had been clearly portended by the previous decisions with respect to colleges and universities. From the perspective of these pages, the significant fact about the federal judiciary as a political force moving in favor of Negro equality is that it is the federal institution furthest removed from state and local influence. (Federal judges are appointed for life tenure by the President, the Senate concurring.) Many southerners and conservatives of other stripe have bitterly criticized the Court. But none of the several possible legislative attacks came seriously close to success, and it is a significant fact that, despite southern protest and obstructionism, including occasional violence, no sustained attempt has been made to overturn the school decision by the prescribed route of constitutional amendment. This is of course difficult, but not so difficult as to be unfeasible if the decision were generally unpopular, as the Eleventh and Sixteenth Amendments bear witness.

I have so far discussed how the pattern of federal-state relationships affects the action of the three principal institutions of the national government with respect to racial relations. Another aspect of federal-state relations, the territorial division of power, goes even further to explain the situation of Negro citizens. Two points need to be made.

The first is the obvious point that the American system devolves heavy responsibilities on state and local governments. Despite Supreme Court permissiveness during the last 25 years, there has not been any considerable extension of exclusive federal functions. Characteristically, when the federal government assumes a new function, it takes up only part of it, leaving substantial discretion and responsibility in state hands. State law is the basic law covering property rights, education, health, employment safety, and welfare, among other fields. The scope of state power was illustrated in the very Supreme Court decision restricting that power with respect to the management of schools. "Education," said the Court, "is perhaps the most important function of state and local governments." And the Court did not impose any national program for enforcing desegregation; instead it invited state and local governments to devise their own desegregation procedures "with all deliberate speed."

The second point is less obvious. Within American political parties, partly as the consequence of constitutional arrangements for federalism, power moves from the bottom to the top, not from the top down. Congressmen and senators can rarely ignore concerted demands from home constituents, especially if those constituents are mayors of large cities or a state governor. But no party leader in Washington can expect the same kind of response when he requests action from state or local leaders. Not even the President can exact obedience from a governor on a matter the latter considers important—short of calling out troops as Mr. Eisenhower did at Little Rock, Arkansas. This is easily explained. The power to nominate and elect resides in the hustings, not in party central headquarters. The periphery can command the center because the periphery largely controls the votes. So it is that the influence of state and local governments in national affairs is generally stronger than the influence of the national government in state and local affairs. American federalism, in sum, not only decentralizes functions, but it also makes difficult central political influence over the performance of those functions.

III. VARIETIES OF DISCRIMINATION AND INTEGRATION

These purely governmental considerations make possible, but they do not explain, the great state-by-state (and even community-by-community) variations in the position of American Negroes. For that explanation one must look at a vast range of historical, cultural, and economic data. Where discrimination is at its worst, Negroes are heavily concentrated, they were once slaves, their exploitation once supported the economy, and they have long been regarded as social and intellectual inferiors. Governmental policies reflect the public temper built upon factors such as these, and American federalism, as we have seen, makes easy the local and state expression of such attitudes.

If American federalism allows for great local and state variation in the pace of granting equal civil rights to Negroes, it will now no longer permit inequality and discrimination to exist undisturbed. Outside the South, Negroes have achieved full legal equality. Their votes are everywhere sought. They have use of all public facilities, although in the largest cities social discrimination has produced segregated Negro neighborhoods which lead to legally unsegregated schools becoming, in fact, all white or all Negro. Save in the South, Negro leaders have won important local and state political positions. In the years immediately ahead, the concentration of Negroes in the larger cities (coupled with the suburbanization of whites) will give them roles of dominance. There is little doubt that within the next 20 years Negro mayors will appear in Baltimore (35 per cent Negro in

1960), Detroit, Philadelphia, St. Louis, Chicago, Oakland (California), or Cincinnati (each more than 20 per cent Negro).

White groups in the North will not accept the development of Negro political primacy without protest. One form of protest will almost certainly be attempts to enlarge city boundaries in order to include within them their predominantly white suburban populations. (Thus the age-old suburban opposition to the city annexation of suburban areas will be overcome. But in the opinion of the suburbanites concerned the move will be justified: they will be annexing the city to the suburb.) It is highly unlikely that white countermeasures to growing Negro power in nonsouthern cities will include violence. This, however, does not mean they will be polite—ordinary American practices of political opposition being what they are.

It cannot be said even in the North that Negroes, except in a few egalitarian enclaves, are accepted as social equals. Increasingly, Negroes are welcomed at hotels, restaurants and theaters, and a relatively few live side by side with whites as amiable neighbors in virtually every large nonsouthern urban center. But the largest number of Negroes face many social and extra-legal barriers in the free choice of places to live, and they are effectively restricted to residences in predominantly Negro areas. A similar situation exists with respect to employment. Outside the South, Negroes are finding acceptance in wider and wider areas of work previously barred to them, including clerical and selling jobs in retail stores, and professional positions. But here, as in housing, only the first—although important— steps to equal status have been taken. The problem is complicated because a larger fraction of Negroes than whites are in the lower economic groups and many are new migrants to northern cities. They have not yet acquired the middle class skills demanded in white collar employment, or the middle class habits of life expected of white collar neighbors. Whites tend to judge the group as a whole, and job discrimination of the fully qualified Negro worker exists, as well as residential discrimination for Negro families whose standards of conduct would be pleasing to a late nineteenth-century British high clergyman.

Community organizations exist everywhere outside the South to aid Negroes overcome discrimination in housing and employment. A Supreme Court decision has made it illegal to make covenants excluding Negroes from residential areas, and New York has made it an offense for certain landlords to discriminate in the sale or lease of property. Several states have laws prohibiting discrimination in hiring practices. Within the framework of a general improvement of the Negroes' social standing, their situation varies greatly from city to city and according to the economic level of the Negroes and whites concerned. Generally, discrimination becomes less evident as one travels north and as one moves from lower to higher income groups. It is also less evident where Negroes are fewer and where determined local leadership works to ease Negro-white relations.

The South also shows marked variations. The idea of the solid South, in race matters as well as politics, is becoming a myth. Before the 1954 school decision 17 states and the District of Columbia made racial segregation compulsory in publicly supported schools. Today [Ed.: 1961] the schools of only three states are completely segregated (Mississippi, Alabama, and South Carolina).§ A map of the South, hatched to show desegregated districts, would have an almost unbroken desegregated territory running across the entire top of the area and around its western edge (including all or virtually all of Delaware, Maryland, the District of Columbia, West Virginia, Kentucky, Missouri, and Oklahoma, as well as scattered counties in the Texas panhandle and in west and south Texas). In these areas schools are desegregated in fact as well as in law. In six states of the Deep South (Florida, Georgia, North Carolina, Virginia, Tennessee, and Louisiana) there has occurred only token desegregation, involving relatively few students in a single or several communities. The total record is not a proud one for those who believe both in lawfulness and in the rightness of the cause, but progress has been and is being made. It will almost certainly become swifter in the years immediately ahead.

Similar variations exist with respect to voting in the South. Negroes in the border states uniformly possess the ballot. Data are difficult to obtain for the 11 states in the far South. The best estimates for those states show a considerable increase, perhaps almost a doubling, in Negro registration for voting between 1947 and 1957. Nevertheless, in the latter year fewer than 25 per cent of the Negroes of voting age were registered. This compares with about 60 per cent of voting-age whites. Some of the difference is accounted for by the low economic status of Negroes in the South (everywhere in the country the least wealthy have the lowest turnout of votes). But a large share of the difference, certainly, is the result of white hostility, expressed as violence, the threat of violence, or (the more usual practice) extravagant tests concerning literacy and constitutional understanding, applied to Negro applicants but not to whites. Where Negroes are most concentrated in the South, they are most likely to face discrimination. But this rule does not hold for voting when rural and urban areas (with equal fractions of Negroes) are compared: everywhere a higher proportion of Negroes vote in cities than in farm areas, and it is likely that they vote

§ Editor's Note: By 1965, token desegregation had taken place in those states as well. The application of the requirements of the Civil Rights Act of 1964 is likely to change this situation considerably by 1967.

proportionally more as city size increases. (This provides a good clue to why the governments of many southern cities are far more liberal than the state governments: the latter are heavily dominated by rural voters. In urban areas, incidentally, educational and income levels are generally higher for both whites and Negroes.) Although school desegregation provoked new harshness in white feelings for Negroes in many southern places, in only one state, Mississippi, have registrations for voting failed to rise in the last five years.

There are two hopeful auguries in these data. One lies in the fact that Negroes are accorded greater legal equality in cities than in rural areas. The dominant population trend, as the South joins the rest of the nation in industrialization, is from farm to city. The second is that as the Negro fraction of the population decreases in a given area, so does the hostility. The massive population movement of the last decades has rapidly decreased Negro population concentrations in rural areas of the South. Hardly one-half of the southern counties now have Negroes constituting more than 10 per cent of their population. Most areas of highest rural Negro concentration (running to 50 per cent or more of the total population) are in Mississippi, Alabama, Georgia, and South Carolina. Here is where the heart of segregation lies and where progress towards equality will be slowest.

IV. FORCES ENCOURAGING CHANGE

What is now notable is that, despite all difficulties, the larger national view is being implemented. We have already seen that the institutional push in this direction is principally supplied by the President and the Supreme Court. Influenced by and influencing these institutions are other forces at work.

One is the sheer force of public opinion. William Faulkner said in 1955, "To live anywhere in the world of [today] and be against equality of race or color, is like living in Alaska and being against snow." Faulkner was himself a deep Southerner. He was speaking in the South. His words are a clue to the most significant factor of all behind the changing status of the American Negro: no significant public opinion, even in the South, can any longer reasonably support inequality in citizens' rights or the particular inequality that characterizes segregation. Opposition to equal legal status for Negroes of course runs strong in many southern states. But it is an opposition less and less likely to appeal to reasoned argument. More and more frequently it is expressed as simple racial hatred or economic exploitation, and by statements of equality masking practices of inequality, as when voting registrars state that they will enroll whites and Negroes alike but in fact make it difficult, if not impossible, for Negroes to register. This sort of disingenuousness, lacking moral and intellectual justification, is the last resort of those fighting for a lost cause. The population groups supporting legal inequality are being squeezed to smaller geographical areas, usually rural, and to smaller population groups, usually the lower economic stratum.

To some extent this shift of opinion, especially in the South, is the consequence of the 1954 school desegregation decision of the Supreme Court. Americans like to think of themselves as obeying the law, however often they may not. The law of the land now clearly proscribes school segregation, just as it does discrimination in the use of other public services and the exclusion of Negroes from the polls. The Supreme Court has reminded Americans, in a fashion never before so striking, of the meaning of "due process" and "equal protection" of the law. And the reaction in the South —the passage of "illegal" laws, laced occasionally with violence—has shown how blatantly these precepts are abrogated. But the net effect has certainly been to strengthen the opinion of most Americans that Negroes must be granted full rights of citizenship everywhere in the land.

Beyond the Court's role, other factors also operate to produce public opinion favorable to equality in civil rights. Less than 40 years ago it could be argued by intellectuals, as well as others, that the inferior status of Negroes was the result of biologically based intellectual and moral qualities. (The anthropologist Boas once gave scientific credence to this point of view which on later evidence and reflection he disavowed.) This is a point of view no longer tenable. Scientific evidence aside, the achievements of nonwhites in all aspects of American life, as well as their accomplishments in Africa, the Pacific Islands, India, and the Far East, have destroyed all reasonable bases for belief in the inferiority of Negroes and other nonwhites. Americans may only dimly apprehend that the century of the nonwhite is upon us; but they cannot deny what is self-apparent with respect to the gifts and accomplishments of Negroes at home and abroad.

The international politics of discrimination is another important factor making for change in public opinion. Discrimination in Little Rock or New Orleans prejudices United States interests in Tokyo and Nairobi. More particularly, the fact of discrimination mocks American claims that their way of life is the way of freedom and justice. Louis Armstrong is an effective representative of American democracy in Africa, but the gerrymandering of Tuskegee, Alabama, effectively barring Negro intellectuals from participating in the city's political life, is more than offsetting: Who can doubt that the articulate citizens of new African nations value participation in an election more highly than expertise on a horn? The worldwide damage to America done by discrimination would be great even if the Soviet Union did not exist. It is all the greater because of the quickness with which U.S.S.R. propaganda seizes upon incidents of American racial strife to turn to the Soviets' benefit.

The existence of the Soviet Union makes itself felt in still another fashion. One need not seriously consider the Soviet boast that in five or ten years it will overtake the United States in production, including the production of consumer goods. Or, if the boast is taken seriously, one need not believe that this tin-lizzie calculus is the most important point of comparison among nations. But the scientific and technological competition of the Soviet Union, as exemplified by its successes in rocketry and the triumphs of intellect and organization implied by those successes, are impressive even to the least perceptive of Americans. In a competition of this sort, it becomes a danger to the nation if a southern Negro, who may have within himself the powers of a Nobel laureate, is by racial discrimination barred from realizing his potential. The nation needs all the brains it can muster. This is an argument for full citizenship rights that many southern whites have found relatively easy to comprehend.

Many Americans find irony in arguments for Negro equality based upon the threat of the Soviet Union. They support full integration not because of national advantage but because it is right. It is right because human equality is part of the basic creed of America and because political equality, and its accompanying civil rights, are guaranteed by the law of the land.

Opinion, to be politically effective, must be translated into action. Many groups now exist, in as well as outside the South, actively promoting the cause of equal status for Negroes. These include every leading church (notwithstanding statements in favor of segregation by individual southern ministers), older organizations like the American Civil Liberties Union, and newer ones organized for the specific purpose of protecting Negro rights in the South, such as the Southern Regional Council (whose leaders include southern whites of the highest professional, economic, and social standing). The most important forces for change, however, are Negro groups themselves.

One sort of political tactic has disappeared among Negroes. This is the tactic of Booker T. Washington, which held that economic and educational progress was the basis of the good life for Negroes and which deliberately avoided even moderately militant steps towards desegregation. Political apathy is widespread among Negroes, but the posture of acquiescence to temporary second-class citizenship, once the most widely accepted posture of leadership, is no longer tolerable. This is as good a clue as any to the momentum of change in United States race relations.

Two sorts of political action groups have grown to primacy in the Negro population. One is represented by the National Association for the Advancement of Colored People. Twenty years ago the NAACP was considered a radical group. Now it represents the more conservative strain. Its principal area of action, and its outstanding successes, have been in the area of litigation. It has played an active role in all the great judicial procedures aimed at discrimination, including the outlawing of the white primary in the South, proscription of the "separate but equal" doctrine in southern professional and graduate schools, and (its crowning success) the prohibition of racial segregation in the public schools.

NAACP leaders are militant. They fill the federal dockets with their suits, they take their fight into the deepest sections of the South, and they are willing to accept nothing less than complete victory. But they have the demeanor of statesmen and the patience to wait upon the slow progress of judicial process. Many Negroes do not share this patience. Consequently, for the first time in modern American history, significant movements for direct action have made their appearance. The first spectacular success of direct action was the boycott of the public transportation system in Montgomery, Alabama, under the leadership of the Reverend Martin Luther King. Since Negro riders constituted a majority of the regular bus users, the economic impact of the action was effective. More than this, the Negro community was successfully mobilized by a religiously based call for absolute passive resistance.

This general tactic has now been taken up in a wide variety of situations. An important impetus to the movement was provided by a group of Negro high school and college students in 1960 with their "sit-ins" at lunch counters in stores of Greensboro, North Carolina. The stores chosen were usually parts of nationwide corporations, thus enabling the demonstrators to bring to bear important economic sanctions through sympathizers in other cities, including northern ones. Desegregation of eating places in more than 100 southern cities has been accomplished through this strategy. (Both the NAACP and the American Civil Liberties Union have supplied legal guidance.) A more recent manifestation of direct action has been the succession of "freedom rides" by groups of whites and Negroes to challenge all extra-legal segregation on interstate buses and trains in the South.

The direct action groups clearly represent a protest against the slow procedures of the law and the even slower action towards nondiscrimination on the part of southern populations and southern governments. Yet it is a remarkable testimony to the faith of most Negroes in the orderly processes of American law that even more extremist action has not been taken. There are several Negro protest groups which espouse white hatred and disbelief in the capacity of American authorities to bring about genuine equality among the races. The violent demonstration by Negroes in the United Nations assembly several years ago was one manifestation of this attitude. Few white Americans believe seriously in the threat of widespread violence by Negroes—an incidental demonstration that Negro faith in peaceful and lawful change is, as with other aspects of Negro culture, a reflex of the larger community. But a realistic observer must certainly expect an increase in extremist action in the event that the movement towards equality does not continue and, indeed, accelerate. A partially satisfied need is felt more strongly than a hopeless one, and those who have tasted equality can never again be expected to live as inferiors.

V. UNDERSTANDING THE FEDERAL POLICY OF RESTRAINT

In the last analysis it should be clear that Negroes in the United States fail to correspond to the usual definitions of what an ethnic group should be, just as they fail to make demands that ethnic groups characteristically make. All of this makes it difficult to think of American Negroes as an ethnic group at all, at least within the usual rubrics of discussion. There is a more useful way of viewing the problem: that is to regard the issue as one of two conflicting minorities—one Negro, one white southerner—both facing the nation with demands that are unfulfilled. The situation of the Negro is difficult enough. But he shares the larger views (however he may suffer from the actions) of the majority, he is protected by the law, and he has the drift of time on his side. The deep southerners, clinging to traditional stereotypes, are far more disadvantaged in the sense that they are far further removed from the rest of the country and world. Certain of their cherished cultural practices are prohibited by the highest authority in the land. They are being asked to give up a whole complex of life ways in the name of a justice that they cannot fully comprehend.

Imagine that southerners were head-hunters occupying some distant island and that the democratic state of which the island is a part has determined that head-hunting, being immoral, must stop. The reform would be sought resolutely and without compromise. But surely it should be achieved in a way to minimize bloodshed (not to make a farce of the original life-saving impetus) and also to minimize possible political disaffection.

Segregationist southerners are not unfairly compared to these aborigines,

THE AMERICAN SYSTEM

and racial discrimination to head-hunting. Further, as lives may be lost in saving lives, so freedom may be lost in enforcing freedom. To add a consideration, national leaders may also be allowed to make a distinction between the existence of power and its use. They may have a regard for preserving political power even while restricting it, for they may judge power as such in state and local institutions to be highly desirable, however much they condemn the use of that power for what they consider evil ends.

White southerners are indeed the most significant American minority, and a case can be made for regarding them as an ethnic minority. In the end they must give up their exotic and dangerous practices of discrimination. Integration of Negroes, everywhere in law and many places in social life, will be achieved, I believe, in a relatively short time, utilizing the possibilities of federalism to overcome the barriers a federal system had previously supported. The trick is to use those possibilities in a way that will also insure the integration of both minorities.

Chapter 12

CENTRALIZATION AND DECENTRALIZATION: THE FAILURE TO UNWIND THE SYSTEM

I. ATTEMPTS TO SEPARATE FEDERAL AND STATE FUNCTIONS

The federal system has been criticized in recent years from two sides. On the one hand, it is said that the strength of special and local interests (including the strength of state and local governments) frustrates national policy. In Congress, this critique holds, the power of the peripheries makes consistent national leadership impossible. Members of Congress, dependent for re-election on local constituencies rather than on national centers of party power, can with impunity sacrifice national goals for special interests. This argument concludes that an expansion of national powers is essential. On the other hand, it is said that the power of the central government is growing to such an extent that it threatens to efface the state and local governments, reducing them to compliant administrative arms of national offices. The "federal octopus" is held to threaten the very existence of the states and to destroy local initiative.

The two critiques are to a large extent contradictory. Yet reforms of the federal system are often proposed as if one or the other of these complaints were totally valid. Those concerned about the federal system uniformly express fear of the federal octopus.

Since the end of World War II there have been four major attempts to reform or reorganize the federal system: the first (1947–49) and second (1953–55) Hoover Commissions on Executive Organization; the Kestnbaum Commission on Intergovernmental Relations (1953–55); and the Joint Federal-State Action Committee (1957–59). All four of these groups have aimed to minimize federal activities. None of them has recognized the sharing of functions as the characteristic way in which American governments operate. Even when making recommendations for joint action, these official commissions take the view (as expressed in the Kestnbaum report) that "the main tradition of American federalism [is] the tradition of separateness." All four have, in varying degrees, worked to separate functions and tax sources.

THE JOINT FEDERAL-STATE ACTION COMMITTEE

The history of the Joint Federal-State Action Committee is especially instructive. In every respect it represents the "hard case" among the four attempts. The committee was inaugurated as a consequence of President Eisenhower's speech at the Governor's Conference at Williamsburg in June, 1957. Mr. Eisenhower delivered a passionate statement that "those who would be free must stand eternal watch against excessive concentration of power in government." He argued that government power must be counterbalanced—"checked, hedged about, and restrained"—and suggested the creation of a Joint Federal-State Action Committee to be composed of high federal officers and governors of the states, charged with three responsibilities:

> One—to designate functions which the states are ready and willing to assume and finance that are now performed or financed wholly or in part by the federal government;

> Two—to recommend the federal and state revenue adjustments required to enable the states to assume such functions; and

> Three—to identify functions and responsibilities likely to require state or federal attention in the future and to recommend the level of state effort, or federal effort, or both, that will be needed to assure effective action.[1]

The governors—who look upon centralization of power in Washington as churchmen look upon sin and who for years have resolved against it—gave their enthusiastic approval to the idea and a committee of distinguished personnel was established (Figure 4).

The committee as established seemed most favorably situated to accomplish the task of functional separation. It was composed of distinguished and able men, including among its personnel three leading members of the

---

[1] The committee initially devoted little attention to this problem. Upon discovering the difficulty of making separatist recommendations, i.e., for turning over federal functions and taxes to the states, it developed a series of proposals looking to greater effectiveness in intergovernmental collaboration. The committee was succeeded by a legislatively based, 26-member Advisory Commission on Intergovernmental Relations, established September 29, 1959.

FIGURE 4.   MEMBERSHIP OF THE JOINT FEDERAL-STATE ACTION COMMITTEE

Appointed by the President

Co-Chairman:
Robert B. Anderson, Secretary of the Treasury

Members:
James P. Mitchell, Secretary of Labor
Marion B. Folsom, Secretary of Health, Education, and Welfare
    (replaced by Arthur Flemming)
Percival F. Brundage, Director of the Bureau of the Budget
    (replaced by Maurice Stans)
Meyer Kestnbaum, Special Assistant to the President
John S. Bragdon, Special Assistant to the President
Howard Pyle, Deputy Assistant to the President
    (replaced by Robert E. Merriam)

Appointed by the Chairman, Governors' Conference

Co-Chairman:
Gov. Lane Dwinell, New Hampshire

Members:
Gov. Victor E. Anderson, Nebraska
Gov. James P. Coleman, Mississippi
Gov. Price Daniel, Texas
Gov. George Docking, Kansas
Gov. George M. Leader, Pennsylvania
Gov. Theodore R. McKeldin, Maryland
Gov. Dennis J. Roberts, Rhode Island
Gov. Robert E. Smylie, Idaho
    (later appointed chairman)
Gov. William G. Stratton, Illinois, *ex officio*

(Replacements)
Gov. LeRoy Collins, Florida, *ex officio*
Gov. J. Caleb Boggs, Delaware
Gov. Michael V. Disalle, Ohio
Gov. Orville L. Freeman, Minnesota
Gov. Mark O. Hatfield, Oregon
Gov. Luther H. Hodges, North Carolina
Gov. Abraham A. Ribicoff, Connecticut

President's Cabinet, the director of the Bureau of the Budget, and ten state governors. It had the full support of the President at every point, and it worked hard and conscientiously. Excellent staff studies were supplied by the Bureau of the Budget, the White House, the Treasury Department and, from the state side, the Council of State Governments. It had available to it a large mass of research data, including the 16 recently completed volumes of the Kestnbaum Commission. There existed no disagreements on party lines within the committee and, of course, no constitutional impediments to its mission. The President, his Cabinet members, and all the governors (with one possible exception) on the committee were in complete agreement on the desirability of decentralization via separation of functions and taxes. They were unanimous in wanting to justify the committee's name and to produce action, not just another report.

The committee started off as if its total and sole task were the devolution of functions by separation, i.e., to hand over functions and taxes from the federal to the state governments. There had been a certain ambiguity in the President's speech: it was not clear if he thought it was possible to devolve some federal functions to the states without equivalent federal taxes being handed over. This ambiguity was soon resolved. The Committee's first conclusion was that there was no federal function that the states would assume and finance without some appropriate relinquishment of federal taxes to them. In fact, the governors were so hostile to this idea that it was never even discussed. There was no consideration of any such possibility in the Committee's first meetings or in its first report; no discussion of the idea at the Governor's Conference in Miami in May, 1958, and none at the two meetings held subsequent to that.

The Committee's Proposals

Almost the entire effort of the Committee was therefore put into finding federal functions that could be devolved to the states along with the relinquishment of federal tax sources so that the states would add to their revenues enough income to pay for the newly assumed services. The Committee worked for more than two years. It found exactly two programs to recommend for transfer from federal to state hands. One was the federal grant program for vocational education (including practical-nurse training and aid to fishery trades); the other was federal grants for municipal waste treatment plants. The programs together cost the federal government less than $80 million in 1957, slightly more than 2 per cent of the total federal grants for that year. The federal share of the vocational education program in 1956 came to $33 million, while the states spent $62 million and the localities $81 million. In addition, $4 million was spent on practical-nurse training and another $228,000 on vocational education for the fishery trades. Federal aid for municipal waste treatment plants averaged $47 million annually in 1957 and 1958, about one-tenth of the total spent for such plants. At that annual rate, it would take 50 years to fully devolve the federal system, even if one counts only grant programs.

To pay for these programs, the committee initially recommended a credit against the federal tax on local telephone calls. If a given state levied a tax equivalent to 4 per cent of the federal tax, then the taxpayer would not have to pay that tax to the federal government. The credit device was used because it was realized that, if the federal government simply gave up the tax, then the telephone lobby would make it impossible to levy the tax in many states. Faced with the choice of paying it either to the federal government or to a state, however, it was felt that the lobby would not object to the latter.

This credit device was strongly criticized by many governors and by a Governor's Conference resolution at the 1958 Miami meeting. The simple 4 per cent credit more than offset the cost of the functions to be assumed by the wealthier states; but in the poorer states, it came to considerably less than the sum of the vocational education and sewage disposal grants. With the tax credit, then, the rich would get richer, and the poor poorer. Congressional criticism of the plan for the same reason was made known early by Congressman L. H. Fountain of North Carolina (a leading expert in intergovernmental relations) and by Congressman Lee Metcalf of Montana. Both served states likely to lose under the proposed plan.

Consequently, the Committee altered its recommendation so as to allow equalizing grants to poorer states: the upshot was a recommendation which, if implemented, would have given every state at least 140 per cent of what it was receiving at the time for vocational education and sewage disposal. Under equalization, then, all states would be more equal than they were; and some states would still be more equal than others: New York, for example, would get from the tax credit more than double what it had been getting from the two grant programs.

WHAT WAS DISCUSSED AND NOT DONE

Many other functions were discussed as being appropriate for transfer to state administration. This led to a phenomenon strange to those who have studied the rhetoric of federal-state relations. The governors are generally the most vocal on the utter necessity of decentralization. But at the meetings, federal administrators were willing to give the states far more than the governors were willing to accept.

The federal side suggested that the federal government stop giving cash for the school Lunch and Milk Program: a total of $158 million plus $132 million in surplus commodities. The governors replied that there were too many parochial schools and too many voters attached to parochial schools, making the political issue too explosive because the states cannot constitutionally give money to parochial schools. The federal people asked: "Why not take a test case to the courts as to whether such aid would violate state constitutional restrictions?" The governors' response (at the time of Little Rock) was classic: "Perhaps Governor Faubus might be willing."

Old age assistance was another program—a big one—which the federal authorities suggested. They were willing to relinquish the entire program, which involved over $1 billion in federal funds, or only the old age assistance supplementing OASI, a $200 million item. Again the governors demurred on the grounds that the item was politically too hot to handle, that there were too many organized older voters.

One governor suggested that the states might assume the federal share of the program's administrative costs, the device the federal government uses to exercise control and to set standards for the over-all program whose annual costs exceed $1 billion, producing the following exchange:

Federal representative: "We would object."
Governor: "For what reason?"
Federal: "We have a billion reasons."

There was much discussion of tax transfers but even here the governors were reluctant. They talked of big lobbies and the difficulty of levying taxes. Many other suggestions produced the same reactions, among them low-rent housing. The governors even used the opportunity to urge greater federal action in the field of civil defense.

Finally, somewhat discouraged by its slow progress in devolving functions, the Committee turned to the examination of cooperative programs, looking for ways to remove the "squeak points" in shared functions. Shortly thereafter it passed out of existence with the change of administrations in Washington.

THE COMMITTEE'S FAILURE: WHY?

It is impossible to overemphasize the dimensions of the Committee's failure:

1. The Committee worked under what seemed to be ideal conditions for devolving and separating functions.
2. Its chief emphasis during its first year and a half of activity was this attempt to unwind the federal system.
3. In the end, it could only recommend two minor programs for separate state administration: those for vocational education and sewage disposal.
4. Finally, the Committee failure is all the more sharp when it is understood, for reasons that will be made clear below, that Congress was unwilling to legislate even those two programs.

Why did the Committee fail? What are the intractibilities making for shared, not separated, functions?

There are many levels at which this might be answered:

1. Why Failure?   The Platonic Answer

Some would say, "The governors are weak; they have no courage; they are demagogues talking out of both sides of their mouths." This is the Platonic criticism. It is a view that demands philosophers for governors, men who are "spectators of all time and all existence," their minds fixed on perfection and their devotion to perfection raising them above "corruptions of office, wealth and honor."

The trouble is that ideal rulers of the ideal state would not be tolerated in any but the ideal state. They could not be elected and certainly not re-elected. We may ask for the ideal, but we will rarely get it in officeholders. Nevertheless, the governors, as a group—in terms of energy, courage, intelligence, desire to accomplish public good—are probably a cut above most other groups, including butchers, businessmen, or even college professors. The conclusion that their lack of courage and foresight led to the failure of the Committee may have some truth. But it is only a partial truth, and it is a truth of no practical or political consequence.

2. Why Failure?   The Answer From Historical Evidence

The effort to devolve functions by separation rests upon a basic mis-apprehension of the nature of the federal system. We have already seen that, historically and today, the federal system is not a layer cake government; but a marble cake. Just as federal law is "interstitial in character," federal functions, as they have expanded, have been dovetailed into state and local ones.

This has been true since the earliest days of the Republic; a reversal of the trend would take a far more powerful group than even the powerful Joint Action Committee. Moreover, historically, the tendency is all toward the flow of power to central institutions—not only in the United States, but all over the world; not only in government, but also in church, business, and labor organizations. To believe that these tendencies can be reversed, even with the sort of effort the Committee made, is to ignore the power of great historical forces.

3. Why Failure?   The Political Answer

In political terms—and they are the most relevant terms for answering the question of "Why failure?"—the Committee failed because of the lack of any solidarity or discipline within the American political parties. Whether the parties are considered dependent on other factors, or independent, or both (which is closest to the truth), functionally, their lack of unity and discipline accounts for the failure of the Committee's separation effort.

Specifically, where national programs exist, any attempt to give them to the states is a threat to recipients of services, and therefore, a threat to the governor's elected position. A governor may in good faith promise that his state will assume a federal function, but there is no guarantee that he can fulfill his promise because even when a governor and a majority of the state legislature are members of the same party, he cannot control the party members in the legislature and therefore cannot guarantee passage of the necessary legislation. This accounts for the governors' reluctance. They ask: "Why alienate a significant fraction of voters?"

The governors' stand did not follow party lines. The President and governors, even when members of the same party, may have quite different views with respect to vocational education and sewage disposal. A Republican President cannot control Republican governors; nor can one Republican governor control others. This sort of party disunity—to say nothing of the diversities when different parties control the presidency and the governor's office—mean that it is impossible to assume the ordered decentralization contemplated by the Committee.

The relationship between governor and state legislator is reproduced in the relationship between President and Congress. The President, even if his party has a majority in Congress, cannot assure the success of the devolution movement and the concomitant tax transfer. When, as was the case during most of the Eisenhower administration, the congressional majority and presidency were held by different parties, such assurances become impossible.

Even if it were assumed that the Democratic leadership and the President agreed upon the desirability of separation, the members of Congress could not be controlled. Consider the congressmen's position. They were already under pressure to disapprove the Committee's recommendations from:

1. United States Conference of Mayors;
2. American Municipal Association;
3. Most mayors, individually;
4. School officers and organizations of officers, including powerful groups of vocational educational specialists;
5. Public health officers of states and municipalities, including their organizations;
6. And many others, including, interestingly enough, many governors![2]

These pressures were unquestionably strong enough to prevent passage of the legislation recommended by the President and his Committee. The same factors that led the governors to reject other programs offered to the

[2] See the testimony of the mayors and governors before the Fountain Subcommittee in 1957 and 1958, *op. cit.*

states by members of the President's Cabinet led Congress to reject even those programs recommended by the Committee. (In these terms the Cabinet members' willingness to go so far can be easily explained: they have no constituencies ready to rise up to punish them.)*

In summary, then, it is lack of party solidarity (a) between governors and legislatures, (b) between President and governors, and (c) between national party leaders and Congress which produced such a picayune set of recommendations from the Committee and which, in turn, doomed these recommendations to failure.

If the President controlled the national Congress and was linked by strong party ties to the state governors and state legislatures, then some genuine separation and devolution of functions would be possible. The failure of the Committee to decentralize government is a measure of the decentralization of the parties which in turn rests upon the diversity of American society.

THE IRONY OF THE FAILURE

Restating the previous paragraph positively: if the political parties were centralized, then an ordered decentralization of government would be possible. Yet this, it should be clear, is an irony, because decentralization would, in fact, not take place if the only way to get it were through centralized parties. Party centralization would lead inevitably to greater governmental centralization, not less. It is not to be expected that the forces leading to party centralization, if they triumphed, would be content with anything less than centralization of government; or, if decentralization occurred, it would be a decentralization of ordered choice, one based upon

* Editor's Note: Complicating the political framework even further were the technical obstacles that had to be overcome by formal action involving the kinds of political changes referred to above. The author had intended at least to list those obstacles as they affected the proposed transfer of the vocational education program to the states. They included actions on several levels:
Congressional:
   1. Repeal of the Smith-Hughes Act authorizing the program. This 1917 act includes an automatic annual appropriation of $7 million. Thus Congress could not simply end the program by refusing to appropriate funds for it as in the case of many other federal programs.
   2. Enact legislation providing for federal relinquishment of part of the telephone excise tax upon enactment of appropriate state legislation.
State Legislation:
   1. Enact legislation providing for operating the program without federal funds and repealing existing legislation establishing the program as a cooperative one.
   2. Enact legislation to assume and collect the telephone tax.
   3. Appropriate the necessary operating funds.
Moreover, the Senate and House committees that had to consider the legislation at the federal level were both headed by outspoken supporters of the existing system: Representative Graham Barden (Dem., N.C.) and Senator Lister Hill (Dem., Ala.).

the central government's power to decentralize.† This kind of decentralization implies also the power to centralize. And one may be permitted to believe that once a national party is powerful enough to bring about an ordered decentralization, it is more likely to choose in favor of an ordered centralization. All the evidence of history and logic, and all our knowledge of social processes, lead to this conclusion. It is a conclusion, incidentally, brilliantly demonstrated by the authors of the *Federalist,* before the Union was completed.

The decentralization that now exists—best described as the decentralization of mild chaos—does not depend upon the sufferance of an organized national party for its existence. If it is less neat and less visible, it is also less fragile and less subject to ordered change.

II. DECENTRALIZATION VIA STRENGTHENING STATE GOVERNMENTS‡

The foregoing argument makes the case that decentralization does not take place because the states have considerable influence over "national" decisions affecting them. The strength of state governments is not often measured in terms of the states' influence on national programs. Rather the strength of the states is most frequently discussed in terms of state inde-

† Editor's Note: The editor, in repeated conversations with the author, urged him to discuss the American system as "noncentralized" rather than "decentralized," a semantic difference that would have heightened the clarity of his argument. In fact, we agreed that the constitutionally based and politically reinforced diffusion of power among multiple centers (most specifically the federal government and the states) meant that there was no "central government" in the simple sense of the term, only a "national" government. If we were to apply the suggested usage to the case presented in this chapter, it could be said that the noncentralized system which gives the states substantial control over the shared programs carried on within their boundaries also gave the states a veto over any attempt to change the format of those programs. This made it impossible for the programs to be decentralized because there is no central government to undertake such a task in a noncentralized system. This should clarify the distinction presented by the author between possible but not probable decentralization by order and the unsuccessful attempt to decentralize by negotiation. The author was clearly receptive to the distinction between decentralization and noncentralization but, to the editor's knowledge, never made a final decision on the matter of usage; hence the original usage has been retained here. For further discussion of the concept of noncentralization see the editor's article on "The Shaping of Intergovernmental Relations in the Twentieth Century," *The Annals,* Vol. CCCLIX (May, 1965), pp. 10–22.

‡ Editor's Note: This section is based on selections from Grodzins' article, "Centralization and Decentralization in the American Federal System," in Robert A. Goldwin (ed.), *A Nation of States* (Chicago: Rand McNally & Company, 1962), pp. 1–23.

pendence, or at least in terms of fiscal and administrative power sufficient to carry out their own functions. From that view, the failure of the Joint Action Committee reflects the states' weakness rather than their strength. This conforms with another traditional view—that federal programs follow the failure of the states to meet their own responsibilities. "By using their power to strengthen their own governments and those of their sub-divisions," the Kestnbaum Commission said, "the states can relieve much of the pressure for, and generate a strong counter-pressure against, im-proper expansions of National action." A distinguished scholar of Ameri-can politics, V. O. Key, expressed the same point, although somewhat more guardedly. He considered deficiencies of representation in state legislatures, constitutional restriction on state power, and state political systems as a "centralizing factor in the federal system."

> Evidently the organization of state politics builds into the government system a more or less purely political factor that contributes to federal centralization. The combination of party system and the structure of rep-resentation in most of the states incapacitates the states and diverts de-mands for political action to Washington.[3]

The argument's simplicity is persuasive. But that does not make it correct. There is no doubt that the inability or unwillingness of state legis-latures and executives to plan a national airport program led to federal grants in that field. But could the states be expected to design and finance such a program? The same sort of question could be asked with respect to housing and urban renewal, the second conspicuous federal-local program of the postwar era. (In both fields, incidentally, the states are given the chance to assume important responsibilities.) The great expansion of fed-eral aid programs came during the depression. Certainly it can be said that the federal government went into the business of welfare on a wholesale scale because the states were unable to do the job. Was state inability the result of the ineffectiveness of state political parties, inequities of legislative representation, and outmoded constitutions? Or was the states' inability the result of a catastrophic depression? The first factors may have had some effect, but they are minor compared with the devastating impact of the depression on state income. And the depression would have demanded action from the federal government (with its virtually unlimited borrowing power) in new fields, whatever the status of the states' political parties or the modernity of their constitutional arrangements might be.

Furthermore, it can be empirically demonstrated that expansion of na-tional programs has not always followed the *failure* of state programs; the

[3] Key, *op. cit.*, pp. 81, 266–67.

nation has also assumed responsibility upon demonstration of the *success* of state programs. Thus requirements for health and safety in mining and manufacturing, the maintenance of minimum wages, unemployment compensation, aid to the aged and blind, and even the building of roads, were all undertaken, more or less successfully, by some states before they were assumed as national functions. So the states can lose power both ways. The national government steps in as an emulator when the states produce useful innovations, making national programs of state successes; and it steps in when a crisis is created as the consequence of state failure, making national programs follow state inadequacies.

The role of the national government as an emulator is fostered by the nationwide communication network and the nationwide political process which produce public demands for national minimum standards. The achievement of such standards in some states raises the issue of reaching them in all. Many reasons exist for this tendency. For example, the citizens of the active states feel that with their higher tax rates they are pricing themselves out of the market. Those in the laggard states can find specific points of comparison to demonstrate that their services are unsatisfactory. National fiscal aid may be essential for the economically disadvantaged states. State legislatures may be less congenial to a given program than the national Congress. Combinations of these and other causes mean that national programs will continue to come into being although, and even because, some states carry out those programs with high standards. The only way to avoid this sort of expansion by the national government would be if all 50 states were politically, fiscally, and administratively able to undertake, more or less simultaneously, a given program at acceptable national standards. This is not likely to happen. Even if it were, those in states less likely to undertake the program are certain to raise public demands for the national government to take responsibility for it.

If both state failures and state successes produce national programs, it must be added that neither of those mechanisms is the most important reason for the expansion of the central government. This expansion, in largest part, has been produced by the dangers of the twentieth century. (War, defense, and related items constitute more than 80 per cent of the federal budget, and federal increases of nondefense activities lag far behind expenditure increases by the states and localities.) War items aside, the free votes of a free people have sustained federal programs in such areas as public welfare, highways, airports, hospitals and public health, agriculture, schools, and housing and urban redevelopment, to name only some of the largest grant-in-aid programs. The plain fact is that large population groups are better represented in the constituencies of the President and Congress than they are in the constituencies of governors and state legislatures. No realistic program of erasing inequities of representation in state legislatures can significantly alter this fact. Only those who hold that "the federal government is something to be feared" (to use the words of Senator Morse, in his minority criticism of the Kestnbaum Commission Report) would wish to make the federal government unresponsive to those national needs expressed through the democratic process, needs which by their very nature will not, and cannot, be met by state action.

In sum, strong as well as weak states refer "demands for political action to Washington." More important, the ability of the central government to meet citizen needs that cannot be met by either strong or weak states, whatever those adjectives mean, also accounts for the expansion, as well as for the very existence, of the federal government. Strengthening states, in the sense of building more effective parties and of producing legislatures and executives who have a readiness and capacity for action, may indeed prevent an occasional program from being taken up by the federal government. The total possible effect can only be insignificant. The only way to produce a significant decline in federal programs, new and old, would be to induce citizens to demand fewer activities from all governments. (The cry, "Strengthen the states," in many cases only means, "Decrease all governmental activity.") This is an unlikely development in an age of universal literacy, quick communications, and heightened sensitivities to material factors in the good life, as well as to the political appeals of an alternative political system. One can conclude that strengthening the states so that they can perform independent functions and thereby prevent federal expansion is a project that cannot succeed.

Historical trend lines, the impetus of technology, and the demands of the citizenry, are all in the direction of central action. The wonder is not that the central government has done so much, but rather that it has done so little. The parties, reflecting the nation's social structure, have at once slowed up centralization and given the states (and localities) important responsibilities in central government programs. Furthermore, political strength is no fixed quantum. Increasing one institution's power need not decrease the power of another in the same system. Indeed, the centralization that has taken place in the United States has also strengthened the states—with respect to personnel practices, budgeting, the governors' power, citizens' interest, and the scope of state action—as every impartial study of federal aid has shown.[4]

[4] See, for example, *The Impact of Federal Grants-in-Aid on the Structure and Functions of State and Local Governments* (a study submitted to the Commission on Intergovernmental Relations covering 25 states) by the Governmental Affairs Institute (Washington, D.C., 1955); and the report of the New York Temporary Commission on the Fiscal Affairs of State Government (the Bird Commission), (Albany, 1955), especially Vol. II, pp. 431–672.

In summary, the argument that weak state governments make for national centralization is far more false than true. The states remain strong and active partners in the federal system. They do so in large part because of their power within federal programs and because of the strengthening effects that federal-state programs have on state institutions. The important reason that state institutions should be further strengthened is so that they may become more effective innovators and even stronger partners in a governmental system of shared responsibilities.

III. PROPOSALS FOR ISOLATING
LOCAL FUNCTIONS§

While public attention in recent years has been focused on attempts to separate federal and state functions, there have been some efforts made to separate state and local functions, continuing a tradition that extends back to the beginnings of the "home rule" movement at the turn of the century. Such efforts have had no greater success than the others.

HOME RULE THROUGH SEPARATE FUNCTIONS
The separation of federal and state functions is advocated on constitutional grounds as appropriate to the letter and spirit of federalism. Since the states are constitutionally unitary governments, this argument is not a valid one (though it is still used—inaccurately—by many). State-local separation is justified on grounds that local self-government is a positive good and must be maximized by allowing every locality the right to exclusive authority over those functions natural or suitable to local control.

The nature of the American system precludes the possibility of distinguishing "naturally" local functions just as it precludes the separation of functions at higher levels. It is impossible to say that some functions are natural or suitable for the local level and unnatural or unsuitable for the state or federal ones. Any separation of functions on the criteria of "naturalness" or "suitability" would leave local governments with little or nothing to do.

The cooperative participation—sometimes the antagonistic cooperative participation—of all American governments in supplying services at the local level has been going on since the beginning of the Union.[5] As has

§ Editor's Note: This section is based on an uncompleted draft manuscript designated for this chapter by the author, supplemented by selections from "Centralization and Decentralization," op. cit.
[5] See above, Chapter Two.

already been shown, means to shape federal and state programs to local purposes are well worked out and well understood.[6] But efforts have never ceased to separate functions among governments in order to carve out "natural" spheres of exclusive activity for the local units.

Municipal officers have been in the forefront of these efforts. Their objective has generally been stated in terms of municipal home rule, and frequently in bitter tones. They have argued that:

> Municipalities should not be required to support state projects, pay for state services, or carry financial burdens imposed on them by the state.
>
> The people of an incorporated city should have the right to handle their own affairs under a constitutional grant of power from the state. . . . They should have authority to raise revenues from any local sources without being required to beg for funds to pay for the services they need. . . .
>
> Local government in the United States should be autonomous as far as practical and consistent with public welfare. . . . While no municipality can have complete autonomy, the cities should have the maximum local authority consistent with their position as constituent elements in a sovereign state. . . .[7]

For their own reasons, the state governors have also paid lip service to the idea of carving out spheres of local freedom. On more than one occasion, governors have pointed out that when local activities are paid out of state-collected funds, "state control of local affairs is likely to follow." Furthermore, the governors have argued that if localities become dependent upon state governments for a large fraction of local income, they are more likely to turn to the states for the solution of essentially local problems. This tends to decrease citizen interest in problems of local government and therefore to decrease the meaning of democracy in the United States. The state governors have in some cases matched their words with deeds. During the postwar period, the most frequent manifestation of this was the extension of tax powers to localities over a wide area, to the extent that localities now tax everything from cats to personal incomes, from bicycles to public utilities, from amusement devices to business receipts. A number of local governments now even collect an income tax.[8]

The merits of home rule as traditionally conceived are debatable; but they are not the issue raised here. That issue is the possibility of defining a

[6] See above, Part Two.

[7] *National Municipal Policy for 1949* (Chicago: American Municipal Association), pp. 2–3. Reprinted by permission of the National League of Cities.

[8] The views of the governors are summarized from discussions at recent annual governors' conferences. See the issues of *State Government* for August of each year for summaries of the conferences.

set of "purely local" functions. The home rule movement is more than 80 years old. But it is an astounding fact that during this time no definition of what may properly be called "local affairs" has evolved. And there is no evidence that cities in home rule states have any greater discretion in substantive programs, including tax programs, than those in nonhome rule states. Certainly home rule has in no measure decreased the collaboration between states and localities in services rendered or regulations imposed. A good case can be made in favor of greater discretion (through either home rule or permissive legislation) for local units of government. But all this is not a case for separation of functions.

The first report of the Joint Federal-State Action Committee recommended that federal grants for municipal waste (sewage) treatment plants be discontinued. The justification for this recommendation was continued in the following words:

> The Joint Federal-State Action Committee holds that local waste treatment facilities are primarily a *local concern,* and their construction should be primarily a local or state financial responsibility. . . . There is no evidence to demonstrate the continuing need for the present federal subsidy of an essentially local responsibility.[9]

The committee at no place tried to justify its statement that waste treatment is "primarily a local concern." Nor could such a justification be sustained:

1. There is no way to distinguish, for example, the "localness" of a sewage treatment plant from the "nationalness" of, say, grants for public health. Sewage treatment plants, no less than public health programs, are aimed at increasing public health and safety. Where there are no adequate plants, the untreated sewage creates health hazards, including higher infant mortality rates. This sewage, when dumped into streams (the usual practice), creates in many cases interstate hazards to health and safety. Every indicator of·"localness" attributed to sewage treatment plants can also be attributed to public health programs. And every attribute of "nationalness" in one is also found in the other.

2. Since all federal aid funds are for specified purposes, there is no basis for claiming that the narrow purpose of the sewage treatment grants abrogates any general principle of federal aid. (The claim that all *specified* grants are wrong is, of course, possible, but that is an unrelated argument.)

3. Since sewage treatment funds are indispensable for public health, it cannot be claimed that grants in the field are for less important purposes

[9] Joint Federal-State Action Committee, *Progress Report No. 1* (Washington, D.C.: Government Printing Office, 1957), p. 35.

than other federal grants—those for rural libraries or vocational education or public roads, for example.

Why did the committee choose sewage plants, rather than public health grants, or federal old age assistance, or the federal school milk program, to transfer to the localities? Clearly not because one program is more "local" than the other. The real basis of choice can be easily guessed. The federal sewage plant program was relatively new, and it did not have as many direct recipients of aid as the other programs. The political risk to the governors of recommending local responsibility for sewage treatment plants was relatively small. To recommend federal withdrawal from public health, or old age assistance, or the school lunch program would have aroused the wrath of numerous individuals and interest groups. Governors cannot alienate such groups and still remain governors. The choice of sewage treatment plants as "primarily a local concern" had little or nothing to do with genuine distinctions between local and national functions.

Furthermore, a detailed analysis would show that any division of functions, along the line of their "local" or "national" character, would leave precious few activities in the local category. Automobile safety, for example, is now largely a local (and private) responsibility with some state assistance. Automobile deaths approach 40,000 annually, while injuries exceed 1.5 million. Before any given weekend, Dwight Waldo recently observed, it can be safely predicted that 15 people will be killed by automobiles in northern California. If a similar number of deaths was the result of an airplane crash, several teams of federal officers, operating under a number of federal statutes, would be combing the area in an effort to prevent further deaths. But there are no federal officers on the scene to prevent further auto deaths, not even if it be shown that some fatalities in California are caused by drivers licensed in New York. Unless the fatalities occur on major state highways, there are not likely to be any state officers on the scene either. In a rational division of responsibilities, assuming that they have to be all federal or all state or all local, would automobile safety remain in the local category? Clearly it would not.

This sort of analysis can be applied to a number of fields in which the localities have important, if not exclusive, responsibility. It is hard to find any area in which the localities would remain in control, if a firm division of functions were to take place. Not even education would be an exception. Pseudo-historical considerations, outworn conceptions of "closeness," and fears of an American brand of totalitarianism would argue for an exclusive local control of primary and secondary education (with state assistance, of course). But inequities of local resources, disparities in educational facilities and results, the gap between actual and potential educational services, and, above all, the adverse national consequences that might follow long-term inadequacies of local control would almost certainly, if the choice had to be made, establish education as the exclusive concern of a higher level of government.

The clear conclusion is that widespread separation of functions would reduce the localities to institutions of utter unimportance. They can no longer sustain the claim that they are closer to the people. Their strength has never been a strength of isolation. Their future depends upon their continued ability to assume important roles in the widening scope of public service and regulation. Their future, in short, depends upon the continuation of shared responsibilities in the American federal system.

The reaction of the American Municipal Association to proposals for federal aid for construction of sewage treatment facilities sums up the matter. The association not only opposed the Joint Action Committee's proposal but simultaneously lobbied for an expansion of that program as it then existed. In a 1959 communication to its members, it advocated doubling the size of the program for national as much as for local reasons:

> While over 1,400 communities have been rendered badly needed financial assistance in the construction of waste treatment plants, the job is far from being completed. Over 3,000 communities still discharge untreated sewage into our streams and of the 7,500 existing treatment plants, 973 should be replaced, 688 should be enlarged and 753 need additions. Local governments simply cannot finance the entire job alone.[10]

Those who work in the municipal vineyard know that one city's untreated sewage dumped into the river affects every city downstream, eliminating any exclusive "localness" of sewage treatment from the outset.

In the last analysis, what is of "national" as opposed to "local" concern cannot be defined in technical terms and, in the interests of the localities, should not be. That definition is the product of the political process. Before the social security acts of the 1930's, aid to the aged was a local responsibility, if it was the responsibility of government at all. The definition of old age assistance as a national responsibility was made in the social security acts themselves. Many people then—and some even now—doubted the wisdom of that definition. But it can be changed only by the same political process.

One point is clear. Any attempt to separate, to define, and to implement exclusive areas of governmental responsibility for local units, on the one hand, and the states and federal government, on the other, would inevitably

[10] American Municipal Association, *National Legislative Bulletin*, March 17, 1959.

result in the elimination of virtually all local units. Here, too, those who would attempt to decentralize functions of government in the United States through the process of separation would, perversely, produce an even greater centralization. It is through the same mild chaos that preserves the strength of the states that the localities continue to exercise important responsibilities over virtually all functions of government.

There is another reason for this conclusion with respect to the smaller local governments. The fiscal and manpower resources of these smaller units of government are so limited that virtually no governmental functions can be cut off and left to their exclusive jurisdiction. A review of the data in Chapter Six makes this clear: almost nothing in these communities is now done without substantial state and federal aid. And, financially at least, it would be far easier for the larger units of government to assume exclusive responsibility for these shared functions than for the smaller ones to do so.

This is not to say that greater areas of local discretion within shared functions could not be achieved through general or block grants that would supply funds to the localities while allowing them a very broad decision-making role. What we do maintain is that *exclusive* functions—usually demanded by those seeking to preserve the strength and vitality of local units—are impossible for localities to achieve.

METROPOLITAN GOVERNMENT AND
PROPOSALS FOR SEPARATION

This also holds true for the largest local units. Advocacy of large-scale metropolitan units is fashionable among both scholars and reformers. It is said that these units are necessary—among other reasons—so that local governments can handle local problems. There can be no doubt that many problems, from a purely administrative point of view, could be more economically and expeditiously solved through larger governments at the local level: for example, by two or three governments instead of (or layered above) the 1,400 governments in the Chicago metropolitan area. But this is not to say that these new larger governments would be able to handle any functions without the collaboration of the states and the federal government. What are the metropolitan problems that the new metropolitan governments are supposed to handle? They are problems of transportation, of air pollution, of water supply, of civil defense, of housing and redevelopment. The catalogue of metropolitan problems is, in fact, a catalogue of national problems, or, perhaps more accurately, national urban problems. Not one of them is a problem that the national government can possibly avoid. If they are problems that can be solved, they will be solved only through the collaboration of the entire federal system. If they are problems that are to be separated out in exclusive packages, there can be little doubt that most if not all of them would be far more likely to turn up under the exclusive jurisdiction of the federal, than of enlarged local government.

IV. CONCLUSION

Elsewhere in this book it has been shown that the characteristic decentralization of American parties produces significant decentralization of government: (1) in legislation, (2) in congressional intervention in the national administration, (3) in the politics of administration, and (4) in the availability of the multiple crack. This is not a controlled decentralization, but rather a decentralization of mild chaos. The power of this chaotic separation is obvious: it prevents the Joint Federal-State Action Committee, even under ideal conditions, from bringing about ordered decentralization through separation of governmental functions. And it prevents home rule cities from operating much more independently of state and federal governments than their less formally autonomous sisters.

These characteristics are hallmarks of modern American federalism. To them can be traced in large part the continued, important participation of the states and localities in virtually all programs of government: what we have called the marble cake of government. They account, with historical considerations added, for the fact that federal law is limited in objective and builds upon the main body of legal relationships established within the states. They indicate the existence of a substantial devolution of power in the American political system.

Any success of a committee like the Joint Federal-State Action Committee or of the local separationists—success predicated as it would have to be on the centralization of parties—would, therefore, be wholly undesirable. This controlled decentralization would, in fact, mean the end of federalism as we know it, an end of those attributes of decentralization through mild chaos that we possess. The failure of controlled decentralization is, in reality, evidence of a truer decentralization, a form of decentralization that is less neat and less visible, but—to the benefit of all those who believe in dispersed governmental power—less easy to change.

EDITOR'S NOTE:
STRAIN AND CONFLICT IN THE FEDERAL SYSTEM

Morton Grodzins was also concerned with strain and conflict in the federal system. In fact, one of his major fears was that his portrayal of the

*system as one of intergovernmental collaboration and essential harmony
between levels and participants would be interpreted as an overoptimistic
exaggeration of political reality. Part of the problem, as he recognized, lies
in the positive connotations attached to the word "cooperation." It was
partly for this reason that he came to favor use of the word "sharing" in
its place. He also spoke of "antagonistic cooperation" to indicate how it is
possible for governments (and people) to participate in joint ventures on a
routinized and regular basis even as they react to each other antagonisti-
cally. While Grodzins did not write about these problems as he had intended, he did leave notes stressing some of the more important aspects of
his thought on the subject.*

STRAINS IN THE SYSTEM

Among the many potential strains in the federal system Grodzins identified the following (the list is far from exhaustive).*

1. The lack of coordination between agencies and programs of the same
government has some important and detrimental by-products. Take the
case of standards of building construction which are a major concern of the
federal agencies operating in the housing field. For all the emphasis of
HHFA and FHA on building inspection, the federal government is one of
the worst violators of sound construction regulations that local building
inspection departments have to deal with. Indeed, the General Services
Administration wants to build its buildings without any local inspection
whatsoever. In effect, one branch of the federal government says to the
local authorities, "upgrade your building inspection standards" while another goes ahead with construction and says "we do not need your
inspection."

In San Francisco, for example, there was a great controversy over the
new federal building, constructed in the late 1950's, on just this point—a
controversy that represented a real strain on the sharing system there.
Ultimately the city-county engineer and architect were responsible for an
alteration in the plans of the federal building that brought it into some
measure of harmony with the city's unique civic center as a whole. The city
architect worked very closely with the General Services Administration in
planning the new federal building. The GSA architects and other officials
came to several civic design meetings. The first building plan that they
showed was a massive square box completely bordering the property line.
Under pressure from the city architect and other members of the city staff,
the federal officers agreed to erect a building set well back from the block
line. The federal officials would very likely agree that as a consequence of

* Editor's Note: All examples are taken from the author's own notes and most are
in his own words.

their cooperation with the city architect, they now have a better building.

2. Interagency competition is found at all levels and always causes strain. This kind of competition is perhaps most intense at the federal level where sheer size makes it difficult for agencies to coordinate activities among themselves and where the high degree of specialization increases the opportunities for interagency conflict. Thus in the late 1950's the National Aeronautics and Space Administration raided the Pentagon for personnel to inaugurate its management of the space program, angering the Defense Department and causing it to seek redress at the highest levels. For years, the Department of the Interior and the Department of Agriculture have maintained a running battle in the conservation and recreation field, based, in part, on their sharing of the management of the federal public domain. Within the Department of Agriculture, some agencies work to help farmers drain marsh lands for cultivation while others seek to convince farmers to retire land from agricultural production. The list could be multiplied indefinitely. In every case, the very openness of the system encourages these agencies to persevere in their respective paths since they can seek support for their activities in Congress and in the states where they develop their own clientele.

3. The ability of local communities to bypass those decisions of their state governments that affect them adversely, taking their appeals to federal authorities puts a strain on the normal mechanism of federalism by encouraging conflict between the federal government and the states. When the New York State Power Authority, under the leadership of the irrepressible Robert Moses, refused to bury certain power transmission lines connected to the new power generating facility it was building in western New York, the city of Niagara Falls, concerned about the aesthetics of the matter, successfully took its case to the Federal Power Commission (on engineering grounds). This caused a major rift within the state and a measure of state-federal antagonism where none had previously existed.

4. The ability of the states and localities to influence Congress on behalf of local interests, preventing federal government action for purposes of efficiency and economy in the national interest, is well known. It is the other side of the arrangement that makes it possible for citizens to protect themselves from arbitrary national actions and is part of the price paid for that freedom. When the Veterans Administration wishes to change the location of a hospital, or the Army Corps of Engineers to shift an office from one place to another, for example, local businessmen are directly affected and their alarm is taken up by the city fathers. As we have seen in Chapter Nine, the route to a national administrative agency on behalf of the locality via the congressional delegation is often the most effective one.

5. The reverse of this is the problem of excessive local dependence on federal programs—installations, contracts, or simply systems of operation. A distant federal action undertaken for national reasons alone may have a direct impact on official city business. In Ann Arbor, Michigan, in 1958, city officials were very much perturbed by a rumor that the Bureau of the Census was going to change its current practice and enumerate students, not as residents of the city at which they were attending university, but rather as residents of their home towns. This purely technical change in the definition of residents by the Census Bureau would have had a drastic effect on the fiscal strength of the city. Of the city's total annual income of slightly more than $3 million, $1 million came from state aid or the return of state-collected taxes, the apportionment of which was largely on the basis of population. Students of the University of Michigan constituted well over a third of the city's total population of approximately 60,000. If students were not counted as residents of the city, this would cut revenues from state sources by one-third and the total city income by one-ninth. A decline of $350,000 in a $3 million budget would have been a major catastrophe.

The case of federal surplus lands in San Francisco is even more to the point. It also represents the "hard case" because the size of that city "should" keep federal decisions on such matters from influencing local government so greatly.

Forty-six per cent of all of San Francisco is publicly owned. This includes the city parks and some state installations, but most of the publicly owned land is held by the federal government, and the greater part is in military reservations of one sort or another. Federal lands provide a big problem for San Francisco, not least of all because they are tax exempt. Since the mid-1950's the federal government has been disposing of some of its property in and around San Francisco and this has created major problems for the city.

Some time ago the General Services Administration announced, without prior consultation with city officials, that it was selling as surplus Fort Funston, 160 acres of San Francisco land adjoining the Pacific, to a private residential developer. The city, through its mayor, strenuously objected, and the mayor made a trip to Washington where he mobilized the state's two senators and a number of congressmen in an assault upon the director of the GSA. The latter, under pressure from the mayor and the congressional delegation, gave way and postponed the sale of Fort Funston for six months. The controversy continued to rage between city officials and the GSA. The city hoped to use most of the land for public purposes, especially for a park. The GSA director seemed to believe that such public purposes are unnecessary and that GSA is obligated to get as much cash as possible from the sale of land. (Sale of surplus land to public authorities is subject to a legislative discount.)

In this case, the business-minded GSA director apparently did not think much of the need for parks under local governmental supervision, or at least put greater value on the higher price he expected to get for such land if he could sell it to private developers. San Francisco officials, on the other hand, believed that he completely overlooked the need for local government to make determinations of the use of such land, once the federal government no longer occupied it. The extensive development of the Fort Funston area, for example, would mean a rather sizable expenditure by San Francisco for the extension of utilities, roads, police protection, and other urban services. San Francisco planning officers were not certain that all of Fort Funston should be used as a park. But they were certain that it should not be sold to a developer until proper plans for the use of this land could be formulated and considered locally. And the San Francisco officials concerned strongly resented the methods utilized by the GSA to dictate to San Francisco how land within the city limits should be used.

6. Yet these drawbacks do not deter localities from seeking all they can get from Washington and enmeshing themselves in the system—a sixth possible strain. A strongly conservative Republican officer of a Michigan town expressed a common view of those who work hard (and competently) to bring federal advantages to their local community when he remarked that if the world were dishonest, all men would have to be crooks. He expressed a distaste for all programs at the local level that are not completely financed and administered by the local government but said, "I go out and get every federal penny I can for my city. We share the tax burden. We need many improvements here and if we don't get the federal money somebody else will."

A NOTE ON THE CHARACTER OF CONFLICT IN AMERICAN FEDERALISM*

Contrary to the verbiage of the traditional exponents of "states rights," the real conflicts in the federal system are not between the federal government and the states, *per se*. Most great national conflicts that take on a "federal-state" dimension find the states divided against each other, some aligned with the federal government and others in opposition to what are enunciated as national policies. The segregation conflict is a case in point. The struggle is not simply between the federal government and the states

*Editor's Note: This section is based on notes left by the author and data from his files.

but between the segregationist states (comprising no more than a quarter of all the states) and the rest of the nation, including the federal government and over 35 states.[11] The 50 states rarely agree among themselves as a group when such issues arise. Moreover, when a majority of the states are agreed on a particular course of action, they are also likely to elect a majority in Congress, thus bringing the national government into alignment with them. This, in turn, shifts public focus to the federal-state aspects of what, under other conditions, might have been considered an interstate (or intersectional) conflict.

In fact, there is more conflict *within* levels of government than between them. Conflicts between professionals and political leaders are commonplace at all levels of government: planners fight with city councils, welfare professionals fight with state legislatures, the State Department fights with Congress.[12] Conflicts between interests are not based on political boundaries except insofar as such boundaries set the outer limits of the conflict area. Even conflicts within the same functional groups are more common. The struggle between the American Farm Bureau Federation and the Farmers' Union has been of longer duration than all but the most vital sectional struggles in this country. It may be said in all truth that the traditional separation of planes of government is less important in generating conflict than professional and interest group divisions. Often what seem to be conflicts between levels are actually reflections of the temporary alignment of different groups with different levels.

Interlevel conflicts are almost invariably over details rather than over general patterns or policies. The segregation issue is an exception to this rule; hence it is far harsher than other conflicts (and potentially more threatening to the future of federalism). But there is no difference of opinion between the federal government and the states as to whether or not there should be public welfare programs. There may be differences over the details of administration of those programs, or the level of benefits they should offer, but there is a nationwide consensus on the merits of the programs themselves. Before this consensus developed, the struggle that took place between prowelfare and antiwelfare forces was only incidentally an interlevel conflict—whatever "states' rights" arguments the latter might have used in an effort to strengthen their case.

[11] Even this is obviously oversimplified, since substantial populations in the segregationist states—Negroes and others—are clearly in opposition to the ruling elements, which may or may not be the majority in their respective states.

[12] The Federalism Workshop has collected data on such conflicts at all levels. Particularly illuminating are the data collected at the state level in Minnesota by E. Lester Levine.

Part V

APPLICATIONS OF THE SHARING HYPOTHESIS

Chapter 13

OUTDOOR RECREATION AND
THE AMERICAN SYSTEM*

I. THE VIRTUES OF CHAOS

Those with a reformist bent or a directive to recommend policy are likely to look aghast at the chaos of services and facilities that exist for recreation purposes in the United States. There is no neatness in the situation. Responsibilities overlap. Concern and effort are widely shared and appear to be poorly coordinated. It is difficult even to describe who is accountable for what or to understand where one government's responsibility begins and another's ends. If for no other reason than to aid his understanding— to bring some order out of apparent disorder—the observer is tempted to recommend that the system be made more simple and therefore more rational. He who recommends policy is by nature a neatener. The first progress report of the Outdoor Recreation Resources Review Commission comes to this sort of conclusion:

> There are a proliferation of policies, a multitude of agencies, ten score activities, and an interest group or clientele for each activity . . . it is this very overabundance of concern and fragmentation of responsibility that complicate, and in part even create, "the outdoor recreation problem."[1]

The opposite view in fact recommends itself. "Overabundance of concern" does not in any sense create the outdoor recreation "problem"; that

* Editor's Note: This chapter is based on the author's contributions to *Trends in American Living and Outdoor Recreation,* Study Report 22 of the Outdoor Recreation Resources Review Commission, 1962. It reflects his application of the sharing hypothesis to the practical problems of outdoor recreation services based on his discussion of those services in Chapter Four.
[1] *A Progress Report to the President and to the Congress by the Outdoor Recreation Resources Review Commission* (Washington, D.C.: Government Printing Office, 1961), p. 62.

concern rather is the best route to solving the problem, however it may be defined. Nor is "fragmentation of responsibility" a source of difficulty. Rather it is the desirable method by which American governments characteristically carry out almost all of their functional tasks.

Why does lack of neatness recommend itself?

First of all, the overlapping concern of many governments in a single problem in no way prohibits, indeed it invites, the establishment of general goals by the national government. It also invites national authorities, usually through grants of money, to stimulate activity by the smaller governments. These are functions of the American national government in virtually every major domestic public program. The national government has carried out these tasks since the beginning of the Union and even before the Union, as in the allocation of public lands for education in the Northwest Ordinance in 1785. In recreation, as in other programs, the goal-setting and stimulating roles do not mean that the national government's program becomes an exclusive program. Typically, it leaves room for a vast proliferation of ancillary, if not competing, programs in the same area. Ours is a nation rarely possessing a single goal in a given field. We specialize in goals.

Second, the existence of many governments operating freely in a single program area preserves a desirable openness in the system. There is no single source of initiative; rather there are many. There is no single standard for determining what is desirable, and no single set of officials with the power to define the desirable and undesirable. Power, as well as function, is dispersed.

Third, a system of many power centers is well suited to meet the infinite variety of expressed needs. It responds quickly (sometimes too quickly) to citizen demand. Because there are many points for decision, citizens and citizen groups have multiple opportunities to influence decision-makers. If a group does not get satisfaction at one place, it can try another. And if the second is unresponsive, there may exist a third or a fourth. This openness in the system for making government decisions is particularly appropriate for recreation because it is not a single, but many, things. The very diversity of activities labeled "recreation" makes it unwise to invest any single set of public officials with the power to make decisions concerning them all. Even for a single recreation need, exclusive responsibility is both difficult to achieve and unwise if achievable. Many points of public power, with different degrees of accommodation to different sorts of recreation demand, mean, in the end, that no reasonably widespread recreation need will be unfulfilled.

Fourth, many governments operating in recreation, even if they do roughly the same thing, are effective in meeting the growing pressure on recreation resources. Parks, like roads, seem to play the role of food in the old Malthusian calculus: rather than relieving the pressures of population on them, new resources produce new use. There is little chance in the foreseeable future of providing too much recreation land, especially since recreation, as a political issue, does not sustain widespread public attention. One recreation area frequently substitutes for another, and development of new recreation facilities by states and localities directly relieves pressure on areas under federal management, and vice versa. All this argues for more duplication of effort, not less.

Many governments doing one job may appear inefficient and wasteful. Neither charge, except for units of small population, has been effectively demonstrated. The situation does lack neatness and this is difficult to comprehend fully. In healthy institutions, ambiguities of this sort must be tolerated. In government, as in family life, business, and educational institutions, the absence of complete direction from above disperses initiative and releases energies. It should be preserved. Hierarchy, order, and the delegation of neatly packaged responsibilities are not adequate substitutes.

II. PERSPECTIVE FOR RECOMMENDATIONS

A number of recommendations are suggested by the consideration of many governments operating in the recreation field. As a background for these recommendations, several points of perspective must be made clear. One concerns the political importance that recreation is likely to have when it is viewed in its largest setting. A second considers the opportunities for political action by recreation groups themselves. And a third restates the desirable organizational model for the provision of public recreation facilities.

Specialists in recreation have been telling each other, and anybody who would listen, that the nation faces a great crisis in outdoor recreation. On the one hand there are many pressures creating an ever-growing demand for recreation resources: more population, more real income, more leisure, and more mobility. On the other hand, there is the pre-emption of open space by new industry and by the growing urban concentrates. The latter growth results partly from increasing populations and partly from the massive farm-to-city movement of Americans. Use of land in urban places increases even faster than population because the population densities of suburban growth areas are far lower than those of older center cities. The result is a serious potential deficit in recreation space, already apparent in the gross overcrowding of desirable park areas at peak use periods. The deficit in urban areas will be particularly serious.

The need for greater recreation space is clear. But it does not follow that this need will exist so acutely that it will be translated, as some recreation enthusiasts have predicted, into a political issue of great saliency. The economic and psychological shift from production to consumption, on which the demand for greater recreation resources is largely predicated, cannot be considered complete or permanent. It is not complete because large fractions of the population—professional as well as the unskilled and ethnically underprivileged—do not share with some white-collar and skilled blue-collar workers equal benefits in the new leisure. More important, ever-increasing leisure is not permanent because the view of easy, sufficient production (on which so much free time rests) is singularly ethnocentric: it ignores a minor fraction of our own population and a major fraction of the rest of the world. The poverty of individuals, as evidenced by inadequate food, shelter, and clothing, and the poverty of public institutions, as demonstrated by inadequate schools, libraries, health facilities, and simple cleanliness, everywhere exist. They exist in many American communities, and they are acute in large areas of South America, Africa, and the Far East. If the task of economic development is squarely faced, the shift from work to play will prove to be an ephemeral tendency in American life.

Recognition of our own needs, and those of the rest of the world, is abetted by the continued existence of a psychology of work that characterized the eighteenth and nineteenth centuries in the United States and Western Europe. It shows itself today in much play being turned into work and in the obvious uneasiness of many loafing and playing people.

The most important factor discouraging the pre-eminence of play lies in the dual threat of communism and annihilation by nuclear weapons. In the event of continuing conflict with communism, economic and other social weapons are greatly preferable to the terrible physical weapons that exist. Even if "settlement" is achieved on some level, competition can hardly cease, and overseas development programs that dwarf any now in existence will certainly come to the fore. Whatever the nonviolent outcome of our relations with the Soviet Union, therefore, the leisure produced, when the nation's boundaries are conceived as the whole relevant area, is likely to be pre-empted as the world becomes more and more the area of our concern. If this pacific outcome does not develop, the augury is that the nation and the globe will contain ample open spaces without recreation (or procreation) of any kind.

All this does not contradict the nation's need for more recreation areas. It does, however, put that need into a proper, larger, context. And it becomes highly doubtful that candidates will stand or fall on their position with respect to greater recreation space. If the analysis is correct, the political saliency of the issue will not become paramount. Recommendations for what is needed in recreation, if they are to be meaningful, must take this lack of saliency into account.

Turning from international to national politics, what most impresses the observer is the extraordinarily large number of citizen groups organized for wilderness, wildlife, conservation, and park purposes. Just to list such groups would require a small volume. The success of these recreation organizations in influencing public policy has not been negligible. But they have not been optimally effective because they are splintered. Groups interested in intensive park development often look upon wilderness adherents as crackpots intent upon preserving unused emptiness. Wilderness enthusiasts in turn view park developers as desecraters of God's glory (the religious metaphor is not inaccurate), and they consider some conservation groups as tools of the gun and ammunition industry, bent upon securing a continuous supply of live targets. These are only samples of a long agendum of conflict.

Clearly, concerted efforts by recreation, wilderness, and wildlife citizens' groups is needed. Only by combining strength can their causes be placed high on the scale of congressional and administrative priorities, and thus relieve pressure on each other. And only through combination can they resist the legitimate demands for open space by lumber, grazing, mining, and farmer-irrigation groups.

Prescription, as always, is easier than action. The Natural Resources Council, loosely organized as it is, has already begun the effort of consolidating political action in support of recreation resources. Further steps in this direction are the best guarantee that outdoor recreation, in all its forms, will sustain a claim to public land and public money in a period that will see claims for other uses grow in power and legitimacy.

The third point of perspective can be briefly stated. The organizational model to be followed by governments in meeting outdoor recreation demands should be an open, pluralistic one. For reasons already given, no attempt should be made to provide, among public agencies, "a clear-cut division of responsibility," as suggested by the first progress report of the Outdoor Recreation Resources Review Commission. Rather, all planes of government (as well as private enterprise) should be encouraged to increase the facilities and services they provide. All of them will do roughly the same sorts of things, and this too has been shown to be desirable. The important need for administrative agencies within and between levels of government is the further development of collaboration and mutual aid.

This can be best achieved through the continued professionalization of workers and the further development of professional organizations.

III. RECOMMENDATIONS

1. There are vast state-by-state and regional differences in the extent of public recreation land and facilities. The following diagram is an attempt to present an analysis of these differences. It shows two facts about each state (excluding Alaska and Hawaii): (1) on the horizontal scale, the acreage of all state and local recreation land (local parks and forests plus state parks and forests) is shown as a percentage of that state's total land area; and (2) on the vertical scale, federal recreation land in each state (national parks, forests, and fish and wildlife acreage) is also given as a percentage of that state's total area. The solid lines are based upon these data calculated for the United States as a whole: state and local parks and forests are 1.7 per cent of all land in the continental United States; and federal parks, forests, and fish and wildlife areas are 9.7 per cent of all United States land. The scatter diagram reveals (as well as conceals) a number of important points.

The upper left portion of the diagram contains "the-more-the-less" states. In proportion to state area, federal recreation holdings are large and state holdings are small. Here are found all of the western states except Washington, Oregon, and Nevada. All of these states, of course, contain far more federal land than shown in the figure, but most of it is residual public domain under control of the Bureau of Land Management, not considered "recreational" for purposes of this analysis. (Nevada does not show "high" with respect to federal recreation land, even though 85 per cent of its total area is federally owned.) New Hampshire also shows this inverse relationship between federal and state-local recreation land, but it has a proportionally higher fraction of state-local facilities than other states in the group.

A consistent but reverse pattern is followed by those states in the lower right portion of the diagram. They have proportionally little federal land for recreation use, combined with a proportionally large amount of state-local recreation land. They are "the-less-the-more" states. New York, ranking close to the very bottom in federal recreation area, has by far the most land for this use in state-local hands (19.5 per cent of the whole state). Minnesota, Michigan, Pennsylvania, and Wisconsin (each with more than 7 per cent of its area used for recreation under state-local management), and Rhode Island, Connecticut, New Jersey, Massachusetts, Maryland, and

FIGURE 5. STATE-LOCAL AND FEDERAL RECREATIONAL LAND AS A PER CENT OF STATE AREA

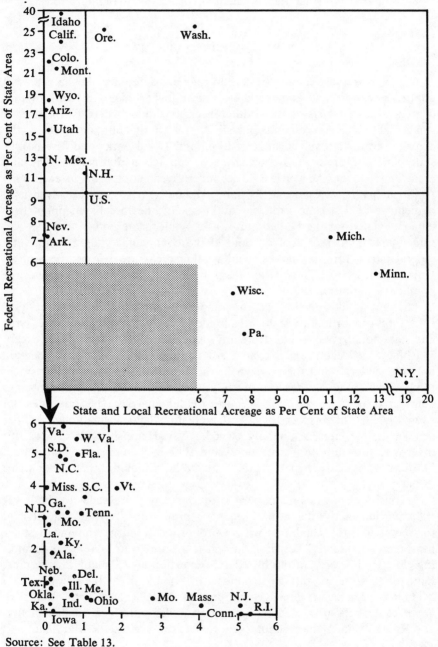

Source: See Table 13.

Vermont complete the group. Eight of these states are in the Northeast, three in the upper tier of midwestern states. All of New England except Maine and New Hampshire is here, and New Hampshire is above the national average in federal recreation lands and close to the average in state-local acreage.

There is no consistency in the patterning of federal and state-local recreation lands in the remaining sections of the diagram. Two states, Oregon and Washington, are in the fortunate, "the-more-the-more" category. They rank high for both federal and state-local recreation areas. The 26 states in the lower left quadrant of the figure rank low on both scores. This group of "the-less-the-less" states contains every southern state. Most of the Midwest is in the same category. Maine is in the group despite having the third most extensive park system in the country: it has no state forests and ranks low in local parks. Iowa, Kansas, Indiana, Texas, Oklahoma, Nebraska, Illinois, Maine, and Ohio are the poorest states in the country in terms of recreation land, when federal, state, and local areas are taken together.

The limitations of this sort of analysis must be made clear. One prime difficulty is the inadequacy of some of the data. The most authoritative available materials with respect to the various categories of land have been used, but some are almost certainly inaccurate. (The greatest inaccuracies are probably those relating to the size of state forests and local parks and forests.) Only when the inventories of the Outdoor Recreation Resources Review Commission are completed can the data on which the diagram is based be fully authenticated. A second inadequacy of available data made it impossible to take into account any of the vast holdings of the Bureau of Land Management. To have included them all in the diagram would have badly skewed the picture, since very large tracts are not used for recreation; but no adequate estimate was available on that portion of the public lands actually utilized for recreation. Similarly, the important TVA recreation holdings are excluded. If BLM and TVA land areas had been included in the computations, the principal result would have been to push all the western states very much higher than they are. Kentucky, Tennessee, and Alabama would have moved slightly higher. A third data inadequacy goes in the other direction. All land of the national forests is included in the calculation, despite the fact that some fraction of the forests is used little if at all for recreation purposes. Data at hand are not sufficient to take this factor into account, and, in any case, the very principle of multiple use would make such a judgment difficult.

Aside from deficiencies in the data, the diagrams must be interpreted

TABLE 13

FEDERAL AND STATE-LOCAL RECREATION AREAS BY STATES AND BY PER CENT OF STATE AREA

	(1) Total Land Area of State (Thousands)	(2) State Park Acreage (Thousands)	(3) State Forest Acreage (Thousands)	(4) Local Park Acreage (Thousands)	(5) Local Forest Acreage (Thousands)	(6) State and Local Recreation Acreage as Per Cent of State Area $(2+3+4+5) \div 1$	(7) National Park Acreage (Thousands)	(8) Service Forest Acreage (Thousands)	(9) Fish and Wildlife Acreage (Thousands)	(10) Federal Recreation Acreage as Percent of State Area $(7+8+9) \div 1$
All States	$1,907,336a	5,487	21,310	706	4,423	1.7	13,947	167,239	4,127	9.7
Alabama	32,690	43	9	3	1	.2	1	632	0	1.9
Arizona	72,688	0	0	53	0	.1	1,445	11,395	0	17.7
Arkansas	33,712	19	0	5	2	.1	1	2,433	122	7.6
California	100,314	677	70	67	0	.8	4,209	19,990	24	24.1
Colorado	66,510	9	72	26	39	.2	518	14,372	1	22.4
Connecticut	3,135	21	123	15	0	5.1	0	0	0	.0
Delaware	1,266	4	5	1	0	.8	0	0	14	1.1
Florida	34,728	73	193	14	14	.8	389	1,189	220	5.2
Georgia	37,429	55	39	4	15	.3	16	783	371	3.1
Idaho	52,972	18	423	1	7	.8	79	20,326	11	38.5
Illinois	35,798	41	10	68	57	.5	0	211	51	.7
Indiana	23,171	44	107	8	8	.7	0	120	0	.5
Iowa	35,869	31	13	9	14	.2	1	5	22	.1
Kansas	52,549	53	0	7	0	.1	0	106	0	.2
Kentucky	25,513	36	41	5	20	.4	51	459	65	2.3
Louisiana	28,904	12	8	4	5	.1	0	592	224	2.8
Maine	19,866	204	0	1	15	1.1	28	50	22	.5
Maryland	6,324	17	118	10	32	2.8	16	0	14	.5
Massachusetts	5,035	32	103	17	50	4.0	0	2	10	.2

State									
Michigan	36,494	182	3,757	41	173	11.4	134	2,565	94	7.7
Minnesota	51,206	105	5,551	14	869	12.8	0	2,791	205	5.9
Mississippi	30,239	14	2	0	0	.1	12	1,134	41	3.9
Missouri	44,305	71	161	11	4	.6	0	1,375	40	3.2
Montana	93,362	9	536	12	0	.6	1,141	18,572	489	21.6
Nebraska	49,064	49	0	6	1	.1	2	340	139	1.0
Nevada	70,265	10	0	1	0	.0	116	5,058	255	7.7
New Hampshire	5,771	43	0	3	46	1.6	1	678	0	11.7
New Jersey	4,814	23	152	17	53	5.1	0	0	12	.3
New Mexico	77,767	5	0	2	0	.0	235	9,251	137	12.4
New York	30,684	2,539	3,055	68	180	19.0	2	14	53	.2
North Carolina	31,422	36	36	8	95	.6	253	1,137	134	4.9
North Dakota	44,836	4	0	3	0	.0	59	1,104	189	3.0
Ohio	26,240	91	153	54	23	1.2	1	106	0	.4
Oklahoma	44,180	57	0	6	1	.1	1	267	79	.8
Oregon	61,642	59	1,367	10	88	2.5	161	14,939	417	25.2
Pennsylvania	28,829	160	1,900	32	134	7.7	3	471	0	1.6
Rhode Island	677	8	15	1	12	5.3	0	0	0	.0
South Carolina	19,395	46	123	1	32	1.0	4	587	126	3.7
South Dakota	44,983	93	86	3	1	.4	159	1,997	50	4.9
Tennessee	26,750	80	158	9	2	.9	240	596	11	3.2
Texas	168,648	62	6	36	2	.1	692	783	75	.9
Utah	52,701	28	0	3	47	.1	286	7,928	74	15.7
Vermont	5,938	12	83	1	16	1.9	0	231	2	3.9
Virginia	25,532	26	48	5	49	.5	250	1,450	13	6.7
Washington	42,743	74	2,371	12	100	6.0	1,133	9,691	86	25.5
West Virginia	15,411	41	78	4	4	.8	0	903	0	5.9
Wisconsin	35,011	19	338	20	2,212	7.4	0	1,466	165	4.7
Wyoming	62,404	152		5	0	.3	2,309	9,140	70	18.5

Source: Columns 1, 7, 8, and 9: Marion Clawson and Burnell Held, *The Federal Lands* (Baltimore: Johns Hopkins Press, 1957).
    Column 2: *State Parks, Acres, Acreages, and Accommodations, 1960*, National Park Service.
    Columns 3 and 5: *Conservation Yearbook*, 1958.
    Column 4: Marion Clawson, *Statistics on Outdoor Recreation* (Washington, D.C.: Resources for the Future, 1958).
ᵃ Total includes 7,550 acres not allocated as to State.

cautiously. It considers neither population, visitors to particular states for recreation purposes, the character of the land, nor privately owned land and facilities available for recreation use. Any one of these factors can affect the evaluation of a state's need for public recreation. For example, the existence of extensive privately owned farm and wooded areas in the Midwest and South (often available for fishing, hunting, and hiking) at least partially accounts for the relatively low level of development of public recreation areas in those sections. Similarly, the relatively greater number of tourists that visit California in comparison with Kansas produces some corresponding difference in demand for recreation space. Finally, some lands, largely in the West—such as Grand Canyon, Yosemite Valley and other national parks as well as the wilderness areas of the Rockies, Sierras, and Cascades—are unique and irreplaceable. Their existence within a state is an accident of nature, and they must be viewed as the special assets of the nation as a whole, not of a given state.

Despite these and other difficulties of interpretation, the diagram is highly suggestive of the differential need for public recreation facilities. The entire South (including Texas) and the Midwest (except Minnesota and Wisconsin) are particularly deficient in current resources for public outdoor recreation. The greatest efforts by all levels of government should be made in these areas.

2. Many parts of the resource-based recreation land under the management of the National Park Service—land of greatest natural beauty—are already overused and will become more so in the years immediately ahead. Yet land of this sort is least readily expanded. One solution that has been advanced is a more intensive development of lands of this caliber. Another widely discussed solution is to limit use. Suggestions include requiring advance reservations, the simple closing of entrances when crowding becomes apparent, or the charging of a fee high enough to discourage many visitors.

An alternative proposal is preferable. Most federal lands, presently or potentially useful for recreation, cannot be distinguished in terms of their intrinsic beauty or historical interest from recreation lands held by other governmental units. Once national policy-makers acknowledge this truth, they can take the desirable step of establishing federal recreation properties, including national parks, throughout the entire country. The present policy has produced the most federal recreation areas where there is least population. An acquisition policy that puts less emphasis upon natural attributes—and that does not limit acquisition of additional recreation land to by-products of other programs—would result in a more rational relationship between people and national parks. It would, moreover, make national parks and other recreation property available to the less wealthy, who are hampered by the cost of transportation.

The addition of federal recreation property to recreation-poor areas of the country should be conceived as a supplement to, not a substitute for, the conservation of tracts of great natural grandeur, largely in the West. Though they are scarce—and because they are scarce—additional lands of this unique high quality should be placed under the sort of federal control that will insure their preservation.

3. There is one irreplaceable national resource, the distribution of which roughly corresponds to high population density. This is the ocean and gulf shore. Of the 3,700 miles of Atlantic and Gulf coastline, only 6.5 per cent is presently in public ownership for recreation (though a larger fraction is accessible for public use).[2] Federal surveys of salt-water shore properties have underscored the rapidly diminishing fraction of shoreland available for recreation use. But the surveys have been lamentably timid in their recommendations for further public acquisitions. A salt-water shore, no less than the Grand Canyon, is an irreplaceable national asset. The reasoning that justifies the public ownership of one is applicable to the other. Further, of the 21 states with ocean or gulf beaches, 17 are below the national average in federal recreation land and 11 are in the recreation-deficient, "the-less-the-less" states.

Direct federal purchase of large segments of these salt-water shores is in many places appropriate, especially in those areas in which federal recreation holdings are now virtually nonexistent. Grants from the nation to the states for shoreline purchase are also recommended. Where outright ownership cannot be acquired, easements and other development control rights should be utilized. Though not immediately possible, the ultimate aim should be public management of the entire shoreline.

4. The Great Lakes shoreline does not precisely fit into the same irreplaceable category. Manmade reservoirs, e.g., the TVA development, approximate the lakes, and it is not beyond possibility that Mr. Edward Teller and his colleagues, given the requisite open space and water sources, could, with clean hydrogen explosives, even more perfectly reproduce the Great Lakes. But public purchases of the existing lake shores would probably be cheaper and safer. Such a program, involving all planes of the fed-

---

[2] *Our Vanishing Shoreline,* the survey of the Atlantic and Gulf Coasts (Washington, D.C.: National Park Service, no date, c. 1955); see also *Pacific Coast Recreation Area Survey* (National Park Service, 1959), and *Our Fourth Shoreline, Great Lakes Shoreline Recreation Area Survey* (National Park Service, 1959). All three studies illustrate the mixture of public and private spheres of responsibility: they were carried out by the National Park Service with a good deal of aid from private groups, and were paid for entirely with private funds.

eral system, is recommended. Not one of the Great Lakes states ranks above the national average in federal recreation lands (relative to total state area); purchases by the federal government would have the advantageous result of spreading national facilities throughout the nation.

5. A federal program of grants to the states should extend beyond shore-line purchases to the general acquisition of recreation properties. The primary purpose of such grants should be to aid states and localities to work out their own programs. Yet legislation should also make possible the use of federal influence in four difficult areas. For one thing, the primacy of problems involving the metropolitan areas of the nation should be recognized. There are the population concentrations most in need of open space. No single local government can adequately meet the recreation needs of metropolitan populations because they spill over many cities and counties and not infrequently involve more than one state. A federal program should make whatever contribution it can to the general goal of providing a more rational governmental structure in such areas. For example, it should not create new governmental entities in areas already surfeited with government units, but rather should use grants for recreation land purchases to strengthen metropolis-wide institutions.[3]

Second, a federal park-purchase program should do what it can to raise the professional standards of park and recreation personnel throughout the country. This is true even where no formal personnel standards are imposed as a condition of the grant, as in the fish and wildlife program. The issue is particularly delicate in the park-recreation field because of the great disparity in professionalization among states and because, indeed, the level of expertise in some states may exceed that in the national government. A federal grant program for parks has to set itself the task of bringing personnel standards in some states up to a minimum level without impeding the achievement of much higher levels in other states. A fully successful program will use the highly professionalized state officers as instructors for the less professionalized ones.

Third, a federal grant program can be used to encourage the further development of professional associations in the park-recreation field.

Fourth, a federal grant program should encourage states to liberalize laws regulating the acquisition of recreation land by local units of government, as more fully described in a later recommendation.

[3] Since these lines were written, Title VII of the Housing Act of 1961 has been passed. It takes a first, significant step in the direction of federal grants for open-space land purchases in urban areas and attempts, though somewhat awkwardly, to encourage greater rationality in the governments of metropolitan areas. This legislation falls far short of the full grant program (and does not attempt to meet the second, third, and fourth points) of recommendation five in the text.

6. Multiple-use policies of the Forest Service and Bureau of Land Management must accommodate, in the years immediately ahead, increased utilization of the public lands for both commercial and recreation purposes. Both uses have valid claims. Their compatibility on the same land is in many cases possible. But each of the several commercial uses of public lands is not compatible with every one of that land's recreation uses, e.g., hunting is possible where there is extensive timber cutting, but wilderness camping is not possible. The Forest Service and the Bureau of Land Management have in recent years demonstrated increased sensitivity to the need for greater land use for recreation (the result—and cause—of legislation to this end). Under the circumstances, the danger of multiple use as it is related to recreation is not so much the danger that all recreation will suffer as commercial uses of lands prosper. It is the danger that some types of recreation, which are incompatible with almost any commerce, will no longer be possible. This contingency is particularly to be avoided because it is irreversible: once a wilderness area (which may be compared in this respect to a great work of art) is destroyed, it can never be replaced. The national forests and the public domain lands must not only accommodate far greater recreation use under multiple-use management; they must also provide more liberally for those recreation practices that are only possible when there is little or no other use of the land. If provision for these practices is not made now, they cannot be known by future generations.

7. A number of federal policy changes would, in one area of the country or another, greatly improve state and local efforts in the recreation field. The minimum-land acquisition policy of the Bureau of Reclamation and the Army Corps of Engineers has often made state and local operation of reservoir shore properties ineffective and costly. Larger purchases of land in the early stages of reservoir planning would prevent these difficulties. This will demand more liberal legislation (which the bureaus involved can aid in achieving) as well as a more liberal method of estimating the economic benefit of recreation use.[4] In a similar fashion, land acquisitions for the interstate highway system as well as for other federal-aid highways should take into account the desirable development of highway stops that provide more than a gas pump and a short order restaurant. The General Services Administration has at times been excessively determined to maximize the dollar return from the sale of federal surplus property, thus impeding discount sales of land to public bodies for recreation purposes.

[4] Both the Bureau of Reclamation and the Army Corps of Engineers have recently moved toward more liberal land acquisition policies. A demonstration of the new policy direction has yet to be made, however.

Greater responsiveness by GSA to local and state determination of recreation needs would be desirable. The sums involved are relatively small, and there seems to be no reason why federal surplus property could not be transferred without cost to states and localities for recreation purposes, as is now the case for historical monuments. In the absence of free transfer, one minor procedural change—which would allow states and localities to await the next budget-making period before payment for surplus property is demanded—is highly recommended.

8. State park departments, participating in a federal grant program, can be expected to become more uniformly professional throughout the country and, within given states, to work on terms of greater equality with fish and game personnel. State park systems badly need support from the kinds of organized citizens' groups that now stand behind fish and wildlife programs. (Indiana's Department of Conservation works closely with no fewer than 800 hunting, fishing, and conservation clubs, a level of public support unmatched by any state park department.[5]) The sustained activity of citizens' groups is indispensable for achieving legislative approval of enlarged state park programs, badly needed in all but a very few states.

9. In any given state, responsibility for recreation is widely diffused. No principle of rationality can bring all agencies concerned under a single department because many state agencies (highways, water resources) contribute heavily to recreation as incidental to achieving other goals. Every state, however, can formally or informally bring together its recreation specialists for purposes of keeping each other informed and concerting, where possible, their efforts. This close collaboration will have a desirable effect on one important responsibility of every state: that of giving professional advice to local units of government. There are many useful ways of organizing these consultative services. Cities and counties should be able to turn to a well-staffed state office for aid in planning, acquiring, and operating recreation properties. Facilities for training local personnel should be available in, or to, such an office. It should also be prepared to aid in the intricate tasks of organizing parks for metropolitan areas, and parks to be jointly operated by several local governments.

10. A few states, as noted previously, have programs of financial aid for local recreation facilities. Many other states have the need and resources for such a program. State funds for planning at the local level would alone be an important stimulus. Loans to localities, serviced by user fees, for parks, boat harbors, and swimming areas, are feasible in some places. In smaller communities, where land tends to be more easily available, small grants or

[5] "Directory of State Outdoor Recreation Administration," *op. cit.,* chapter on Indiana.

loans for development would purchase large increments of land for recreation use.

11. A needed legislative development in the states is the general loosening of restrictions on local governments with respect to the acquisition of recreation facilities. Limitations of some sort exist almost everywhere. In only three states (California, New York, and Maryland) can local governments acquire easements in order to maintain open places on lands not purchased outright [As of 1961: Ed]. Many states do not allow localities freedom in acquiring recreation land by gift or through tax delinquency suits. A complete list of such restrictions would be a sizeable catalogue of horrors. What is needed is permissive legislation that would allow local units of government, alone or in collaboration, to acquire recreation property through a wide range of action. Various techniques of acquisition should be available, including purchase, condemnation, lease, tax delinquency suits, land fills, and street closings. Local governments should be allowed to accept gifts in cash or land as well as gifts of land use. They should be free to develop recreation areas by utilizing general funds, general obligation and special revenue bonds, and benefit assessments. Local governments should also have discretion in the use of a wide variety of devices for protecting open space, short of outright purchase. These include leases, leasebacks, easements, development rights, covenants or other forms of contract, agriculture, forestry, flood plain, and recreation use zoning. Subdivision ordinances of several sorts should include those that require builders to dedicate a fraction of newly developed land for park purposes.

These sorts of local freedom can be obtained only through state legislative action, but the states can be encouraged by the federal government to take this action, especially if a federal grant program to states for park development becomes a reality. Many acquisition techniques involve intricate legal and tax problems, and not all localities will choose—or be able —to utilize them. But almost every larger city could; and smaller places could if legal permissiveness is accompanied by state technical assistance.

Planning the recreation system for a joint state-federal reservoir several months ago, a state officer discovered that he had to work closely with a congeries of governmental officials. The Bureau of Reclamation, paying a sizeable fraction of the cost of the dam, was of course involved. So was the National Park Service which acted as the federal agent for recreation development. A large fraction of the dam water would be in a national forest, and this brought the state planner into consultation with the Forest Service. His own state park department designed the park areas and their amenities, for which task the National Park Service was again consulted. The state highway department and federal Bureau of Roads were called upon to supply new access highways. Federal and state health officials gave advice on sanitation facilities and measures for insuring the purity of drinking water. The state conservation department (using federal fish and wildlife personnel and standards) aided in defining the boundaries of the reservoir area. The conservation department would also stock the reservoir with fish. Two counties and one city (and several dozen businessmen) were consulted about contracts for building and operating specific recreation facilities. There will be a city park at the reservoir. Or is it a state park? Or a national one? Reality makes the old nomenclature inadequate. To be accurate, it is a park of the federal system.

The above recommendations are designed not only to increase the nation's outdoor recreation facilities but also to encourage the development of even greater collaboration in recreation among the many American governments. The governments can be many because the system is one.

Chapter 14

THE FARMER COMMITTEE SYSTEM
AND RURAL GOVERNMENT*

The United States Department of Agriculture's system of farmer committees is the product of the great economic crisis of the depression and almost
30 years of subsequent history. It has been shaped by the several power
centers within the Department of Agriculture; by the Congress, its committees and subcommittees; and by the internecine warfare between
farmers and farm organizations. The Agricultural Stabilization and Conservation county and community committees—the heart of the system—
are regarded by their partisans as an unqualified good. Their deficiencies
are believed to be minor and easily corrected. The committees are considered examples of grass roots democracy at its best, of elected neighbors
serving neighbors, of local control avoiding the evils of a national bureaucracy. In fact, however, the virtues of the committee system are by no
means unambiguous.

What is said to be ideal local democracy is also, *par excellence,* a device
of manipulation and control from the top. Counting only committee members and ignoring their elected alternates, the 3,000 county and 26,500
community committees involve some 90,000 rural dwellers. All of them
are paid, although most of them not very much. They are paid not only to
administer farm programs but are also expected to support and promote
them.[1] Committees are inundated with instruction from Washington and
state headquarters, they are jacked up weekly by visits from farmer field-
men (the name given to regional supervisors) and commodity specialists,

---

* Editor's Note: This chapter is based largely on the separate statement submitted
by the author to Secretary of Agriculture Orville Freeman in 1962, in conjunction
with his service as a member of the study committee appointed by Secretary Freeman
to review the USDA's farmer committee system.

[1] The promotional activities of the committees are discussed in the majority report
of the Study Committee under the awkward euphemism, "Popularization of Specialized Information."

and they are urged to greater and more effective action in state and regional meetings. The democratic grass roots committees are spoken of in Washington as "federal instrumentalities." Democratic forms may camouflage central control. To the extent that Washington officials preserve the committees in order to mask central control, or make it more palatable, they are guilty of using democratic forms in an authoritarian manner.

Further, whatever may have been the case in the depression days of three decades ago, today ASC elections are not regarded as being of first importance by the farming communities. Fewer than 23 per cent of the eligible voters participated in the election of community committees in 1961. Among the ten midwestern states, not one showed a turnout in excess of 15 per cent. (In Illinois it was 4.8 per cent.) In a significant number of communities the number of people elected was as large as or larger than the number of people voting. Nor is it true that leading farmers play principal roles. Many community and county committees are the captives of superannuated veterans of the old agricultural wars, retained in their posts because of voter apathy plus their own efforts to insure for themselves some income and something to do.

If the committee system is something less than ideal as an exemplar of grass roots democracy, it also has obvious shortcomings as an administrative device. Supervision from Washington of the ASC programs is an altogether natural fact of administrative life. Programs handled by the ASC committees are, taken together, the most expensive domestic federal activity. The Secretary of Agriculture is by law charged with the effective expenditure of these funds. He would be grossly derelict in his duties if he did not do everything within his power to see that the committees carry out their functions honestly and efficiently. But the attributes of grass roots democracy which are ascribed to the committees imply that they must have a considerable measure of freedom, including freedom from central control. Supervision that otherwise would be regarded as ordinary administrative prudence is, under the circumstances, often looked upon as evil, bureaucratic action. The logic of the committee system turns ordinary supervision into manipulation. This is an absurd burden for central administrators to bear. Yet if the Secretary took seriously the charges that he manipulated the committees and withdrew a considerable measure of the supervision given to them, he would surely not escape reprimand by forces in Congress (and the Bureau of the Budget and General Accounting Office). He would be guilty of slack administration, of unlawful administration of funds, of failing to exercise due diligence in meeting legislative objectives. In this matter, the Secretary is damned if he does and damned if he doesn't. In this way, absurdity is compounded.

The ASC committee system has still other administrative defects. In a poll conducted by this study group, the county committee chairmen were asked:

What is your reaction to the present approach of the U.S. Department of Agriculture to the farm problems?

The responses were:

20% Very favorable
43% Favorable
20% Neutral
12% Opposed
2% Very opposed
3% No response

A staff analysis of this response said:

If we assume that those committeemen who are in sympathy with the Department's approach to the farm problem would not hesitate to mark their returns as "favorable" or "very favorable" then our evidence suggests that 37% of the respondents are not in sympathy with the present approach of the Department. (I.e., the neutral responses must be counted among those not in sympathy with the Department.) They do not endorse the present Department's approach, even though they are not necessarily hostile toward administration of farm programs as authorized by law.

The remaining 63% of the respondents are an important part of the Department's "supporting force" in the counties across the nation.

It must be recalled that the county chairmen are the most important persons at the point of farmer contact in the ASC administration. They set the effectiveness and tone of the whole operation. Their expectations and standards determine how well or poorly county managers and office staffs will perform their tasks. Those looking for solace may take comfort that 73 per cent of the county chairmen are a "supporting force" for ASC programs. Those concerned with efficiency—and with the Secretary's responsibility to Congress and the electorate as a whole—will be more impressed with the fact that one out of every four elected county chairmen is not in sympathy with the very programs he is charged by law with administering.

The character of the committees as instruments of grass roots democracy is prejudiced by the fact that they are closely directed—perhaps manipulated is the better word—by central headquarters. But, given the character of our society and the system of electing committee members, the central manipulation cannot be complete. Enemies of the program are elected to serve as program administrators. The result clearly allows one to presume that alternative modes of administration of considerably greater efficiency could be devised. The committee system, in my view, is deficient both as an institution of democracy and as an instrument of efficient administration. And any attempt to correct one of these deficiencies is likely to exacerbate the other.

It is more difficult to pass judgment on the committees in a third area. The very nature of what is called supply management engages those applying the regulations in matters of a quasi-judicial nature. Should Farmer Jones have his productivity index (which governs the dollar amount he receives for diverted acres) raised two percentage points? If so, since the county operates within a fixed total limit, whose index will be lowered? When the Krueger brothers divide up their father's farm, who gets the cotton allotment? Is the partnership formed for the growing of rice a *bona fide* partnership or does it represent manipulation of the legal forms for the illegal transfer of rice allotments? Should Mr. Carlson, who has had cows grazing intermittently on acreage supposedly lying fallow, be given his conservation payment on his plea that the kids coming home from the rural school have just for fun allowed the cattle to roam where they ought not? Such questions—and others far more complex—are frequently put before county committees. The decisions rendered are of great consequence to the farmers (and the farm corporations) concerned. Although discretion of the county committees has consistently declined through the years—not least of all because of the committees' insistence that central direction relieve them of judging the nasty cases—there will always be an irreducible number of these quasi-judicial matters before a local office.

Does justice follow when decisions on these matters are made by a locally elected committee? Would alternative modes of adjudication produce greater justice? The Department of Agriculture has never faced these questions with sufficient seriousness to gather the basic facts upon which they could be answered with any confidence. As a consequence, our further discussion of the issue is purely speculative.

Is it reasonable to suppose that a farmers' committee is well qualified for adjudicating issues concerning neighboring farmers merely because both the judged and judging are neighbors? To be sure, the judges have an intimate acquaintanceship with the issues at hand. Such close acquaintanceship is not likely to be matched by any alternative adjudicators, whether an appointed statewide committee of farmers or a specially trained panel of civil servants. On the other hand, there are reasons (still on speculative grounds) that lead one to believe that county committees perform their quasi-judicial tasks poorly. Intimate acquaintanceship with and participation in the local community may lead not to even-handed justice but to subservience to the powerful and neglect of the weak. (It is worth noting that in all the county committees of the South there has never been, as far as I can discover, a single Negro member.) Justice, in other words, may be hindered by intimacy and fostered by aloofness. This is especially so in a rural community where powerful people have a great opportunity to punish their local opponents with a wide range of economic and social, as well as political, weapons. The linkage in many counties between political organizations and ASC committees is also prejudicial to justice. Where this relationship exists it at least implies that the dominant political organization in the county can prevent certain people from holding membership in the committee; at most, it means that the political organization can consistently receive special consideration in committee adjudications for its adherents.

In sum, it can be speculated that a more even-handed justice might follow from alternative methods of adjudication. The data are not in hand to say this with certainty. But clearly the deficiencies of the committees as exemplars of democracy and as effective administrative units are not offset by their virtues as a source of justice. On the contrary, it is likely that a badly needed, close examination of the committees as sources of justice might condemn them on that ground, too.

On one score the committee system must provisionally be given high grades. There exists a substantial degree of farmer acceptance of supply management programs. Without acceptance there would be no program. For example, in the Midwest, limitations of feed-grain acreages (and payments for diverted acres) are effective only if an individual farmer volunteers to participate. Similarly, the Agricultural Conservation Program depends upon voluntary participation. In both cases, considerable regulations accompany the financial incentives. In establishing marketing quotas to bring about reduction in the supply of such products as cotton, rice, tobacco, wheat, or peanuts, approval by at least two-thirds of the eligible producers must be secured in a referendum. (Price supports then become effective for the crop concerned.) Such provisions are written into law for various reasons, not least of all because Congress is uncertain where wisdom and justice lie, which in turn reflects the bitter division of opinion among those working in agriculture and related industries. A substantial segment of that opinion believes no supply limitation program of any sort should exist on any but a temporary basis.

The Department of Agriculture must therefore persuade farmers to be its clients before most ASC programs can become effective. Historically, community and county committees were inaugurated precisely so that they would aid in this persuasion job. And more than 25 years ago—when the programs were new, farms were smaller, roads were bad, rural telephones a scarcity, and television nonexistent—committees may have been the only effective persuasive device.

It is by no means certain that they still are. The whole matter can be discussed only in the most tentative terms because, as in so many matters facing the study group, the data necessary for firm conclusions are not at hand. The committees exist, and so does farmer acceptance, the latter ranging from tolerable to excellent. This has brought many farm leaders to the easy conclusion that the committees are indispensable to acceptance, and that without the committees there would be no acceptance. But the conclusion may be false. For one thing, no other systematic means of persuasion has ever been tried. For another, there are great regional variations in the farmers' willingness to participate in ASC programs (tobacco and cotton growers are more willing than corn growers) which are not explained by variations in the effectiveness of the committee system. The causality, on the contrary, may go in the opposite direction, i.e., high farmer acceptance may produce more effective committees. Most important, acceptance of ASC programs depends in very large measure on the financial incentives offered, almost $4 billion in direct subsidies in 1962. The committees are secondary to the cash in persuading farmers to participate in ASC programs. This alone suggests that it should not be difficult to find substitutes for the committees in their role as persuaders.

Nevertheless, in my view the best justification for retaining the committee system is that it effectively encourages the voluntary participation necessary to the existence of ASC programs. Since other means of persuasion have not been tried, one is justified in seeking, at least in the short run, improvements in the committee system rather than its abolition. Assuming that ASC programs are desirable, something less than the best administrative system is for a time acceptable, if this acceptance insures the programs' existence. I believe that a good deal of the cant about the committees as proud local democracies and as efficient administrative arms is evidence of a general unwillingness to recognize them as, primarily, program sales units. And doubts about the committees as purveyors of justice are fortified: since they must spawn *gemütlichkeit,* justice is harder born.

All these considerations (and others) make me considerably more skeptical than the majority of this study committee's members about the utility of the ASC committee system. I believe a prudent Secretary of Agriculture would, while improving the system, look to its eventual demise. Immediately, in my view, the committees should be deprived of their administrative, as opposed to their quasi-judicial and persuasive, functions. The county managers would be directly responsible in the administrative chain of command to the Secretary of Agriculture. The managers and their staffs would be full civil servants of the United States. The issue of accountability to the Secretary would be solved, and the anomaly of a Cabinet member operating a program with a substantial fraction of key personnel inimical to it would be substantially liquidated.

I believe these steps could be taken without threat to program acceptance. County committees would, for a time at least, exist for the performance of the quasi-judicial and promotional functions. An effort should be made to determine more exactly than is now known how well the first of the functions is performed, and which of the many substitutes for the committees as promotional devices might be politically feasible. If, as I suspect, better methods can be found for both functions, the county committees would in time disappear. (So would community committees. Indeed, they even now do too little to justify their existence.)

In most domestic programs of the federal government, administration is accomplished through cooperative arrangements with states and localities, ranging from grants-in-aid (as in public assistance and roads) to more informal collaboration (as in law enforcement). The Department of Agriculture's experience with this mode of administration has not been a happy one: the state extension services (and county agents) have often been more responsive to the Farm Bureau or other political influences than to central leadership. As if in reaction to this difficulty, the Department in other programs has ignored the constitutionally designed system of state and local governments.[2] Moreover, Agriculture has established, through one device or another, its own system of local governments, directly in the cases of the elected committees for the ASC and for the Farmers Home Administration. (The federally sponsored local governments for the soil conservation program require state enabling legislation.)

Rural local governments in the United States, with a few exceptions, are by common consent the nation's most deficient ones. They suffer from having too little to do. They suffer from voter apathy and therefore control by "courthouse gangs." They suffer from inadequate organization, low-grade personnel, and services performed at a low level of efficiency. Causes for these conditions are numerous and would exist if there were no United States Department of Agriculture. Nevertheless, the Department has contributed to the low state of rural (especially county) local government.

[2] In early legislation for the ASCS (the Soil Conservation and Domestic Allotment Act of 1935, as amended in 1936) section 7 provided that the program should be carried out by the states through federal grants. Authority to the Secretary to carry out the program directly, without going through the states, was originally limited to two years. National administration was continued under successive temporary extensions of grants of power to the Secretary until 1962, when the old grant-in-aid provisions were finally repealed. The 1935–36 grant system provided for specially elected ASC county and community committees as well as state administration. For reasons suggested in the text I think it highly advantageous that this legislation was never implemented.

First, ASC offices in every rural county compete with the county government in attracting leaders, skilled personnel, electorate attention, and in other ways. In many areas, county operations are dwarfed by the ASC programs, as measured by dollar expenditures or impact on the resident, or both. This competition has without doubt been deleterious to county government. More important, by not working collaboratively with local (or state) governments the Department of Agriculture has deprived these governments of significant advantages. Grant programs in other fields have been used to raise standards of personnel, organization, and performance. They have increased the scope of activity of states and cities and have added to the stature of those institutions.

I believe that the Department of Agriculture has been seriously deficient in ignoring local and state governments in the administration of the ASC (and other) programs. There are great difficulties in the way of overcoming the deficiency. For example, standards of organization and personnel established by the Department might require such a basic overhauling of county governments that amendments to state constitutions would be necessary. (Ordinarily, grant programs involve only legislative and administrative action by states and localities.) Safeguards would have to be constructed to insure that ASC programs should not become the preponderant part of —and therefore swamp—rural county functions. This would argue for initiating cooperative action for only a part of what the ASC committees now do. In turn, there arise the enormously complex tasks of phasing programs from one form of administration to another.

Despite all difficulties, there seems to me great merit in the Department's turning to a system by which it shares its responsibilities for ASC programs with the duly constituted system of local governments. This would end the Department's current game of charades with local democracy. It would, given the changes demanded of county governments, supply an effective working force at the local level. (But the quasi-judicial function would have to be given to some specially constituted body.) And it would contribute to the substantial upgrading of that local government which needs it most. Many problems (both old and new) would of course remain. The federal-state-local partnership is not a panacea; it is a viable relationship that with time becomes more rather than less effective.

These are considerations that can only be effectuated over a long span of years. One effective rural local government at the county level may be achievable in time; two seem too much even to hope for. In that happy day when the world, rather than the nation, is the focus of agricultural policy and supply—and curtailment programs therefore only a memory—a radical upgrading of county governments might be the only permanent monument to the principal ASC programs.

Chapter 15

STATE-CITY FISCAL RELATIONS AND THE SHARING APPROACH[1]

The late Henry Simons left as part of his intellectual legacy a remarkable "political credo" which says, in part:

> Modern democracy rests upon free, responsible local government and will never be stronger than this foundation. . . . A people wisely conserving its liberties will seek ever to enlarge the range and degree of local freedom and responsibility. In so doing, it may sacrifice possible proximate achievements. Doing specific good things by centralization will always be alluring. It may always seem easier to impose "progress" on localities than to wait for them to effect it themselves. . . . Progress to which local freedom, responsibility, and experimentation have pointed the way may be accelerated for a time and effected more uniformly by the short cut of central action. But such short-cutting tends to impair or to use up the roots of progress in order to obtain a briefly luxuriant bloom.[2]

This is a statement of political values to which municipal and state officials, and their professional associations, almost unanimously give support. The position is taken not only by the state governors in their relationships with the national administration and not only by municipal officers in their negotiations with state offices. It is also expressed, at least verbally and frequently in concrete measures, by state officials and state legislators in dealing with municipal officers and municipal affairs.

The history of state-local relations in the United States during the past

[1] I have had the advice and criticism of Carl Chatters and Winfield Best, both of the American Municipal Association; Frank Bane and Frank Smothers, both of the Council of State Governments; Charles Conlon and Ray Garrison, both of the Federation of Tax Administrators; and I. M. Labovitz and Bernard Larner, both of the U.S. Bureau of the Budget. The responsibility for what is said is entirely my own.

[2] Henry C. Simons, *Economic Policy for a Free Society* (Chicago: University of Chicago Press, 1948), p. 13. Copyright 1948 by the University of Chicago. For a parallel statement by John Stuart Mill, see *On Liberty* (Everyman's Library Edition; New York: E. P. Dutton & Company, 1910), pp. 168–69.

several years is characterized by an attempt to formulate a specific program for the achievement of "free, responsible local government." This program has been largely expressed by the states in the granting of new tax powers to municipalities and by municipalities in the levying, for the first time, of a wide variety of nonproperty taxes.

The purpose of the following paragraphs is to assess this development in terms of the value of "free, responsible local government."

I. THE NEW TREND IN TAXATION

The plight of most city governments is not a happy one. They have been faced during the past several years with a steadily rising price index and with consequent rapidly rising costs for commodities and personnel. They have been faced with insistent demands for new and expanded public services. They have been faced with the bleak necessity of war-delayed plant expansion and plant maintenance. They are currently faced with increased welfare costs in the face of automation and unemployment generated by new technologies.

These are new manifestations of old complaints, aggravated by inflationary conditions. The response of city officials has been the widespread demand for new tax powers. These demands have been coupled with a drive for general municipal home rule and have been made in the following terms: municipal governments are entitled to sufficient revenue to finance the activities required of them by custom or by law. Where the local citizens demand a local service they must expect to pay for it. Unless the state provides adequate revenue by other measures, municipalities which can administer them should be authorized to use as local taxes the payroll-income tax, local sales taxes, license taxes based on volume of business, cigarette and tobacco taxes, amusement or admissions taxes, hotel taxes, liquor taxes, utility taxes, and various service charges.[3]

From the point of view of the states (which face grave fiscal problems themselves), there are also good reasons for increasing municipal freedoms, especially in the field of taxation. They have been expressed by the state governors as follows:

1. Just as it is essential that overcentralization be prevented in Washington, so it is necessary that overcentralization be prevented within the states. When local activities are paid for out of state-collected funds, state control of local affairs is likely to follow.

[3] *National Municipal Policy for 1949, op. cit.,* pp. 2–3.

2. If localities become dependent upon the state governments for funds, the localities will be likely to turn to the states for the solution of essentially local problems. This decreases citizen interest in problems of local government. The way to maximize citizen participation in local affairs is to make localities, to every extent possible, fiscally responsible for their own activities. This citizen participation in local government is fundamental to the strength of the national state.

3. Furthermore, extensive state-aid programs encourage both wastefulness and extravagance. If local governments, themselves, raise the money they spend, those governments will call for fewer services and administer their affairs more economically.

4. By giving localities control over their own affairs, local officials and local citizens will understand the difficulties of apportioning limited funds. They will become conscious of the pressure groups which legislators find difficult to oppose.[4]

The states have matched their words with laws increasing local tax powers, particularly by expanding local powers to levy nonproperty taxes. The growth of local nonproperty taxes is a phenomenon of current public financing. It is the outstanding single trend in the development of state-local relations. Localities now tax everything from cats to personal incomes, from bicycles to public utilities, from amusement devices to business receipts. In some states localities still do not utilize nonproperty taxes to any appreciable extent, and property taxes still remain by far the most important source of municipal revenue. Nevertheless, nonproperty taxes are rapidly increasing in number and rapidly becoming more important in the tax collections of American cities.

Another indication is a resolution of the 1948 Governors' Conference which favored "the extension of local powers of taxation in order to strengthen local government and its capacity to meet the needs of its people and to discourage the present trend toward centralization of government in the states."[5] And the 1949 program of suggested state legislation developed by the Council of State Governments and circulated to all states includes a model "Municipal Tax Levying Enabling Act." This law, largely modeled on Pennsylvania's 1947 statute, "would give local governments wide discretion in the field of taxation. Home rule from a fiscal standpoint would become a reality."[6]

[4] Summarized from discussions at the 1948 and 1949 Governors' Conferences. See *State Government*, August, 1948, pp. 171–74; August, 1949, pp. 202–3.
[5] *State Government*, August, 1948, p. 174.
[6] Interpretive statements, attached to "Municipal Tax Levying Enabling Act," *Suggested State Legislation, Program for 1949* (Chicago: Council of State Governments, 1948), pp. 25–30.

II. THE UNDERLYING ARGUMENT

The arguments advanced by both state and local officials in support of enlarged municipal taxing powers reflect a strongly separatist attitude and express a concern for status and for personal and institutional prerogative. The quotations above indicate this. But there are even more revealing statements. For example, an official policy statement of the leading organization of municipalities says: "Municipalities should not be required to support state projects, pay for state services, or carry financial burdens imposed on them by the state."[7] And the state governors reach agreement on the proposition that "the 'pleasure' of spending public monies (by localities) must be linked with the 'pain' of levying and collecting taxes."[8]

The movement for increasing the taxing powers of municipalities can be understood only as one phase of a larger and more fundamental power controversy. This is the familiar controversy over "centralization": just as municipal officials believe they suffer loss of freedom as the result of state fiscal policies and state legislative and administrative practices, so the state official reacts to federal programs.

The laments expressed cannot be regarded simply as the crocodile tears of political conservatives or the natural attempts of men to arrogate power to themselves and their positions. These factors are undoubtedly present. But there also exists a sincerely expressed fear of overcentralized government and a conviction that the strength of the national democracy rests on the strength of government at the local (and state) level. Furthermore, the complaints about overcentralization result from genuine embarrassments: from policies of the higher government impeding the discretion and resources of the lower one.

From this perspective, the enlargement of local taxing powers becomes only one phase of the larger struggle over the allocation of political power in the American federal system. It cannot be doubted, for example, that the state governors' willingness to grant new taxing authority to municipalities is closely connected with their own efforts to effect a division of tax resources with the federal government. Nor can it be doubted that the willingness of certain taxpayers' groups to support enlarged local taxes rests upon a belief that, in the long run, these taxes are more amenable to group pressures than the taxes of the national government.

The issues in the whole controversy are clouded because of the ambiguity of such phrases as "free and responsible" or "strong and vital"

[7] *National Municipal Policy for 1949, op. cit.*
[8] *State Government,* August, 1948, p. 161.

municipalities. Everybody can readily agree on the importance of "strong" and "vital" cities. But what do the adjectives mean? If they mean the functional activities of cities, then cities are stronger and more vital than ever before in their history: despite the cries of "centralization" they are spending more money, doing more things (and probably more efficiently), and touching the lives of citizens more frequently than ever before. On the other hand, if the desirable attributes of municipal government mean independence of action, then there can be no doubt that cities are less strong and less free than at some periods in the past.

In the latter sense of these words, the cities (and states) are sharing in a fundamental social trend which has affected all institutions. The simultaneous increases in population, in technical effectiveness, in the division of labor, and in contacts between individuals, groups, and nations have produced an interdependence within the social structure which has, inevitably, decreased the scope of absolute freedoms. When the consequences of free activity may result in dangers to the whole society, then freedoms must be limited. This is true for the constitutional freedom of individual American citizens. It is no less true for social institutions. The controls exercised over businesses, labor unions, and lobbying groups are a case in point. The decline in the unfettered discretion of cities and states is a related case. If municipal freedoms result in tax policies that are inimical to the national economy or in public health programs that endanger the lives of whole population groups, then it is quite clear that those freedoms should not be exercised.

The grant-in-aid technique by which municipal (and state) functions are stimulated and municipal (and state) freedoms are sometimes simultaneously curtailed is, at present, the favorite whipping boy of those opposed to "centralization." But the grant-in-aid, obviously, is a symptom, not a cause. It symbolizes government's reaction to the interdependence of governmental activity. It is also a device for meeting the demands of that interdependence while retaining flexibility of administration and that degree of local (and state) discretion not inconsistent with the larger national need.

All this does not mean that the demands for greater municipal and state powers are without merit. It does not mean that steps cannot be taken to strengthen the fiscal position of states and localities. It does mean that municipal freedom, responsibility, vigor, and strength cannot be measured in parochial terms; and it also means that the full meaning of these alluring adjectives must be fully understood before intelligible policy can be established.

The issue of how much local freedom still remains. It cannot be resolved in absolute definitions or in platitudinous appeals to the past. Local freedoms, in the sense of local discretion to meet local problems, are of course important; they are important in terms of administrative efficiency and in terms of encouraging participation of citizens in the affairs of government. But this desirability must be equilibrated with a realistic view of modern governments operating in a tightly geared economy and a highly interdependent culture. To ignore these factors in a discussion of local powers and the trend to "centralization" is to miss the only relevant context for such a discussion.

III. THE WIDER VIEW

Governments are means, not ends, and exist in the United States to fulfill the people's goals. Democratic governments properly serve no other purpose. Neither a state nor a municipality has a vested interest in a revenue to be collected or a function to be performed. Their larger goals are identical. And their functions are bound together.

States and localities and the national government share functions. There is virtually no field (not even foreign affairs) that is the exclusive province of the national government. There is virtually no field (not even schools) that is the exclusive province of the states and localities together. There is virtually no field (not even traffic control for localities, not even highway construction for the states) for which states and localities do not in fact share responsibility.

The freedom of municipalities is therefore only a relative matter. Local governments cannot disengage themselves from the larger state and federal mechanisms. They cannot be "freed" from constitutional obligations or from the numerous legislative demands that make it necessary for them to provide educational facilities, public protection, health services, judicial processes, and a multitude of additional services. Even if they could be freed from these responsibilities, they should not be. To do so would be to destroy a historic pattern of governmental operations, to dissipate a tradition of cooperative services, and to revert to an untenable feudalism.

The expansion of local nonproperty taxes must be assessed from the perspective of the interdependent culture, of shared responsibilities, and of common purpose. The following disadvantages of most of these taxes then become of preponderant importance:

1. Most of the locally collected nonproperty taxes bear hardest on those

least able to pay. This is true of the gross receipts taxes, the numerous general and specific sales taxes, many of the general business licenses, and the type of flat (i.e., nonprogressive) income tax levied by Philadelphia and most other cities using the income tax.

2. Most local taxes are harder to enforce and easier to evade than taxes levied by larger jurisdictions. Enforcement can seldom be adequate in small jurisdictions.[9] The honest taxpayer is penalized for his very honesty.

3. Though no data are yet available, it seems certain that the proportion of administrative expenses to taxes collected must inevitably increase as one multiplies the number of taxing units for any given tax. Further, it becomes progressively more difficult to bring about effective cooperation activities in tax administration as the number of taxing bodies, and the number of taxes, increase.

4. There is a further expense to the taxpayer. His cost of compliance increases directly as the number of taxes and tax jurisdictions increases. This is especially burdensome for businessmen operating in several localities; it is a greatly reduced burden when a given tax is levied by the larger jurisdiction.

5. Local taxes tend to have undesirable economic effects, as in the movement of businesses and residents from high- to low-tax areas.

6. Dependence on local taxes makes for tax inequities. A severance or business tax levied by a municipality may unduly burden a small segment of the population. On the other hand, it may act as a windfall for other taxpayers, relieving them of even minimum responsibilities for supporting local services.

7. The multiplication of local taxes makes it more difficult to keep the nation's public finance system sensitive to changes in the business cycle. Local revenues dip sharply during depression, and local borrowing capacities are not sufficient either to fill revenue gaps or to meet extraordinary depression expenditures.

Local fiscal systems, as a whole, lack the flexibility needed to offset fluctuations in consumption and investment. Yet the new trend in municipal finance has the purpose, and the effect, of throwing cities upon their own resources. This autonomy, if maintained, can lead in depression only to

[9] It has been estimated that the sales taxes collected by California cities "are only about 70 per cent as effective in raising revenues as would be state taxes imposed at the same rates in the same areas." See Dixwell L. Pierce, "Why State and Local Sales Taxes Should Be Coordinated," *Revenue Administration, 1948* (Chicago: National Association of Tax Administrators, 1948), p. 21. For a number of reasons local tax administration in California is probably a great deal more efficient than it is in most states.

undesirable results: the transfer of functional activities to other governments, the decrease in municipal services, or the increase in municipal tax
rates. The first consequence is discussed below; the other two have undesirable effects in terms of countercyclical financing. To the extent that
cities strive to become fiscally self-sufficient, the possibility of achieving
successful compensatory fiscal policies is decreased. Those policies can be
achieved at the local level only through aids from other governments.

An individual city official may solace himself with the thought that his
taxes and expenditures are of utmost insignificance in the total economy.
But in the aggregate, local tax systems loom large. Their impact on the
national economy is great.[10]

8. All of this has a very real importance in terms of larger local freedoms. During depression, the revenues of localities inevitably fall when the
expenditures of cities must inevitably increase. And the new nonproperty
taxes will decline in yield faster than property taxes. Dependence on the
new taxes thus threatens the functional role of cities in the American
federal system.

This threat is especially menacing because the expansion of municipal
nonproperty taxes is accompanied by a decline in state-aid programs. A
system of revenue raising which provides a continuous mechanism for the
transfer of funds from states to localities (and from the national government to the states) supplies a ready means for states to bolster local
finances during a depression period. With this administrative readiness,
localities can normally expect to continue their responsibilities in providing
services financed with state and federal aid. This administrative readiness
is periled by the new emphasis on local nonproperty taxes. Without it, there
is a far greater likelihood that municipal services will be curtailed or that
the larger unit (either the state or the federal government) will step in and
assume wholesale the functional responsibilities of impoverished cities.
Thus, "freeing" municipalities to dependence on their own resources may
lead during depression to their ultimate collapse, fiscally and functionally.

Expanded and refined systems of state grants-in-aid and locally shared
state taxes are clearly preferable to the multiplication of local nonproperty
taxes. The states, by virtue of their very size, are better suited than municipalities to be revenue collectors. From their own resources and from
their position as channelers of federal funds in the national system of
intergovernmental grants, states can develop revenue and loan receipt programs that avoid the inherent defects of numerous local nonproperty

---

[10] For evidence of the perversity of municipal *and state* fiscal policies, see Alvin
H. Hansen and Harvey S. Perloff, *State and Local Finance in the National Economy*
(New York: W. W. Norton and Company, 1944), Ch. 4.

taxes.[11] The states' responsibility for supplying state-collected funds to municipalities springs, essentially, from the common purposes of states and municipalities. And this responsibility has been institutionalized in many ways: in the use that states make of cities as vehicles of administration; in the practice of states in establishing minimum standards of performance, thus obligating local expenditures; in the limitations states impose on local taxation and borrowing; in the very legal superiority of states over municipalities.

State-aid programs can do two things that the proliferation of local taxes cannot do. The aid programs can stabilize local revenues at adequate levels, and they can relieve localities from the burden of sharp expenditure increases during periods of depression.

State-aid programs have many further advantages. They can be coupled with the establishment of minimum standards of performance and with programs of technical advice and assistance. They can be designed consciously to increase the taxable wealth of municipalities (as in housing and industrial development programs), thus contributing to the development of sound local revenue systems. They can be used to eliminate those units of local government which are archaic, inefficient, and representative of no genuine community interests, and thus can aid in the development of municipalities that are large enough and wealthy enough to achieve effectiveness of operation and a progressively greater fiscal sufficiency. They can be used in accordance with principles of local fiscal capacity and local fiscal need.[12] They can further cement the bonds of common purpose that exist between governments at both the state and local levels, and between them and the federal government.

IV. THE ROLE OF THE FEDERAL GOVERNMENT

The last point deserves emphasis. Just as a citizen of a municipality is a citizen of his state, so is he a citizen of the United States. Advances in tech-

[11] Vast improvements are needed in the states' own fiscal programs. Most importantly, many state taxes are heavily regressive and fiscally perverse. And the policy of stringently limiting state debts by constitutional provision is unsound, both fiscally and politically. It is fiscally unsound because it makes countercyclical financing impossible. It is politically unsound because, during depression, it leaves the states so dependent upon federal financing that it invites the very centralization the governors oppose.

[12] Local nonproperty taxes, of course, are most productive in the wealthiest areas and cannot bring fiscal relief to those municipalities that need it most. For those grants given to equalize resources or to insure the maintenance of service standards, it is feasible to construct tests of municipal wealth and municipal tax effort and to allocate grants accordingly.

nology (e.g., the disappearance of the frontier as a result of new modes of communication) and changes in the economy and in the public conscience (e.g., the demand that government take responsibility for the care of the aged) have made this common citizenship at once more apparent and more the concern of all citizens, everywhere. The history of government in the past half-century has been the history of big government at the center becoming evermore concerned with problems that once were the exclusive province of small governments at the periphery. This has inevitably been accompanied by the assumption of greater revenue raising burdens by the central government and the disbursement of some of those revenues to other governments for specified purposes in the national interest. This course of action has been validated by the votes of free people; so long as those people remain free, there seems little likelihood that the trend will be reversed.

In terms of fiscal programs, this says only that just as the states must, and should, continue to supply fiscal aid to municipalities, so the national government must, and should, supply aid to the states. The national government is far less subject to economic stress than the state governments. Even during depression the national government has tremendous resources to levy progressive taxes, to borrow, and to create its own deposits through the Federal Reserve System. It is difficult to foresee any future in which national grants to states will not continue to exist and will not carry with them beneficent effects in terms of the services citizens receive and the strength of the component units of the federal system.

Constitutional lawyers are fond of saying that hard questions make bad law. The fiscal plight of cities confronts American federalism with a hard question. The total pattern of analysis presented above indicates strongly that the answer being evolved (in the form of statute, ordinance, and practice) is the wrong one. The policy of expanding municipal nonproperty taxes is, in the long run, self-defeating for the cities and, by that very fact, damaging to the federal system.

It is the crisis nature of the situation facing cities that makes the wrong answer seem the only one to the people working out that answer. The factors discussed above play their role; both state and local officials define the situation in particularist terms; both lag behind (a typical sociological phenomenon) in recognizing the degree to which the several levels of government are basically interrelated; both strive for power and for functional autonomy, their motives being only partially related to the state rationale. But over and above these factors, the squeeze on the city finances is a very real one. And, most importantly, the alternatives to enlarged local taxing powers are difficult to achieve. They are blocked by the whole legal gamut of a complex federalism;[13] by political considerations arising from interlevel government; and by the very parochialism of both local and state officials. The last point has a special importance in the cycle of action. The factors leading to the multiplication of local nonproperty taxes are also those factors blocking consideration of such measures as the careful working out of schemes for locally imposed, state-collected taxes or for the consolidation of local goverments.

In such a situation, the increase in local nonproperty taxes is seized upon. Better ways of solving local fiscal problems may be acknowledged, but this way is, apparently, the only immediately feasible one. As one city official has put it: "The other solutions are wonderful. But in the interim, cities cannot live on love."

The point is well taken. But its short-run logic cannot deny its medium- and long-run consequences. Those consequences are dangerous.

There is, further, a good deal of self-defeatism in arguing for enlarged municipal taxes because other ways of solving the fiscal problems of cities are more difficult. The prediction of difficulty confirms itself. When state and local officials tell themselves that the improvement of property tax administration (or any of the other programs outlined above) is hard to achieve, by that very act they tend to make it so. They succeed so completely that they divert their efforts from these programs in favor of the relatively easy—and undesirable—multiplication of local taxes.

A realistic assessment of the difficulty of achieving desirable state-local fiscal programs is, of course, a prerequisite to intelligent action. And no argument is made here that those programs are *not* difficult to establish. But is it argued that the good cannot be equated with the easy, and that the difficult is preferable when the easy is evil.

This puts a heavy burden on state and local officials. Their problem is a joint one and its solution rests equally upon both. State officials face perhaps the heaviest responsibility because their position makes it easy for them to slide away from the problem. They can pay lip service to "local home rule," and simultaneously comfort themselves with the knowledge that if the policy is wrong, local officials are digging their own graves. Yet the states' legal and fiscal superiority makes the problem no less a state than a local one.

In the long run, power lost by cities as the result of unwise fiscal policies

[13] A recent court decision in West Virginia, for example, has declared unconstitutional the state's sharing with municipalities profits from the state's liquor monopoly (54 S.E. 2d 729 [1949]).

will not revert to the states. Indeed, the states' position is even more vulnerable than the cities'. As a single integrated organism the states and municipalities may decline together during fiscal crisis. But, alternatively, the states may witness the proliferation of direct national-local programs, and the resuscitation of cities by national action. As middlemen in the federal system, state officials have everything to lose and nothing to gain in abetting municipal fiscal systems whose total effect is to weaken municipalities.

All this adds up to a hard practical point. If the right solutions to local fiscal difficulties are difficult solutions, no purpose can be served by shying away from them. As a matter of fact, the solutions themselves are clear enough. What is lacking are means—specific steps through which the programs outlined above can be molded into law and action. These must be fitted to local situations. They will emerge only from the research of students and from the ingenuity, sensitivity, and intelligence of political and administrative leaders.

The principal contemporary means taken by states and localities to achieve "free, responsible local government" is through the granting of wide tax powers to municipalities and the consequent multiplication of local nonproperty taxes. In the preceeding pages it has been argued that this trend in fiscal relations is unwise.

It is unwise for a long series of important economic reasons. It is unwise because it separates governments at a time when the logic of public finance, the legal framework of state-local relations, and the deveolpment of government as a service institution in our culture all push in the direction of cooperative government action.

The multiplication of municipal nonproperty taxes is unwise, most of all, because it will produce results contrary to its objectives of "free, responsible local governments." The probable depression results of dependence on these taxes all argue of reverse consequences. These include reduction in the quantity and quality of municipal services and the widespread transfer of local functions to higher levels of government.

These possibilities are directly courted by the rapid extension of municipal taxes. They are indirectly courted by the emphasis of both states and localities on promoting these taxes, thus diverting their interest from more solid, if politically more difficult, avenues of approach to vigorous, local self-government.

The freedom and responsibility currently sought by American municipalities is not the freedom and responsibility to declare their own demise. Rather, it is to maintain and increase their effectiveness for the populations they serve.

Chapter 16

THE FUTURE OF
THE AMERICAN SYSTEM

I. TRENDS IN AMERICAN FEDERALISM

As one of several major societal institutions, government in the past half-century has increased in importance and scope. It has taken over functions previously allocated to the family (as in social security), and the church (as in providing community centers); and has assumed new responsibilities for demands that prior to 1900 were unfelt or minor—as in public health and road building. This growth of government is not wicked, not insidious. It is simply a response to the major social developments of our time.

The trend in family living provides a simple example of this: in 1900, there were almost five persons per family in America and a majority of the nation's families lived on farms and in small towns. Old age assistance could be, and to a very large extent was, a family problem. Children were available to take care of aged parents; living space was available; and land plots were available for growing food if cash income was low.

Between 1900 and 1950 the proportion of people over 60 years of age has doubled as a result of decreases in early mortality. Simultaneously, the number of persons per family has decreased to an average of three and the population has become largely urbanized. The care of the increased number of aged can no longer be a family problem. Conceivably, assistance to the aged might have devolved upon the church, but this did not happen. The responsibility became the government's.

In a similar way, we can find in the industrialization of the nation, the urban concentration of population, the increase in educational level and other *social* factors, ample justification for the increase in functions and cost of government. These increases have been shaped by crisis—wars and depression—but they have been validated by the free votes of a free

371

people. To deprecate them as evidences of totalitarianism is a confusion of terms and a distortion of history.

FISCAL DEVELOPMENTS

A few figures reveal the essential, relevant facts about how this growth of government has affected the federal system. First there is the growth of all governmental expenditures from $1.6 billion in 1902 to $57.8 billion in 1947 and then to $175.8 billion in 1962 (unadjusted dollars). The composition of this increase is important. In 1900 state and local expenditures were more than twice as great as national expenditures. In 1947, national expenditures were almost three times as great as those of state and local governments combined. But, in 1962, the former were only 50 per cent greater than the latter. A third point is of particular interest. In 1962, the national government spent just under $8 billion more from its own sources than for its own functions. The state and local governments spend an equal sum—just under $8 billion more than they collected from their own sources. This is, of course, the same money, transferred by the grant-in-aid device from the national to the state-local column. This sum covers a major share of the nation's social service activities. Moreover, national grants today are 16 times as great as the total federal expenditure in 1902 and five times as great as the total expenditure of all governments that year. The federal grant expenditures actually equal the total federal expenditures in the last pre-World War II years.

The reversal of the roles of the national government, on the one hand, and the state and local governments, on the other, is even more striking. In 1902, the national government spent 32 cents of every public dollar, the localities 56 cents. In 1947, the national government spent 74 cents of every public dollar, the localities 14 cents. In 1962, the national share had dropped to 56 cents, and the local share increased to 27 cents. The percentage spent by the states remained relatively constant between 1902 and 1947 but increased between 1949 and 1962.

The extent of the increase in total expenditures can be better understood by this very fact. Despite the fact that state expenditures, in terms of percentages of total costs, remained roughly the same for many years and have not increased proportionately, state expenditures in terms of unadjusted dollars increased from $182 millions in 1902 to $7.9 billion in 1947 to $36.3 billion in 1962.

Some examples of the meaning of this growth help place it in perspective:

New York spends more today for the care of its insane than its total state budget in 1902.

Illinois spends more today than all the states combined in 1902.

California's annual state and local expenditures combined exceed the federal budget of the late 1930's.

Chicago spends more today on police and fire protection than its total expenditure in 1902.

The national government pays for veterans' pensions today an amount approximately eight times its total expenditures in 1902.

New York City spends well over three times as much today as total national expenditures in 1902.

The interest (not payments on principal) on the national debt today is nearly six times as large as total government expenses—national, state, and local—in 1902.

Within this dominant trend of mushrooming services and costs, there have been two vitally important supplementary developments: first, the dominance of the national government as a collector and spender of revenue; and second, the device of transferring funds collected by the national government to be spent by states and localities for nationally determined purposes.

A parallel development has occurred within the state-local system to an even more marked degree.

The grant-in-aid technique does not tell the whole story; but it tells a good part of it. It is a story of growing expertise; growing professionalization, growing complexities; it is a story most of all, of an ever-increasing measure of contact between officials of the several levels of government within the federal system. Contact points bring some disagreements and produce misunderstanding and some enmity. But most of all, they have produced cooperation, collaboration, and effectiveness in programming and steering the multiple programs of modern government.

This development of cooperative, or collaborative, federalism is not a sudden development of the twentieth century, though it gained its greatest impetus as the result of the depression of the 1930's. Despite the Civil War and despite the decisions of the Supreme Court, the American system was a collaborative administrative system of intermeshing governments well before 1900.

The year 1913 can be taken as a significant bench mark for further building in the cooperative system of administration. In that year the national income tax was established on a permanent basis. A readily expandible source of revenue, the income tax, collected by the national government whose very size made it the most efficient collector of mobile wealth, was a profoundly important factor in sharpening the twentieth-century trend of the American federal system. That same year the Smith-Lever Bill was enacted, establishing the Agricultural Extension Service on a continuing basis with an initial appropriation of unprecedented size. This was soon followed by other important grants: the Federal Aid Road Act of 1916; the Smith-Hughes Act of 1917 for vocational education; the Chamberlain-Kuhn Act of 1918 for public health. With the depression of the 1930's, the nation was ready for huge grant programs—to bring both temporary relief and permanent social security. At one point during the depression, federal grants totalled almost 50 per cent of total state revenues. Administratively, therefore, the trends since 1900 have been in the direction of collaboration between the national government and the states. The grant system has been the most notable example of this collaboration since it brought intimate contact between governments, as in the provision of national personnel standards.

Even in those areas where it is said that the national government "bypasses" the states, one can nevertheless find ample evidence of national agencies taking full account of the talents, capabilities, and sensibilities of state and local officers. TVA, for example, is frequently cited as a breakdown of the traditional federal relationship between national government and states. But one cannot read about TVA without being strongly impressed with the collaborative bonds the agency has forged with officials in city halls, county courthouses, and state capitols throughout the region it serves. In the formally cooperative programs this is even more noticeable. Agricultural extension, for example, heavily financed by national funds, has become an important voice for state interests as scholars and practitioners have discovered.

While it is undeniable that initiating power and prestige have flowed to the national government, it is no less undeniable that states and localities have participated as partners in the new national programs, have gained functions, and have played important administrative roles.

JUDICIAL DEVELOPMENTS

Until the New Deal, decisions of the Supreme Court tended to separate the several governments of the federal system. In the earlier years of the nineteenth century, the Court, influenced by Marshall, was heavily weighted with those who successfully sought to extend the national power. At times, these efforts were at the expense of state power. *Gibbons* v. *Ogden* of 1824 is a good example; it was the first case interpreting the commerce clause of the Constitution, and in it, Marshall defined the national power over interstate commerce as sovereign and complete.

In the later years of the nineteenth century, and, indeed, up to the 1930's, the Court was more inclined to cut down the national powers and reserve more rights to the states—unless the latter tried to exercise them to regulate business. It was in this period, roughly from the end of the Civil War to the New Deal, that the Supreme Court tried to set the national and state governments at arm's length. *Hammer* v. *Dagenhart* in 1918 well illustrates the tendency and, incidentally, stands as a good contrast to *Gibbons* v. *Ogden*. In *Hammer* v. *Dagenhart* the Court declared unconstitutional an act of Congress prohibiting the interstate transportation of goods in the manufacture of which children had taken part. The Court held that "the grant of authority over a purely federal matter was not intended to destroy the local power always existing and carefully reserved to the states in the tenth amendment to the Constitution." The decision insisted upon the doctrine that interstate commerce must be regulated by Congress as commerce and not for "ulterior" purposes.

In terms of power, the two decisions—*Gibbons* v. *Ogden* and *Hammer* v. *Dagenhart*—were contradictory. The first extended the powers of national government; the second limited them. In terms of separating the governments within the federal system, however, the second was completely consistent with the first. It confirmed the duality of powers in the very act of redressing a balance between them.

This whole doctrine of the Court has been almost completely upset within the past generation. The Court no longer views the Constitution in such inflexible terms; it tends to conceive it as a general framework of rules through whose adaptability the national purpose can be realized. It has approved efforts of collaborative federalism, for example, by approving the grant-in-aid mechanism. And it has allowed both states and the federal government to move freely into each other's traditional areas of power.

In *Carmichael* v. *Southern Coal & Coke Co.,* the 1937 case in which the Court found in favor of the Federal Social Security Act, it stated:

Together the two statutes now before us embody a cooperative legislative effort by state and national governments, for carrying out a public purpose common to both, which neither could fully achieve without the cooperation of the other. The Constitution does not prohibit such cooperation.

But the Court has gone much further than approving the practices of collaborative federalism. It has recognized the general welfare clause of the Constitution as the basis for broad federal power (*U.S.* v. *Butler,* 1936; *Stewart Machine Co.* v. *Davis,* 1937; *Helvering* v. *Davis,* 1937). In so doing, it can be argued that the Court has made it legally possible for the national government, if it so desires, to destroy collaboration by assuming, under the authority of the general welfare clause, full authority for the administration of many activities traditionally considered as reserved for the states. Thus we have an interesting paradox: in the process of validating the legality of state-national collaboration, the Court has apparently paved the way for the national government to assume, in wholesale, new functions without state participation. This means, in effect, that substantial legal impediments to completely national programs "promoting the national welfare" no longer exist; legal considerations will be less and less important in determining the content and form of government action. More and more, programs will be determined on their political grounds—in terms of criteria of administrative efficiency and social productivity. The further development of the federal system is thus no longer strictly guided by legal considerations. This is of crucial importance.

POLITICAL CONSIDERATIONS

Unlike the judicial field, the political patterns of American federalism have remained relatively stable. It is in the political field, above all others, that states and cities have retained the primacy of their role. The national parties continue to have little unity; they continue to depend upon the strength and vitality of state and local organizations.

A recent example illustrates this point well. It was widely stated, following the 1960 elections, that Kennedy's victory was a vote for big government in the image of FDR. This is certainly true. But the vote for big government was built upon the political efforts of state and city political organizations. In almost every case, Kennedy ran behind, and was carried by, state and local candidates.

The political potency of the local organization has a very important effect on national policy. In at least one sense, it makes a counterweight against the tendency to centralize power in Washington. The history of legislation with respect to many important programs—highways, social security, water pollution, airport construction, to mention but a few—shows national legislators writing national legislation with a sensitive ear to state and local political leaders. This is a natural tendency in the light of political realities: the American national legislator considers himself the representative of district and state interests because his position is secured through the efforts of state and district—not national—political organizations. This accounts for the lack of political solidarity among our national parties, so much lamented by those who compare our system with the British.

The undisciplined parties affect the character of the federal system as a result of senatorial and congressional interference in federal administrative programs on behalf of local interests. Many aspects of the legislative involvement in administrative affairs are formalized. The Legislative Reorganization Act of 1946, to take only one example, provided that each of the standing committees "shall exercise continuous watchfulness" over administration of laws within its jurisdiction. But the formal system of controls, extensive as it is, does not compare in importance with the informal and extra-legal network of relationships in producing continuous legislative involvement in administrative affairs.

The widespread, persistent, and in many ways unpredictable character of legislative interference in administrative affairs has many consequences for the tone and character of American administrative behavior. From our perspective, the important consequence is the comprehensive, day-to-day, even hour-by-hour, impact of local views on national programs. No point of substance or procedure is immune from congressional scrutiny. A substantial portion of the entire weight of this impact is on behalf of the state and local governments. It is a weight that can alter procedures for screening immigration applications, divert the course of a national highway, change the tone of an international negotiation, and amend a social security law to accommodate local practices or fulfill local desires.

The political system as it is presently constituted compels administrators to take a political role. The administrator must play politics for the same reason that the politician is able to play in administrations: the parties are without program and without discipline.

In response to the unprotected position in which the party situation places him, the administrator is forced to seek support where he can find it. One ever-present task is to nurse the Congress of the United States, that crucial constituency which ultimately controls his agency's budget and program. From the administrator's view, a sympathetic consideration of congressional requests (if not downright submission to them) is the surest way to build the political support without which the administrative job could not continue. Even the completely task-oriented administrator must be sensitive to the need for congressional support and to the relationship between case work requests, on one side, and budgetary and legislative support, on the other. "You do a good job handling the personal problems and requests of a Congressman," a White House officer said, "and you have an easier time convincing him to back your program." Thus there is an important link between the nursing of congressional requests that largely concern local matters and the most comprehensive national programs. The administrator must accommodate to the former as the price of gaining support for the latter.

One result of administrative politics is that the administrative agency may become the captive of the nationwide interest group it serves or presumably regulates. In such cases no government may come out with effective authority: the winners are the interest groups themselves. But in a very large number of cases, states and localities also win influence. The politics of administration is a process of making peace with legislators who for the most part consider themselves the guardians of local interests. The political role of administrators therefore contributes to the power of states and localities in national programs.

Finally, the way the party system operates gives American politics their over-all distinctive tone. The lack of party discipline produces an openness in the system that allows individuals, groups, and institutions (including state and local governments) to attempt to influence national policy at every step of the legislative-administrative process. Here, again, is the "multiple crack" attribute of the American government providing myriad points of access and possibilities to wallop the system.[1] The party system functions, as we have seen, to devolve power. And the American parties, unlike any other, are highly responsive when directives move from the bottom to the top, highly unresponsive from top to bottom. Congressmen and senators can rarely ignore concerted demands from their home constituencies; but no party leader can expect the same kind of response from those below, whether he be a President asking for congressional support or a congressman seeking aid from local or state leaders.

The political strength of the states and localities thus has a profound effect throughout the entire federal system. Its principal result, I believe, is to act as a balance against the many factors—including the circular self-generating ones—that tend to centralize power in Washington. I am tempted to say that it is only a disagreement among the local centers of power—disagreement that emerges sectionally—or between the states, on the one hand, and the cities, on the other—that makes possible the degree of national power that now exists. This, though, would caricature the true situation: there are, after all, as already indicated, substantial social and economic reasons compelling the national government to increase the scope of its authority and the sweep of its action.

[1] See Chapter Ten, pp. 274–76.

II. ASSESSMENT:
THE PRESENT SITUATION OF AMERICAN FEDERALISM

We now turn to an evaluation of the trends—fiscal, administrative, legal, political—that we have discussed so far. By what standards, what criteria, should we judge the developments of the past half century?

Government is not only a producer of services; it is also a process. The citizen is not only a client of democratic government; he is also its creator. I suggest that it is not only important to judge government in terms of the services it produces, but also in terms of what those services do to the structure of his government and his relationship to it.

Specifically, the standard of evaluation I would like to consider is the strength of the various units of government within the federal system. Theorists since Aristotle have argued the importance of the strength of local government. Ignazio Silone has put it very well in his neglected work, the *School for Dictators*. Silone says:

> The school of democracy is in local self-government. For a worker to take a serious part in the life of his trade union, or for a peasant to take part in the life of his village, there is no need of higher education. The first test to be applied in judging an alleged democracy is the degree of self-governing attained by its local institutions. If the master's rule in the factories is absolute, if the trade unions are controlled by bureaucracies, if the province is governed by the representative of the central government, there can be no true and complete democracy. Only local government can accustom men to responsibility and independence, and enable them to take part in the wider life of the state.[2]

Many people who survey American federalism today assert that, in terms of this criterion, American federalism is dead. This is the view of many who decry national centralization.

If one examines this conclusion, one can see it is based on the following specific considerations:

1. Less independence, less discretion: the activities of the national government have removed large areas of discretionary power from the hands of state and local officials. When states are offered grants on a matching basis, it is a foregone conclusion that they will appropriate their own resources for the nationally supported activity. A large share of the policy-making power of state authorities is consequently transferred to the national government.

[2] Ignazio Silone, *School for Dictators* (New York: Harper & Brothers, 1938), pp. 291–92.

2. Administrative dependence: the same grant device has removed a measure of administrative control from state to national officials.

3. Skewed budgets: the national programs have seriously skewed state budgets and total state programs. No true system of national grants exists. Instead, the national government operates a series of uncoordinated separate grant programs. By concentrating on some activities and emphasizing others, the national government virtually requires states to support some activities (e.g., old age assistance) while they may be neglecting equally important activities, (e.g., general welfare).

4. Tax conflicts: the national system of taxation has been expanded outward, upward, and downward. Simultaneously, state revenue needs have increased. Tax conflicts are numerous, and, more important, state revenues have been seriously limited by the priority and magnitude of the national government's needs.

5. Shifted popular attention: the magnitude of national operations has shifted popular attention away from local and state governments and towards the national government. Citizens look to Washington for the solution of their problems. They deprecate and deplore conditions in states and municipalities; but they do not participate in the activities of the governments closest to them.

These are, of course, serious charges. And they are for the most part, true. (They also have, to some degree, their own correctives, as in the reallocation of tax sources and the rationalization of the national grant system.)

If one analyzes these statements claiming that states and cities are no longer "strong," it is clear that what is meant is that local units of government do not have the near-absolute independence they once were supposed to have. I have tried to demonstrate that this independence was always qualified. But it is certainly true that they have less independence today than they once had. And this is so because cities and states are sharing in a fundamental social trend which has affected all social institutions. The simultaneous increases in population, in technical effectiveness, in the division of labor, and in the contacts between individuals, groups, and nations have produced an interdependence within the social structure which has, inevitably, decreased the scope of absolute freedoms. When the consequences of free activity may result in dangers to the whole society, then freedoms must be limited. This is true for the constitutional freedom of individual American citizens. It is no less true for social institutions. The controls exercised over businesses, labor unions, and lobbying groups are a case in point. The decline in the discretion of cities and states is a related case. If state or city freedoms result in social policies that are inimical to the national economy or in public health programs that endanger the lives of whole population groups, then it is quite clear that those freedoms should not be exercised.

State and municipal strength thus must be viewed from the perspective of a tightly geared economy and a highly interdependent culture. In this context, "independence" in the traditional sense becomes a relatively unimportant and highly unrealistic attribute. It is unimportant because it is undesirable in the context of modern society. It is unrealistic because it is impossible to achieve. Independence is impossible and unrealistic for states and municipalities in the same manner and for roughly the same reasons that the national government cannot be independent of events in Europe— or Viet Nam.

What is needed is an intricate balance between national dominance, where the national interest is primary, and local discretion, where the local opinions are more important than national ones. And this is the balance which we as a nation have attempted to strike.

A far more valid measurement of the strength of states and municipalities is the extent to which these governments are constructively involved in the great public service functions. From this point of view, no one can doubt that the states and municipalities are strong. They are spending more money, doing things more effectively, touching more people in more important ways than ever before in their history. And they are doing this in fruitful collaboration with the national government. Virtually all functions of government in America are shared functions. And the sharing of the states and localities in these functions is not simply passive participation. One sees at every turn, states and localities contributing to planning, policy, and administration.

This constructive involvement of states and municipalities in the nation's business is, of course, the result of the factors we have previously discussed.

Obviously the political strength of the states and municipalities has, to a large measure, been responsible for establishing the great social service programs on a federal-state basis. In Chapter Ten we saw that Rexford Tugwell was an unwilling witness to the effects of that political strength. We can be sure that this conclusion rested on political grounds. In that case and in many others we see national programs consciously used to bolster the strength of the states. At the same time, vesting administrative control of the grant programs—highway building, social security, public health— in the states has been an important factor in maintaining the potency of state and local party organizations, thus increasing their political strength.

We pointed out that the grant-in-aid was one of the most important fiscal developments of the past half-century. It is popular in some quarters to damn the grant-in-aid as a device of centralization; it would be more accurate to recognize the grant as an admirable device to utilize the best resources of the national and state governments. The national government, as the most effective revenue raiser and as the central determiner of popular demands, supplies and equalizes funds, establishes and maintains service standards. The grant-in-aid thus is a symbol of government's reaction to the interdependent social institutions in a modern society. The grant is a device for meeting the demands of the interdependence, blending the needed direction from the center and the equally needed discretion at the periphery. The grant, in short, is an admirable invention for the promotion of collaborative federalism.

And, it should be added, the grant system has had many by-products highly advantageous to states and localities.

1. The cooperative, federal system has provided needed standards of service according to a national minimum in many fields, service that many states alone would find it impossible to supply. In addition to decreasing inequalities of service, the system has raised the level of all aided services.

2. The system, as we have emphasized, has added to the activities of the state governments, contributing to their resources and expanding their services in programs that directly touch the day-to-day life of every person.

3. The system has avoided many undesirable alternatives from the viewpoint of the states. The national government, for example, has not assumed functions that can be better administered by the state governments, while services demanded by citizens have been performed well. If the states were left to their own resources, these services would have been in many cases performed badly.

4. The cooperative system has improved the administration of many state activities: national administrative standards (as in welfare work) and national advice (as in police work) have done much to increase the professional skill and effectiveness of state administrators.

Thus we can see how the fiscal, administrative, and political trends of the past 50 years have produced the collaborative federal system we possess today. The Supreme Court's acquiescence has contributed to the development; but it must be recalled that the Court's new position is a two-edged sword. It has made collaborative federalism possible; yet its broad constructions also make possible a vast multitude of direct national services without state collaboration.

It is clear that such a future development, whether desirable or undesirable, is a very likely one. It might occur, for example, if the national party organizations were strengthened and party lines solidified on national issues. More probably, however, if it does take place, it will do so as the result of the ground swell of conservatism that constantly presses from certain quarters. This "states rights'" opinion is frequently a mask: it demands that government power be exercised by the states and localities; it actually demands a cessation or decrease of the activity of governments. The power of state governments is likely to decline according to the extent that this opinion is successful at the state level. For it is a truism that the only way a government can preserve authority is to exercise its powers. As Elihu Root said long ago, "The only way to maintain powers of government is to govern."

III. EVALUATION:
THE VIRTUES OF THE SYSTEM

We can conclude that the states and localities are strong because they continue to be important, active, and constructive partners within our system of government. We must still answer the question: Why is it important to be strong even in this sense? I would answer:

First, because officials who are part of the community they serve can understand local problems in all their detail and diversity to a greater degree than others from the outside even when the outsiders are stationed in the locality. This is not the same as arguing that local government is closer to the people. It is not an argument of closeness but of understanding. This argument certainly does not assume that local opinion leaders are always right, or that it may not be necessary to overrule them in the cause of larger interests and even in the cause of certain politically unexpressed local interests. It only says that, other things being equal, judgments by neighbors are more apt to be correct than those by strangers. There is ample anthropological evidence to support this view.

Secondly, local and state involvement in government is important as an antidote to complete centralization. This is so in two senses. The first is from the viewpoint of power politics and is familiar to all. The second sense has to do with human reactions to centralized government.

Forces that widen the distance between people and governments are very strong. The complexity of modern life and of issues of government, the growth of huge metropolitan areas, and many other factors have contributed to the bewilderment of the voter and to his difficulty in making rational decisions. One defense against these forces is through the devolution of powers and activities. It cannot be doubted that the situation in some cities and some states is more confusing to the citizens than is the national government. This does not argue for shifting all burdens to the national government; it only argues for making local governments more responsible.

Finally, the activity and strength of state and local governments is important as a force in solidifying the national allegiance of democratic citizens. There is a fascinating interplay between local, regional, and national loyalties. Theorists have speculated that strong loyalties to locality are important ingredients of the larger national allegiance. Yet the balance is a delicate one. When local loyalties grow, national ones may become effaced. Our Civil War was one demonstration of this.

It is nevertheless true that loyalties to nation can spring largely from the human satisfactions that emerge from personal, face-to-face relationships. From this point of view, satisfactions gained in family, work, church, and peer group relations are the primary ingredients of national loyalty. Modern life tends, however, to minimize these satisfactions. And totalitarian countries have attempted to capitalize on this process by destroying all groups not directly controlled by the central government. It should be remembered that Hitler destroyed not only the independence of the German states and municipalities; he also tried to replace the family with new Nazi institutions.

To build loyalties on the single relationship between the individual and the central government may be possible—and indeed phenomenally successful in the short run. But it is a loyalty quick to sour and relatively easy to subvert. Far more stable loyalties are built upon those satisfactions that spring from the many and varied group relationships freely chosen and widely devolved. This has been the source of democratic strength in the past; so long as democracies exist, it must continue to be their strength.

Active state and local governments, doing important jobs, can be an important source of community and group cohesion, and of human satisfaction. This is one important reason for justifying our system of collaborative federalism. It constitutes a well from which larger democratic allegiances are drawn.

IV. GOALS FOR THE SYSTEM OF SHARING

THE GOAL OF UNDERSTANDING

Our structure of government is complex, and the politics operating that structure are mildly chaotic. Circumstances are ever changing. Old institutions mask intricate procedures. The nation's history can be read with alternative glosses, and what is nearest at hand may be furthest from comprehension. Simply to understand the federal system is therefore a difficult task. Yet without understanding there is little possibility of producing desired changes in the system. Social structures and processes are relatively impervious to purposeful change. They also exhibit intricate interrelationships so that a change induced at point "A" often produces unanticipated results at point "Z." Changes introduced into an imperfectly understood system are as likely to produce reverse consequences as the desired ones.

This is neither a counsel of futility nor of conservatism for those who seek to make our government a better servant of the people. It is only to say that the first goal for those setting goals with respect to the federal system is that of understanding it.

TWO KINDS OF DECENTRALIZATION

The recent major efforts to reform the federal system have in large part been aimed at separating functions and tax sources, at dividing them between the federal government and the states. All these attempts have failed. We can now add that their success would be undesirable.

It is easy to specify the conditions under which an ordered separation of functions could take place. What is principally needed is a majority political party, under firm leadership, in control of both presidency and Congress, and, ideally but not necessarily, also in control of a number of states. The political discontinuities, or the absence of party links, (1) between the governors and their state legislatures, (2) between the President and the governors, and (3) between the President and Congress clearly account for both the picayune recommendations of the Federal-State Action Committee and for the failure of even those recommendations in Congress. If the President had been in control of Congress (that is, consistently able to direct a majority of House and Senate votes), this alone would have made possible some genuine separation and devolution of functions. The failure to decentralize by order is a measure of the decentralization of power in the political parties.

Stated positively, party centralization must precede the governmental decentralization that exists today in the United States. It may be called the decentralization of mild chaos. It exists because of the existence of dispersed power centers. This form of decentralization is less visible and less neat. It rests on no discretion of central authorities. It produces at times specific acts that many citizens may consider undesirable or evil. But power wielded even for evil ends may sometimes be desirable power. As we have said elsewhere, to those who find value in the dispersion of power, decentralization by mild chaos is infinitely more desirable than decentralization by order. The preservation of mild chaos is an important goal for the American federal system.

OILING THE SQUEAK POINTS

In a governmental system of genuinely shared responsibilities, disagreements inevitably occur. Opinions clash over proximate ends, particular ways of doing things become the subject of public debate, innovations are contested. These are not basic defects in the system. Rather, they are the system's energy-reflecting lifeblood. There can be no permanent "solutions" short of changing the system itself by elevating one partner to absolute supremacy. What can be done is to attempt to produce conditions in which conflict will not fester but be turned to constructive solutions of particular problems.

A long list of specific points of difficulty in the federal system can be easily identified. No adequate congressional or administrative mechanism exists to review the patchwork of grants in terms of national needs. There is no procedure by which to judge, for example, whether the national government is justified in spending so much more for highways than for education. The working force in some states is inadequate for the effective performance of some nationwide programs, while honest and not-so-honest graft frustrates efficiency in others. Some federal aid programs distort state budgets, and some are so closely supervised as to impede state action in meeting local needs. Grants are given for programs too narrowly defined, and over-all programs at the state level consequently suffer. Administrative, accounting, and auditing difficulties are the consequence of the multiplicity of grant programs. City officials complain that the states are intrusive fifth wheels in housing, urban redevelopment, and airport building programs and that the federal authorities impose overly rigid restrictions on local innovation in the same programs.

Some differences are so basic that only a demonstration of strength on one side or another can solve them. School desegregation illustrates such an issue. It also illustrates the correct solution (although not the most desirable method of reaching it): in policy conflicts of fundamental importance, touching the nature of democracy itself, the view of the whole nation must prevail. Such basic ends, however, are rarely at issue, and sides are rarely taken with such passion that loggerheads are reached. Modes of settlement can usually be found to lubricate the squeak points of the system.

A pressing and permanent state problem, general in its impact, is the difficulty of raising sufficient revenue without putting local industries at a competitive disadvantage or without an expansion of sales taxes that press hardest on the least wealthy. A possible way of meeting this problem is to establish a state-levied income tax that could be used as an offset for federal taxes. The maximum level of the tax which could be offset would be fixed by federal law. When levied by a state, the state collection would be deducted from federal taxes. But if a state did not levy the tax, the federal government would. An additional fraction of the total tax imposed by the states would be collected directly by the federal government and used as an equalization fund, that is, distributed among the less wealthy states. Such a tax would almost certainly be imposed by all states, since not to levy it would give neither political advantage to its public leaders nor financial advantage to its citizens. The net effect would be an increase in the total personal and corporate income tax.

The offset has great promise for strengthening state governments. It would help produce a more economic distribution of industry. It would have obvious financial advantages for the vast majority of states. Since a large fraction of all state income is used to aid political subdivisions, the local governments would also profit, though not equally as long as cities are underrepresented in state legislatures. On the other hand, such a scheme will appear disadvantageous to some low-tax states which profit from the immigration of industry (although it would by no means end all state-by-state tax differentials). It will probably excite the opposition of those concerned over governmental centralization, and they will not be assuaged by methods that suggest themselves for making both state and central governments bear the psychological impact of the tax. While the offset would probably produce an across-the-board tax increase, wealthier persons, who are affected more by an income tax than by other levies, can be expected to join forces with those whose fear is centralization. (This is a common alliance and, in the nature of things, the philosophical issue rather than financial advantage is kept foremost.)

Those opposing such a tax would gain additional ammunition from the certain knowledge that federal participation in the scheme would lead to some federal standards governing the use of the funds. Yet the political strength of the states would keep those from becoming onerous. Indeed, inauguration of the tax offset as a means of providing funds to the states might be an occasion for dropping some of the specifications for existing federal grants.

The income tax offset is only one of many ideas that can be generated to meet serious problems of closely meshed governments. The fate of all such schemes ultimately rests, as it should, with the politics of a free people. But much can be done if the primary technical effort of those concerned with improving the federal system were directed not at separating its interrelated parts but at making them work together more effectively. Temporary commissions are relatively inefficient in this effort, though they may be useful for making general assessments and for generating new ideas. The professional organizations of government workers do part of the job of continuously scrutinizing programs and ways and means of improving them. A permanent staff, established in the President's office and working closely with state and local officials, could also perform a useful and perhaps important role.

THE STRENGTH OF THE PARTS

Whatever governmental "strength" or "vitality" may be, it does not consist of independent decision-making in legislation and administration. Federal-state interpenetration here is extensive. Indeed, a judgment of the relative domestic strength of the two planes must take heavily into account the influence of one on the other's decisions. In such an analysis the strength of the states (and localities) does not weigh lightly. The nature of the nation's politics makes federal functions more vulnerable to state influence than state offices are to federal influence. Many states, as the Kestnbaum Commission noted, live with "self-imposed constitutional limitations" that make it difficult for them to "perform all of the services that their citizens require." If this has the result of adding to federal responsibilities, the states' importance in shaping and administering federal programs eliminates much of the sting.

The geography of state boundaries, as well as many aspects of state internal organization, are the products of history and cannot be justified on any abstract grounds of rational efficiency. A complete catalogue of state political and administrative horrors would fill a sizeable volume. Yet exhortations to erase them have roughly the same effect as exhortations to erase sin. The boundaries of the states are fixed in the national constitution and defy alteration for all foreseeable time. Urban underrepresentation in state legislatures, often a major cause of the perpetuation of constitutional and administrative archaisms, serves the overrepresented groups, including some urban ones, and the effective political organization of the deprived groups must precede reform.

Despite deficiencies of politics and organizations that are unchangeable or slowly changing, it is an error to look at the states as static anachronisms. Some of them—New York, Minnesota, and California, to take three examples spanning the country—have administrative organizations that compare favorably in many ways with the national establishment. Many more in recent years have moved rapidly towards integrated administrative departments, statewide budgeting, and central leadership. The others have models-in-existence to follow, and active professional organizations (led by the Council of State Governments) promoting their development. Slow as this change may be, the states move in the direction of greater internal effectiveness.

The pace toward more effective performance at the state level is likely to increase. Urban leaders, who generally feel themselves disadvantaged in state affairs, and suburban and rural spokesmen, who are most concerned about national centralization, have a common interest in this task. The urban dwellers want greater equality in state affairs, including a more equitable share of state financial aid; nonurban dwellers are concerned that city dissatisfactions should not be met by exclusive federal, or federal-local, programs. Antagonistic, rather than amiable, cooperation may be the consequence. But it is a cooperation that can be turned to politically effective measures for a desirable upgrading of state institutions.

If one looks closely, there is scant evidence for the fear of the federal octopus, the fear that expansion of central programs and influence threatens to reduce the states and localities to compliant administrative arms of the central government. In fact, state and local governments are touching a larger proportion of the people in more ways than ever before; and they are spending a higher fraction of the total national product than ever before. Federal programs have increased, rather than diminished, the importance of the governors; stimulated professionalism in state agencies; increased citizen interest and participation in government; and, generally, enlarged and made more effective the scope of state action.[3] It may no longer be true in any significant sense that the states and localities are "closer" than the federal government to the people. It is true that the smaller governments remain active and powerful members of the federal system.

CENTRAL LEADERSHIP: THE NEED FOR BALANCE

The chaos of party processes makes difficult the task of presidential leadership. It deprives the President of ready-made congressional majorities. It may produce, as in the chairmen of legislative committees, powerholders relatively hidden from public scrutiny and relatively protected from presidential direction. It allows the growth of administrative agencies which sometimes escape control by central officials. These are the prices paid for a wide dispersion of political power. The cost is tolerable because the total results of dispersed power are themselves desirable and because, where clear national supremacy is essential, in foreign policy and military affairs, it is easiest to secure.

Moreover, in the balance of strength between the central and peripheral governments, the central government has on its side the whole secular drift towards the concentration of power. It has on its side the national leader-

[3] See the valuable report, *The Impact of Federal Grants-in-Aid on the Structure and Functions of State and Local Governments,* submitted to the Commission on Intergovernmental Relations by The Governmental Affairs Institute (Washington, D.C., 1955).

ship capacities of the presidential office. The last factor is the controlling one, and national strength in the federal system has shifted with the leadership desires and capacities of the chief executive. As these have varied, so there has been an almost rhythmic pattern: periods of central strength being put to use alternating with periods of central strength dormant.

Following a high point of federal influence during the early and middle years of the New Deal, the postwar years were, in the weighing of central-peripheral strength, a period of light federal activity. Between 1947 and 1961, excepting the Supreme Court's action in favor of school desegregation, national influence by design or default was not strong in domestic affairs. The danger then was that the central government was doing too little rather than too much. National deficiencies in education and health required the renewed attention of the national government. Steepening population and urbanization trend lines produced metropolitan area problems that could be effectively attacked only with the aid of federal resources. New definitions of old programs in housing and urban redevelopment, and new programs to deal with air pollution, water supply, and mass transportation became necessary. Since 1961, the pendulum has begun to swing in the other direction. The new administration immediately recognized that the federal government's essential role in the federal system is that of organizing and helping to finance such nationwide programs and began a new cycle of federal activism to fulfill that role.

The American federal system exhibits many evidences of the dispersion of power not only because of formal federalism but more importantly because our politics reflect and reinforce the nation's diversities-within-unity. Those who value the virtues of decentralization, which writ large are virtues of freedom, need not scruple to recognize the defects of those virtues. The defects are principally the danger that parochial and private interests may not coincide with, or give way to, the nation's interest. The necessary cure for these defects is effective national leadership.

The centrifugal force of domestic politics needs to be balanced by the centripetal force of strong presidential leadership. Simultaneous strength at center and periphery exhibits the American system at its best, if also at its noisiest. The interests of both find effective spokesmen. States and localities (and private interest groups) do not lose their influence opportunities, but national policy becomes more than the simple consequence of successful, momentary concentrations of non-national pressures if it is guided by national leaders.

This book is in happy disagreement with the prophets of doom who are so fashionable today. Our federal system at mid-century does creak at its joints. But these are creaks indicating a healthy flexibility. We have, principally, tried to demonstrate three things: first, that the past half-century has produced a fruitful, collaborative federal system; second, that along side the inevitable growth to primacy of the central government, the cities and states have maintained their strength, in the only terms with which that strength can be meaningfully measured; and third, that this strength is important because it is one basis of the vitality of the nation as a whole.

INDEX

Acker, Earl V., 112n
Adams Act, 34
Administration, legislative involvement in, 260–70
Administrative interaction, nongrant: legislative, 38; regarding elections and dual officeholding, 38; and regulatory cooperation, 39–40
Administrative streams (1800–1913), 38–40. *See also* History, perspectives of
Administrator: as politician, 270–74; and Congress, 377. *See also* Political parties
Adrian, Charles R., 156n
Advisory Commission on Intergovernmental Relations, xiii, 308n
Agar, Herbert, 281
Agricultural Conservation Program, 199–200
Agricultural Extension Service, 43, 160, 374
Agricultural Stabilization and Conservation Committees. *See* Farmer Committee System
Agriculture, Department of, xi, 139, 186n, 200; Bureau of Plant Industry, Soils, and Agricultural Engineering, 185; and special government units, 191–93; and Congressional liaison, 267; and Farmer Committee System, 351–58
Air Force, Department of, 96n; Office of Legislative Liaison, 266–67
Alabama, 35; and classification law, 180n–81n; and parks, 341
Alabama Power Co. v. *Ickes,* 47
Alaska, 138, 295n; and criminal law, 99–100
Alcohol Control Division (Treasury), 162
Alcohol Tax Unit (Treasury), 95, 96n, 110
Allegan, Mich., and Federal Power Commission, 188

Allen, Francis A., xiii, 97n, 101n
Aluminum Company of America, 173
Aman, Albert F., 113n
Amendment process, in hands of states, 27
Amendments, constitutional, and cooperation, 27–28
American Association of State Highway Officials, 74
American Bar Association, 100n
American Civil Liberties Union, 303–304
American Institute of Park Executives, 147, 149
American Legion, 234–35, 246
American Library Association, 248
American Municipal Association, 215n, 218, 221, 224–25, 236, 314, 324
American Printing House for the Blind, 36
American Public Welfare Association, 224
American Red Cross, 186n
American Well Water Co. v. *Lane and Bouler Co.,* 87n
Anderson, Clayton E., 135
Anderson, Robert B., 309
Anderson, William, 8n, 71n
Anslinger, H. J., 111n
Anti-Federalists, 24
Appleby, Paul H., 261n, 271
Arabian-American Oil Co., 150
Arizona: Employment Security Commission, 158; University of, 160; Chiefs of Police Association, 162
Armed Services Committee, House, 263, 264n
Armstrong, Louis, 302
Army Corps of Engineers, 31, 128, 131, 137, 140–41, 143, 146, 185, 186n, 188, 247–49, 262, 328, 347n
Army Provost Marshal School, 108
Articles of Confederation, 17, 151
Ashcraft v. *Tennessee,* 101n
Ashtabula, and U.S. Corps of Engineers, 188
Atomic Energy Commission, 151